Surviving Jewel

The Global Story of Christianity Series
History, Context, and Communities

Seven One-Volume Books

SERIES EDITORS
Emma Wild-Wood & Mark A. Lamport

SERIES ASSISTANT EDITOR
Gina A. Zurlo

SERIES INTRODUCTION
Dana L. Robert

BOOK EDITORS
Mitri Raheb *(Middle East)* | Amos Yong *(Asia)* | Wanjiru Gitau *(Africa)*
Alex Ryrie *(Europe)* | Raimundo Barreto *(Latin America)*
Upolu Vaai *(Oceania)* | Christopher Evans *(North America)*

SERIES EDITORIAL ADVISORY BOARD
Edwin Aponte *(Louisville Institute)*
Elias Bongmba *(Rice University)*
Arun Jones *(Candler School of Theology/Emory University)*
Brett Knowles *(University of Otago)*
David Maxwell *(University of Cambridge, UK)*
Elizabeth Monier *(University of Cambridge, UK)*
Dana L. Robert *(Center for Global Christianity and Mission/Boston University)*
Nelly van Doorn-Harder *(Wake Forest University)*
Stephanie Wong *(Valparaiso University)*

SENIOR EDITORIAL CONSULTANT
Joshua Erb

"With energy and verve, *Surviving Jewel* examines the kaleidoscope of Middle Eastern Christianity. Readers will appreciate the volume's impressive historical and geographical sweep, attention to Christian diversity, and clear analysis offered by an array of experts in the field."

—**Heather J. Sharkey**, University of Pennsylvania

"*Surviving Jewel* tells the rich story of Christianity in the Middle East. It provides an accessible account of the Christian experience in the Middle East from origins to the present day by exploring the historical context, the diversity of experiences of Christian communities, and contemporary issues."

—**Fiona McCallum Guiney**, University of St Andrews

"This volume tells an absorbing story that illustrates both how the Middle East shaped Christianity and how Christianity shaped the Middle East. This story not only illustrates the diversity of Christian life in the Middle East but is also a vital element in the study of global Christianity today."

—**Elizabeth Monier**, University of Cambridge

"Imaginatively conceived and with a variety of different approaches, this appropriately titled book offers a panoptic overview of Christianity in the Middle East, with an emphasis on the contemporary situation."

—**Sebastian Brock**, Oriental Institute, Oxford University

"Christian-Muslim relations are not defined by Muslim relations with the West. This rich resource brings together in one place a vast array of data and insight, informing readers about the mosaic of churches in the Middle East and providing vital context for understanding Christian-Muslim relations in the region and beyond."

—**Martin Whittingham**, director, Centre for Muslim-Christian Studies, Oxford

"*Surviving Jewel* is a very welcome introductory volume to Eastern Christianity. It is concise and largely comprehensible for newcomers to the subject. . . . This book will appeal both to young students in the academia and to the general public globally. Authors and editors are to be commended for this important effort."

—**Martin Accad**, Arab Baptist Theological Seminary

"This book takes the reader on a journey from past to present, unfolding the rich and kaleidoscopic world of Middle Eastern Christianity. . . . Each chapter is an invitation to dive deeper into the culture, history, and theology of the different communities. This book is a much-needed addition to the growing field of Middle Eastern Christianity and a must-read for students of world Christianity, history, the Middle East, and many more fields of study."

—**Pieternella van Doorn-Harder**, Wake Forest University

"For far too long, the history of Christianity has been told from a Western perspective alone, with little recognition that it spread equally to East and West. It is more than gratifying that this series begins with the cradle of Christianity in the Middle East. . . . It is most welcome that the scope of the book is extended to Western influences and the present challenges."

—**Dietmar W. Winkler**, University of Salzburg

Surviving Jewel

The Enduring Story of Christianity
in the Middle East

EDITED BY
Mitri Raheb
AND
Mark A. Lamport

CASCADE *Books* • Eugene, Oregon

SURVIVING JEWEL
The Enduring Story of Christianity in the Middle East

The Global Story of Christianity Series, vol. 1

Copyright © 2022 Wipf and Stock Publishers. All rights reserved. Except for brief quotations in critical publications or reviews, no part of this book may be reproduced in any manner without prior written permission from the publisher. Write: Permissions, Wipf and Stock Publishers, 199 W. 8th Ave., Suite 3, Eugene, OR 97401.

Cascade Books
An Imprint of Wipf and Stock Publishers
199 W. 8th Ave., Suite 3
Eugene, OR 97401

www.wipfandstock.com

PAPERBACK ISBN: 978-1-7252-6319-2
HARDCOVER ISBN: 978-1-7252-6320-8
EBOOK ISBN: 978-1-7252-6321-5

Cataloguing-in-Publication data:

Names: Raheb, Mitri [editor]. | Lamport, Mark A. [editor].

Title: Surviving jewel : the enduring story of Christianity in the Middle East / edited by Mitri Raheb and Mark A. Lamport.

Description: Eugene, OR: Cascade Books, 2022 | The Global Story of Christianity Series, vol. 1 | Includes bibliographical references and index.

Identifiers: ISBN 978-1-7252-6319-2 (paperback) | ISBN 978-1-7252-6320-8 (hardcover) | ISBN 978-1-7252-6321-5 (ebook)

Subjects: LCSH: Christianity—Middle East | Middle East—Church history | Christianity and other religions—Middle East | Christianity

Classification: BR1070 R34 2022 (print) | BR1070 (ebook)

05/04/22

For *Mitri*—To the resilient Christians of the Middle East

For *Mark*—To the memory of *Kenneth Latourette* (a pioneer in the recovery of global Christian history, 1884–1968); and to *Clement of Alexandria* (theologian, ca. 150–215); *Eusebius of Caesarea* (historian, ca. 260–340); *Abraham of Kashkar* (father of the Assyrian monastic revival, ca. 492–586); *Jacob al-Barādʻi* (bishop of Edessa, ca. 542–78); *Catholicos Timotheos I* (patriarch of the Church of the East, ca. 740 to 823); and to the faith-inspiring courage in the face of persecution and degradation of legions of Christians in the Middle East throughout the last two thousand years.

Contents

Series Introduction—DANA L. ROBERT | ix

List of Editors and Introducers | xix

Preface—GINA A. ZURLO AND MARK A. LAMPORT | xxi

Acknowledgements | xxxi

List of Contributors | xxxii

Book Introduction—SOURAYA BECHEALANY | xxxv

Section One
The Story of Christianity Narrated in Historical Context

1. The Expansion and Dispute of the Christian Movement (First to Sixth centuries)—CLAUDIA RAMMELT | 3

2. Conquest and Christian-Muslim Relations during the Islam Era (Seventh to Eleventh centuries)—MICHAEL KUHN | 19

3. Imperialism and Mission during European Rule (Twelfth to Nineteenth centuries)—JAMES C. SKEDROS | 36

4. Christianity in the Twentieth Century—MITRI RAHEB | 52

Section Two

The Story of Christianity Expressed in a Grand Church Family Mosaic

5. The Coptic Story—Wafik Wahba | 71

6. The Syriac Story—George Kiraz | 86

7. The Armenian Story—Hrayr Jebeljian | 103

8. The Greek Story—Nicholas Abou Mrad | 118

9. The Assyrian Story—Karl Pinggéra | 133

10. The Catholic Story—David Bertaina | 147

11. The Protestant Story—Mitri Raheb | 164

Section Three

The Story of Christianity Encounters Twenty-First-Century Issues

12. Diaspora and Middle Eastern Christianity—Mariam Youssef | 183

13. Women in Middle Eastern Christianity—Pamela Chrabieh | 199

14. Interfaith Relations with Middle Eastern Christianity
—Najib Awad | 215

15. Public Theology and Middle Eastern Christianity
—Anne E. Zaki | 232

Timeline—Brett Knowles | 248

Appendix: Christian Communities in the Middle East | 257

Index | 259

Series Introduction

The Global Story of Christianity

History, Contexts, and Communities

DANA L. ROBERT

WHAT DOES IT MEAN *to tell the story* of global Christianity? Storytelling is important for personal identity, for community life, and for shared humanity. When people tell their own stories, both individually and as communities of faith, they share who they are and who they hope to become. When people make friends, they swap stories. They introduce themselves. They discuss their work, or where they went to school. They might talk about the sports teams they support, or what activities they enjoy. As people get to know each other better, they exchange stories about their families, or politics, or other important issues. Friends do things together—and the being together creates memories that launch new stories they recall when they see each other again. In listening to each other, people's stories merge and create a common basis for relationships—even across boundaries or divisions.

Global Christianity is the story of a huge extended family. Christians are rooted in a common ancestor, Jesus Christ. For two thousand years, the followers of Jesus of Nazareth have traced their spiritual lineage through him to the God of ancient Israel, as spoken through the prophets and written in the Bible and celebrated in worship and outreach. Christianity is now the world's largest religion, encompassing one third of the world's peoples. During the twentieth century, the family of faith burst out of European frameworks and began growing rapidly in Africa, Asia, and Latin America. By 2018, Africa had become the continent with the largest number of Christians, followed by Latin America, and Europe, with Asia soon to become second in numbers.[1] Christianity as a global story reminds me of the chatter at a giant family reunion, where the relatives get together and reminisce

---

1. https://www.gordonconwell.edu/blog/who-owns-global-christianity/. See Johnson and Zurlo, *World Christian Encyclopedia*.

about their distant family history, and the departed saints that they remember—and the old family arguments that never seem to end. For better or worse, whether or not they know each other personally, the people who call themselves Christians are spiritual brothers, sisters, and long-lost cousins. Shared family history connects them.

And yet, nobody has only *one* story. This book series on the global story of Christianity embodies many stories that have unfolded across two thousand years of time, and that inhabit wide-ranging geographic and cultural spaces. The sheer size and complexity of the global Christian family means that a shared history is composed of multiple memories, from thousands of contexts. Being part of a community means organizing the stories into a convincing whole and claiming a common identity through them. Communities can be direct sets of relationships, such as families, neighborhoods, sports clubs, therapy groups, and local churches. They can also be "imagined" and thus composed of people who may never meet in person, but whose groups—including ethnicities, cities, political parties, and even nations—share common interpretations of experiences. For Christians, both personal and imagined faith communities use shared narratives to organize their spiritual realities. And yet, the meaning and identity of faith communities also changes over time, depending on the context. Depending on one's purpose or needs, different parts of one's story become more important than others. I am reminded of a friend who was the new pastor of a small church. Each week, no matter how hard he tried to get the old-timers to move, nobody would sit in the front section of the church. Finally, in frustration he asked one old man why he wouldn't move toward the front of the church. "I've been sitting in this pew for forty years," he replied. "It is not my fault that the people who used to sit in front of me have died or moved away." In his mind, the old man was still sitting in his imagined community made up of previous generations of friends and neighbors who had composed his church. But the new minister, looking out every week, saw nothing but empty front pews, waiting to be filled with new faces and new stories. Because the context had changed, the church community had changed; and because the community had changed, the context had changed—even though the old man had not moved anywhere at all. And yet, until the old man shared his story, the history of his community, the new minister couldn't understand the old man's resistance to his request.

History, contexts, and communities—all these pieces are important frameworks for organizing the many stories that together paint a global picture of Christianity. The connection among history, contexts, and communities was beautifully expressed by the late Andrew Walls, Scottish historian and expert on African Christianity, and a founder of the field of "world

Christianity."² Walls asked his readers to imagine a visitor from outer space, a professor of comparative religions, who visits Earth for field work every few centuries, to observe the practices and beliefs of representative Christians. First the space man visits the original Christians in Jerusalem, a few years after the death of Jesus. He finds that they are Jewish and follow Jewish customs, including offering animal sacrifices, worshiping on the seventh day, and reading old scrolls in Hebrew. They identify the Messiah, Son of Man and Suffering Servant, with their teacher who just died, Jesus of Nazareth. They live in close-knit families and eat meals together in each other's homes. When the visitor from space next returns to earth, he observes a big church meeting of church leaders around 325 C.E., in Nicaea (now in Turkey). Hardly any are Jewish and most are unmarried. To them, sacrifice means a ritual meal of bread and wine and they worship God on the first day of the week, not the seventh. They talk about Jesus, but they are debating whether the Greek words *homoousios* or *homoiousios* better characterize his nature. They argue a lot about theology.

Walls goes on to describe the space visitor's next field visit, Ireland in the 600s. There monks are gathered on a rocky coastline reciting the psalms. Some are going into a small boat with a box of beautiful manuscripts heading toward nearby islands to ask the inhabitants to give up worship of multiple nature divinities. Other monks sit alone in caves, denying themselves food. Upon examining the manuscripts, he finds they are the same writings he saw on his last visit, and he hears the monks recite the same basic statement of belief or creed he heard at Nicaea in 325. Yet these monks seem much more interested in being holy than in debating theology. Next the space visitor returns to earth in 1840s London. He finds a convention of mostly white Christians hearing speeches about the desirability of promoting Christianity and trade in Africa. To eliminate the slave trade, they are planning to send missionaries, lobby the government, and promote the education of black Africans. He sees many people carrying printed Bibles and finds out they accept the creed of Nicaea. They talk about holiness but would be shocked at the thought of praying alone in a cave. Rather, they are well fed and committed to political activism.

Finally, the space visitor returns in the 1980s to Lagos, Nigeria, in time to see a white-robed procession of people dancing and chanting through the streets. They are inviting people to come with them and

2. Walls preferred the term "world Christianity" to what this book series is calling "global Christianity." On the use of the terms "world" versus "global," see Robert, "World Christianity as a Revitalization Movement," 17–18; Sanneh and McClymond, *The Wiley Blackwell Companion to World Christianity*, 4–6; Johnson and Kim, "Describing the Worldwide Christian Phenomenon," 80–84.

experience the power of God. They talk about healing and driving out evil spirits. They say they accept the creed of Nicaea, but they are not really interested in theological creeds or in political activism. They do care passionately about personal empowerment through prayer, preaching, and healing. Back on his own planet, the professor must figure out what it all means. He notes that the location of the Christian heartland has shifted each time he has visited. How does he conclude what it means to be a Christian? Is there any coherence across time? What do Christians around the world have in common, despite the visible differences in culture, race, locations, ethnicities, and practices that he observed?

Andrew Walls' fantasy about the space visitor illustrates the complexities of telling the global story of Christianity. What each era had in common was its historical connection. Like links in a chain, history connected the different communities to each other. Jews from Jerusalem preached to Greeks and led to the events of Nicaea in 325. Emissaries from the Mediterranean planted the seeds that became Irish Christianity. Celtic missionaries launched what became the religion of London in the 1840s, and the British evangelical lobby sent the messengers that energized churches in Africa. To bring the story up to the present, today Nigerian churches send missionaries around the world, including to London. In fact, some of the largest churches in Europe have African pastors. Other historical connections involve a "continuity of consciousness" across time.[3] In each group's story, Jesus Christ "has ultimate significance." They use the "same sacred writings," though in different formats and languages. Writes Walls, "Each group thinks of itself as having some community with the others," continuous with ancient Israel, even though they are no longer Jews.[4] These elements of continuity, however, are embedded in very different contexts, ranging from the Middle East to West Asia, to Europe, Africa, and beyond. In each context, the space visitor found worshipping communities, ranging in form from house churches to bishops' gatherings, from monasteries to conferences and popular processions. The shape of the Christian communities and what they do differs according to their local cultures, politics, and historical period. And yet, taken together, the many stories echo the shared memory of Jesus Christ, passed down through the ages.

---

3. Walls, "The Gospel as Prisoner and Liberator of Culture," 6.
4. Walls, "The Gospel as Prisoner and Liberator of Culture," 6–7.

About this Book Series

To tell the global story of Christianity, each book in this series is organized into a common format. If we think about what goes into telling our stories, the elements are common to the books in the series. The *first* thing to notice is that the books each cover a different *geographic region*. In other words, they are organized by "neighborhood." This organization allows the editors, who come from each region, to explore the "historical context" and to answer the questions: Where are we from and how did we get here? Who are the people who brought Christianity? How did the Christian story change in each part of the globe, and what difference did it make? How are the followers of Jesus in that region anchored in his heritage? What is the testimony of the people of each region about their Christian identity, and how did they become part of the global story of Christianity? There are a range of answers to questions like "where are we from and how did we get here?" including stories of migration and mission, slavery and coercion, violence and resistance, joy and struggle. Analyzing where they have come from also allows the editors to build toward where they think their region might be going.

The *second* section of each book in the series talks about the kind of *faith communities* found in each geographic region, and the issues they face. Communities reflect group identities shaped by such factors as theology, ethnicity, language, or persecution. In the case of the volume on Asia, a vast continent with thousands of different ethnic groups, the communities described are organized by sub-region. The North America volume discusses some of the fundamental theological and organizational issues behind different groups of North American Christians. In Christian parlance, faith communities shaped by shared theologies and histories are often called "denominations," organized groups of Christians that recognize each other as brothers and sisters but have different stories to tell about how they got to be where they are today. Some faith communities are rather like private clubs, with high membership fees and strict rules as to who can belong. Others are more like groups of sports fans, open to anyone who feels like supporting the team and participating in its activities. In all cases, the discussion of different communities shows how their identity reflects both its local context and its participation in the global story of Christianity. Communities each have their own special saints, prophets, and leaders—people who have guided them and symbolize their identity to the world. They have their own favorite religious practices. Conversations internal to each community spill into the outside world, and sometimes attract others to join them. Contexts shape communities, and communities shape contexts. Faith communities are where the global story of Christianity forms church families and creates spaces in which they build a home.

The *third* section of each volume discusses *global issues* that are important to each region today. This is where the urgency behind each volume becomes clear. What are the passions that drive the communities in context? What problems do they face? What political and social issues are vital to their well-being? Some of the volumes explicitly discuss what churches call "ecumenism," churches cooperating and joining together to pursue shared ideals and common goals. Important twenty-first century issues such as climate change, racism, interfaith relations, war and peace, gender, church-state relations, and religious persecution are global issues that affect people on every continent. It is often these pressing issues that connect Christians in solidarity with others across geographic boundaries.

Elements of a Global Story

Although each book in the series stands alone, putting them into dialogue with each other paints a bigger picture of what is called "global (or world) Christianity." As already mentioned, Christianity in the twenty-first century has become a multi-cultural religion practiced by one third of the world. The fact that it exists nearly everywhere means that to tell the story of Christianity in one region affects the story of Christianity in another region. To think of Christianity as a global story requires seeing each region as connected. In scholarly terms, this idea is called "entanglement," an important concept in global history. The idea of historical entanglement means that each region is shaped by its relationship to the others. To think of Christianity as a global story means looking for ways in which the local and the global are entangled—all mixed up together, influencing each other, and not easily separated. As people in each region embrace what they see as the universal story of Jesus Christ, the way they practice their faith affects the nature of the religion as a whole. To be "global" means that regional stories are linked, with and through their Christian faiths.

Looking for interconnections among the regions is a way to trace how the assumption of entanglement creates a global story out of what are usually thought of as separate stories. As you read the different books in this series, also zoom out and look for common themes that bind the regions together to create a global story, though from different perspectives and angles. What follows are three major themes that intersect all the volumes—movement, translation, and public theologies:

- *Movement* is central to the global story of Christianity. Without new people entering old spaces, or people on the move, Christianity could not spread from one place to another. The New Testament journeys of Paul throughout the Mediterranean modeled how Christians moved from place to place in spreading their faith. Migration and "global diaspora" are features of the global Christian story, especially today when more people are on the move than ever before. When people deliberately cross boundaries to spread their faith, they are often called missionaries. During the era of colonialism, Europeans sent missionaries around the world. Today missionaries go from everywhere to everywhere, including especially from Korea, Brazil, Nigeria, and North America.[5] Sometimes movement to new areas causes migrants to embrace Christianity as a new way of life. Although migrants typically seek economic security over religious change, sometimes the act of moving to a new place can inspire them to launch missions of their own: Central Americans moving to North American cities, and Africans moving to Eastern Europe have started numerous churches. Forced migration can also spread Christianity. In a monstrous crime against humanity, over ten million Africans were sent to the Americas as slaves. Many of their descendants became Christians and reshaped the faith into a vehicle of resistance. Migrating people—whether forced or by choice—bind together their places of origin with their destinations and change both places in the process.[6]

- *Translation* is another theme that makes Christianity a global story. In literal terms, translation of the Bible into thousands of languages has been the foundation of Protestant missions for centuries, and the basis for faith-sharing across linguistic and cultural boundaries. Once people have the Bible in their own language, they interpret it according to their own cultural norms and needs.[7] During the twentieth century, many indigenous prophets—equipped with the Bible in their own language and inspired by dreams and visions—launched new Christian movements in Africa, Asia, and Latin America. Studies of conversion show how new Christians translate the Christian faith into their own personal contexts, or use it to revitalize their surroundings.[8] At a more theoretical level, translation can refer to cultural processes

5. Robert, *Christian Mission*.
6. See Frederiks and Nagy, *Religion, Migration, and Identity*; see also, Hanciles, *Migration and the Making of Global Christianity*, and *Beyond Christendom*.
7. Sanneh, *Translating the Message*.
8. Kling, *A History of Christian Conversion*.

of hybridization, of adopting the Christian message and reframing it to fit new contexts and to energize Christian communities.[9] Since all communication comes packaged in particular cultural forms, the process of translation is necessary for sharing the Christian faith across all kinds of ethnic, cultural, and geographic barriers. As Christians encounter other cultures and live alongside persons of other religions, their faith is often stimulated into renewed life. The translation process, both on personal and social levels, is an endlessly rich source of innovation that feeds into the global story of Christianity.

- *Public theologies* also shape the global story of Christianity. In the modern West, people often think of faith as a private matter, separate from politics or social life. But the idea that religion is a matter of personal choice, irrelevant to community life, is a fairly recent cultural innovation that itself assumes a public theology of secularism.[10] In most of the world, in most periods of history, religion carries practical implications for how people live in community. Christianity shapes people's attitudes toward authority, power, nature, gender relations, and human rights. Such ideas as "the doctrine of discovery," or the "priesthood of all believers," or "one nation under God" express the relationship of Christianity to peoples, politics, and land. The global story of Christianity consists of theological flows that spread around the world through migration and social media.[11] Public theologies require analyzing flows of power, including the supernatural and spiritual power embedded in Christian belief itself, the unequal political and economic power of Christians who use faith to justify control of others, and the tenacious power of resilience by Christians who are suffering or persecuted. By the late 1900s, evangelicalism, liberation theologies, and Pentecostal practices were all vehicles for political power, especially in Africa and the Americas. Christian charitable outreach through non-governmental organizations remains a major social factor throughout the world, especially in poor communities. Half of all Christians are Roman Catholics, a worldwide faith network with a central teaching authority lodged in the pope and the Vatican. Public

---

9. For a postcolonial analysis and typology of historical religious encounters, including syncretism and selection, see Lindenfeld, *World Christianity and Indigenous Experience*, 1–30. See also, Jones, ed., *Christian Interculture*; and Gruber, *Intercultural Theology*.

10. Casanova, *Public Religions in the Modern World*.

11. Schreiter, *The New Catholicity*.

theologies—the globalization of religious ideas, institutions, power, and practices—are a key feature of Christianity as a world religion.

Conclusion: From Local Stories to Global Story and Back Again

To tell the global story of Christianity requires reconstructing the entangled histories of communities down through the ages, in different regions. It requires retracing their historical contexts and learning how communities respond to the urgent issues of the day. As this series shows, only as different Christian communities tell their own stories—and listen to the stories of others—can the global story of Christianity be glimpsed in all its fullness.

For Further Reading

Casanova, José. *Public Religions in the Modern World*. Chicago: University of Chicago Press, 2011.
Frederiks, Martha, and Dorottya Nagy, eds. *Religion, Migration, and Identity: Methodological and Theological Explorations*. Leiden, The Netherlands: Brill, 2016.
Gruber, Judith. *Intercultural Theology: Exploring World Christianity after the Cultural Turn*. Göttingen, Germany: Vandenhoeck & Reprecht, 2018.
Hanciles, Jehu J. *Beyond Christendom: Globalization, African Migration, and the Transformation of the West*. Maryknoll, NY: Orbis, 2008.
———. *Migration and the Making of Global Christianity*. Grand Rapids: Eerdmans, 2021.
Johnson, Todd M., and Gina A. Zurlo. *World Christian Encyclopedia*. 3rd ed. Edinburgh: Edinburgh University Press, 2019.
Johnson, Todd M., and Sandra S. Kim. "Describing the Worldwide Christian Phenomenon." *International Bulletin of Missionary Research* 29, no. 2 (2005) 80–84.
Jones, Arun, ed. *Christian Interculture: Texts and Voices from Colonial and Postcolonial Worlds*. University Park, PA: Penn State University Press, 2021.
Kling, David. *A History of Christian Conversion*. New York: Oxford University Press, 2020.
Lindenfeld, David. *World Christianity and Indigenous Experience: A Global History, 1500-2000*. Cambridge: Cambridge University Press, 2021.
Robert, Dana L. *Christian Mission: How Christianity Became a World Religion*. Hoboken, NJ: Wiley-Blackwell, 2009.
———. "World Christianity as a Revitalization Movement." In *World Christianity: History, Methodologies, Horizons*, edited by Jehu Hanciles, 17–18. Maryknoll, NY: Orbis, 2021.
Sanneh, Lamin O. *Translating the Message: The Missionary Impact on Culture*. Maryknoll, NY: Orbis, 2009.

Sanneh, Lamin, and Michael J. McClymond. "Introduction." In *The Wiley Blackwell Companion to World Christianity*, edited by Lamin Sanneh and Michael McClymond, 1–18. Malden, MA: Wiley-Blackwell, 2016.

Schreiter, Robert J. *The New Catholicity: Theology between the Global and the Local*. Maryknoll, NY: Orbis, 2004.

Walls, Andrew. "The Gospel as Prisoner and Liberator of Culture." In *The Missionary Movement in Christian History Studies in the Transmission of Faith*, 3–15. Maryknoll, NY: Orbis, 1996.

Editors and Introducers

Series Editors

Emma Wild-Wood (PhD, University of Edinburgh) is director of the Centre for the Study of World Christianity, University of Edinburgh School of Divinity, and senior lecturer of African Christianity and African indigenous religions (Scotland). She is the former director of the Cambridge Centre for Christianity Worldwide and lecturer in World Christianities in the Faculty of Divinity of the University of Cambridge. Wild-Wood is the Editor of *Studies in World Christianity* journal and a fellow of the Royal Historical Society.

Mark A. Lamport (PhD, Michigan State University) has been a professor for more than thirty-five years at graduate theological schools in the United States and Europe. He is author of *Nurturing Faith: A Practical Theology for Educating Christians* (2021); and editor of *Emerging Theologies from the Global South* (in press, 2022); *Christianity in the Middle East* (2 vols., 2020); *Encyclopedia of Christianity in the Global South* (2 vols., 2018); *Encyclopedia of Martin Luther and the Reformation* (2 vols., 2017); *Encyclopedia of Christianity in the United States* (5 vols., 2016); *Encyclopedia of Christian Education* (3 vols., 2015).

Gina A. Zurlo (PhD, Boston University) is co-director of the Center for the Study of Global Christianity at Gordon-Conwell Theological Seminary (South Hamilton, Massachusetts). She is the co-author of the *World Christian Encyclopedia* 3rd ed. (Edinburgh University Press) and co-editor of the *World Christian Database* (Brill). Zurlo was named one of the BBC's 100 most inspiring and influential women of 2019 for her work quantifying the religious future, and the role of women in it.

Book Editors

Mitri Raheb is the founder and president of Dar al-Kalima University College of Arts and Culture in Bethlehem. The most widely published Palestinian theologian to date, Dr. Raheb is the author of eighteen books including: *Bethlehem: A Sociocultural History; I Am a Palestinian Christian; Bethlehem Besieged; Faith in the Face of Empire: The Bible through Palestinian Eyes*. His books and numerous articles have been translated into eleven languages.

Mark A. Lamport—see above

Series Introduction

Dana L. Robert (PhD, Yale University) is Truman Collins Professor of World Christianity and History of Mission, and director of the Center for Global Christianity and Mission at Boston University School of Theology. She is a member of the American Academy of Arts and Sciences and in 2017, she received the Lifetime Achievement Award from the American Society of Missiology. Recent books include *Faithful Friendships: Embracing Diversity in Christian Community* (2019); *African Christian Biography: Stories, Lives, and Challenges* (2018). An active lay United Methodist, in 2019 Roberts spoke at the 150th anniversary of the United Methodist Women.

Book Introduction

Elie Souraya Bechealany (PhD, Theology, Centre Sèvres, Jesuit Faculty of Paris; PhD, religious studies, University of Saint Joseph, Beirut, Lebanon) is the former secretary general of the Middle East Council of Churches. She is professor and director of the Research Center of the Faculty of Religious Sciences at the University of Saint Joseph (Lebanon) as well as a member of the Board of the Ecumenical journal *Proche-Orient Chrétien* (Christianity in the Middle East). Bechealany is a founding Member of the Jean Corbon Foundation.

Preface

GINA A. ZURLO & MARK A. LAMPORT

IT IS FITTING THAT the first volume of *The Global Story of Christianity: History, Context, and Communities* focuses on the Middle East, the historic home of Christianity. As the faith first took root in the region, the first Christians were technically Asian and until the year 923, the global South was home to half of all Christians in the world. (See Graph 1.) In Jesus' lifetime, the movement was itinerant, rural, Jewish, and contained in Palestine. Primarily led by the apostles, whose primary languages were Aramaic and Hebrew, it spread through synagogues and its teachings inscribed and disseminated on scrolls, even though the movement did not have an official name. However, in the subsequent seventy-five years, until the death of Ignatius, as we learn from his writings, this small movement had changed. It had become urban, Roman and Greek; its adherents met in churches and were led by gentiles and bishops. Its writings were disseminated in codex (or book form); and those who gave their lives to its cause were called Christians.

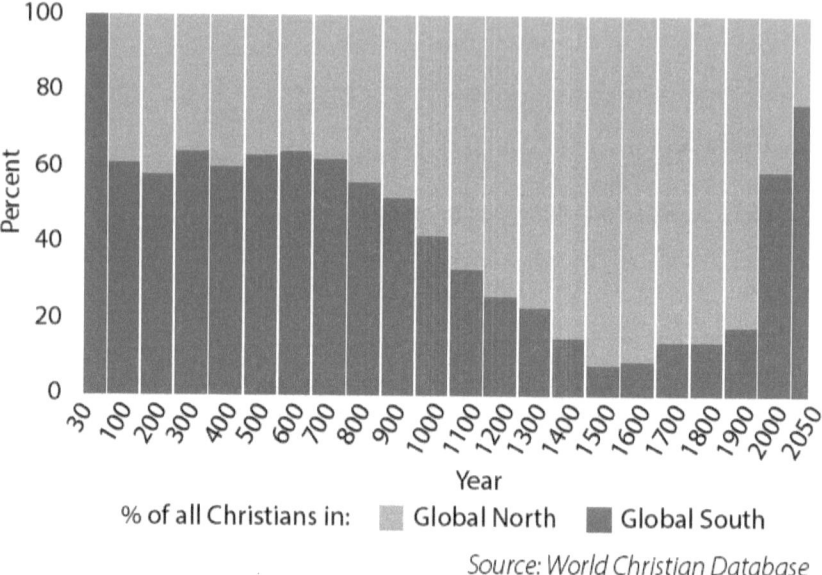

Graph 1: North/South Distribution of Christianity

Source: Todd M. Johnson and Gina A. Zurlo, *World Christian Encyclopedia*, 3rd ed. (Edinburgh: Edinburgh University Press, 2019), 4. Used by permission of the authors.

These expansive changes occurred in a very short time span and were accomplished when the church was relatively powerless, beset by many obstacles and persecutions. The movement that would become Christianity was spread throughout various geographic areas and languages, and had grassroots elements due to its charismatic and itinerant missionaries.[1] Though the church distanced itself from Judaism, it still clung to its foundational story in the Hebrew Bible. The church survived by adapting, but never wavering from its central message of the gospel as it expanded beyond the confines of Judaism and Rome.

One of early Christianity's greatest achievements was its missional consciousness in geographical expansion. Considered at first an offshoot of Judaism, Christianity spread from the Roman world into the Persian Empire and Armenia, where its adherents constituted the majority of the population from the third through sixth centuries. Christianity reached

1. Edwards, *From Christ to Christianity*, 249–55.

China in the seventh century via the Silk Roads, when Islam was beginning its own expansion. Islam significantly altered the status of Christianity in its original homelands in Asia and Africa. While Coptic and Ethiopian Christianity survive in Africa to this day—although greatly reduced through its encounter with Islam—Byzantium continued in Asia for centuries.

Once representing the faith's center of gravity, Middle Eastern Christianity is now a picture of struggle, sacrifice, and survival. Its history typifies Andrew Walls' "serial expansion" view of the faith—that upon moving into new geographic areas, Christianity eventually dies out in previous places, despite prior numerical strength. Over the course of the twentieth century, Christianity shifted from the global North (Europe, North America) to the global South (Asia, Africa, Latin America, Oceania), but this North/South typology unintentionally overlooks the Middle East. Located technically in the South, the Middle East, though having received Christianity before the North, is not a region where Christianity is growing or flourishing.

Country	Pop_1900	Pct_1900	Pop_1950	Pct_1950	Pop_1970	Pct_1970	Pop_2000	Pct_2000	Pop_2020	Pct_2020	Pop_2025	Pct_2025	Pop_2050	Pct_2050
Bahrain	200	0.3	900	0.8	5,900	2.8	94,500	14.2	205,000	12.1	208,000	11.1	251,000	10.8
Egypt	1,552,000	14.8	2,722,000	13.3	4,574,000	13.3	7,751,000	11.3	9,473,000	9.3	9,988,000	8.9	12,027,000	7.5
Iran	116,000	1.2	186,000	1.1	268,000	0.9	300,000	0.5	579,000	0.7	693,000	0.8	1,102,000	1.1
Iraq	144,000	6.4	259,000	4.5	401,000	4.0	949,000	4.0	186,000	0.5	135,000	0.3	114,000	0.2
Israel	29,700	8.0	71,200	5.7	79,000	2.8	145,000	2.4	188,000	2.2	177,000	1.9	183,000	1.4
Jordan	14,600	5.8	27,300	5.7	83,400	4.8	138,000	2.7	141,000	1.4	135,000	1.3	159,000	1.2
Kuwait	200	0.3	6,200	4.0	38,600	5.2	200,000	9.8	508,000	11.9	550,000	12.2	678,000	12.6
Lebanon	317,000	77.4	855,000	64.1	1,436,000	62.5	1,404,000	36.5	2,339,000	34.3	2,155,000	33.7	2,120,000	32.5
Oman	20	0.0	480	0.1	2,700	0.4	91,300	4.0	185,000	3.6	203,000	3.6	253,000	3.7
Palestine	30,300	11.7	74,900	8.0	53,200	4.7	69,900	2.2	45,100	0.9	40,500	0.7	32,000	0.4
Qatar	70	0.4	1,200	4.7	3,900	3.6	69,100	11.7	400,000	13.9	423,000	13.6	518,000	13.4
Saudi Arabia	50	0.0	2,400	0.1	18,300	0.3	901,000	4.4	2,102,000	6.0	2,250,000	6.0	2,755,000	6.2
Syria	316,000	18.1	481,000	14.1	667,000	10.5	1,525,000	9.3	672,000	3.8	524,000	2.3	316,000	1.0
United Arab Emirates	80	0.2	2,200	3.1	9,300	4.0	394,000	12.6	1,114,000	11.3	1,128,000	10.9	1,340,000	12.9
Middle East (as defined)	2,520,220	13.9	4,689,780	17.7	7,640,300	19.0	14,031,800	14.6	18,137,100	10.1	18,609,500	9.0	21,848,000	5.7

Table 1: Christianity in the Middle East by Country, 1900–2050

Data source: Todd M. Johnson and Gina A. Zurlo, eds., *World Christian Database* (Leiden: Brill, accessed August 2021)

Table 1 displays the fourteen countries considered the "Middle East" for the purposes of this volume, with their Christian populations and percentages from 1900 to today and projections for the future. Together, these fourteen countries were 14 percent Christian in 1900, but this figure dropped to 10 percent by 2020. For perspective, the wider North Africa/Western Asia region (defined by the United Nations) was 16 percent Christian in 1900 and 5 percent in 2020, showing a more substantive decline due to the emigration of Christians from Algeria, Morocco, Tunisia, and Turkey over the twentieth century. Over the same period, Islam increased in these fourteen countries together from 89.6 percent to 90 percent, with a projected increase to 91 percent (table 2).

Year	1900		1970		2000		1900-2000 % p.a.
Religious	28,699,000	100.0	94,751,000	99.6	219,805,000	99.1	2.06
Muslims	25,707,000	89.6	84,103,000	88.4	198,796,000	89.6	2.07
Christians	2,521,000	8.8	7,640,000	8.0	14,032,000	6.3	1.73
Orthodox	1,915,000	6.7	5,497,000	5.8	9,304,000	4.2	1.59
Catholics	541,000	1.9	1,759,000	1.8	3,736,000	1.7	1.95
Jews	249,000	0.9	2,481,000	2.6	4,833,000	2.2	3.01
Nonreligious	1,000	0.0	366,000	0.4	2,062,000	0.9	7.93
Agnostics	1,000	0.0	294,000	0.3	1,825,000	0.8	7.80
Total population	28,700,000	100.0	95,117,000	100.0	221,867,000	100.0	2.07

	2015		2020		2000-2020 % p.a.	2050	
Religious	302,828,000	99.0	330,218,000	99.0	2.06	476,308,000	98.9
Muslims	275,055,000	89.9	301,173,000	90.3	2.10	439,420,000	91.2
Christians	17,729,000	5.8	18,138,000	5.4	1.29	21,847,000	4.5
Orthodox	10,149,000	3.3	10,263,000	3.1	0.49	12,319,000	2.6
Catholics	6,433,000	2.1	6,625,000	2.0	2.91	7,410,000	1.5
Jews	6,371,000	2.1	6,890,000	2.1	1.79	10,001,000	2.1
Nonreligious	3,005,000	1.0	3,283,000	1.0	2.35	5,277,000	1.1
Agnostics	2,654,000	0.9	2,902,000	0.9	2.35	4,721,000	1.0
Total population	305,832,000	100.0	333,500,000	100.0	2.06	481,585,000	100.0

Table 2: Religions in the Middle East, 1900–2050

Data source: Todd M. Johnson and Brian J. Grim, eds., *World Religion Database* (Leiden/Boston: Brill, accessed August 2021)

The most pronounced declines from 1900 to 2020 occurred in Lebanon (77% to 34%), Syria (18% to 4%), and Palestine (12% to 1%). Lebanon is a unique case: despite its decline, it still has the highest proportion of Christians of any country in the Middle East, and Christians have an outsized influence in government and economics. Most Lebanese Christians are Catholics of many different rites: Maronite, Melkite, Armenian, Syrian, Chaldean, and Latin.

However, the story of Christianity in the Middle East is more nuanced than simply one of decline. There are *three* categories of churches in the region: (1) the historic Orthodox and Catholic churches, (2) the modern Protestant and Independent missionary-founded churches, and (3) immigrant churches of many traditions (see Map 1 for the geographic spread of Christianity in the region).[2] The Orthodox are the largest, and most historic, segment of Middle Eastern Christianity, found especially in Egypt (Coptic), Cyprus (Greek), and Syria (Armenian, Greek, Syrian). These churches have been profoundly impacted by persecution and emigration over the last 120 years. For example, countless Christians were martyred in Syria (3.8% Christian, two-thirds of whom are Orthodox) with the rise of ISIS during the civil war that began in 2011. Under ISIS, Christians were given four options: convert to Islam, pay the *jizya* tax and accept *dhimmi* status, leave the country, or die. Two archbishops of Aleppo, Boulos Yazigi and Mor Gregorious Youhanna Ibrahim, were abducted in 2013 and their status is still unknown. Many of the Christians who fled will likely never return.

Protestant and Independent churches in the Middle East are comparatively newer, with some dating to the nineteenth century and later. These churches have grown in recent years, but mostly due to people switching from Orthodox churches, rather than via converts from Islam, which contributes to tense relations between historic and missionary churches. Chinese Christians have prioritized mission in the region with the Back to Jerusalem Movement, which aims to send missionaries along the ancient Silk Road routes from China to Israel. Independent churches also include "underground" or "Muslim background believer" networks of Christians, sometimes of people who choose to publicly remain Muslim for security but privately profess Christ.

Perhaps the most underestimated network of churches in the Middle East are those composed of foreign workers. Filipinos, Indians, and others are working in the region, many of whom are men in the oil industry and women in domestic service and retail. Many consider their work as "missionary," not simply working to send money back home. The presence of these Christians has certainly complexified religion in the region. The growth of Christianity in Qatar (0.4% to 13.5%), Bahrain (0.3% to 12%), and Kuwait (0.3% to 11.6%) is essentially due to these foreign Christian workers. While many of these workers are Catholic (primarily Filipinos), there are substantial Pentecostal/Charismatic communities among them in

---

2. See Appendix in the back of the book for a fuller description of the various Christian communities of the Middle East. This construction derives from imminent scholar Sidney Griffith who prefers to sort the branches of the church in reference to their origins, including those who later changed affiliations, like those groups from within certain communities, some of whose congregations eventually came into union with Rome.

these Muslim majority countries. For instance, in Kuwait, 2.4 percent of the population is Pentecostal/Charismatic because of the large community of Indian Christians from Kerala, south India. They represent a wide variety of Pentecostal churches, including the Assemblies of God, Indian Pentecostal Church, and the Pentecostal Maranatha Gospel Church.

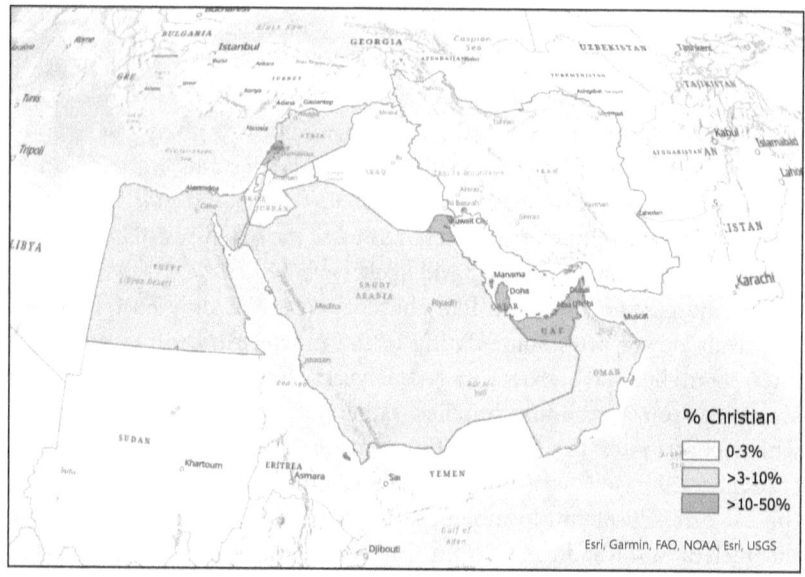

Map 1: Christianity in the Middle East

Data source: Todd M. Johnson and Brian J. Grim, eds., *World Religion Database* (Leiden/Boston: Brill, accessed August 2021)

Life for Christians in the Middle East is not easy. Social hostilities (by individuals, organizations, social groups) and governmental restrictions (laws, policies) on religion have both been on the rise, leading to persecution, death, and emigration of Christians from the region. However, one unexpected trend among Middle Eastern churches is a different kind of Christian unity than typically found anywhere in the world. Under a shared strife, Christians of all traditions have forged a kinship under pressure, bringing them together despite theological differences. This kind of mutual understanding is sometimes institutional, such as in the Gulf Churches Fellowship (established 2013) that represents the needs of Christians to their respective governments. Other initiatives to unite are more grassroots, such as in the United Arab Emirates, where buildings and complexes are routinely shared by different churches.

The Evangelical Church in Abu Dhabi (established 1975), for example, is shared among more than sixty different congregations.

The future of Christianity in the region is uncertain, as Christians' fate is often tied to the whims of those with political power, both domestic and foreign. Christianity is likely to continue declining to perhaps 5.7% by 2050. However, these projections are based on current Christian emigration trends; should political and/or social conditions worsen, these figures could be much lower.

Concept and Mission of the Book

The story of Christianity in the Middle East spans centuries, entailing historical interactions of people, politics, cultures, languages, and religions, with far-ranging and long-lasting consequences. The challenge of our task in telling this story herein is to describe (not prescribe), report (not take sides), and interpret (not prejudice). However, our purpose in this volume is clear: should our collective efforts reveal the protean nature of the ancient and modern faith of Christianity as it has existed for twenty centuries—thriving and floundering, triumphalist and tenacious—then we will have succeeded. Whatever else may be said, the story of Christianity in the Middle East survives history as a rare, multifaceted jewel.

But jewels can be lost and found. Though Christianity was born in the Middle East and flourished there for centuries, the ascendance of Islam sent it to the margins, putting it at great peril in a hostile political and religious climate. Of course, the story of Christianity over the last 1,300 years is not solely one of conflict; it is as much about accommodation, interchange, and cooperation as it is about marginality and persecution.

Despite its presence in the Middle East and Ethiopia, and even to some extent in India, Christianity is today mostly identified as a European or Western religion. It is not that Christianity "became" a European or Western religion, but Western scholarship and culture became focused mainly on Western Christianity as "orthodox" while other forms were marginalized or declared to be heretical. To blame this on a single factor alone, such as Islam, is erroneous, a stereotype to be avoided. The importance of this project is that it highlights the rich history and present situation of Christianity that is often either unknown or neglected.

With the phenomenon of Christian migration out of the Middle East in the middle and end of the twentieth century, we focus our studies on how Christianity has fared in the ancient home of its founder and birth. This compendium of up-to-date scholarship examines with broad strokes the religious landscape of the sixteen Middle Eastern countries in the beginning of the twenty-first century.

Concept and Mission of the Series

This is the first book of a seven-book series. *The Global Story of Christianity* series is designed as a set of accessible introductions for those who wish to understand the emergence of the Christian faith and its global church presence today. The concept of "story" (as explained in the Series Introduction by Dana Robert) will be the featured motif in each book; in turn, we intend for an evident symmetry in each of the seven books. To do so, each book presents fifteen chapters organized around three main subheadings:

> Section One: The Story of Christianity Narrated in *Historical Context*
>
> Section Two: The Story of Christianity Expressed in a *Grand Church Family Mosaic*
>
> Section Three: The Story of Christianity Encounters *Twenty-first Century Issues*

With many Christians detached from the complexity of churches beyond their own, let alone the history of Christianity's spread and unique expressions around the globe, we are compelled to tell the story of global Christianity through the centuries. Though the history of Christianity can appear to be a bewildering array of national churches and ethnic jurisdictions, the purpose of this survey series is to provide a clear overview of the global church for the non-specialist—preferably, the student in academic coursework—by furnishing basic information about these arrayed elements and indicating the relationships among them. Each church is placed in its historical, geographical, doctrinal, and practical context.

We concede edited volumes are not as selective as textbooks may be, especially those of single-authored volumes. Some volumes or series lack cohesion when read cover-to-cover. With this in mind, we have written these volumes intentionally as textbooks and general reference books, with their primary aim for use in the classroom: student- and reader-friendly.

The following is a chart detailing the series, including the top-flight editor for each book as well as the release date for the seven publications. They are organized not only by geographical region but also by a rough chronology of when Christianity was introduced to that region. Our desire is that a more comprehensive understanding of Christianity's geographic breadth and its cultural interactions will further an appreciation for those who have come before and for the status of the Christian faith in its contemporary world context.

The Global Story of Christianity *series*

Book Title	Year of Release	Editors
Surviving Jewel: The Enduring Story of Christianity in the Middle East	Book 1: 2022	Mitri Raheb *(Dar al-Kalima University College, Bethlehem)* & Mark A. Lamport
Uncovering the Pearl: The Hidden Story of Christianity in Asia	Book 2: 2023	Amos Yong *(Fuller Theological Seminary)* & Mark A. Lamport
Globalizing Legacies: The Intermingling Story of Christianity in Africa	Book 3: 2023	Wanjiru M. Gitau *(St. Thomas University, Miami)* & Mark A. Lamport
Entangling Web: The Fractious Story of Christianity in Europe	Book 4: 2024	Alec Ryrie *(University of Durham, UK)* & Mark A. Lamport
Engaging Coloniality: The Liberative Story of Christianity in Latin America	Book 5: 2024	Raimundo César Barreto, Jr. *(Princeton Theological Seminary)* & Mark A. Lamport
Restoring Identities: The Contextualizing Story of Christianity in Oceania	Book 6: 2023	Upolu Vaai *(Pacific Theological College, Fiji)* & Mark A. Lamport
Expanding Energy: The Dynamic Story of Christianity in North America	Book 7: 2024	Christopher H. Evans *(Boston University)* & Mark A. Lamport

For Further Reading

Eastman, David L. *Early North African Christianity: Turning Points in the Development of the Church.* Grand Rapids: Baker Academic, 2021.

Edwards, James R. *From Christ to Christianity: How the Jesus Movement Became the Church in Less Than a Century.* Grand Rapids: Baker Academic, 2021.

Griffiths, Sidney. *Church in the Shadow of the Mosque: Christians and Muslims in the World of Islam.* Princeton, NJ: Princeton University, 2007.

Ross, Kenneth R., Mariz Todros, & Todd Johnson, eds. *Christianity in North Africa and West Asia.* Edinburgh: Edinburgh University Press, 2018.

Sharkey, Heather J. *A History of Muslims, Christians, and Jews in the Middle East* Cambridge: Cambridge University, Press 2017.

Womack, Deanna Ferree. *Neighbors: Christians and Muslims Building Community.* Louisville, KY: Westminster John Knox, 2020.

Acknowledgements

THE GERM OF AN idea pollinated into a book-length treatment of the history, plight, and experiences of the multi-faceted expressions of Christianity celebrated in the church. We have been more than a little assisted by the comments, guidance, and perspective of sensational scholars Philip Jenkins, Erica Hunter, Wafik Wahba, Harold Suerman, Akram Khater, Jonathan Swift, Deanna Ferree Womack, and Michael Ghiz. Thanks one and all for your friendship and collegiality in the spirit of collaboration. Thanks so to Michael Hahn for smoothing out the voices in the Preface.

The following were instrumental in shepherding the contents of the book into production-worthy copy—Joshua Erb (senior editorial consultant) and Philip Bustrum and Mel Wilhoit for tremendous skill and detail in indexing the contents.

Further, we are beholden to Michael Thomson, acquisitions and development director for Wipf & Stock Publishers. He tracked Mark down in the produce aisle of a large grocery chain in Grand Rapids and proposed *this* book to him (and to persuade Mitri to join in)! A year later Mark came back to Michael and pitched a seven-book series to tell the global story of Christianity with this book as its starting point. Michael is at once analytical and spontaneous, perceptive and intelligent, exacting and gracious. This is Mark's second and Mitri's first project with Michael. We are pleased that an additional large international edited book is also in process under Michael's guidance describing "emerging theologies from the global south" (Cascade Books, 2023). Thank you for cheering on our vision.

Finally, we feel great respect for Christians in the Middle East, many of whom have experienced desperate pain and unthinkable loss merely for pledging allegiance to Christianity. May God given strength and courage to be faithful during dire times, and may God teach us lessons in faithfulness because what we now know about our brothers and sisters in the faith.

Contributors

Najib George Awad (PhD/DrTheolHabil), originally from Syria is a theologian, author, and poet. He was the professor of Christian theology and Eastern Christian thought and the director of the PhD program in Islamic Studies and Christian-Muslim Relations in Hartford Seminary, Connecticut. Recent publications are *Orthodoxy in Arabic Terms: A Study of Theodore Abū Qurrah's Trinitarian and Christological Doctrines in an Islamic Context* (2015); *Umayyad Christianity: John of Damascus as a Contextual Example of Identity-Formation in Early Islam* (2018); and *After-Mission, Beyond Evangelicalism: The Indigenous 'Injīliyyūn' in the Arab-Muslim Context of Syria-Lebanon*.

David Bertaina (PhD, The Catholic University of America) is a professor in the History Department at the University of Illinois at Springfield. He researches encounters between Christians and Muslims in Late Antiquity and the medieval Middle East, including the use of the Bible and Qur'an in religious disputations.

J. Scott Bridger (PhD, Southeastern Seminary) is associate professor of Global Studies and World Religions at Criswell College in Dallas, Texas. He formerly taught Islamic Studies at The Southern Baptist Theological Seminary in Louisville, Kentucky. He is the author of *Christian Exegesis of the Qur'ān: A Critical Analysis of the Apologetic Use of the Qur'ān in Select Medieval and Contemporary Arabic Texts* (Pickwick, 2015).

Pamela Chrabieh (PhD, University of Montreal, Canada) is a scholar, university professor, senior researcher and consultant, visual artist, and activist based in Lebanon. She is the director SPNC Learning & Communication (Beirut), and her publications include areas of war memory and peacebuilding, sciences of religions, human rights, visual arts, and interreligious/intercultural dialogue in Western Asia.

Ani Honarchiansaky (PhD, Near Eastern languages and cultures—Armenian Studies, UCLA; MA, Iranian Studies, UCLA) is postdoctoral research associate at Princeton University at Seeger Center for Hellenic Studies supported by the Committee of the Study of Late Antiquity. She works on religion, taxation, and violence in late antique Armenia with a focus on both Roman and Sasanian connected histories.

Hrayr Jebejian is general secretary of the Bible Society in the Gulf. He holds a Doctor of Ministry degree in Bible engagement from the New York Theological Seminary. Jebejian is the author of three books, along with articles published in academic journals and encyclopedias. He is a recipient of the Ambassador of the Motherland medal from the Ministry of Diaspora of the Republic of Armenia.

George A. Kiraz (PhD, Cambridge) is a senior research associate at the Institute for Advanced Study, Princeton, and the director of Beth Mardutho: The Syriac Institute, Piscataway. He has written extensively on Syriac studies and computational linguistics. Recently, he wrote a history of the Syriac Orthodox in North America, 1895–1915 (2019) and edited a new Syriac-English edition of the Syriac New Testament (2020).

Brett Knowles (PhD, University of Otago) is a retired associate professor of church history and teaching fellow, formerly of the Sydney College of Divinity and the Theology Programme, University of Otago, New Zealand. His publications include *A Timeline of Global Christianity: 1,000 Significant Dates for Christianity across the Planet—and Beyond* (Wipf & Stock, 2019); *Transforming Pentecostalism: The Changing Face of New Zealand Pentecostalism, 1920–2010* (Emeth, 2014); and *New Life: A History of the New Life Churches of New Zealand, 1942–1979*, 3rd ed. (Emeth, 2015).

Michael F. Kuhn (PhD Middlesex University, UK) has lived extensively in the Middle East. His research interests are in the areas of Trinitarian theology and Christology, particularly how Eastern Christians engaged with Muslims concerning the nature of God. His publications include *God Is One: A Christian Defence of Divine Unity in the Muslim Milieu* and *Finding Hagar: God's Pursuit of a Runaway*.

Karl Pinggéra (DrTheol, Philipps-Universität Marburg) is professor for church history at Marburg University (Germany). His publications cover different fields of Near Eastern Christianity with a focus on theology and history of the churches of Syriac tradition. Pinggéra is active member of inter-church consultations between the Evangelische Kirche in Deutschland and the Oriental-Orthodox Churches.

Claudia Rammelt (PhD, Universität of Marburg) is a professor at the Faculty of Protestant Theology in Bochum, Germany at the chair of church history and intercultural theology. Since her studies at the Near East School of Theology in Beirut, she is engaged in topics of the Middle East, especially the Oriens Christianus. A recent book collected inter alia stories of violence, flight and displacement.

James C. Skedros (ThD, Harvard Divinity School) is the Michael G. and Anastasia Cantonis Professor of Byzantine Studies at Holy Cross Greek Orthodox School of Theology (Brookline, MA). His teaching and publications focus on popular religious practices in Late Antiquity, Byzantine Christianity, and Christian-Muslim relations.

Wafik Wahba (PhD, Northwestern University; ThM, Princeton Seminary) is global Christianity professor at Tyndale University & Seminary, Toronto, Canada. His publications include areas of global Christianity and Islam, and religion and politics in the Middle East. Wafik taught theology, global Christianity, Islam and cultural contextualization in the USA, Middle East, Africa, South East Asia, and South America.

Mariam Youssef (PhD, religion/MA, applied women's studies, Claremont Graduate University) is a lecturer in the Women's, Gender, and Sexuality Studies department at California State University, Long Beach. She is the author of *Gendered Paradigms in Theologies of Survival: Silenced to Survive*.

Anne E. Zaki (PhD, Fuller Theological Seminary; MDiv, Calvin Theological Seminary; MA, The American University in Cairo) is professor of preaching and practical theology at the Evangelical Theological Seminary in Cairo, a marriage and family counselor, and an international speaker.

Book Introduction

SOURAYA BECHEALANY

"THE SURVIVING JEWEL": WHAT a daring title! Through metaphor, this book takes over the past and the present of the Christians in the Middle East, without overestimating their value, nor reducing it. Yet, what makes these Christians added value? To whom are they so precious? What mystery wraps and allows them to survive? From whom and from what must they preserve themselves? Are they genuinely under threat? So many questions that this book attempts to answer.

A Gospel Page: When a Merchant Finds What's Being Sought

I invite you to open the Gospel at a page. Here we are in Matthew's Gospel, where Jesus is teaching the crowd through parables. Let's listen to him: "Again, the kingdom of heaven is like a merchant looking for fine pearls; when he finds one of great value he goes and sells everything he owns and buys it" (Matt 13:45–46).

It is about the kingdom of heaven. The kingdom of heaven that is not compared, following what some might assume, to a pearl of great worth, but rather to the dynamic that moves a man, a merchant, to seek this pearl and end up finding it. It is an active search that implies a tenacious drive, the absolute certainty of the find, and perseverance to the end. This drive that moves the merchant through his faith allows him to reach the aim of his quest: the precious pearl. To his surprise, the value of the sought-after pearl goes beyond his expectations. It is indeed of great worth. This discovery makes him sell all that he possesses to buy this extraordinary pearl. He sells the "whole" to acquire the "singular." This singular thing is indeed worth the whole and much more. It is to this unique, sought-after, found, and bought "thing" that the kingdom resembles.

He who sets off to look for the kingdom does not need other acquisitions. He is this merchant who is ready to lose everything to earn the priceless. To choose the kingdom above all is the required attitude of the one who finds the pearl, the hidden treasure. The joy of its discovery triggers an unexpected bliss, it is the kingdom's joy that surpasses all expectations. The kingdom, that is Jesus amongst us and in us, is the fundamental reason for this human quest. When he is found, the man, the disciple, leaves everything, abandons everything, father, mother . . . to earn him, that is, to follow him (Matt 19:29).

On a different note, the parable also implies that the one who is searching and who is forgoing everything to buy a pearl "Since [he] regard[s] it as precious" (Isa 43:4) is the Lord himself. "For the Son of Man has come to seek out and save what was lost" (Luke 19:10), a priceless pearl, a humanity present and hidden at the heart of each forgotten people and each afflicted disciple.

The Parable and the Christians in the Middle East

To introduce this book by bridging the metaphor of its title—the jewel, an enduring story of Christianity in the Middle East—on one side, and this biblical parable on the other side might unsettle some readers. Yet, the comparison is justified. To approach the reality of the Christians in the Middle East through a metaphor and a parable allows the reader to discover these Christians afresh. Such a metaphoric approach dismisses any dull, static, and museal reading of their rich history and critical present. Admittedly, the pearl does not identify to a jewel; the former is precious through the works of nature and the waters, the latter the combined effort of matter and human craftsmanship. Nevertheless, didn't it take humans to seek out the pearl and others to cut it? It is to say that the history of mankind is constructed with time by the craft of men who carve into it their joys and sorrows. Thus, the metaphor and the parable inscribe the Christians in a precious heritage. It projects them into a life dynamic where they are taken, at times as the merchant, at other times as the jewel pearl, and to, a certain more dialectic extent, as both at once.

As merchants, these Christians, like their Master Jesus, can renounce everything—comfort, security, and stability—to seek out and find the priceless pearl-humanity that lies in the depths of all the afflicted Middle Eastern populations. That pearl is Jesus Christ and his kingdom. Some might understand this quest as an act of recovery or even proselytism. Beware of these reductionist interpretations since the way of the gospel is completely different. To look for the pearl is to be at the service of men and women of all affiliations and all denominations. It is to reveal to them the noblest parts they hold inside themselves: their precious jewels. The journey of this book will show that judiciously.

Merchants, these Christians themselves are also the pearl of great worth. These men and women come from a long history of 2,000 years. A history that is written with their strengths and weaknesses; their loyalties and disloyalties; their glories and failures; their wounds and blessings. Like a pearl of great value that is buried, covered, hidden under the rubble of life's struggles, they are here, and they are surviving.

By now you must have figured it out: it's about an enduring history; a history of men and women who carry on, who endure the struggles of time; a history that was, that is, and that is yet to come; the pages of which are still being written.

Merchants and priceless pearl-jewel, these Christians in the Middle East are both at once. Rooted in this region torn by wars and conflicts and moved by an eschatological strain, they are waiting for the true merchant, the Christ. He shall seek them out, find them, and comfort them during those troubled times, struggles, and persecutions. The Christ will redeem them and would cut them into precious jewels. Only then, and in their turn, will they make amends for the harm their brothers and sisters in the Middle East have lived. The *enduring story* is a history of hope and life.

When the Personal Experience Witnesses

This book is a travel in time. It will allow you to discover the Christians in the Middle East throughout history. It will open for you the doors of their homes; will make you discover the context where they were born and have grown, their pages of glory, but also their disarray and distress. It will propel you back to their heritage; will make you realize their serious historical disputes; will show you their current unstable existence, their "here and now," and the uncertainties of their future. It will show you the sanctity of their ways as much as the disloyalty to their bi-millennial mission.

Through this book, many amongst you will better know these Christians and measure more their real value. This discovery will probably be conclusive.

Yet some of us know them more closely because they have shared their roots and their fate with us. I am one of those. I endure what they are enduring, and I delight myself in what makes their joy, their honor, and their dignity. I especially had the blessing to visit them as a pilgrim and a bursar-guardian, while serving as secretary general of the Middle East Council of Churches (MECC, 2018–20). I have visited them where they lived, crossed their paths, walked into their footprints, exchanged fellowship with them. I have born witness to their daily life, to their joys and sorrows, to their fear and confidence. I know them by their names and through what they have chosen to reveal of themselves. I receive their faces and I pay a tribute to them. They are here and they are alive.

Hereby, a reality imposes itself. The future of these Christians is intrinsically tied to that of their fellow citizens. An analysis of their future situation that isolates them from their context will inevitably be lacking. It would be inaccurate to treat them as victims unbeknownst to their fellow Middle Eastern citizens—their persecution is known. Such a denial would betray the reality of history. We owe it to ourselves to be faithful to the truth. This necessarily requires a global approach to their reality. Yet, their context in the Middle East is very complex. It demands multidisciplinary approaches that consider all the historical aspects of their lives as much as their present. This guiding line forces itself on each researcher and seeker of meaning. The book that you are holding in your hands will reveal to you the appropriate and essential keys to such examination.

Oh, Reader, You are the Merchant, and You are the Jewel!

Merchants or priceless jewels, the Christians in the Middle East survive. They live through the ages and defy the centuries. They are recognized and mysterious; buried at times, conspicuous at others, sold and bought back; lost and found; merchants-researchers and seekers of God. In all cases, they are of high worth, they are unique if I dare say so, without any equal in the world. More than a jewel amongst others, it is *The* jewel that survives, *The enduring story of hope and life!*

By revealing who they are, this book shows you that you too are pearls of great worth. By preserving them you will preserve yourselves. For they say a lot about your mystery. To allow others to bury them will put you at a high risk of being yourselves sold at a low price! To lose them is to lose the reason for your existence. For you would have sold or forgone the Christ hidden in them, your cradle, your Christian roots, your foundations. You are called to follow the drive of the merchant to seek what you already know: look for them, find them, and redeem them.

Redeem them, how? It does not come down to me to give you the relevant instructions. I invite you to dive into this book and to let yourself be taken by their mystery. Make your way through to meet them. Forge a communion with them. Only then, from the depth of a bruised survival, theirs, and perhaps also yours, life will spring out as from a source that never runs dry.

Section One

The Story of Christianity Narrated in Historical Context

1

The Expansion and Dispute of the Christian Movement (First to Sixth Centuries)

CLAUDIA RAMMELT

FROM ITS VERY BEGINNINGS, the faith community founded on the message of the cross and the resurrection saw itself as a global movement that was not confined to existing boundaries. Faith in Jesus Christ started to expand after Pentecost as an inter- and transcultural confession both within the cultures and languages of the Roman Empire and beyond (Acts 1:1–13).[1] From the very first, it took on varied forms (1 Cor 1:10–17). This heterogeneous constitution provoked further processes of differentiation, which also implied struggles for power and hegemony, orthodoxy and heresy. A main reason Christianity's heterogeneous shape contributed to a further increase in diversity is that the question of how to understand Jesus Christ arose in different contexts. Consequently, the plurality of the Christian faith became anchored in the structure of Christianity. From a certain point onwards, "Oriental"[2] Christianity existed in different confessions.

This chapter outlines of the processes with which the Christian faith moved through the ancient world, before exploring the developments that resulted in the rich heritage of those churches that are at the center of this volume, the churches that confessional studies discuss under the names of the Oriental-Orthodox churches and those of the Byzantine imperial church.

---

1. Rammelt and Hornung, "*Begegnung in der Glokalität*," 15–28.

2. I am using the term "Orient" in the awareness of the many nuances it has, notably in the Orientalism debate inspired by Edward Said. I understand the Orient as a region that is not dependent on the political boundaries of the Roman and Sasanian Empires, but will focus instead on those regions in which the processes in question have played a prominent role.

To the Ends of the Earth (Acts 1:8): Christianity Reaches the Cultures of the Orient

The Roman Empire held sway over vast parts of the "Orient." Adjacent in the East was the empire known as that of the Parthians (from the third century BCE into the third century CE), later as that of the Sasanians (224/226–642). This realm likewise occupied large areas of what is often called the Orient. The pantheon of the Roman deities and likewise the religious diversity in the Parthian and Sasanian Empires, represented by fire altars or popular rites, do not suggest a religious vacuum that would have been filled by Christianity—to the contrary. Life in the Orient took place within a multitude of religious possibilities. Within the boundaries of the Roman Empire, an exceptional position was occupied by those Jewish traditions from which Christianity emerged—the community whose faith was rooted in the crucified and risen Jesus Christ and that expanded from its initial basis in Jerusalem. I wish to give an outline of this expansion as a process that reaches various places in the Orient and in which Christianity establishes itself within its respective societies.

Expansion into the Orient

The resurrection was the most significant event for the expansion of Christianity. Believers narrate the life of the crucified and risen Lord while expecting his return (Luke 24). They preached the gospel in Jewish congregations, and soon gentiles likewise took to the message, like the centurion named Cornelius (Acts 10). The Acts of the Apostles further recount how Paul always took synagogues as starting points for his missionary activities, as for example in Thessalonica (17:1–9). A certain image of the gatherings of these first Christians emerges: they live and pray in communion (2:42). Baptism is constitutive of this fellowship (2:41). Yet these communities were not spared internal conflicts, for faith in Jesus Christ questions existing convictions and customs (e.g., Acts 15).

Soon the proclamation of the gospel was no longer limited to Jerusalem. The followers of Jesus Christ were first called Christians in Antioch (Acts 11:26). Peter takes on a prominent role in the expansion of this group (9:32), but so does Barnabas (11:22). Eventually, however, the apostle Paul became the driving force behind the foundation of congregations in the most varied metropolitan centres (from Acts 9 onwards). Paul's missionary journeys (Acts 13–21) appear as a goal-oriented endeavor taking him into the various cities of Asia Minor and Greece, where the foundation of congregations ensued.³ That the expansion of Christianity was due to the activities of a large number of additional people can be seen from the reports about Priscilla and Aquila (18:1–3,19–21), but also from the lists of greetings in Paul's letters (prominently in Rom 16:21–23). We also know that the gospel reached the most varied areas of the ancient world through merchants, travellers, soldiers as well as itinerant preachers. We often lack the historical sources to trace these events in detail; only a few archaeological finds give testimony to these religious developments. Eventually, literary sources will mention Christian theologians and their oeuvre, chronicles will report of churches and later of bishops, implying that congregations had taken shape before.

Christianity expanded to Asia Minor via the area known as the Syro-Palestinian region, reaching Greece, North Africa, and moving onwards into the East and the West. Although Jerusalem remained out of bounds also for Jewish Christians, due to the political conflicts between Jews and Romans, we soon hear from congregations in Antioch, Ephesus, and Corinth, but also in Alexandria and Carthage. Via the area of Osrhoene, congregations were established in Northern Mesopotamia, in Adiabene, and soon even further in the East. Since the fifth century at the latest, Christians in those areas recognized the episcopal seat of Seleucia-Ctesiphon. Congregations were also founded in the area known as Armenia and Georgia.

In these places, the spirit of the apostolic beginnings was very much alive, for example in the tradition of tracing the bishop's office back to the times of the apostles. This awareness sustained Christians across all internal differences, and all traditions laid claim to their respective founding fathers. In this sense, Peter was often considered the first bishop of Antioch (Gal 2:11–12); tradition viewed his disciple Mark as the first representative in Egypt. The list of bishops in Jerusalem begins with James, the brother of the Lord (Gal 2:9–12), Thomas was held not only to be the founder of the bishopric of Seleucia-Ctesiphon, but even of the Christian congregations in India and China. Another tradition recounts how Thomas commissioned Thaddeus (Addai in Syriac) to preach in Edessa, who then installed the first bishop of Arbela and supposedly reached Armenia. Likewise, Bartholomew was held to have been active in Persia, Armenia, and India. Georgians refer to Andrew as their first missionary, while Ethiopians invoke Matthew, with whom numerous missionary legends are associated that were meant to bolster the legitimacy of the apostolic origins, as was the case with all the other prominent apostles.

---

3. In this sense, see Koschorke, "Religion and Migration," 60.

Navigating the diverse cultures of the Orient

The empires of this larger area, which were usually in rivalry with each other, contained the most varied regions that were home to people who often differed from each other in language, ethnicity, culture, and religion. They lived together or alongside each other, engaged in commerce, competed with each other, or maintained close personal connections. The "cultures" of the Orient were diverse and complex. Within this diversity, people started to articulate and practice their faith in Jesus Christ: in Jerusalem as in other places, Jewish believers in Christ confessed their faith; in Edessa, Christian traders said their prayers, and in Egypt, Christian prayers were likewise heard from the lips of the faithful in the metropolis of Alexandria. In the mountains between the lakes Van, Sevan, and Urmia, Armenians who had embraced Christianity prayed and reflected in Armenian. Numerous linguistic traditions were present in these places, as were other cultural traditions and forms of thought. People from various social strata, milieus, and geographic regions came together in the name of Jesus Christ, practicing their faith, but also discussing it and struggling for its truth and authenticity.

This faith was the context in which the *ekklesia*-congregation emerged, the group that faced the challenge of finding a language to understand the gospel, to live and communicate it.[4] The severing of ties from the congregation of the synagogue shows that in precisely these congregations, processes of contrastive delimitation and the negotiation of identity took place. People struggled with others regarding commandments of circumcision and ritual purity as well as forms of organization and thought. A look at the metropolitan centres shows that these processes of negotiation did not result in a uniformity of Christian faith, but rather in an increase in diversity. The gospel was explicated in the Greek tradition of the *logos*, while in the vicinity of Alexandria and Antioch, people appropriated the language of ascesis, shaping the Christian faith in the tradition of austerity. Those who reflected on the faith in the context of gnostic convictions, as in Alexandria, wrote cosmic dramas of creation. So did the adherents of Bardaisan, who lived in Edessa. Their faith was articulated the way he had laid it down in his "Book of the Laws of the Countries," the only extant work of his. In Edessa they were known as Marcionites and Bardaisanites, and likewise the group that would later retain the upper hand against them as representing the "catholic" church was named after

---

4. Kahl, "Re-Lektüre der Apostelgeschichte aus der Perspektive von Flucht und Migration," 4.

its own founding figure. This was a man named Palut, which resulted in the name of Palutians for the "catholic" Christians in Edessa.[5]

Christianity turned out to be a social phenomenon shaped by migration, moving through the spaces and into the societies of the Orient as a faith that developed in diverse ways regarding theologies, forms or organization, and also languages.[6] In varying degrees, processes of identity-formation took place by contrastive delimitation, assimilation, and transculturalism. In this process, communities repeatedly asked themselves what constituted what constituted the essential aspects of the faith, implying repeated struggles about what was indispensable in the midst of change. Questions of orthodoxy and heresy were continuously discussed and negotiated, resulting in ever more specific views of what it means to be Christian. This process also involved struggles for power and influence.

Origen is exemplary of the wider movement in supposing an original unity in Christianity, which was later on harmed by heresies: "When they were beginning . . . they were few and were of one mind; but since they have spread to become a multitude, they are divided and rent asunder, and each wants to have his own party. For they wanted this from the beginning."[7] Lists of heretics or writings refuting certain views and convictions give expression to precisely this wrestling about truth, or truths.[8] Repeatedly this led to acts of condemnation and exclusion that marginalized certain theological trends and views, while other forms of the faith became more dominant, representing the Christian faith from now on.[9]

Differentiation of Christianity in the Orient

The Christian faith was a multi-faceted reality within the boundaries of the Roman Empire, but also far beyond this realm. The biblical canon resulted from the struggles surrounding both the various shapes the Christian faith took and its essentials. Christians in the Orient likewise

---

5. Ephrem the Syrian, *Contra Haereses* 12.5, 169–70.

6. Koschorke, "Religion und Migration," 58–59.

7. Origen, *Contra Celsum*, 134 (III, 10).

8. Particularly prominent are Irenaeus of Lyon's *Adversus Haereses*, Tertullian's vigorous objections against the heretics, and the *Panarion* ("First Aid Kit") by Epiphanius of Salamis, intended for those who have been bitten by the snake.

9. As Origen's views show, the usual assumption was that in the beginning, Christianity was unified in the true faith, after which an increasing number of heretics split off. Walter Bauer inverted this view in, Kraft and Krodel *Orthodoxy and Heresy in Earliest Christianity*. Bauer assumes that diversity or heresy came first, and unity was achieved later.

achieved consensus regarding the understanding of God as the Father, Son, and Holy Spirit, as reflected in the acknowledgment of the decrees of the councils of Nicaea (325) and Constantinople (381). After Christianity was deemed *religio licita* in 31, councils became an instrument chosen to discuss controversial questions and deliberate about ecclesial matters. In the hope to achieve peace and maintain unity in religious matters, decisions were considered binding. Doctrinal unity was considered crucial for legitimate worship, on which the divine favor of the Roman Empire and the maintenance of *salus publica* depended.

After the Trinitarian debates, the bishops sought to overcome the deep controversies in the understanding of Jesus Christ, hoping to achieve religious unity. The conciliar decision dealing with the teaching about Jesus Christ from 451, however, failed to produce the church unity that was both demanded politically and desired within the church.

Christological controversies as a boundary marker

The question of how to understand Jesus Christ deals with the very heart of Christian identity. Those who investigated this question in the ancient world understood that with such reflection the church pursued no mere theoretical interest but explored the chief factor that shaped theology and piety. In the first place, theologians were dealing with the question of how a person's salvation would be possible, which defines the technical area of soteriology, and so they turned to expressions of the faith that were condensed in various kinds of texts. Readers encounter certain Christological views already in the writings of the New Testament. While the tenets that were basic for the doctrine of Christ had at first been preserved and expressly proclaimed as a *depositum fidei*, theologians went on to discuss various understandings of the matter in an increasingly controversial sense. With Apollinaris of Laodicea (d. 390), the discussion received the broader public attention of prominent theological debates, and the controversy gained in urgency. Since no one less than God was able to destroy sin and death, the bishop reasoned that Christians cannot envision the Son of God merely as a human person equipped with extraordinary divine power or inspiration. In his understanding, then, the *Logos* itself replaced Jesus Christ's human intellect (*nous*) as the highest aspect of his soul, functioning as the personal subject. Apollinaris encapsulated this understanding of the Son of God in the formula "of the one incarnate nature of the God Logos." Especially the expression "the one nature" provoked repeated controversies in the Christological debates. It created the impression of a divine-human fusion, which would denigrate the mystery of God. For that reason, Apollinaris was repeatedly condemned as a heretic, starting in 377.

The proper controversy was triggered in 428, with the question of which title to assign to Mary. Nestorius (381–453), the bishop of Constantinople, had suggested that as a compromise, theologians should speak of Mary neither as the God-bearer (*Theotokos*) nor as one who had given birth to a human person, but as the Christ-bearer (*Christotokos*). The proposal was rooted in the kind of Christology that is commonly called Antiochene and which had been devised notably by theologians like Diodore of Tarsus (d. 394) and Theodore of Mopsuestia (352–428). The latter emphasized that Jesus must be thought of as a person in body and soul, precisely to rule out Apollinaris' suspect views. For if the root of sin lies in the soul, the Second Adam must be attributed a human soul so that he can redeem it. Jesus Christ must, by consequence, be envisioned as a complete human and a complete divine nature, which are connected in him (by means of a *synapheia*, an indwelling). Cyril (375/80–444), bishop of Alexandria, responded passionately to Nestorius' proposal, favouring the title God-bearer for Mary (*theotokos*). Were Mary merely the Christ-bearer, she would give birth to the human person Jesus, but not the Son of God. Cyril disparaged Nestorius repeatedly with the charge of having fallen for the heresy of Paul of Samosata (bishop of Antioch from 260–68). God had not come *into* a human person, but had truly *become* even a human being, without ceasing to be God. On this basis, Cyril conceived of the union of the Son of God as an essential union, pressing the notion of one nature again and again. The two opponents were the highest-ranking clergy in two prominent, rival patriarchal seats, Constantinople and Alexandria, and a council was required to solve the theological controversy. Emperor Theodosius II (r. 408–50) convened a council, which met in Ephesus in 431. When the situation escalated in the ancient metropolis, the emperor dissolved the council. Finally, Cyril's partial synod was recognized as the Third Ecumenical Council, while Cyril, under pressure, in turn declared his respect of the Formula of Union from 433. Although the Formula of Union was aimed at a rapprochement, advocates of a Christology in the Alexandrian mold faced off with those favoring the Antiochene concept. The demarcation lines ran through these regions and cities themselves, rather than merely between them.

This situation became palpable in Edessa, for example, where evidently a sense of religious competition had popularized the Christological discourse. Clergy, monks, people from the wider monastic milieu, but also artisans, agricultural labourers, Roman administrative officers, and various municipal dignitaries jostled for the proper understanding of Christology. The question of how to understand Jesus Christ had apparently thrown the entire city into turmoil. Yet the conflict was kept burning not merely because of the theological question; crucially it was also a conflict about the proper regard of authority figures and their lifestyles. Monastically minded circles harshly criticized the loose way of life of Bishop Ibas. Especially in the year 448, the Christological question triggered a dispute about power and influence in the northern Mesopotamian metropolis.

On the level of the wider church of the empire, theological discourse was likewise beset with controversy, especially relating to the theology of Eutyches (378–456). The allegiances of this abbot of a monastery in Constantinople lay with the Alexandrian camp. While he affirmed Jesus Christ's two natures, he emphasized particularly the "one nature" that resulted when Jesus' humanity was absorbed with the unification of the natures. Following a complaint about the archimandrite, the endemic synod deposed him in 448. Taking sides with Eutyches, Dioscurus of Alexandria (d. 454) brought numerous supporters around in the monk's favor, and in 449, the emperor felt forced to convene yet another council. Dioscurus presided over the meeting, which achieved notoriety as the "Robber Council." The meeting was bound to have a clear tendency, and Leo's Tome, a doctrinal letter that Leo the bishop of Rome sought to insert into the discussion, was not taken into account. Emperor Marcian (450–57) again convened a general council in 451. The atmosphere was tense when the opposing theological camps sought to make their cases. During the entry of Theodoret of Cyrus (393–460) and Dioscurus, one side was shouting: "Out with the teacher of Nestorius!"[10] The opposite side cried: "Out with Dioscurus the murderer!"[11] Because the opponents cast each other's positions in stereotypical terms, robust theological disputes were increasingly dominated by the fear of committing blasphemy. When opponents were unable to agree with the critique of the opposing side, they instrumentalized heresy charges for excluding others from church communion, without having fully engaged their theological arguments.[12]

Insisting on an expression of the unity of the faith, it was asked for a definition of the faith that would complement the Nicaean Creed. The Confession of Chalcedon, phrased as one single sentence, first states the unity of the person of Jesus Christ and then, in the second part, specifies the way this unity is real "in two natures." In the latter context, the formula makes

---

10. Gesta Chalcedonae, *Acta Conciliorum Oecumenicorum*, vol. II.1.1, 55–70, 69:18–19.

11. Gesta Chalcedonae, *Acta Conciliorum Oecumenicorum*, vol. II.1.1, 69:27.

12. Mühlenberg discusses the question of whether Chalcedon should be considered a struggle between phantoms. Mühlenberg, "Das Dogma von Chalcedon," 253–56.

use of four alpha privatives: inconfusedly, unchangeably, indivisibly, inseparably.[13] Chalcedon associates the two aspects in Jesus Christ with the concept of nature, while the unity is denoted with the concept of *hypostasis*. This is a gain in specificity that helps prevent misunderstandings. Later research has especially discussed the question of which sources the Chalcedonian Creed drew on, and here Cyrilian, western, or Antiochene influences have been proposed, depending on the interpretation of the formula. Yet even if we do not decide for any of these options, developments subsequent to the council show that this amalgamation of theological positions has been unable to conclude the search for theological truth for everyone involved.

How differences became more entrenched with the Christological debates

From the emperor's point of view, the definition of the faith of Chalcedon had forged a consensus: "What we urgently and fervently desired has come to pass: the quarrel about the law of the orthodox Christian has been ended; finally the remedies against sinful error have been found, and the disagreement among the nations has turned into complete agreement."[14] However, the creed that had been designed in order to achieve unity provoked disagreement as well: "And we anathematize the Council of Chalcedon also because it distinguisheth in one Lord Jesus Christ, the Only-begotten Son of God, . . . and it agreth with the wicked Nestorius who is accursed and doomed to perdition."[15]

Events taking place in various locations of the Roman Empire illustrate the disagreements openly. In Palestine, large groups of monks expelled their bishop, Juvenal (422–58), because he had changed sides at the council. Inciting the crowds, the monk Theodosius took the lead in cleansing the province of the Chalcedonian confession. It took Emperor Marcian until 455 to re-install the ousted Juvenal, after the monks engaged in a veritable battle with the military. In Alexandria, the pro-Chalcedonian bishop, Proterius (451–57), had to resort to military violence to prevail against his anti-Chalcedonian rivals Timothy Ailurus (d. 477) and Peter Mongus (d. 490). After the death of the former patriarch, Dioscurus, Timothy Ailurus, an adherent of Cyril, was elected patriarch of Alexandria in a secret vote; in office he vigorously pursued anti-Chalcedonian propaganda. In Edessa, the

---

13. "Definitio Fidei," *Acta Conciliorum Oecumenicorum*, vol. II.1.2, 127–30, 129.

14. "Marcianis Imperatori Edictum," *Acta Conciliorum Oecumenicorum*, vol. II.1.3, 120:15–20.

15. "The Creed of Philoxenus," *The Discourses of Philoxenus, Bishop of Mabbôgh, A.D. 485–519*, xxxiii–xxxvii, xxxv–xxxvi.

Chalcedonian position also won the day, but anti-Chalcedonian forces likewise sought to displace proponents of the Antiochene position. Notably the so-called "Persian school" was instrumental in asserting the Alexandrian position, which resulted in the shutdown of the school in Edessa in 489, if not before, due to the zealous activity of the local bishop and the emperor's command. Especially in the region around Antioch, a number of prominent bishops gained a foothold with their anti-Chalcedonian theology. Philoxenos of Mabbug (ca. 440/50–523) and Severus of Antioch (ca. 456–538) are probably best known in this regard.

This rough outline of events, which could be complemented with numerous details from the various provinces and cities from the era, shows clearly how those theological convictions classically known as Antiochene Christology developed their potential, especially outside of the boundaries of the Roman Empire. Within these boundaries, the imperial church wrestled with those forces indebted to a Christology as devised by Cyril of Alexandria. Such events show dynamics: critical theological questions against decisions of the council went hand-in-hand with resistance against a compromise that was politically motivated. In turn, theological disagreements were answered in political terms: once conflict threatened to break out openly or the declaration of the council was met with open resistance, any flexibility in carrying out the decisions of the councils came to an end. Besides disagreements in theological matters, a discrepancy emerged between centralized political aspirations, which asserted a Greco-Roman heritage, and those local forces in the cities and regions that were shaped by greater religious heterogeneity, reflecting the pluralist societies of the Orient.

From this point onwards, the religious history of the Roman Empire takes place as a back and forth between the rival theological positions. Emperor Basiliscus (r. 475–76) and Anastasius (r. 491–518) decided for an anti-Chalcedonian politics. Emperor Zenon (r. 474–91) sought to reconcile the competing positions by implementing the so-called Henotikon, but failed. In the ensuing years, the Henotikon was interpreted both in anti- and pro-Chalcedonian ways. In the sixth century, however, Justin (r. 518–27) gave imperial religious politics a new direction, rigorously seeking general recognition of Chalcedon. Pursuing this goal, the emperor did not flinch from coercive measures. Personal politics, including notably the installation of bishops, played a crucial role for him. In its decrees, the Council of Chalcedon had regulated the rights and duties of bishops and other clerics more clearly than before. Justin demanded that bishops follow him in his resolute striving to secure absolute recognition of Chalcedon. Not everybody agreed, and in the region of Antioch, Justin deposed forty bishops; in the Euphratensis region he dismissed half of the bishops and even three quarters in Osrhoene. Yet the exiled bishops sought to continue their administrative activities and to go on providing pastoral guidance in their original churches. The emperor realized that an increasing number of Christians participated in the Eucharist celebrated by the non-Chalcedonian priests. His successor Justinian (r. 527–65) continued Justin's approach, even if among his chosen instruments were more elegant efforts to win over reluctant Christians with religious colloquies. Even here, constructive dialogue and the discussion of terminological differences was rarely at the center; rather the interest lay in the preservation of formulae and concepts. Routinely theologians invoked the authority of past thinkers, in the assumption that certain figures represented heresy itself and that their demonstrative refutation would preserve orthodoxy intact. These procedures culminated in the Council of Constantinople in 553 that sacrificed the two prominent representatives of Antiochene thought and one further representative document, Theodore of Mopsuestia, Theodoret of Cyrus, and the letter of Ibas of Edessa.[16] The fathers of the council assumed that by refuting these thinkers and this document, they would free the Chalcedonian creed from the charge of Nestorianism. Names and persons had been reduced to mere instruments in the struggle between heresy and orthodoxy. In this era, the theological initiative of so-called Neo-Chalcedonianism was not beyond such means. Neither were the seventh-century efforts in the monergetic and monotheletic debates able to advance a proper mutual theological understanding and achieve reconciliation.

Differences stabilize, heterogeneous church structures emerge

Central authorities renewed their efforts again and again to find a path back towards unity. The long struggle shows how much the emperors and church officials had invested to maintain and assert the ideal of a unifying formula, which was politically motivated. Yet Christianity was simply unable to be as unified as the empire and its own self-understanding wanted it to be. Post-Chalcedonian developments implied that church unity, demanded by political interests and sought by church representatives, was simply not to be found anymore. Only in further ecclesial differentiation did the conflict come to an end: a differentiation into Chalcedonian and Anti-Chalcedonian strands between those who saw themselves in the tradition of a Cyril of Alexandria and those who continued to hold up the theology of Theodore of Mopsuestia. In the Sasanian Empire, the Chalcedonian dogma did not turn out to be a powerful factor, nor did anti-Chalcedonian forces in the tradition of Cyril

16. *Acta Conciliorum Oecumenicorum*, vol. IV.1, 219.

of Alexandria end up dominating Christian thought. Nevertheless, the dogmatic confession has preserved the form of Christological reflection that had been uprooted in the Roman territory and has favoured a Christology in the tradition of Theodore of Mopsuestia's. In the fifth century, synods of the so-called Apostolic Church of the East precisely adopted this confession, going on to establish structures in the Sasanian territory.

If we are to bring out tendencies more vigorously that have been implicit in these developments, ultimately the conclusion would be that these latter procedures amount to a struggle that was at odds with the ideas of unity promoted in Roman circles and supported among Christians. Theological truth was recognized as such even apart from conciliar decrees. It was absorbed together with the question of how belief in this truth can be expressed in such a way that its shape is recognizable to others who may perceive it in concrete ways. The answer must include the development of independent church structures. Such processes took on concrete form when Emperor Justin demanded loyalty to Chalcedon from the bishops. Initiatives in the establishment of an independent hierarchy received new energy when the council of 536 declared Severus of Antioch a heretic. Things became yet again more concrete when non-Chalcedonian Jacob Baradaeus was consecrated as bishop, along with an Arab. Empress Theodora (d. 548) supported this, having become a patron of the non-Chalcedonians over the years.

Once the consecration of anti-Chalcedonian bishops was possible, the theological differentiation received a firm structural foundation in the religious institutions. The establishment of non-Chalcedonian communities raised the question of the institutional shape of the church in more concrete terms. If the newly affirmed communities were legitimate churches indeed, church unity had ruptured for the first time in such a way that abiding parallel church structures had emerged. Considered in another way, in the altered historical and political circumstances of the time after Constantine, the heterogeneous identity of Christianity received a new basis, which was manifest in the development of different churches or structurally discrete communities. Precisely this procedure both bolstered up various given constituents of a religious multiplicity and made them visible for the first time. A plurality of ways to live the Christian faith, together with particular cultural and ethical orientations, stabilized or continued to develop their particular shapes.

The different linguistic traditions and the way they became tied up with particular faith traditions are a prominent example. In large parts of the patriarchate of Antioch, people spoke Aramaic dialects. In Edessa, the language called Syriac developed from this Aramaic tradition. In Egypt,

Coptic was the vernacular. Moreover, there were the languages of "Rome," Latin and Greek. Certainly, in the regions of the Orient, Greek was particularly prominent. In the region of Antioch in particular, however, higher social strata regarded Syriac as the language of the barbarians. John Chrysostom (347–407), for his part, made a point of preaching precisely in Greek, avoiding Syriac in order indicate his social location. A translation project at the so-called Persian school in Edessa illustrates yet another trend: people did not use their language skills to exclude others, but to disseminate the Greek theology of the Orient in the Syrian milieu. Christians in Edessa did not wish to favor any particular side within that wider constellation that Theodor Mommsen characterized, surely appropriately, as the "double civilisation" of the Syrian region.[17] Rather, people intended for both sides of the wider tradition to be recognized and to merge. In the areas speaking Syriac or Coptic, this dual linguistic tradition takes on a more differentiated shape in the controversies about the proper understanding of Jesus Christ, because the anti-Chalcedonian circles appear to have been more familiar with the local languages, which then became established as the languages of the respective communities. These developments were possible because both in Egypt and in the Syrian region, local communities had been firmly rooted in the Christian faith. In Edessa, translations of the Hebrew Bible into Syriac go back even into the first century. The Peshitta—the Syriac "simple version"—is known to have existed in numerous manuscripts in the fifth century. We have to assume, then, that Christians in the Syriac-speaking region relied precisely on this version. In just the same way, Coptic versions of New Testament writings are among the oldest in use by the Christians in that region. Even though the demarcation lines between languages were more fluid and open than I can reconstruct in this context, the trend emerges that ultimately, individual languages become identity markers within their respective traditions.

Moreover, languages were associated with liturgical traditions. Christians celebrating rites in Syriac used the liturgy of James, which was rooted in Jerusalem along with numerous other liturgies. The *Euchologion* of Serapion of Thmuis documents liturgical texts used by Christians in Egypt, while in the imperial church, the Greek liturgy of John Chrysostom became prevalent. When communities established themselves, they favoured the languages that had traditionally been familiar in the respective regions—as was the case with Syriac, Coptic, and with Armenian, as well as Greek for Christians in

---

17. Mommsen, *The History of Rome*, vol. VIII: *The Provinces of the Roman Empire*, 125.

the tradition of the imperial church. These trends asserted themselves in the use of particular writings and of liturgical forms.

The obvious association of different language traditions with the anti-Chalcedonian position shows that the opposition to the creed was not restricted to a few regional centres. Rather, the phenomenon can be observed in those regions whose cultures tended towards heterogeneity already. Presumably, that means that the anti-Chalcedonian opposition became a powerful factor in those areas in which indigenous populations were dominant alongside Greco-Roman citizens. Yet the opposition takes shape within the regional character of ethnic groups and cultures, or as a twofold structure in the traditional bishoprics of the Orient. The principle of the antique church—"one city, one bishop"—become obsolete when twofold ecclesial structures were established. Additionally, the aspect of anti-Chalcedonian convictions also helps trace ethnic aspects within the traditional boundaries of the great patriarchates: the indigenous communities saw themselves as Syrians, Armenians, or inhabitants of Egypt who preserved and cultivated the Christian heritage within their own respective languages. Their designation as national churches strengthens and elevates the national aspect of these emerging communities, just as, alternatively, their characterisation as anti-Chalcedonians would reduce them to their opposition to Chalcedon. As Christians of the Orient, for centuries they have lived the Christian faith in a multi-faceted, differentiated way. In this faith, they have never been able to ignore the question of the inviolable truth of the understanding of Jesus Christ, and this has influenced basic decisions in church politics up to today.

Conclusion: The Rich Heritage of the Christian "Orient"

With a view to the political demands that Roman society made of religious practitioners, the developments in church history sketched here appear tragic: they can be seen as a process of loss, even of failure—with the underpinning sense that the inviolable theological truth held by the majority is continually faced with a minority whose position would never become the consensus. This lies in the nature of the common historical concept of this wider process, and that is the way historians have come to understand it.

The process that church historians, with their training in doctrinal matters, see as resulting in a loss of unity, due to doctrinal differences, also implies the aspect of productivity and creativity. In other words, the uncompromising commitment to one's own tradition harbors a force that "creates" churches, preserving or bringing forth particular cultures of lived religion. This raises the question as to whether this process should indeed be characterized as one in which new boundaries come to separate former neighbors, or whether in this process, differences emerge and stabilise as well. Considerations by Christoph Markschies may point in the direction of the latter aspect:

> It does not seem to be due to chance that in the mid-fifth century, a theological division came about that stabilised eventually, separating the core of the Mediterranean region and these regions at the periphery. . . . Moreover, in analysing this schism, we should not overlook the contrast between the provincial regions, shaped more by monasteries and rural villages, and the urban centres, shaped more by the bishops, a differentiation, then, within the great geographical regions.[18]

The split preserved theological positions and cultures of lived religion that otherwise would be lost to reflection. Likewise, linguistic traditions have remained alive that would otherwise certainly have been forgotten. Once this perspective is embraced, the events surrounding the reflection on Jesus Christ appear as a differentiation within the Christian faith that is inherent in Christianity itself. This differentiation reflected:

- theological convictions that emerged from conflicts and struggles around the understanding of Jesus Christ,
- political views and efforts that were impossible to be shared by everyone, and
- diverging formations in culture and lived religion that became visible and stabilized.

In this process, intercultural and ecumenical themes gain clearer shape: the universality of the message can find expression only within the particularity of historical contexts and in the struggle between the powers of the day, and this expression cannot be monolithic. Alexandrian, Antiochene, and eventually, Chalcedonian ways of reflecting on Christ, as well as the debates surrounding these positions, have arisen precisely within such particular situations. In the Orient, the necessity to engage in dialogue and reach some joint settlement on intercultural and ecumenical issues emerges already at the waning of late antiquity.

---

18. Markschies, *Das antike Christentum*, 31–32.

For Further Reading

Amirav, Hagit. *Authority and Performance: Sociological Perspectives on the Council of Chalcedon.* Göttingen: Vandenhoeck & Ruprecht, 2015.

Bauer, Walter. *Orthodoxy and Heresy in Earliest Christianity.* Edited by Robert A. Kraft and Gerhard Krodel. Philadelphia: Fortress, 1971.

Budge, E. A. Wallis, ed. *The Creed of Philoxenus: The Discourses of Philoxenus, Bishop of Mabbôgh, A.D. 485–519.* London: Asher, 1894.

"Definitio Fidei." In *Acta Conciliorum Oecumenicorum,* vol. II.1.2, edited by Eduard Schwartz. Berlin: de Gruyter, 1933.

Ephrem the Syrian. *Contra Haereses 12.5: Des heiligen Ephraem des Syrers Hymnen contra Hareses.* Edited and translated by Edmund Beck. Corpus Scriptorum Christianorum Orientalium. Louvain: Secretariat du Corpus Scriptorum Christianorum Orientalium, 1957.

Frend, W. H. C. *The Rise of the Monophysite Movement: Chapters in the History of the Church in the Fifth and Sixth Centuries.* Cambridge: Cambridge University Press, 1972.

"Gesta Chalcedonae." In *Acta Conciliorum Oecumenicorum*, vol. II.1.1, edited by Eduard Schwartz. Berlin: de Gruyter, 1933.

Grillmeier, Alois. *Christ in Christian Tradition,* Vol. 1 and Vol. 2,1–4. Oxford: Oxford University Press, 1975–2013.

Harnack, Adolf von. *The Mission and Expansion of Christianity in the First Three Centuries.* 2 vols. New York: Williams and Norgate, 1908.

Leuenberger-Wenger, Sandra. *Das Konzil von Chalcedon und die Kirche: Konflikte und Normierungsprozesse im 5. und 6. Jahrhundert.* Supplements to Vigiliae Christianae 153. Leiden: Brill, 2019.

"Marcianis Imperatori Edictum." In *Acta Conciliorum Oecumenicorum,* vol. II.1.3, edited by Eduard Schwartz. Berlin: de Gruyter, 1935.

Markschies, Christoph. *Das antike Christentum: Frömmigkeit, Lebensformen, Institutionen.* Munich: Beck, 2006.

Mommsen, Theodor. *The History of Rome, vol. VIII: The Provinces of the Roman Empire from Caesar to Diocletian,* part 2. Translated by William P. Dickson. London: Bentley, 1886.

Origen. *Contra Celsum.* Translated and edited by Henry Chadwick. Cambridge: Cambridge University Press, 1965.

Price, Richard, and Michael Gaddis, eds. *The Acts of the Council of Chalcedon.* Translated Texts for Historians 45. Liverpool: Liverpool University Press, 2007.

Rammelt, Claudia, and Esther Hornung. "Begegnung in der Glokalität: Christliche Migrationskirchen in Deutschland im Wandel der Zeit." In *Begegnung in der Glokalität,* edited by C. Rammelt, E. Hornung, and V. Mihoc, 87–102. Leipzig: Evangelische Verlagsanstalt, 2018.

2

Conquest and Christian-Muslim Relations
during the Islam Era (Seventh to Eleventh centuries)

MIKE KUHN

Proximity and Antipathy

THE STORY OF ISLAM's origin is full of intrigue, perhaps matched only by its near confessional neighbor, Christianity. Located at the conflict nexus of two major world civilizations—Rome and Persia—Islam emerged from the arid lands of the Arabian Peninsula with a dynamism and elan that would startle and, at times, terrify both of its larger precedents. Cities and lands that were once the prize jewels of the Mediterranean would fall to Islamic dominance in rapid succession. The desert trader herald of the Islamic faith saw himself as the final prophet in the long tradition of seers, thought by Christians to have culminated in Christ. The other scriptures had arisen from this long tradition of Jewish prophets. Would Muhammad himself have been mystified that his prophetic message came to be understood as inveterately opposed to the primary tenets of Christianity? How the two faiths intersected and shaped one another is the story of this eventful period of history.

The Qur'anic revelation purported to be in continuity with the precedent revelations. "We sent to you [Muhammad] the scripture with the truth, confirming the scriptures that came before it, and with final authority over them . . ." (Q5:48).[1] Furthermore, the adherents of the early prophetic revelations were present and available to corroborate the message: "So if you [Prophet] are in doubt about what We have revealed to you, ask those who have been reading the scriptures before you" (Q10:94). Such exhortations lead to the conclusion that Muhammad viewed his own revelation

---

1. Unless otherwise indicated, all Qur'anic references are from *The Qur'an*, by M. A. S Abdel Haleem.

as being in agreement with Moses, David, Jesus, and the other prophets. The difference being that the revelation given through Muhammad was in a clear Arabic tongue—a prophetic word to unite the Arab tribes around the worship of the one God—Allāh: "Truly, this Qur'ān has been sent down by the Lord of the Worlds: the Trustworthy Spirit brought it down to your heart [Prophet], so that you could bring warning in a clear Arabic tongue. This was foretold in the scriptures of earlier religions" (Q26:192–96). From an initial posture of proximity, we move through our period of concern to the threshold of the Crusades—a military and territorial conflict waged with and around the symbols and landmarks of two world faiths, now rivals. How did proximity turn to antipathy? The question's complexity reverberates through history down to the present day.

We begin by Muhammad's encounters with Christians, preserved in the literature of Islam's religious heritage, the *Ḥadīth* (the collected sayings and actions of Muhammad) and the *Sīra al-Nabawiyya* (the biography of the prophet).

The Prophet of Islam Encounters Christians

It is important to note, at the outset, that each of these encounters are narrated by Muslims. In academic circles, the *Hadith* of Muhammad as well as his biography, penned by Ibn Ishaq (d. 767/150) and edited by Ibn Hishām (d. 833), are subject to question as they both come to their final form more than a century after the death of Muhammad. This chronological distance from the events narrated leads to the accusation that subsequent political powerplay may have shaped the prophetic narrative more than concerns for historicity. Nevertheless, it *is* the surviving narrative of early Islam and therefore deserves consideration.

The prophet of Islam had significant encounters with Christians. We consider four.

Baḥira

As an adolescent (age twelve) Muhammad accompanied his uncle and guardian, Abū Ṭālib, as he directed a trader caravan north into Syria. An enigmatic monk emerged from his desert cell having noticed a cloud overshadowing the young boy. Tree branches stooped over him where he stopped. BaḤira invited the caravan to dine with him, though the caravan leaders had passed by him many times before. When Muhammad was left to tend the baggage as he was but a young boy, BaḤira insisted that everyone come and enjoy the meal. BaḤira questioned him and received answers in keeping with his expectation of the boy's unique gifts. He also observed a seal of prophethood—a physical mark between the young boy's shoulder blades. BaḤira informed the caravan traders of the boy's unique calling and role and instructed them to guard him carefully, especially from the Jews, who would certainly seek to harm him.[2]

Waraqa Ibn Naufal

Waraqa is another enigmatic figure, related uniquely in the biography of the prophet. He was one of four members of the Quraysh tribe who, disenchanted with tribal religion, sought to worship the one God.[3] He was knowledgeable of the previous revelations, known as one who translated the Gospel from Hebrew into Arabic.[4] Moreover, he was a cousin of Khadija, Muhammad's first wife and prominent caravan owner of Mecca. Upon receiving his initial revelations by means of a vision of the angel Gabriel, Muhammad repaired to Khadija relating an experience so traumatic that he contemplated suicide. Angelic assurance came to affirm the prophetic call: "O Muhammad! Thou are the apostle of God and I am Gabriel." Khadija's confidence in Muhammad's moral integrity was unwavering, professing her hope that Muhammad would be the prophet of the nation. She left to consult Waraqa concerning this unique revelation. His response: "Holy! Holy! I swear to Him in whose hands the life of Waraqa is that the law of Moses has been bestowed on him and he is the prophet of this nation! Tell him to stand firm." Later, Waraqa encountered Muhammad at the Kaaba. He warned the young prophet, "Thou wilt be accused of falsehood, thou wilt be persecuted, exiled, and attacked." He promised his allegiance to Muhammad and hoped that he would live to offer him protection.[5]

The Negus of Axum

In the year of sadness (619), so-called because Khadija passed away that year as well as Muhammad's uncle and guardian, Abū Ṭālib, persecution of the new Muslim community began to increase. The tragic events led to an

---

2. Goddard, *A History of Muslim-Christian Relations*, 20. Ibn Hisham, *Sirat Rasūl Allāh*, 79–81.

3. Ibn Hisham, *Sirat Rasūl Allāh*, 99.

4. Recent scholarship accepts the plausibility of a gospel tradition existing in Hebrew. See Edwards, *The Hebrew Gospel*.

5. Ibn Hisham, *The Life of Muhammad*, 106–7.

early flight from Mecca known as the first hijra to the Kingdom of Axum (Abyssinia), in what is today Ethiopia. It was a Christian kingdom and the account of the reception of these Abyssinian Christians of the Muslim community has also found its way into the narrative of Islamic origins in the Sira of Ibn Hishām. Although not a direct encounter of the prophet himself, the story is significant as it conveys a Muslim perspective on how Islam was understood by the Monophysite Christians of Axum.

The story relates that two emissaries of the Quraysh (Muhammad's tribe which had turned against him) were sent to the Negus (a title for the sovereign of Axum) to extract the Muslims and return them to Mecca. The king wisely refused to relinquish the Muslims until he questioned them directly. Ja'far ibn Abū Ṭālib, the leader of the Muslim community speaks on its behalf relating the transformation that had taken place among Muslims as a result of Muhammad's prophetic ministry:

> O King, we were an uncivilized people, worshiping idols, eating corpses, committing abominations, breaking natural ties, treating guests badly, and our strong devoured our weak. Thus we were until God sent us an apostle, whose lineage, truth, trustworthiness, and clemency we know. He summoned us to acknowledge God's unity and to worship him. . . . He commanded us to worship God alone and not to associate anything with him. . . . Thereupon our people attacked us. . . . So, when they got the better of us, treated us unjustly and circumscribed our lives, and came between us and our religion, we came to your country, having chosen you above all others.[6]

Being assured of the Negus' favor, the Muslims' antagonists resorted to a ruse telling the king that these Muslims say of Jesus that he is a creature. In response to the Negus' query, Ja'far responds, "We say about him that which our prophet brought, saying, he is the slave of God and his apostle, and his Spirit, and his word which he cast into Mary the blessed virgin." Upon hearing this response, the Negus took a stick from the ground and declared that Jesus does not exceed what the Muslims expressed the length of the stick.[7]

The Christian delegation from Najran

A final encounter of Muhammad with Christians takes place after his hijra from Mecca to Medina in 622. He is now ensconced as a leader and is

---

6. Goddard, *A History of Muslim-Christian Relations*, 20–21.
7. Ibn Hisham, *The Life of Muhammad*, 152–53.

approached by a Christian delegation ostensibly to secure terms of peace. The delegation originated from Najran, a city in the south of the Arabian Peninsula, near the contemporary border of Saudi Arabia with Yemen. The Christians were invited to submit (embrace Islam)[8] at which they responded that they had already submitted. By this, they meant only that they were in submission to God. Muhammad replied that their consumption of pork, their belief in the cross and that Jesus was the Son of God prohibited their submission. After receiving the revelation of the first part of Sura Al-'Imran, concerning the oneness of God and the nature of Jesus, and the unique status of Mary his mother, the prophet invites the Christians into a *mubāhala*—a mutual invocation of God's curse. The Christians decline and return home with permission to practice their faith.[9]

The four encounters of Muhammad (and Muslims) with Christians preserve the view of Islam towards the early Christian community scattered throughout the regions Islam would soon overpower. Sincere and humble Christians (e.g., BaḤira and Waraqa) quickly recognized Muhammad as a prophet promised in the Christian scriptures. Through the narrative of the first *hijra*, the Negus of Axum is the mouthpiece of early Muslim historians to state that Muslims had a correct view of Christ. Finally, in the delegation from Najran, we find Muhammad, after his hijra to Medina, correcting the view of Christians toward their own Messiah. He supplies an elevated view of Christ as a prophet, while eschewing the Christian claim of his divinity. As mentioned above, we need not be overly confident in the historical veracity of the accounts. Rather, they allow us to perceive the view of Muslims towards Christians during the Umayyad Caliphate (661–750), the time of the composition of these narratives.

The Rashidun Caliphate (632–61) and the Umayyad Caliphate (661–750)

In the 120-year period following the death of Muhammad, Islam rapidly spread, controlling much of the east and south Mediterranean basin. Former Christian strongholds appeared to wilt in subjugation to the Muslim expansion. Cities of ancient Christian pedigree—Jerusalem, Antioch, Alexandria, Damascus, and Baghdad—became the domains of an emergent

---

8. Note that "to submit" is the root meaning of the word "Islam." By inviting the Christians to "submit" Muhammad was, in effect, inviting them to embrace Islam.

9. It is thought that the third Caliph 'Umar ibn al-Khaṭāb relocated the Christians of Najrān to Iraq. See Hitti, *History of the Arabs*, 61.

Islamic dominance. Who were these Christians of the East and how did Islam achieve such a rapid expansion among them?

Who were the Christians of the East?

Beginning with the Emperor Constantine, the ecumenical councils were convened by Rome to adjudicate in matters disputed among Christians across the empire. Though the councils were intended to unite Christendom, the deeply held views of bishops, expressed in liturgies, were matters of utmost importance in the Eastern churches. None was so important, nor so disputed, as the nature of Christ, more correctly, the two natures of Christ (divine and human) and how they inter-related. The Council of Chalcedon was meant to heal the breach, but ironically made the disagreements more apparent. Ecclesial politics exacerbated the differentiation, which often fell along the lines of linguistic and cultural divides. Chalcedon determined that Christ was two natures in one person and one hypostasis. The bishop of Egypt (Cyril) insisted on the one incarnate nature of the divine Logos. The East Syriac communities insisted that the hypostasis was essential to the nature and therefore there were two hypostases, corresponding to the two natures, in the one person of Christ.[10] While the dispute may sound arcane in today's world, for the Christians of the East, it concerned salvation and was therefore of first importance.

So, it was that Islam encountered three distinct Christian communities, who viewed each other with deep suspicion, often characterizing one another as infidels and appealing to the dominant political power (Rome or Persia) to persecute the other confession.[11] The dominant group adhered to Chalcedon and were referred to as the "King's people" or the Melkites for their adherence to the Roman emperor. Those who insisted on the one nature of the divine Logos were the "Monophysites" (*mono* "one" and *physis* "nature"). Though history has bequeathed the moniker of "Nestorians" to those who insisted on two hypostases in the one person of Christ, it is, in fact, a misnomer. The more fitting title is "the Assyrian Church of the East" or more simply, "the Church of the East." As they insisted on a separation between the two natures (Greek, *physeis*) of Christ, they are also described as "Dyophysite."[12]

---

10. In Syriac, the moniker *qnome* is translated in Greek as *hypostasis*. Part of the confusion stemmed from different usages of the Syriac word vis-à-vis the Greek. See Brock, "The 'Nestorian' Church," 23–35.

11. Troupeau, "Christianity in the Early Islamic Decades," 453–70.

12. This moniker fails to capture a distinction from the Melkites who also held to

In summary, Islamic invaders challenged the dominance of the Melkites. The Monophysites and Dyophysites were disempowered politically and generally welcomed the overthrow of the Melkites.[13] Christian division over the nature of Christ abetted a rapid Islamic advance in the Christian homelands of the Middle East. Between 650 and 1050CE, twelve of thirty Catholicoi (patriarchs) of the Church of the East were appointed by Muslim rulers.[14] It must not be forgotten that these Christian lands had also been subject to a long and bitter conflict between the armies of Rome and Persia.

Monophysite and Dyophysite responses to Muslim armies

The mysterious Arab invaders were unknown to the Christians of the East. The Arabic they spoke would have been unintelligible to their Greek minds, though Syriac was a closer linguistic cognate. In the early decades as Christians assimilated how Muslims differed in their worship and service to Allāh, a movement to monasteries became observable. There, Christians would preserve their identity and heritage through manuscript production and copying.[15]

Syria, Iraq, and Palestine were overrun by Islam within seven years of Muhammad's death. Egypt fell soon after, coming under Islamic control by 645. The historical record indicates that Christians were involved in the negotiations that handed these prominent cities over to Islamic rule. The Chalcedonian patriarch, Sophronius, negotiated the handover of Jerusalem. Mansūr ibn Sarjūn, grandfather of St. John of Damascus (discussed below), was involved in the handover of Damascus. We have indicated that divisions in Christian dogma were intensified by political rivalry which contributed to Muslim takeover. Recurrent military conflict in the region between Rome and Persia, accompanied by the victor's taxation, created a malaise that also tacitly welcomed the new administration.

---

a distinction in the two natures. The truer moniker would be "dyohypostatic" as the Church of the East held that the two natures implied two distinct hypostases.

13. Gerard Troupeau summarizes the location of the various sects. Nestorians were under Sassanid domination in Babylonia and Mesopotamia, though there were Monophysites around Tikrit. The patriarchates of Alexandria and Antioch were split into Chalcedonians and Monophysites. Similar expressions of Christianity existed in the Arabian Peninsula with Dyophysitism in the east (Bahrain, Qatar, Oman) and monophysitism in the south (Banū al-Harith) and north (Banū Ghassān). Troupeau, "Christianity in the Early Islamic Decades," 453–54.

14. Baum and Winkler, *The Church of the East*, 43.

15. Baum and Winkler, *The Church of the East*, 44.

Indicators in the historical record reveal that Christians viewed the Islamic incursion as a punishment from God on the dominant Melkite Chalcedonians: "The Lord abandoned the army of the Romans as a punishment for their corrupt faith, and because of the anathemas uttered against them by the ancient fathers, on account of the Council of Chalcedon."[16] Michael the Syrian (fifth century) elaborates: "The God of vengeance . . . raised up from the south the children of Ishmael to deliver us from the hands of the Romans. . . . It was no light benefit to us to be freed from the cruelty of the Romans, their wickedness, anger and ardent cruelty . . . ."[17]

Testimony from stones and statutes

The stately Dome of the Rock is a familiar place marker of the skyline of Jerusalem. It also serves as the oldest architectural artifact indicating the Muslim view of the Christian faith in the Umayyad period (632–750). Commissioned by the Umayyad Caliph 'Abd al-Malik in 692, the Dome precedes manuscripts of the Qur'an as the earliest extant testimony to Islamic belief. The massive edifice marks the spot of Muhammad's nocturnal journey to the seventh heaven. Mystifyingly, there is no indication of that fact in the Arabic calligraphy that lines the expansive edifice. Rather, the Dome is an apologetic (defense) of the Islamic Christ and a polemic against the Christian Trinity, citing Suras 112, 17, and 19. Allah is one and begets no son. Christians must desist from saying "three," as Jesus was only an envoy (*rasūl*) and servant of God. The point of the Dome inscription, placed auspiciously at the heart of the city where Christ was crucified, is that Christian belief is misplaced and that the new Muslim overlords are correcting this error.[18]

The Pact of 'Umar

The historical development of Islam through the medieval period saw the science of jurisprudence (Arabic *fiqh*) take on increasing importance. Its corollary, deductive reasoning on the nature of God (theology; Arabic, *kalām*) was Islam's version of scholastic theology. Jurisprudence (*fiqh*) sought the right application of the will of Allāh, expressed in the Qur'an and through the moral example of the prophet, to all aspects of life. A key

16. Goddard, *A History of Muslim-Christian Relations*, 37, cited from Frend, *The Rise of the Monophysites*, 353.

17. Goddard, *A History of Muslim-Christian Relations*, 37, cited from Frend, *The Rise of the Monophysites*, 353.

18. Brown, *A New Introduction to Islam*, 122–26.

question that *fiqh* addressed was the status of non-Muslims in society. As Christianity was the prominent community in the new territories Islam had acquired, the question was urgent. The Pact of 'Umar (or Code of 'Umar) survives as a statement of Muslim state policy towards the protected (*dhimmī*) non-Muslim religious communities. The origin of the Pact is uncertain. Though it is named after 'Umar, it likely postdates the second Caliph of Sunni Islam by that name. By modern standards the Pact appears stringent but, relative to its time, it represented a status-quo treatment of disempowered religious communities. By the ninth century, it represented the Muslim consensus on inter-religious social relations.[19]

Among other clauses, the Pact stipulates that, in exchange for Muslim protection, Christians agree, "not to build a church, convent, hermitage, or cell, nor repair those that are dilapidated, nor assemble in any that is in a Muslim quarter, nor in their presence, not to display idolatry nor invite to it, nor show a cross on our churches, nor in any of the roads or markets of the Muslims . . . ."[20]

It is likely that the implementation of the Pact was not consistent, depending largely on the will of the Muslim governor. Nevertheless, the Pact portrays a social devolution of the Christian communities existent in Muslim-ruled territories.

John of Damascus

An outstanding figure of the Umayyad period is John of Damascus, whose family was from the upper echelons of Damascus society. His grandfather—Sarjūn—was involved in the negotiated handover of Damascus to Muslims. As a Melkite, his writings come down to us in Greek, though his employment in Damascus, where he was known among Muslims as Mansūr ibn Sarjūn, would have required a knowledge of Arabic. Though his ecclesial loyalty was toward Byzantium, his context drew him deeply into the vital discussion points between Muslims and Christians. His chef d'oeuvres was the *Fount of Knowledge*. The second part of that work consists of a descriptive list of heresies. The final one is "the heresy of the Ishmaelites." John's tone is polemical as he seeks to respond to an implicit Islamic attack on his Melkite confession and, indeed, Christianity broadly considered. His objective is to undermine the credibility of Islam in the minds of Christian inquirers.[21] John is the first in a long line of Eastern theologians who would

19. Levy-Rubin, "The Pact of 'Umar."
20. Goddard, *A History of Muslim-Christian Relations*, 45.
21. Griffith, *The Church in the Shadow of the Mosque*, 40–43.

engage Islam through an exposition of the historic Christian faith. The areas of concern were many but chief among them was the Christian conception of God as three hypostases in one essence, the nature of Christ as divine and human, and the authority of the Christian scriptures, especially vis-à-vis the absence of a clear announcement of a subsequent prophet named Muhammad. Muslims had claimed that the *paraclete* of John's Gospel was, in fact, a prophetic announcement of Muhammad. The *Biography of the Prophet* indicates that this figure was the "*Munahemana*"—a Syriac word (meaning "comforter" or "consoler"), conflated by the author of the Biography with Muhammad's name. The confusion perhaps arises from Syriac liturgical readings overheard enthusiastically by Arabic speakers as a reference to their prophet.[22]

John is an important figure because it is through him that we first hear a Christian assessment of Islam. The Islamic narrative of its own origins represents sincere Christians acknowledging the truth of Islam and affirming Muhammad's prophetic call from their own Scriptures. John and his Eastern successors react to the Muslim polemic against their cherished doctrine of God and understanding of Christ. Through John, we perceive that the table is set for a polemical confrontation. That confrontation will reach its pinnacle in the ninth century under the new Abbasid administration in Baghdad.

The Abbasid Caliphate (750–1258)

The early Abbasid Caliphate based in Baghdad proffered a flourishing of Islamic thought as well as engagement with other faiths in the region. Among these faiths, none figured as large as the Christian community, represented by the Melkite Chalcedonians, the Monophysites of West Syria, and the Church of the East (dyophysite). The Caliphs of the Abbasids fostered a renewal of knowledge, particularly the philosophy and science of the Greeks. Baghdad became the home of the *Bayt al-Hikma* (House of Wisdom), which functioned as a literary and translation movement that brought much of the Greek intellectual heritage into Arabic.[23] The Christians of Baghdad and its environs achieved notoriety as the translators of the new and highly prized knowledge of the ancients. In addition to their native Syriac and Arabic, the Christians of the East were knowledgeable of Greek. Their translation efforts were not limited to philosophy, but also involved medicine, astronomy, philology, rhetoric, history and, of course, religion.

22. Ibn Hishā, *Sirat Rasūl Allāh*, 104.
23. See Dimitri and van Bladel, "Bayt Al-Ḥikma," in *Encyclopedia of Islam Three*.

Church of the East monks had penetrated deep into China by this time. One of many outstanding translators arising from the Church of the East was Hunayn ibn Ishaq. Referred to as the Erasmus of the Islamic renaissance, he translated over 260 works and authored more than 100.[24] The combination of the Abbasid desire for knowledge and the scholarly abilities of Eastern Christians culminated in the Abbasid renaissance.

It is ironic, though perhaps predictable, that this flowering of knowledge coincided with a hardening of Muslim attitudes towards Christians. Caliphs al-Mahdī (775–85CE) and al-Ma'mūn (813–33CE), credited with establishing the *Bayt al-Hikma*, established policies that led to the flight of many Christians.[25] As mentioned above, the *paraclete* passages of John's Gospel were marshalled by Muslims as a herald of a future prophet who would arise to lead his people into all truth. However, Christians understood those promises to speak of the Holy Spirit, who was given at Pentecost. The failure to identify a clear prophetic oracle concerning Muhammad contributed to the contention that the scriptures of the Jews and Christians had been corrupted (*taḤrīf*). The most convenient culprit for this corruption was the Jewish pharisee-Christian convert—the apostle Paul.[26] Aided by their newly acquired taste for deductive reasoning, the Abbasids needed only to demonstrate the utter superiority of their monotheistic faith (*tawḤīd*) over their Trinitarian counterparts. This they accomplished with a ruthless adherence to strict logical reasoning. *Kalām*, or theological deductive reasoning, became an established branch of Islamic science and the chief intellectual tool to defeat the Christian claim of one God in three persons or one Christ in two natures.

Following are some of the outstanding Christian spokespersons who sought to defend their faith and their Muslim counterparts.

Christians defend their faith

Very early in the Abbasid era (781/165), a renowned catholicos (patriarch) of the Church of the East was invited to give an exposition of his faith in the court of the Abbasid Caliph al-Mahdī (775–785).[27] The religious debate officiated by the caliph in his royal courts became a recurrent theme through

---

24. Baum and Winkler, *The Church of the East*, 66–67.
25. Baum and Winkler, *The Church of the East*, 59.
26. Reynolds and Samir, *Abdul Jabbār: Critique of Christian Origins*, 90–91, 98–105.
27. Mingana, "The Apology of Timothy the Patriarch before the Caliph Mahdī," 171–91.

the period.[28] The Christian was Timothy I, whose forty-three-year tenure as catholicos combined with his administrative skills allowed the Church of the East to spread its territorial reach in diverse areas such as China, Yemen, and the Caspian Sea.[29] Al-Mahdī's interrogation of Timothy I covered the waterfront of the theological disputes that would characterize the intersection of Islam and Christianity through the Abbasid period and indeed through history, including the Trinity, the incarnation, and Christian scriptures.[30] For instance, the Caliph thought the title "Son of God" applied to Christ must indicate a biological sonship and thus a physicality of God. The idea of two natures residing in one person was implicitly illogical to al-Mahdī. If the belief in Christ's divinity was accurate, how could it be claimed that Christ also died? For al-Mahdī, such a shameful execution would not befit a prophet, much less divinity incarnate.

Though Timothy and his Muslim counterpart were not able to agree, the fact that such a public and high-level debate was held informs us of the spirit of inquiry of the Abbasids. Though it would be anachronistic to conceptualize it as religious tolerance, it represented, nonetheless, a willingness to engage with the religious other in an intellectual pursuit of truth. What becomes apparent in the hindsight of history is that al-Mahdī's canon of truth was derived uniquely from his Muslim formation. A truer engagement with the religious other would necessitate a willingness to see from the vantage point of the other—a skill that few of the medieval period, or even the modern period, were able to acquire.

Theoldore Abū Qurra (d.c. 830) hailed from the Melkites (Chalcedonian). Timothy I's dialogue with al-Mahdī appears to have been held in Syriac with Arabic translation. Abū Qurra is distinguished as the first Arabic-writing theologian of the East and he is best known for his exposition of the faith in the Caliphal court of al-Ma'mūn (813–33) in 829 CE. Manuscript copyists have enhanced Abū Qurra's prowess, who goes on the attack of his Muslim interlocutors. One must recall that the written record of these caliphal debates went beyond the purpose of preserving history to education and even entertainment of its Christian reader.

Abū Qurra is interrogated by a series of Muslim leaders, beginning with the Caliph himself. With each question, Abū Qurra manifests his skill in debate and often seals his points through recitation of the Qur'an. The crux of the debate centered on Christ. When the Christian demurred to respond, ostensibly for fear of his own safety, the Caliph intervened with the Qur'anic

---

28. See Griffith, "The Monk in the Emir's Majlis."
29. Baum and Winkler, *The Church of the East: A Concise History*, 60.
30. Beaumont, *Christology in Dialogue with Muslims*, 23.

injunction that arguing with the people of the book should be conducted "in the best way" (Q 29:46). Abū Qurra proceeds to show there could be no division between God and his word. Thus, the Qur'anic title of Christ as "a word from God" upheld the Christian claim of divine incarnation. Al-Ma'mūn comes to the defense of his Christian interlocutor more than once, showing his even-handedness in the pursuit of religious truth.[31]

Abū Qurra's exposition reveals a deepening antipathy between the two religious communities. As mentioned, the extant text is almost certainly the product of copyist emendations. Nevertheless, Abū Qurra's willingness to impugn Islamic belief is noteworthy. He supplies a Christian meaning to the *Fātiḥa* (the opening chapter of the Qur'an) suggesting that those on whom God has been gracious are the Christians while those going astray are the very ones who repeat the *Fātiḥa* in their daily prayers—the Muslims. His questions amount to a Christian polemic. He even asks who will marry Muslim women in paradise as Muslim men are occupied with the *huris* (female companions granted as part of the reward of paradise).[32]

A hardening Islamic polemic

Unfortunately, the Abbasid period manifests a hardening of polemical rhetoric between the two faith communities. It has been well-summarized by David Thomas:

> Through the course of the shared history of the faiths these . . . attitudes have led to . . . the mistaken point that each faith has represented the other in its own terms, to a reduction of the other down to a subsidiary form of itself, and then to demonization, enmity, and the sanction of bloodshed.[33]

While the historic enmity was multi-faceted, including social and cultural aspects, a theological tenet became the point of the spear that drove the divisive wedge ever deeper. It is the Muslim doctrine of God's unicity or *tawḥīd*. God's absolute transcendence became the core element of Islam, rooted in Qur'anic declarations and nurtured by the unassailable logic of *kalam*. The Christian understanding of God in three persons, one of whom became incarnate and thereby indelibly associated with humanity, rendered the Christian faith unconscionable and blasphemous. The corresponding transgression of *tawḥīd* was *shirk*—the unpardonable act of associating

---

31. Griffith, "The Monk in the Emir's Majlis," 38–44.
32. See Qur'an 52:20 and 56:22–23. N.b. the identity of the *huris* is debated.
33. Thomas, "Past and Future in Muslim-Christian Relations," 33–42.

uncreated divinity with created material.³⁴ The claim that Christ was both human and divine provided a "case in point" for Muslim polemicists who demonstrated the necessary inferiority of a faith that blatantly transgressed the "gold standard" of *tawḥīd*.

One of the most rigorous and sustained polemics against Christianity was wielded by Abū ʿĪsā ibn Hārūn ibn Muḥammad al-Warrāq (d. soon after 864/250). He obtained a detailed knowledge of the various Christian sects and challenged each in their distinctive beliefs. Abū ʿĪsā's *Refutation of the Three Christian Sects* was the most extensive polemic against Christianity until the fourteenth century. The scope and detail of his interrogation of Christianity rendered a Christian response virtually impossible. Indeed, the response of the Melkite Yaḥya ibn ʿAdī came nearly a century later. Abū ʿĪsā relentlessly probes the internal inconsistencies of a God who is three in hypostases and one in essence against the backdrop of an unmitigated divine unicity revealed in the Qurʾan and expounded by the *mutakallimūn* (rational Muslim theologians).³⁵

A further example is Abū Bakr Muḥammad al-Bāqillānī (d. 1013/403) whose polemic against Christianity was both dismissive and derisive. His prolific literary output coupled with his sharp polemic tone earned him the epithet "sword of the Sunna and spokesman of the nation." al-Bāqillānī was an example of an entrenched polemical view that refused to consider the perspective of the religious other. Christians had long referred to the essence of deity as *jawhar* (substance). al-Bāqillānī took issue with the moniker, declaring it to be tantamount to material conception of God or physicality.³⁶ Moreover, he ridiculed the Christian limitation of the essential attributes of God to three (as in the doctrine of the Trinity) as arbitrary and without rational foundation.

Although polemical examples of Muslim-Christian engagement dominate the period, there is at least one example where a respectful defense of the Christian faith gained a hearing and even acknowledgement by a Muslim official that Christians were indeed monotheists. It concerns the *Sessions* of Elias bar Shinaya of Nisibis with the Marwanid vizier (minister) Abū al-Qāsim ibn Alī al-Maghribī (995–1027). The literary corpus consists of both a written account of seven tete-a-tetes that took place between the two as well as an epistolary exchange. Taken together, they reveal a warm bond of respect and the rare quality of "agnostic inquisitiveness" on the part

---

34. See Qurʾan 4:116 and 39:65.
35. Thomas, *Christian Doctrines in Islamic Theology*, 124.
36. Thomas, *Christian Doctrines in Islamic Theology*, 128.

of Abū al-Qāsim.[37] The Muslim vizier reveals a willingness to forego his previous understanding that Christians were infidels (*kuffār*) and idolators (*mushrikīn*) as a result of his experience of healing in a Christian monastery. He appeals to a wise and renowned bishop of the Church of the East (Elias was a revered sage) to fill in the gaps of his understanding. As a result, he declares that Christians are indeed worshippers of the one God.[38]

The Crusades: religions at arms

The end of the eleventh century witnessed the beginning of the Crusades—the long series of Christian armed incursions into the Middle East to wrest "Christian" lands from Muslim hands. Fear of the encroachment of Islam became palpable in Western Europe. Indeed, remnants of the Umayyad Empire remained entrenched on the Iberian Peninsula since the early eighth century. A frantic apocalypticism among Spanish Christians anticipated the impending demise of Islam. Christians publicly denounced Muhammad at the cost of their lives. In another hotspot, the antics of the so-called "Mad Caliph" (al-Ḥakim bi-Amr Allāh, 996–1021) of the Faṭimid dynasty of Cairo included the destruction of the Church of the Resurrection in Jerusalem. The more pressing issue for Christians in the West was the closure of pilgrimage routes that had previously been easily accessible. As tensions escalated, the bishop of Constantinople (Alexius I Comnenus 1081–1118), under threat from the Ottomans, issued a summons for help from the West never imagining that it would lead to a breach between Eastern and Western Christendom that would haunt global Christianity nearly a millennium later.[39] For Muslims, the Crusades remain a historic symbol of a strident and insecure Western Christendom.

Conclusion: Religious Antipathy

The period offers little hope in terms of peaceful and harmonious coexistence. While scholarly conjecture continues concerning the attitude of the prophet of Islam towards Christianity, there can be little doubt that

---

37 Thomas, "The Past and the Future in Muslim-Christian Relations," 41. Thomas describes agnostic inquisitiveness as "an attitude of open inquiry into the religion of the other that puts preconditions about its truthfulness or its divine origins to one side and attempts, as far as is possible for an outsider, to discover its core beliefs and diversity of expressions with respect and attentiveness."

38. Kuhn, *God is One*, 122–25.

39. Madden, *The New Concise History of the Crusades*, 5.

the two faiths hardened in their dogmatic positions, leading to a mutual exclusion. The conflicts of those days continue to cast their shadow over Christians of the East and their Muslim counterparts. Perhaps we may find a good outcome in that both Muslims and Christians now recognize that their faiths, despite points of conflict, have many areas of mutual concern. Recent efforts such as the Common Word allow Christians and Muslims to recognize their commonalities and discuss their divergences with mutual respect and dignity.

Bibliography

Baum, W., and Dietmar Winkler. *The Church of the East: A Concise History*. Translated by Miranda G. Henry. London: RoutledgeCurzon, 2003.

Brock, Sebastian. "The 'Nestorian' Church: A Lamentable Misnomer." *Bulletin of the John Rylands University Library of Manchester* 78 (1996) 23–35.

Brown, Daniel. *A New Introduction to Islam*. Oxford: Wiley-Blackwell, 2009.

Dimitri, Gutas, and van Bladel. "Bayt Al-Ḥikma." In *Encyclopedia of Islam Three*, edited by Kate Fleet, Gudrun Kramer, Denis Matringe, John Nawas, and Everett Rowson. Amsterdam: Brill, 2009. http://dx.doi.org/10.1163/1573-3912_ei3_COM_22882

Edwards, James R. *The Hebrew Gospel and the Development of the Synoptic Tradition*. Grand Rapids: Eerdmans, 2009.

Frend, W. H. C. *The Rise of the Monophysite Movement: Chapters in the History of the Church in the Fifth and Sixth Centuries*. Cambridge: Cambridge University Press, 1972.

Goddard, Hugh. *A History of Christian-Muslim Relations*. Chicago: New Amsterdam, 2000.

Griffith, Sidney H. "The Monk in the Emir's Majlis: Reflections on a Popular Genre of Christian Literary Apologetics in Arabic in the Early Islamic Period." In *The Majlis: Interreligious Encounters in Medieval Islam*, edited by Hava Lazarus-Yafeh, 13–83. Wiesbaden: Harrassowitz Verlag, 1999.

Griffith, Sidney. *The Church in the Shadow of the Mosque: Christians and Muslims in the World of Islam*. Princeton, NJ: Princeton University Press, 2008.

Hitti, Philip Khuri. *History of the Arabs from the Earliest Time to the Present*. New York: Macmillan, 1951.

Ibn Hisham. *The Life of Muhammad: A Translation of Ibn Ishaq's Sirat Rasul Allah*. Oxford: Oxford University Press, 2004.

Kuhn, Michael. *God Is One: A Christian Defense of Divine Unity in the Muslim Golden Age*. Carlisle, UK: Langham Global Library, 2019.

Levy-Rubin, Milka. "The Pact of 'Umar.'" In *Christian-Muslim Relations: A Bibliographical History*, edited by David Thomas and Barbara Roggema, 360–64. Leiden: Brill, 2009.

Madden, Thomas F. *The New Concise History of the Crusades*. New York: Barnes & Noble, 2007.

Mingana, Alphonse. "The Apology of Timothy the Patriarch before the Caliph Mahdī." *Bulletin of the John Rylands Library* 12, no. 3 (1928) 171–91.

The Qur'an: A New Translation. Translated by M. A. S Abdel Haleem. Oxford: Oxford University Press, 2004.

Reynolds, Gabriel Said, and Khalil Samir. *Abd Al-Jabbar: Critique of Christian Origins: A Parallel English-Arabic Text.* Provo, UT: Brigham Young University Press, 2010.

Thomas, David. *Christian Doctrines in Islamic Theology.* History of Christian-Muslim Relations. Leiden: Brill, 2008.

Troupeau, G. E. "Christianity in the Early Islamic Decades." In *Christianity: A History in the Middle East*, edited by Habib Badr, 453–70. Beirut: Middle East Council of Churches, 2005.

3

Imperialism and Mission during European Rule (Twelfth to Nineteenth Century)

JAMES C. SKEDROS

THE DIVERSITY OF CHRISTIANITY in the Middle East continued during the eight centuries following the arrival of crusader armies at the end of the eleventh century to the eve of the breakup of the Ottoman Empire at the end of the nineteenth century. The traditional groupings of Christians into the three main theological polities—Chalcedonian, non-Chalcedonian, and Nestorian—with their associated ethno-linguistic groupings (Chalcedonian: Greek, Georgian, and Arabic; non-Chalcedonian: Coptic, Syriac, Armenian; Nestorian: Syriac) was maintained with some significant demographic reductions. However, the Christian landscape expanded to include Latin Catholic Christians, Eastern Christian churches in communion with Rome, various Protestant denominations, along with the widespread adoption of Arabic as the language of communication within many of these communities.

Nearly all Christians during this period lived under Islamic political domination and therefore were part of a long trajectory of second-class status within their regional locations. These communities have their own unique and vibrant histories, producing theological responses to the challenges of Islam and providing for the continuation of the Christian faith of their forebears. Strong ties to their cultural-linguistic heritage and a deep commitment to their Christian confession, in spite of the unavoidable economic and social burdens required of *dhimmi* under Islamic law, provided for the continuation of these Christian groups. Increased contact with Western Christians, nineteenth-century nationalist movements, and Ottoman reforms provided new hope and energy for Middle Eastern Christians. As the twentieth century dawned, these Christian communities could not have foreseen the disastrous political and social upheavals of the coming century that would reduce their communities by significant numbers.

From the Crusades to the Ottomans (1098–1517)

The capture of Jerusalem by Western crusaders in July 1099 ushered in a new period for the indigenous Christians of the Middle East. Latin Christianity, and Latin Christians in particular, had been present in and around Jerusalem since the fourth century; but with the Crusades, Latin Christianity entered a new phase in its presence in the Middle East. Indigenous Christians now living under crusader suzerainty in the newly established crusader states (County of Edessa, 1098–1144; Principality of Antioch, 1098–1268; County of Tripoli, 1109–1268; and Kingdom of Jerusalem, 1099–1187, to name the most important) did not fare much better, in general, than they did under Islamic rule. Latin patriarchs were appointed in Antioch and Jerusalem under which all Christians were subordinated. The Orthodox,[1] the most numerous of indigenous Christian communities living within crusader territory, had the most to lose since they were closely tied to the Byzantine (Greek) world, which had recently (1054) entered into schism with Rome; their patriarchs were forced to relocate to Constantinople.[2] The other Christian communities fared better, in part because their patriarchal leadership resided outside of crusader territory.

Christians in Mesopotamia and Egypt were, initially, not directly affected by the Crusades. However, with the fall of Jerusalem to Saladin in 1187, successive Crusades focused attention on Egypt. In retaliation, and in fear of Christian support for the Crusades, the Ayyubids in Egypt destroyed the Church of St. Mark in Alexandria (1219; the historic seat of the Coptic papacy), additional taxation was imposed, and Christians became the focus of Muslim hatred towards the crusaders. Muslim attitudes were impacted by the presence of the crusaders and Western hegemony. Native Christians retained their status as dhimmi who were protected by

---

1. In this chapter, the term "Orthodox" refers to those Christians in the Middle East who belonged to the historic patriarchates of Constantinople, Alexandria, Antioch, and Jerusalem and accepted the decisions of the Council of Chalcedon (451). Given their close ethnic and theological ties to Byzantine Christianity, the Orthodox were identified by the adjective *Rum* ("Roman"). Although these Christians are often referred to as Melkite (derived from the Semitic root *m-l-k* meaning "royal" or "imperial"), the term Melkite will be used here to identify former Orthodox Christians who entered into communion with Rome in the eighteenth century.

2. In 1366, the Orthodox patriarchate of Antioch permanently relocated to Damascus.

Islamic law and custom; whereas Muslims viewed the crusaders as infidels who, coming from abroad, must be resisted by force. Such negative views were readily transferred to local Christians. For example, in thirteenth-century Damascus, local Christians were now be referred to as "infidels" (*kuffâr*).[3] The impact of aggressive Western Christians negatively colored the image of Christianity under Islam.

The Crusades also provided for increased contact between the Eastern churches and Rome. This led, over time, to several attempts, mostly on the personal level, at reconciliation between Rome and some of the local communities. In the 1230s, under Dominican influence in Jerusalem, Jacobite, Coptic, and Nestorian bishops professed personal obedience to the see of Rome. With the coming of the Mongols and the demise of the crusader presence at the end of the thirteenth century these attempts at rapprochement fizzled. Successful reunion was obtained with the Maronites who, claiming they had never broken ties with the West, (re?)entered into formal union with Rome in 1182. The founding of Dominican and Franciscan orders in the thirteenth century and their subsequent presence in the Middle East will establish a precedent of Western missionary efforts among indigenous Christians.

As cultural and religious contacts with Latin Christianity increased during the Crusades, the Arabization of indigenous communities was nearing completion. Orthodox Christians were the first adopters of Arabic for theological, scriptural, and liturgical use beginning in the ninth century.[4] Orthodox episcopal leadership, often coming from Greek-speaking areas of the Mediterranean, at times reverted to Greek as the liturgical language and as a language of communication, whereas the use of Arabic in everyday life had become common among Palestinian and Syrian urban communities. Among the Coptic Church in Egypt, the adoption of Arabic came somewhat later due to strong ethno-religious ties to the Coptic language. The Coptic Patriarch Gabriel II ibn Turayk (1131–45), who prior to his elevation as patriarch had served as a civil servant in the Fatimid administration, issued canonical legislation requiring bishops to ensure that the faithful memorize the Doxology, the Lord's Prayer, and the Creed in Arabic so that at least they will understand these basic texts. The same patriarch translated into Arabic the books of the Old and New Testament as well as liturgical rubrics in order that the faithful could understand these as well.[5] Although Coptic was still the liturgical language in the twelfth century, it

---

3. Micheau, "Eastern Christianities (eleventh to fourteenth century), 385.
4. Griffith, "The Bible in Arabic," 126–67.
5. Swanson, *The Coptic Papacy in Islamic Egypt*, 72–74.

was not a language known to the majority of Coptic Christians. During the first half of the thirteenth century, the Coptic church experienced a sort of theological and intellectual renaissance that was sparked in part by the presence of Christian Arabic texts from Syria and Iraq now made accessible to Coptic Christians by Coptic Orthodox scholars. This period also saw the production of the first scholarly Coptic grammar. Although spoken Coptic is attested in the twelfth century among some isolated communities in Egypt, nothing is written in Coptic after the eleventh century.

Among Jacobite and Nestorian Christians, the pace of Arabization was slower. Syriac and other Aramaic dialects continued to be the vernacular of these Christians. Syrian Jacobite communities retained Syriac as its liturgical language. As a literary language, Syriac witnessed a significant revival in the thirteenth century, a century that is seen as the "golden age" of Syriac literature.

The Armenian community maintained its use of Armenian as both a liturgical language and the language of communication among its faithful due, in part, to the establishment of an independent Armenian state in southeastern Asia Minor which lasted from the end of the eleventh to the end of the fourteenth century. With such a strong enclave of Armenians here as well as in historic Armenian lands in the Caucuses, the Armenian language was never replaced liturgically by Arabic nor was the extent of Arabization very great among the Armenian Church.

Monasticism remained an important element within the fabric of Eastern Christianity; although numerically and economically diminished. The general demographic and economic decline of Christian communities, expansion of Turks and Mongols, and Bedouin extortion reduced both the number and size of monastic communities. A decreasing number of Christians also meant reduced financial support through gifts and endowments which had always been the economic backbone of monastic communities. Nonetheless, monasteries continued to provide places for spiritual retreat/pilgrimage, literary activity (mostly copying and storing of liturgical, hagiographical, and historical texts), and as a feeder for episcopal appointments. Important monastic communities included Mar Barsaum (Taurus Mountains), St. Catherine (Sinai), St. Sabas (Palestine), and St. Antony (Egypt). From the Mamluk period onwards, Jerusalem comprised a plethora of monastic communities (often small) representing the various Christian ecclesial communities.

The expansion of the Mongols into the Levant in the 1250s brought momentary hope to Christian communities. Non-Muslim and having knowledge of Christianity, the Mongols were initially favorable towards Christians. Muslim chroniclers record the jubilation expressed by the

Christians of Damascus when the Mongols triumphantly entered Damascus in 1260. The celebration was short-lived. Once the Mamluks took Damascus from the Mongols in the same year they set upon reprisals towards the Christians of the city. By the end of the thirteenth century all of Syria, Palestine, and Egypt was tied to the Mamluks. Christians under Mamluk rule fared poorly. In 1301, a general purge of Christians and Jews who held positions within the Mamluk administration in Egypt took place along with the imposition of a particular dress code. Christians were required to wear blue turbans and a special belt (*zunnar*) and were prohibited from riding horses or mules.[6] The year 1354 saw an added increase in discrimination against Christians in which, in addition to the traditional restrictive measures, the Mamluk authorities confiscated some 10,000 hectares of church property. Periodic renewal of anti-dhimmi regulations by the Mamluks increased pressure upon the upper-class Coptic community for conversion to Islam, which in turn meant a reduction in economic and human resources for the church.[7]

Increased pressure from Mamluk authorities towards the Christian population resulted in an increase in conversions to Islam and thus a reduction in the overall Christian population. It has been estimated that Christians formed nearly half the population of Syria and Palestine at the beginning of the Crusades; by the end of the thirteenth century their numbers had dropped dramatically as a result of anti-Latin and thus anti-Christian sentiment among Muslims, but also due to the rise of the Ayyubids, the devastation of the Mongols, and the arrival of the Mamluks. In 1200, there were 2,048 churches and 834 monasteries belonging to the Coptic Church in Egypt; in 1430, only 193 churches and seventy-four monasteries are recorded; and by the end of the sixteenth century, there were 112 churches and five monasteries.[8]

The Black Death of the fourteenth century impacted Christians and Muslims alike and certainly contributed to the reduction in the number of churches and monasteries during this period. Some estimates place the decline of residents in rural Egypt due to the plague to be as high as 80 percent. It was the Copts living in villages who were deprived most significantly of their religious identity due to lack of churches and clergy.

Another factor in the reduction of the Christian population in the Middle East around this time was due to the destruction of the vast irrigation networks in Upper Mesopotamia. This destruction was the result of

---

6. Ye'or, *The Dhimmi. Jews and Christians under Islam*, 192–94.
7. Swanson, *The Coptic Papacy in Islamic Egypt*, 120.
8. Guirguis and van Doorn-Harder, *Emergence of the Modern Coptic Papacy*, 6.

successive migrations and military action associated with various movements of Steppe peoples, most significantly those of the Mongols. Christian communities in these areas consisted primarily of agricultural communities dependent upon irrigation. With the destruction of irrigation networks, Christians relocated either to the north or west. Nomadic expansion also occurred in Anatolia following the successful military campaigns of the Seljuk Turks at the end of the eleventh century. Christians migrated to mountainous regions in Cappadocia as well as the more wooded and coastal areas of Bithynia, Pontus, and Cilicia. The final blow to Christian-populated agricultural areas came in the wake of Timur's brutal expansion into the Levant and Anatolia. The abandonment of agriculture and its replacement by nomadic expansion resulted in the total disappearance of Christians in central and lower Mesopotamia. By way of example, in the early fourteenth century the Church of the East (Assyrian Church) claimed some thirty metropolitan sees and 200 suffragan bishops. Over the next two-hundred years, this same church had been reduced to a small community of Assyrians living in what is now eastern Turkey.[9]

The three centuries between the First Crusade (1098) and the end of Mamluk rule (1517) saw significant changes for Christians in the Middle East. The fall of Constantinople in 1453 solidified Islamic political control over Anatolia. The number of bishoprics in Anatolia under the patriarchate of Constantinople declined dramatically during this period. Western attempts at creating a Christian kingdom in the Levant through the Crusades failed but had a lasting impact on the Christian communities of the Middle East. The Black Death impacted both Christian and Muslim alike. Yet not all was doom and gloom. In Egypt, Coptic Christians continued to maintain important positions as scribes within the Fatimid and Ayyubid governments. Their presence, and their general strong financial position, provided the Coptic community with the access and economic resources for the maintenance of the physical structures of their churches, endowments for monasteries, and the production of liturgical texts. In the middle of the thirteenth century, there were approximately fifty Coptic dioceses and ninety monasteries.[10] Syriac literature witnessed a renaissance, and one of the most important Christian authors of the period, Bar Hebraeus, wrote in Syriac and Arabic and recognized the importance of Islamic scientific and intellectual developments. In the midst of continuous political vicissitudes, Christians persevered.

---

9. Roberson, *The Eastern Christian Churches*, 16.
10. Panchenko, *Arab Orthodox Christians under the* Ottomans, 50.

Ottoman Rule (1517–1798)

Ottoman expansion under Sultan Selim I (1512–20) resulted in the complete annexation and destruction of the Mamluks in 1517 bringing the Arab world, the traditional Middle Eastern areas of the first Islamic empires, under Ottoman control. Ottoman organizational structures were well established by the early sixteenth century and Ottoman engagement with Christian communities, dating back to the fourteenth century, followed traditional patterns of earlier Islamic states, with a few exceptions. Organizationally, Ottoman society was not much different from other late medieval societies: an autocratic ruler with complete authority under whom was a ruling class consisting of the military and civil service. The remainder of society included the masses of Muslim faithful and dhimmis. Traditional historiography of Christians living under Ottoman rule presents a further organizational category for dhimmis: the millet system.[11]

According to this view, the three major dhimmi groups (Orthodox, Armenians, and Jews) were allowed to operate as semi-autonomous entities whose spiritual head located in Constantinople served as leader of these groups. Members of each millet were allowed to adjudicate civil issues (marriage, inheritance, family ties, etc.) within their own legal and administrative structures. As with earlier Islamic societies, "people of the Book" were allowed to hold their own legal civil proceedings as long as the plaintiff and defendant shared the same religious affiliation. Recently, the millet "system" has come under scrutiny by historians who, utilizing the voluminous Ottoman archives, internal histories of the Orthodox patriarchate of Constantinople, and the regional histories of the patriarchates of Alexandria, Antioch, and Jerusalem, observe a much less centralized organization of *dhimmi* groups. Rather, as with much of Ottoman society, regional/local leaders, power brokers, and religious figures (Muslim and non-Muslim alike) played a more significant role in the day-to-day lives of dhimmi communities than did the spiritual leaders in Istanbul.[12] A new interpretive paradigm of Christian communities (especially the largest millet, that of the patriarchate of Constantinople) under Ottomans has emerged suggesting that "the Ottoman state considered the Greek Orthodox ecclesiastical hierarchy primarily as tax farmers (*mültezim*) for cash income derived from the Church's widespread holdings rather than as community leaders."[13]

---

11. The millet "system" is best articulated by Gibb and Bowen, *Islamic Society and the West*.

12. Braude, "Foundation Myths of the Millet System," 69–88.

13. Papademetriou, *Render unto the Sultan*, 11.

The Ottomans inherited and adopted the legal and customary of their Islamic predecessors that regulated dealings with Christians. At times, certain clothing restrictions were implemented; special taxes in addition to the jizya were imposed; and Christians who converted to Islam and then reverted to Christianity were put to death as apostates. The *devshirme* system was a particularly harsh Ottoman practice. Conducted mainly among Christians and Jews in the Balkans (although it was periodically carried out in Anatolia), this child-levy program forcibly abducted young boys from their families who were then converted to Islam and trained as future members of the Janissary Corp–an elite military group governed directly by the Sultan.

The shift in paradigms from the centralized millet system to viewing Christian communities as tax farms suggests a more localized view of Christians living under the Ottomans. Generalizations need to be made regarding Christians under Ottoman rule, yet such generalizations need to be tempered by regional and local variations and circumstances. One such regional area deserves attention: Jerusalem and the Holy Land. Prior to the Crusades, the Orthodox were the dominant Christian community in and around Jerusalem. Most, if not all, of the holy sites were under Orthodox possession. Armenians constituted the second largest Christian presence in the Holy Land prior to the Crusades. An Armenian patriarch of Jerusalem was appointed as early as 640 CE and the patriarchate occupied the large complex of the monastery of St. James. Georgian monks began to populate monasteries in Jerusalem and its environs during the Ayyubid period and increased in number under the Mamluks. Ethiopian and Coptic Christians held privileged status under the Mamluks and their presence in Jerusalem was secured during this period.

The Crusades brought Latin Christians to the Holy Land who now laid claim to various holy sites. By the sixteenth century, the Orthodox patriarchate of Jerusalem with its Greek-speaking hierarchy and its majority Arabic-speaking faithful was still the largest Christian group in Palestine. The two most contested holy sites remained the Holy Sepulcher (Church of the Anastasis) and the Church of the Nativity (Bethlehem). The various Christian groups vied for ownership and liturgical primacy of these sites. During the sixteenth to eighteenth centuries, Ottoman authorities, locally and in Istanbul, shifted their support from one Christian community to the other in Jerusalem with respect to the holy sites. Determining a consistent Ottoman policy towards the Christians in Jerusalem and the ubiquitous disputes over ownership and access to holy sites is fraught with inconsistencies; such shifts in Ottoman policy were most probably the result of financial influence and political connections that fluctuated between the various Christian denominations based on economic needs and resources.

Jerusalem remained a significant focal point for outside political powers by virtue of its importance in Christian pilgrimage. Latin Christian presence increased from the middle of the sixteenth century onwards due to the political/economic enactments of capitulations between the Ottomans and Western powers. These treaties, the first one agreed to with the French in 1536, provided freedom of travel and trade within Ottoman territory for French merchants or those under French protection. Capitulations enacted with other Western powers during subsequent centuries provided economic trade advantages to Western merchants and introduced Latin Christians, small in number, in many important Ottoman cities and regions of trade.

Additionally, capitulations opened the door for Catholic missionary efforts among Orthodox and Oriental Orthodox Christians. The Congregation for the Propagation of the Faith, established in 1622 by the Roman Catholic Pope Gregory XV, had as one of its main objectives the reunion of Orthodox Christians with Rome. By 1626, Capuchin Franciscans had established houses in Constantinople and Aleppo. A year later, Carmelites and Jesuits founded missions in Aleppo and by the end of the seventeenth century Dominicans could be found in several areas throughout the Middle East.

Roman Catholic activity resulted in several splits within the Orthodox and Oriental Orthodox communities. Small Armenian, Coptic, and Syrian ecclesial bodies entered into communion with Rome. Two larger groups appeared in the areas of Lebanon and Syria: the Maronites and the Melkites. Maronites, located in the rugged region of Mount Lebanon, proclaimed union with Rome through the crusader state of Antioch in the twelfth century, with more formal and direct ties to Rome being established in the sixteenth century. A contested election for the Orthodox patriarchal see of Antioch in 1724 resulted in schism and the recognition of one of the candidates as the Catholic patriarch of Antioch by Pope Benedict XIII in 1729. For several decades, a bitter rivalry between Catholic Melkites and Orthodox ensued primarily in Aleppo and Beirut, with the Ottoman authorities usually siding with the Orthodox hierarchy. Known as Eastern-rite Catholics, these Christian communities laid claim to their historical Christian roots in the Middle East while adopting and adapting to Latin liturgical and organizational practices. They remained important ecclesial bodies contributing significantly to the Christian identity of the region.

The success of Roman Catholicism among Christians in the Middle East was due, in part, to economic benefits arising from trade between Eastern-rite Catholics with the Western mercantile class present in major Syrian towns and cities. Additionally, external resources such as educational opportunities and institutions offered by Western Christianity (with Rome as a centralizing educational, political, and symbolic magnet) and the offering of missionary-style preaching and exposure to the Christian gospel attracted Middle Eastern Christians. Not that Orthodox and Oriental Orthodox communities lacked these opportunities; rather it was an issue of degree. Initially, Aleppo was the epicenter of the Melkite Catholic community but from the 1780s onwards Melkites began to relocate to the Syro-Palestinian coast and the area of Mount Lebanon where their communities flourished. It has been estimated that approximately one-third of Arabic-speaking Orthodox eventually became Catholic Melkites.

Tsarist Russia played an important political and economic role for Orthodox Middle Eastern Christians. Both the Greek Orthodox patriarchs of Jerusalem and Antioch sent several embassies (1541, 1558, 1619, 1648, 1655, 1709 to name some of the more important ones) to Russia and the Danubian provinces of Moldavia and Wallachia in search of economic support from their fellow Orthodox Christians. Russian Orthodox pilgrimage to the Holy Land increased in the eighteenth and nineteenth centuries, and the Crimean War (1853–66) between Russia and the Ottoman Empire was ostensibly started over protecting the rights of Christians in the Holy Land. Some seventy-five years earlier, Russia had won concessions from the Sublime Porte in 1774 in which Russia was given "authority" to be the "protector" of Orthodox Christians throughout the entire Ottoman Empire. More of a political statement than anything, this reflects European and Russian interests and support of the well-being of Christian minorities in the Ottoman world.

Egypt is an interesting case study that reflects how local Christian leadership (lay and ecclesiastical) interacted with local Ottoman authorities. With the destruction of the Mamluks, Cairo, once the center of political power, became one of many cities in the vast Ottoman Empire. The mid-seventeenth century marks an important shift within the Coptic community of Egypt.

The role of the Coptic popes, who appropriately figure largely in the history of the Coptic community, is eclipsed by lay individuals with high economic and social status. This coincided with a weakened centralized Ottoman government in Istanbul which provided local Egyptian authorities more freedom and less of a focus on institutional structures. For the next 150 years, this group of lay Copts held important positions in the financial and administrative apparatus of Ottoman Egypt. Therefore, "dealings within the Coptic community increasingly relied on the patronage of influential persons and not necessarily on the canonically established clerical hierarchy."[14] Lay leaders were directly involved in the appointment

---

14. Guirguis and van Doorn-Harder, *Emergence of the Modern Coptic Papacy*," 32.

of the Coptic pope and some of them are even mentioned in the Coptic Synaxarion. A similar increase in the authority and prestige of Greek Orthodox lay notables in Constantinople, known as Phanariots, can be detected at the end of the eighteenth century.

During this period, there was a resurgence in the public demonstration of religious ritual in Egypt. Pilgrimages (local and to Jerusalem) were organized, Holy Saturday evening festivals anticipating Easter Sunday were widely attended (even drawing the attention of Muslims), the consecration of a new pope was a public event, and the production of the holy *mayrun* (myrrh or *myron*) used in the sacrament of Chrismation attracted many. The production of *mayrun* was an ancient ritual that involved several days and included multiple bishops. On two occasions the cost of the production of the *mayrun* (which included the acquisition of numerous and exotic oils, herbs, and fragrances) was borne by lay notables.

Islamic law, in Egypt and elsewhere, consistently forbade the building of new churches and strictly limited the renovation and repair of church edifices. A constant theme throughout the entire period covered by this article was the attempt by Christians to gain permission for refurbishing their houses of worship. Reflective of the relative laxity of Islamic authority and the increased influence and prestige of Coptic lay notables in the eighteenth century, there is hardly one historic Coptic church or monastery in Egypt today that does not show signs of eighteenth-century renovations.[15] Coinciding with building restoration was an increase in the copying of texts as well as a rebirth of church iconography dated to the eighteenth century, all financially supported by the lay notables.

The nearly three centuries of Ottoman rule over the historic lands of Christians in the Middle East provides the backdrop for the main contours of Christian identity and location in these areas up to the twentieth century. With a weak centralized government in Istanbul, Christian communities negotiated their world through contact with local Ottoman and Muslim officials and leaders. Christians in Constantinople, with their own level of economic wealth, educational status, and political connections dealt with Ottoman authorities on a different level. A quick comparison between the number of changes to the seat of the patriarchs serving the see of Constantinople during the eighteenth century (thirty-three) with those serving the Copts of Egypt (six) or the Orthodox of Antioch (six) make this clear. The increased presence of Roman Catholic missionaries in the Levant and their success in establishing ecclesial bodies in communion

---

Lay leaders were referred to as *arakhina* ("distinguished notables").

15. Guirguis and van Doorn-Harder, *Emergence of the Modern Coptic Papacy,"* 43.

with Rome reflect the regional commitments and histories of the Christians in the Middle East. Christians remained second-class citizens, but increased Western interests, contacts, and hegemony would lead to dramatic changes to Christian communities in the following century. For now, the distinctive ecclesial identities of Christians in the Middle East were firmly established for the foreseeable future.

European Imperialism, Nationalism, and Ottoman Reform (1798–1900)

Towards the end of the eighteenth century, European powers, which previously had been content with their economic and political relations with the Ottomans through capitulations, increased their contacts and interests in the Ottoman world. This was partly the result of a desire to gain advantages over trade routes to India via Egypt and Iraq. However, the Middle East soon became an arena in which the struggles between European powers were played out. Napoleon's invasion of Egypt in 1798, ostensibly in support of the Sublime Porte against the regional uprise of Mamluk authority, was a means by which France could challenge Britain's rising trade advantage with India as well as exert military and economic pressure on Britain. Ultimately unsuccessful, the French military intervention in Egypt was a precursor of later European military involvement by Britain, Austria, and Russia. Each of these four European powers feared the other's gain through Ottoman losses and therefore pursued a policy of propping up the Ottoman Empire as a means of maintaining the balance of power.

Increased attention on the Ottoman world coupled with the Ottomans' desire to adopt Western military and industrial advances led European powers to become more cognizant of the plight of Christians and Jews within the Ottoman Empire. Additionally, nationalist movements among the peoples of the Balkans (Serbians, Greeks, Romanians, Bulgarians) spurred on by ideals of the French and American revolutions, and supported both morally and materially by Western powers, fueled a reform (*tanzimat*) movement among Ottomans in which Western ideas of individual rights and the equality of all citizens (at least male) were supported. National aspirations, religious freedom, and Ottoman reforms created an environment of promise and hope for Christians in the Middle East during the nineteenth century.

With the exception of the Armenians (and perhaps the Greeks in western Anatolia), the nationalist movements of Balkan Christians lacked counterparts among Middle Eastern Christians. Rather, the patriarchate of Constantinople published under the name of Anthimos, patriarch of

Jerusalem, an exhortation to its faithful vilifying Western ideas of individual rights. Known as the "Paternal Instruction" and issued in 1798, Christians were warned that the devil "has devised in the present century another artifice and pre-eminent deception, namely the much vaunted system of liberty, which perhaps on the surface appears to be good. . . . It is, however, a trap of the devil and a destructive poison, to drive the people headlong into corruption and confusion."[16] Unlike their Balkan co-religionists, religious and personal freedoms for Christians in the Middle East were to come in the appearance, at least on paper, of Ottoman reforms.

In 1839, Sultan Abdülmecid I promulgated the Hatt-i Şerif of Gülhane. This firman guaranteed the life, property, and personhood of all Ottoman subjects. A later decree, the Hatt-i Hümayun of 1856 affirmed the equality of subjects, regardless of religion or race. Collectively known as the Tanzimat Reforms, these new Ottoman laws provided all Ottoman subjects with Western rights of equality before the law. Given the regionalism of the Ottoman Empire and the weakness of the central government, the actual implementation of these news laws was not universal. They did, however, lead to the creation of local advisory municipal councils on which non-Muslims could serve and become involved in civic affairs. This new openness also allowed for the creation of cultural and educational organizations among the dhimmis that were led by groups of lay and ordained individuals and not necessarily tied directly to the head of a religious community. Oriental and Eastern-rite Catholic communities were recognized with their own millets.

During the nineteenth century there was an increase in the presence of Western, non-Orthodox Christians in the Middle East. European and American missionaries were encouraged to settle in Syria during the decade of the 1830s under the rulership of Ibrahim Pasha, viceroy of Egypt under Ottoman rule. American Evangelical missionaries could be found throughout the Ottoman world at this time. Even with the Tanzimat Reforms, it was still impossible for Muslims to convert from Islam. Therefore, missionaries in the Ottoman world focused their efforts on Christian communities. Though not as successful as they hoped, these missionaries did establish schools, hospitals, and orphanages where Christians could turn for social and educational opportunities. The "conversions" were realized from those who were already Christian and even though local religious leaders had little political and institutional resources to counter Protestant missionary activity, "conversions" were numerically small. An additional important consequence of Evangelical missionary efforts was the push towards reading scripture in the vernacular, influencing Bulgarians, Copts, and Armenians in particular.

---

16. Clogg, "The 'Dhidhaskalia Patriki,'" 105.

Further, American missionaries provided an introduction to American culture and society, which may have assisted emigration among Syrians and Lebanese in particular to America.[17] Important educational institutions, such as St. Joseph University (Jesuits; 1875) and the American University of Beirut (American Board of Commissioners for Foreign Missions; 1863) aided in the Westernization of Middle Eastern Christians.

Nineteenth-century Ottoman legal reforms repudiated Islamic law with respect to the status of the dhimmi population where "people of the book" were protected by the state (local authorities) upon payment of the jizya or head tax. Centuries of Islamic rule had solidified the view of Christians within the Middle East as legally inferior to Muslims but tolerated based on their religious heritage and were allowed to maintain their religious identities within limits. Such long-held and deeply engrained views did not dissipate easily. Throughout the Ottoman world of the nineteenth century, the implementation of the Tanzimat Reforms with respect to Christian communities met with indifference by local Muslim leaders and often physical resistance. The reforms empowered Christian communities to challenge entrenched communal norms and relationships. Unsurprisingly, conflict between the two communities arose and European observers noted the incongruency between pronouncements of reform and the reality on the ground. Ottoman tax reforms, which did away with the jizya and required all adult males, Muslim and non-Muslim, to pay taxes, along with the increasing wealth of Christians who had better commercial ties with their European counterparts increased tension between Muslims and Christians. Significant eruptions between the two communities occurred in Aleppo (1850), Jiddah (1858), and Damascus (1860), the last being the result of tensions between the Druze and Maronite Christians in the area of Mount Lebanon dating back several decades. Damascus and Aleppo were two important Syrian urban centers that saw an increase in Christian population from sixteenth to the eighteenth centuries most likely through migration from rural areas. Damascus consisted of five Christian communities listed in order of size from largest to smallest: Orthodox, Syrian Jacobite, Maronites, Armenians, and Latin Christians (merchants); while the main Christian communities in Aleppo were Orthodox, Armenians, Syrian Jacobites, Maronites, and Chaldeans.

Nineteenth-century nationalist movements among Middle Eastern Christians were limited primarily to the Armenians. The Armenian Church, like the other ethnic churches in the Balkans and Christian churches in general in the Middle East, were a prime vehicle for the preservation and

---

17. Sharkey, "American Missionaries in Ottoman Lands," 9.

continuation of cultural and linguistic identity. In the last decades of the nineteenth century, an Armenian nationalist movement emerged, which was suppressed by Ottoman authorities determined to stamp out any nationalist movements. Thousands of Armenians were slaughtered between 1895–96; a precursor to the Armenian genocide of the following century.

At the end of the nineteenth century, Christians in the Middle East had much to be hopeful for. Independence movements in which religious freedom coincided with national aspirations had succeeded among Eastern Christians in the Balkans; and the drive for Bulgarian independence was afoot. The Christian nations of the West (including Russia and America through its missionary presence) continued their interest in the plight of Christians in these historic Christian lands. A new movement know as Zionism was slowly impacting parts of Palestine. New cultural and educational institutions were being established within the various Christian communities. Yet, age-old antagonisms, cultural and political stratification, and the overwhelming Islamic identity of the Middle East did not dissipate. Additionally, nineteenth-century "Ottomanism" was about to be replaced with a brutal and relentless Turkish nationalist movement and Arabism. The latter would initially include Christians but would eventually acquiesce to a strong Islamic identity in the coming century. Looking back to their forebears of previous centuries, Christians should have been optimistic with regards to their improved status. They were heirs of a religious tradition that began in their backyard and given their circumstances they had done their very best to pass this faith on to their descendants while remaining steadfast in its message of hope and love.

For Further Reading

Braude, Benjamin. "Foundation Myths of the Millet System." In *Christians and Jews in the Ottoman Empire: The Functioning of a Plural Society*, edited by Benjamin Braude et al., 69–88. New York: Holmes and Meier, 1982.

Clogg, Richard. "The 'Dhidhaskalia Patriki' (1798): An Orthodox Reaction to French Revolutionary Propaganda Author(s)." *Middle Eastern Studies* 5 (1969) 105.

Doğan, Mehmet Ali, Heather J. Sharkey, and Middle East Studies Association of North America. *American Missionaries and the Middle East: Foundational Encounters*. Salt Lake City: University of Utah Press, 2011.

Gibb, H. A. R., and Harold Bowen. *Islamic Society and the West: A Study of the Impact of Western Civilization on Moslem Culture in the Near East*. London: Oxford University Press, 1957.

Griffith, Sidney. *The Bible in Arabic: The Scriptures of the "People of the Book" in the Language of Islam*. Princeton, NJ: Princeton University Press, 2015

Guirguis, Magdi, and Nelly van Doorn-Harder. *The Emergence of the Modern Coptic Papacy: The Egyptian Church and Its Leadership from the Ottoman Period to the Present*. The Popes of Egypt 3. Cairo: American University in Cairo Press, 2011.

Jenkins, Philip. *The Lost History of Christianity: The Thousand-Year Golden Age of the Church in the Middle East, Africa, and Asia—and How It Died*. New York: HarperOne, 2008.

Micheau, Françoise. "Eastern Christianities (eleventh to fourteenth century): Copts, Melkites, Nestorians, and Jacobites." In *The Cambridge History of Christianity* 5, edited by M. Angold, 371–403. Cambridge: Cambridge University Press, 2006.

Panchenko, Constantin A. *Arab Orthodox Christians under the Ottomans, 1516–1831*. Translated by B. Noble and S. Noble. Jordanville, NY: Holy Trinity Seminary, 2016.

Papademetriou, Tom. *Render unto the Sultan: Power, Authority, and the Greek Orthodox Church in the Early Ottoman Centuries*. Oxford: Oxford University Press, 2015.

Roberson, Ronald G. *The Eastern Christian Churches. A Brief Survey*. 5th ed. Rome: Pontificio Instituto Orientale, 1995.

Runciman, Steven. *The Great Church in Captivity: A Study of the Patriarchate of Constantinople from the Eve of the Turkish Conquest to the Greek War of Independence*. London: Cambridge University Press, 1968.

Sharkey, Heather J. "American Missionaries in Ottoman Lands: Foundational Encounters." An online catalogue edited by Renata Holod and Robert G. Osterhout for the exhibit on Archaeologists and Travelers in Ottoman Lands, Penn Museum, Philadelphia, September 26, 2010–June 26, 2011.

Sharkey, Heather J. *History of Muslims, Christians, and Jews in the Middle East*. Contemporary Middle East 6. New York: Cambridge University Press, 2017.

Swanson, Mark N. *The Coptic Papacy in Islamic Egypt*. Cairo: American University in Cairo Press, 2000.

Tejirian, Eleanor Harvey, and Reeva S. Simon. *Conflict, Conquest, and Conversion: Two Thousand Years of Christian Missions in the Middle East*. New York: Columbia University Press, 2012.

Ye'or, Bat. *The Dhimmi. Jews and Christians under Islam*. Rutherford, NJ: Fairleigh Dickenson University, 1985.

4

Uncertainty in the Twentieth Century[1]

Mitri Raheb

For many Christians of the Middle East the nineteenth century ended with a bold promise for the people and the churches of the region. The end of the Ottoman Empire was at hand. Churches were prospering and their buildings, institutions, and schools were thriving. With the approach of the twentieth century the best seemed yet to be. Within a century, however, from the outbreak of the First World War to the outbreak of the so-called "Arab Spring," Christianity in the Middle East underwent immense changes and challenges, so much so that the question of the very survival of Christianity in the region called the Middle East is a valid one.

The First World War

The end of WWI brought major change to the Middle East. Four hundred years of imperial Ottoman rule over the region came to an end. On the other hand, the region was divided by the Sykes-Picot Agreement, officially the Asia Minor Agreement of 1916, into a series of artificial states whose boundaries were drawn to suit the interests of the two victorious Western powers, France and Great Britain. France took mandatory control over what became Syria and Lebanon. Iraq, Palestine, and Transjordan came under British Mandate, with Egypt remaining under British rule. The Balfour Declaration (1917) began the process that ultimately gave Palestine to the Zionist movement, and thus paved the way for Palestine's colonization.

WWI brought serious consequences for the Christians of the region. The Russians and Germans lost both ground and influence in the region

---

1. This chapter is an edited and shorter version of my, "Christianity in the Middle East, 1917–2017," 375–95, and used with permission. For extensive research with a detailed biography, see Raheb, *The Politics of Persecution*.

because of the war and their missions in the Middle East were hit badly. Following the First World War German missionaries were deported, their institutions either abandoned or administered by others, and funds to run their programs were cut. The Russian Revolution also brought an end to Russian missionary activities that were vital for the empowerment of Orthodox Christians in the region. The demographics of the region had also shifted since much of the Armenian, Syriac, and Greek population of Anatolia was either massacred or became refugees fleeing to Syria, Lebanon, and Palestine or to Greece in the population exchange of 1925. During WWI the Christian community in Palestine lost 13 percent of its total population due to migration.[2] The same is true for the Christians of Lebanon where the annual rate of migration between 1900–1914 was 15,000 persons, 85 percent of whom were Christians.[3]

The Era between the Two World Wars, 1925–39

By 1925 it was clear that the Sykes-Picot Agreement and the "nation" states that had been created by the European powers were in the region to stay for some time. A sense of a nationalism in search of independence from foreign control was not only a feature of the political establishment of the interwar era, but also a feature of the church in that era. This is seen clearly in the development of two denominations: the Greek Orthodox and the Protestant churches. Within the Greek Orthodox Church and through Russian involvement in Palestine and Syria, an educated Greek Orthodox Arab movement arose in the late nineteenth century and began calling for the Arabization of the church against the exclusively Greek hierarchy. Against an exclusive Greek Fraternity at the Jerusalem patriarchate, arose Greek Orthodox Arab laity who started working actively to provide for equal numbers of Arabs and Greeks, in addition to fostering theological education for Arab clergy candidates. To that end three "Arab Orthodox Congresses" were organized in 1923, 1931, and 1944, followed by another one in 1956. Unfortunately, none of their demands were met and the struggle for Arabization and independence continues to the present. This interwar era was thus characterized by strong Christian lay movements. In 1942 Bishop George Khodr founded, together with fifteen other students in Beirut and Latakia, the Orthodox Youth Movement, a lay organization that became important in the life of the Orthodox Church of Antioch.

---

2. Raheb, *Palestinian Christians*, 11.
3. Abdelhady, *The Lebanese Diaspora*, 6.

The culture of independence from Western hegemony was felt in the Protestant churches as well. The Synod of the Evangelical Episcopal Church throughout the Mandate years, 1920–48, fought with no success to be recognized as a "*millet.*" Not only were the British authorities against such recognition but so too was the British Anglican bishop in Jerusalem. The interwar era, therefore, saw a quest among Middle Eastern Protestant Christians to unite as a native indigenous Protestant community. American missionaries called in 1919 for the United Missionary Conference for Syria and Palestine to coordinate the work of the different mission agencies and to discuss issues related to indigenization. In 1920 the National Evangelical Synod of Syria and Lebanon was formed, followed in 1924 by the Union of the Armenian Evangelical Churches in the Near East. The relationship of the Christians of the Middle East to the Christians in Europe and the U.S. was one of the main topics at the Second World Mission Conference held in Jerusalem in 1928. This conference marked the start of the growing independence of the Protestant European-based missions in the region and both their Arabization and the beginning of a Protestant ecumenical movement.

A similar process took place in Palestine in the German missions. Between 1929 and 1931 two local churches emerged from the German Protestant mission and started organizing themselves: the first was the Palestinian Evangelical Congregation in Jerusalem, and the second was the Evangelical Arab Congregation in Bethlehem. In 1931 the National Evangelical Church in Kuwait was established from the American mission. It is no coincidence that many of these churches and synods established within the interwar era had words like "national" or "Arab" in their titles.

A different development took place in the Maronite Church in Lebanon.[4] The Maronite patriarch, Elias Hoayek (1843–1931) was the head of the Lebanese delegation at the Versailles Peace Conference in 1919. Because the Maronite Church had had an affinity with France for several centuries, his interest was first and foremost for Lebanon to come under the French and not the British Mandate. He endeavored to leverage the kind of state that best suited his church. Within the Maronite Church there were two movements with a distinct vision for Lebanon. One group called for a "Petit Liban," a predominantly Christian state covering only Mount Lebanon and Beirut whereas another group, the "Grand Liban," envisioned a greater Lebanon to include Tyre and Saida as well as the Beqaa Valley, areas with predominantly Muslim populations. Grand Liban found its expression in the National Pact (*al-Mithaq al-Watani*) drafted by al-Khouri and the Muslim Sunni leader Riad al-Solh, which laid the foundation for the current

---

4. Harris, *Lebanon*, 147–92.

sectarian political system in Lebanon and which is based on the sharing of power between the different religious communities according to their numbers in the 1932 census. This agreement remained the basis for the Lebanese political system until its revision in al-Ta'ef in 1989.

Politics along sectarian lines also became the rule in Syria. The French Mandate divided Syria by identifying four main distinct entities: Aleppo, Damascus, the Alawite region, and Jabal al-Druze. The two religious communities, the Alawites and the Druze, were recognized by the French Mandate as a separate *millet*. It is interesting that the French, known for their secularism and their strict separation of church and state introduced, for their own political ends and to have a better grip on the areas they controlled, one of the most sectarian political systems in the Middle East.

A different development took place in Iraq, which was occupied in 1917 by British troops, who divided up the country, appointing a Hashemite king to rule under their mandate. The Assyrians did not understand themselves as a purely religious group, but also as an ethnic group. During the interwar era Assyrians were active within the Iraqi Levies, the first Iraqi military forces established by the British. However, most Assyrians were unhappy with the British handing over the country in 1932 to a Sunni-dominated government and advocated autonomy within a united Kingdom of Iraq, a demand that led to the Mosul massacre in 1933, to the emigration of large numbers of Assyrians, including the catholicos himself to Chicago, and later to integration as a religious minority. The call for a "Nineveh Plain province with a federated Iraqi state" still echoes to this day.

The British Mandate government reinvented a sectarian system in Palestine of Jews against Arabs/Muslims. This led in 1928 to the disintegration of a unified multi-religious Jerusalem municipality into two separate entities: a Jewish one in West Jerusalem and an Arab one in the Eastern part of the city. Prior to World War I Arab Christians in Palestine seemed destined to play a central role in the construction of a post-Ottoman political order. By the time the Mandate ended in 1948, their role in political life was vanishing.

Another dynamic was seen within the Coptic Orthodox Church in Egypt.[5] Many of the Copts were involved with the struggle for independence from Britain, especially within the Wafd Party. This era witnessed a strong sense of national unity between the Copts and their Muslim neighbors. It was in this context that the Copts refused the British proposal for a Coptic quota within the projected constitution of an independent Egypt. For the Coptic Orthodox Church the struggle in the interwar era was mainly

5. Sharkey, *American Evangelicals*, 149–78.

between the patriarch and clergy on the one hand and the lay council (*al-Majlis al-Milli*) on the other. The educated laity of the church were asking for greater rights and more say within the church structure.

A European way of life

The transition era, between two world wars of French and British rule also brought major economic changes to the region. Under the political control of the European powers, the economy of the Middle East lost its independence, which had been distinguished by internal trading and became marginal and subservient to Europe's economies. European goods soon started flooding the markets of the Middle East. This new way of life required that bourgeois quarters and villas be constructed on the outskirts of major cities along with accompanying infrastructure, gardens, and European-style architecture. A middle-class lifestyle thus became a new and important element of Middle Eastern Christianity.

Western-style education became the norm at private Christian schools attended by many of the Middle Eastern Christians and elite Muslims. Students in private schools became fluent in English, French, and German in contrast to the growing majorities who attended the expanding system of mono-lingual public schools. As a result, a gap was created between Western-educated Arab Christians and the elite Muslims on the one hand and the Muslim masses on the other. This growing gap became, with time, a recipe for instability in the region.

Arab socialism

The changing pattern of the economy, driven especially by the capitalization of agriculture, pushed many people from the countryside into the cities. Beginning in the 1930s a new group of urban migrants and unemployed began to emerge in many Middle Eastern cities. Nationalism by itself failed to address this phenomenon adequately, which thus encouraged the emergence of a new Arab ideology based on social values. Michel Aflaq (1910–23), a Syrian Christian born to a middle-class family who studied at the Sorbonne, must have felt the discrepancy between the bourgeoisie and the migrant workers. For Aflaq, liberation from foreign rule and fighting for social justice were two sides of the same coin. For him, socialism meant the sharing of the country's resources by its citizens. Separation of church and state was a prerequisite for the equality of all citizens. This ideology of the Arab Socialist Baath Party dominated Syria and Iraq for several decades, attracting many

Middle East Christians. Another approach was developed by Anton Saadeh (1904–49), a Greek Orthodox Christian from Mount Lebanon, who in 1932 founded the Syrian Social Nationalist Party and who advocated the idea of "Natural Syria," a multi-religious, multi-ethnic, and multi-lingual geographic entity that included the Levant, Palestine, Jordan, Lebanon, Syria, Iraq, part of the Gulf region, as well as part of southern Turkey.

The Muslim Brotherhood

The changes brought by WWI and the interwar era produced yet another ideology within the Arab world, particularly in Egypt. One group that emerged from this context came to be known as the Muslim Brotherhood, established in 1928, whose ideology was crafted by Hassan al-Banna (1906–49). Al-Banna was able to make a Salafist brand of Islam fashionable and to establish the Muslim Brotherhood as an alternative authority to the Islamic Al-Azhar University. Although the Brotherhood's ideology was adopted by many Muslims in Egypt and beyond during the interwar period, it wasn't until 1945 that his followers took to the streets protesting the economic crisis and volunteering in 1948 to fight for Palestine.

The Second World War

The 1940s brought another major shift to Europe and subsequently to the Middle East. The rise of Nazi Germany had two immediate consequences for the Middle East. First, Nazi ideology and policy drove large numbers of Jews to flee Germany and other European countries, many immigrating to Palestine where great social and political instability was created. Second, the German occupation of France led to the weakening of the French Mandate's grip on the Middle East. Indeed, both Lebanon and Syria gained their independence while France was occupied by Germany.

By the end of the war the United States and the Soviet Union had emerged as key players with major political and economic power as well as vast manpower. By the end of World War II Britain was forced to withdraw from most countries in the Middle East. In 1946, The Hashemite Kingdom of Jordan was established, ending the British protectorate there, while on 15 May 1948 Britain withdrew its forces from Palestine. The very same day the Jewish community declared the State of Israel, a declaration that resulted in an attack by Arab forces. The Arab-Israeli War of 1948 was devastating for the Palestinians. Three-fourths (77%) of historic Palestine was lost, becoming the State of Israel. This defeat was called *an-Nakbah*, the Catastrophe.

The Arab-Israel War of 1948 had catastrophic consequences for the 700,000 Palestinians who were driven out of their homes and instantly became refugees. Among them were more than 50,000 Christians. According to the British census of 1931, around 80,000 Christians (10 percent of the Arab Palestinian population) were living in Palestine at that time. By the end of the 1940s, the figure had risen to some 135,000 and constituted a thriving community. In the War of 1948, 35 percent of all Christians living in Palestine lost their possessions, their work, their land, and their homes. The percentage of Christians in Palestine dropped from around 8 percent to 2.8 percent within just a few months.[6]

In 1947, the Lutheran World Federation was created in Lund, Sweden and began work in the West Bank reaching out to the thousands of refugees. An emergency relief program was initiated providing food, shelter, clothing, and medical care. In 1948, a group of international and local clergy and lay leaders established the Department of Service to the Palestinian Refugees (DSPR) that was later integrated into the Middle East Council of Churches. On 18 June 1948, Pope Pius XII established the Pontifical Mission for Palestine, to feed, clothe, and educate Palestinian refugees.

The era of the Arab republic

The loss of Palestinian land and the devastating defeat of the Arab countries in the War of 1948 brought major changes to the political landscape of the Middle East. First, the prevailing governments lost their credibility in the eyes of their peoples, which led to numerous coups. In 1949, a military coup overthrew the Syrian national government. King Abdullah of Jordan was assassinated in 1951 during a visit to Jerusalem's al-Aqsa Mosque. In the same year, George Habash, a Greek Orthodox Palestinian Christian refugee from Lydda founded an Arab Nationalist Movement that soon aligned itself with the ideology of Nasser. Nasser, together with a group of Egyptian officers, was able to seize power in Egypt in 1952, dispose King Farrouk, and proclaim Egypt a republic. The nationalization of the Suez Canal in 1956 was seen as a long-awaited success story, thus elevating Nasser to the status of regional hero. In 1958, civil war broke out in Lebanon while in that same year the Iraqi Hashemite king was killed and Iraq was declared a republic.

This period marked the peak of pan-Arabism. But it was in this era too that Arab socialism reached its zenith. The growing influence of the USSR, the Communist Party in China, and nationalist socialist movements in Asia gave rise to the idea of Arab socialism. The concept espoused by the Syrian

---

6. Raheb, "Palestinian Christians," 12.

Christian Michel 'Aflaq, that there was only one Arab nation in which Arabs possessed the right to live in a single united state, became official state ideology when the party assumed power in Syria in 1961 and in Iraq in 1963.

Changes to Middle Eastern Christianity

The quest of the Arab states for independence from foreign occupation in the 1950s and 1960s brought about the transformation of Protestant missions into national churches. In the wake of Arab nationalism, the National Evangelical Synod of Syria and Lebanon, which was formed in 1920, in 1959 became fully independent from the Board of Foreign Missions of the Presbyterian Church, USA. Similarly, the National Evangelical Church of Beirut together with nine other Presbyterian churches became in the early 1960s the National Evangelical Union of Lebanon.

In Palestine, and with the support of the Lutheran World Federation, a process of consultation and organization with local Protestant congregations that had emerged from the German missionary enterprise resulted in the establishment of the Evangelical Lutheran Church in Jordan, which was officially recognized by the Jordanian government in May 1959.

A similar process took place within the Anglican Church. The Jordanian government recognized the Protestant Anglican *millet* and published its name in the 1938 official list of recognized churches. On 29 October 1947 the Jordanian cabinet accepted the new name of the Anglican Church as the Arab Evangelical Episcopal Church, adding it to the official list. In 1958, the first Arab Anglican bishop for Jordan, Lebanon, and Syria was consecrated.

Likewise, the Egyptian revolution of 1952 was an important turning point in the life of the Coptic Evangelical Church.[7] Celebrating its centennial in 1958, the Evangelical Church of Egypt gained its independence committing to complete self-governance and self-support. Acknowledging its Coptic (i.e., Egyptian) heritage, it became known as the Coptic Evangelical Church. Under the leadership of its general secretary at the time, Samuel Habib, the church started new outreach programs to combat poverty and foster self-development and became known under the name of the "Coptic Evangelical Organization for Social Services" (CEOSS).

The churches of the Middle East were deeply influenced by the quest for Arab political unity. The first to be so influenced were the Protestants. In 1955 representatives of all the major Protestant churches (Presbyterians, Episcopalians, Lutherans, Reformed, and the Church of God), gathered in Beirut and the possibility of forming "The United Evangelical Church of the

---

7. Sharkey, *American Evangelicals*, 191–210.

Arab East" was discussed. The blueprint was the Church of South India. Although the idea of a single united Evangelical church did not materialize, the quest for deeper unity led to the formation in 1964 of the Near East Council of Churches, originally a completely Protestant endeavor, known today as the Fellowship of the Middle East Churches (FMEEC). The quest for unity was influenced, however, not only by the pan-Arabism of the region, but also by the era's spirit of ecumenism. This was the time of the Second Vatican Council, which brought momentous change to the Roman Catholic Church. During this period, Pope Paul VI and the ecumenical patriarch of Constantinople, Athenagoras, met in Jerusalem in 1965, expressing their willingness to overcome their differences, to convey regret for their mutually unreconciled theologies, and to espouse their common desire for justice.

The Near East Council of Churches evolved in 1974 into the Middle East Council of Churches adding to the Protestants and Syrian Orthodox, the Greeks, Copts, and Armenians and expanding in 1990 again to include the Catholics, both Latin and Orientals.

Pan-Arabism, however, had a fatal consequence for many Christians in the Middle East. The Suez Canal crisis led in 1956 to the nationalization of the Suez Canal by Nasser. Nationalization spread quickly across the region. Many Middle Eastern Christians were consequently substantially affected by the policy of nationalization, which was implemented largely in Egypt, Syria, and Iraq. Private individuals and also monasteries lost much of their property at this time. For the administration of the remaining endowed properties, known as *waqf*, the Coptic Orthodox Pope Kyrillos VI (Cyril, 1902–71) was able to establish a joint board of monastic and lay leaders.[8] The impact of Coptic Orthodox education was also in turn diminished since virtually all schools out of financial necessity were given to the state, becoming so-called "subventional schools." In 1974, the Baath government in Iraq nationalized religious schools across the country, including all Christian schools. Consequently, many in the Middle East in the 1960s lost much of their land, capital, livelihood, and influence. This forced large numbers to emigrate.

The 1967 War

The 1967 war between Israel on one side and Egypt, Syria, and Jordan on the other was a turning point for the region. The defeat of Nasser was not only a deep disappointment for the Arab world; it also brought a devastating disillusionment with pan-Arabism. The Arab World woke up one morning to

---

8. Hasan, *Christians versus Muslims*, 57–101.

discover that the remainder of Palestine (the West Bank and the Gaza Strip) along with Syria and the Golan Heights were occupied by Israel.

The first to be disillusioned were the Palestinians, who as early as 1964, under the umbrella of the Arab League, had established the Palestinian Liberation Organization. Regime changes also took place in Iraq in 1968 bringing Saddam Hussein to power. In 1969, military coups saw Qaddafi take power in Libya, and Numayri in Sudan, followed by Assad in 1970 in Syria. The death of Nasser in 1970 marked the end of a pan-Arab era and the beginning of a new one.

The defeat of Nasser also meant disillusionment with the existing political regimes and ideologies and a turn to a more religious discourse. The outcome of the 1967 war boosted Jewish religious nationalism, specifically among extremist Jewish groups within Israel, which started their settler colonial project in the West Bank claiming that it was ancient "Judea and Samaria," a title that was not so much a geographical description as it was a religious designation with a political agenda. The defeat gave boost also to an Islamic discourse. Israeli's 1967 victory had an enormous impact on Christians worldwide. Christian Zionism experienced a renaissance. A post-Holocaust theology that took hold after 1967 was often an attempt to gain liberal Protestantism's support for Israel.[9]

Palestine

On the Palestinian side, with the establishment of the Palestinian Liberation Organization (PLO), the liberation of Palestine became the new focus for the Palestinians, with Beirut as their center of activity. Within the context of the Cold War, Christian leaders emerged adopting Marxist ideologies. Just a few months after the war, George Habash (1926–2008) went on to establish the Popular Front for the Liberation of Palestine (PFLP), adopting a Marxist-Leninist approach. A year later, Nayef Hawatmeh (b. 1938), a Jordanian Christian who was influenced by Maoist ideology, broke away from Habash to found the Democratic Front for the Liberation of Palestine. In this era there was clearly a shift by Middle Easterners in general and Middle Eastern Christians from pan-Arab ideologies to Marxism.

9. Haynes, "Christian Holocaust," 553–85.

Egypt

Disillusioned by Nasser's pan-Arabism, many young educated Coptic Orthodox in Egypt turned to the desert, to the ancient monasteries of their church, searching for their spiritual roots. The number of monasteries tripled in less than two decades. Pope Kyrill (Cyril VI, 1902–71)[10] a former monk, and Matta al-Meskeen (1919–2006) were the two most important figures in promoting this monastic life and spirituality. Monasteries in the Egyptian desert became not only a magnet for young, educated Copts but also their springboard into the church hierarchy as most of the bishops and metropolitans in the post-1967 era came from that milieu. In 1971 another monk, Shenouda III (1923–2012),[11] was elected pope of the Coptic Orthodox Church. Pope Shenouda's election coincided with a change in the political leadership of Egypt. At Nasser's death in 1970 Anwar al-Sadat (1918–81) became his successor. Disappointment with Nasser contributed to Pope Shenouda becoming a popular national leader in the Coptic Church. Pope Shenouda was unwilling to support the Camp David Peace Treaty between Israel and Egypt. In Shenouda's stance Sadat saw an attempt to delegitimize his leadership and the pope himself assuming the role of a tougher national leader than Sadat. Pope Shenouda was also unhappy with Sadat's attempt to Islamize Egyptian society and its laws; he was not afraid publicly to protest against that development. Consequently, in 1980 Sadat ordered Pope Shenouda to be placed under house arrest in one of the monasteries at Wadi Natroun. Pope Shenouda's monastic house arrest was lifted in 1985 by President Mubarak, who was interested in normalizing relations between the Egyptian state and the Coptic pope. Pope Shenouda was in turn, therefore supportive of President Hosni Mubark to the latter's very end.

Lebanon

In Lebanon, the context was different for the Christian leadership. The Maronite Patriarch Khreish, who served from 1975–85, was faced with the reality of a civil war (1975–90). His own Maronite community was divided into different parties and armed factions and his authority was thus minimized to that of moral leadership with little political depth. The patriarch's interest was to maintain the sectarian system, to keep a Maronite as president of Lebanon, and to restore interfaith and intercommunal relations. Nasrallah Sfeir, who was elected the Maronite patriarch in 1986 and served

---

10. Van Doorn-Harder, ed., "Kyrillos VI (1902–1971)," 231–43.
11. Van Doorn-Harder, ed., "Signposts to Biography," 244–54.

to 2011, backed the Taif Accord of 1989, which provided the basis for the ending of the civil war and the return to political normalcy in Lebanon.[12] Following the cessation of the civil war, the role of the patriarch again became important as Maronite political leaders lost a great deal of credibility, being accused of serving their own political ends at the expense of the larger Christian community. In 2001 Patriarch Sfeir urged the withdrawal of the Syrian army from Lebanon, a move which restored his popularity within and beyond the Maronite community.[13]

The War of 1973

A major change took place in the Middle East in October 1973 when Sadat launched a sudden attack on Israel. The war and its aftermath resulted in increased American influence in both Egypt and the Gulf. The oil embargo compensated the Arab world for its defeat in 1967 giving them a sense of power, influence, and wealth. Within few years annual revenues from oil in the Arab oil-producing countries grew enormously. This wealth resulted in the launch of countless large infrastructure projects in those countries attracting millions of migrant workers from poorer Arab countries. Many of those migrant workers were Christians. While the Christian migrants in the 1950s and 1960s were from the highly educated middle class, this new wave of migration to the Gulf states attracted workers of every skill level. In the late twentieth century with large infrastructure projects underway in the United Arab Emirates, Qatar, and Oman, hundreds of thousands of Asian migrant workers also went to work in the Gulf, many of whom were Christian. As of 2017, the Gulf is the only place in the Middle East where the number and percentage of Christians is on the increase.

The oil embargo and the growing affluence resulting from petrodollar income has brought another important change to the region. With Saudi Arabia, the main beneficiary of this oil wealth, an extremely conservative form of Islam, known as Wahhabism was advocated and exported with increasing intensity and funding. Saudi Arabia saw itself as the protector of Sunni Islam and called for the spreading of Islam throughout the region and world. This assertion expressed itself in the building of mosques, supporting Islamic charities, and a policy of general Islamization. Sudden Saudi wealth saw natural allies in many Muslim movements.

Yet Saudi Arabia was not the only country supporting the Islamization of society. The Iranian Revolution, under the leadership of Ayatollah Khomeini

---

12. Henley, "Politics of a Church," 353–69.
13. McCallum, *Christian Religious Leadership*, 159–90.

in 1979, brought a distinctive Shiite version of Islam to power. With major reserves of oil and gas, the Islamic Republic of Iran went on to "export the revolution," especially to countries with Shiite populations such as Iraq, Syria, Lebanon, and Yemen. This policy has ultimately led to increasingly bitter competition between Sunni Saudi Arabia and Shiite Iran, a confrontation that has caused sectarian polarization of the region, a growing arms race, and intra-regional conflicts. Although the Christians of the Middle East were not a direct target of either of these Islamization models, they have indirectly paid a heavy price as collateral damage.

The 1970s and 1980s were characterized not only by great affluence but also by conflicts and wars that exerted a heavy toll on the Christian communities of the region. From 1975 to 1990 Lebanon was wracked by civil war and the harsh Israeli occupation of southern Lebanon (1982–2000) that proved to be devastating for the country in general and for the Christian community in particular. The seventeen-year war destroyed Lebanon's economy and infrastructure, resulted in thousands being disabled, and produced a quarter of a million fatalities. One million people (40 percent of the total population) migrated during the war. While about half of those migrants went to the oil-producing countries of the Gulf, the other half went to Europe, the Americas, Africa, and Australia. All religious groups were affected by this migration, but Christian migrants constituted some 75 percent of the total.

Iraq was yet another country devastated by war. The Iran-Iraq war from 1980–88, followed by the invasion of Kuwait in 1991, and the war to liberate Kuwait, the sanctions imposed on Iraq after that, and then the invasion of Iraq by the U.S. in 2003 took a major toll on the country in general and on Christians particularly. Many Christians fled Iraq during the Iran-Iraq war often to avoid being drafted into that deadly conflict. Christian migration accelerated after the 1991 conflict, mainly to the U.S., but also to Europe, Australia, and New Zealand. Sanctions in the 1990s led 30 percent of the population to emigrate. It is estimated that of the 2 million Iraqis who emigrated between 1980–2003 an eighth (250,000) were Christians.

Following the invasion of Iraq in 2003 over a million more Christians fled Iraq to neighboring countries like Jordan, while many migrated to North America and Australia. Additionally, there was a substantial migration of Christians within Iraq from the north to the south and later to Irbil.

On 8 December 1987, the first Intifada or uprising against the Israeli occupation started bringing a new socio-political consciousness. In response, new theological centers promoting contextual theology evolved in Palestine. This period was characterized by an abundance of Palestinian theological publications by theologians from diverse backgrounds. The first Palestinian Intifada compelled the heads of the Christian churches to unite and to issue individual statements expressing the prophetic voice of the church that condemns injustice and rejoices in justice.[14] In 2009, a group of Palestinians Christians from diverse denominations issued the Palestine Kairos Document.

Aftermath of the "Arab Spring"

The so-called Arab Spring that began on 17 December 2010 in Tunisia raised the expectations of the people of the Middle East for a better future and triggered a ripple effect throughout the Arab World. It resulted in a revolution in Egypt on January 25, 2011 and a day later a civil uprising in Syria. These two states are key for the Christian presence in the Middle East. The largest Christian community in the region lives in Egypt and Syria was known for the most secular ideology in the region.

The course that the Arab Spring has taken in later stages has presented a huge challenge for the people of the Middle East in general and the Christians of the region. Christian response to this challenge assumes different forms, ranging from political engagement to the development of diverse types of contextual theologies, the strengthening of civil society, service to the needy and vulnerable, and a greater engagement in ecumenical and interfaith dialogue. In the last ten years a major focus has been on exploring new ways in looking at faith and citizenship. The Statement of the Christian Academic Forum for Citizenship in the Arab World (CAFCAW) published in 2014 under the title "From the Nile to the Euphrates: The Call of Faith and Citizenship" is a good expression of such a new Christian response to the larger situation in the Middle East today. Another excellent example is the document "Choosing Life: Christians in the Middle East: Towards Renewed Geo-Political and Theological Choices" published in 2021 by a group of independent theologians from diverse churches of the Middle East.

Conclusion

What started, in the minds of many, as a promising century for the Christian community in the Middle East has reached a stage a hundred years later of becoming a nightmare. The survival of the Christian communities in the Middle East is affected by all the socio-political and economic challenges that face the region as a whole. It is not possible to consider the situation

---

14. Raheb, "Displacement Theopolitics," 9–32.

of Christians apart from the more general context, one that is marked by the absence of democracy, modernity, and economic and political stability. Throughout the twentieth centuries Christian communities in the Middle East have endured several waves of displacement, leading them often to emigration. With a low birth rate, it is foreseeable that several Christian communities may not survive in certain areas of the Middle East.

Christianity may well cease to exist in the land of its origins but survive in the diaspora. As a result, diasporic and hybrid identities may, therefore, become an important feature for Christians with Middle Eastern roots. Maronite diaspora in the U.S., France, Latin America, and some African countries is estimated to number from 4 to 5 million. Between 16 to 20 million people of Lebanese origin live in the world today. Over half a million Latin Americans with Palestinian roots live as fourth- and fifth-generation Palestinians in Latin America alone, with over half of them just in Chile, where they comprise 3 percent of the population.

The Syrian Orthodox community which was almost eradicated from Turkey has survived today in several major cities, with large Syriac populations residing in Sweden. While there is only a remnant Assyrian Christian community in Iraq, immigrants have found new homes in Chicago, California, and Michigan. Today the Coptic Church has several dioceses and centers in Western Europe, the U.S., Canada, and Australia serving over half-a-million Copts, while the Armenians who lost their homes in eastern Turkey have a population of around 3 million in Armenia with seven million scattered all over the world, with large concentrations in Russia, the U.S., France, and other countries constituting a vibrant transnational community.

For Further Reading

Abdelhady, Dalia. *The Lebanese Diaspora: The Arab Immigrant Experience in Montreal, New York, and Paris.* New York: New York University, 2011.

Donabed, Sargon. *Reforging a Forgotten History: Iraq and the Assyrians in the Twentieth Century.* Edinburgh, UK: Edinburgh University, 2016.

Doorn-Harder, Nelly van, ed. *Between Desert and City: The Coptic Orthodox Church Today.* Reprint, Eugene, OR: Wipf & Stock, 2012.

Haiduc-Dale, Noah. *Arab Christians in British Mandate Palestine: Communalism and Nationalism, 1917–1948.* Edinburgh: Edinburgh University, 2013.

Harris, William. *Lebanon: A History, 600–2011.* Oxford: Oxford University, 2014.

Hasan, S. S. *Christians versus Muslims in Modern Egypt: The Century-Long Struggle for Coptic Equality.* Oxford: Oxford University, 2003.

McCallum, Fiona, John Anderson, and Raymond Hinnebusch. *Christian Religious Leadership in the Middle East: The Political Role of Patriarch*. Lewiston, NY: Mellen, 2010.

Raheb, Mitri, "Christianity in the Middle East, 1917–2017." In *History of Global Christianity III*, edited by Jens Holger Schjørring and Norman Hjelm, 375–95. Boston: Brill, 2018.

———. "Displacement Theopolitics." In *The Invention of History: A Century of Interplay between Theology and Politics in Palestine*, edited by Mitri Raheb, 9–32. Bethlehem: Diyar, 2011.

———. "Palestinian Christians in Modern History: Between Migration and Displacement." In *Palestinian Christians: Emigration, Displacement and Diaspora*, edited by Mitri Raheb, 9–28. Bethlehem: Diyar, 2017.

———. *The Politics of Persecution: Middle Eastern Christianity in the Age of Empire*. Waco, TX: Baylor University Press, 2021.

———. *Sailing through Troubled Waters: Christianity in the Middle East*. Bethlehem: Diyar, 2013.

Robson, Laura. *Colonialism and Christianity in Mandate Palestine*. Austin, TX: University of Texas Press, 2012.

Sharkey, Heather J. *American Evangelicals in Egypt: Missionary Encounters in an Age of Empire*. Princeton, NJ: Princeton University Press, 2015.

— Section Two —

The Story of Christianity Expressed in a Grand Church Family Mosaic

5

The Coptic Story

WAFIK WAHBA

SINCE THE FIRST CENTURY of Christianity, the Egyptian Christians, known as *the Copts*, kept the lamp of faith burning amid much turmoil and many hardships till our modern time. The word "Copts" is derived from the Greek word for Egypt, *Aigyptios*. Since the Arab invasion of Egypt in the seventh century, the word Copts have been used to describe native Egyptians referring to the indigenous Christians of Egypt. Today, there are over 12 million Copts in Egypt, making Egyptian Christians the largest Christian community in the Middle East.

According to Coptic tradition, St. Mark the Evangelist (one of Jesus' disciples and the writer of the Gospel of Mark) brought Christianity to Egypt. The book of Acts makes a reference to Egyptian Jews being in Jerusalem on the Day of Pentecost (Acts 2:10) who most probably brought Christianity back to Egypt. The book of Acts also references one of the early church leaders, Apollos, who was an Alexandrian from Egypt (Acts 18:24). During the early years of Christianity, Alexandria, Egypt enjoyed a prominent position as a one of the major metropolitan hubs in the Roman Empire. For a millennium, from the third century B.C. until the Arab invasion in the seventh century, Alexandria was the intellectual capital of the ancient world and a great commercial center. It is not surprising that Christianity reached Egypt through Alexandria and by the close of the first century Christianity flourished in this great metropolis of the Roman Empire. The great historian Eusebius made a reference to the Alexandrian eleventh patriarch, Julian (d. 188) overseeing several parishes in Alexandria whereas by the close of the second century Julian's successor, Demetrius (190–233), a well-known Christian figure, presided over a large Christian population in the city.

By the third century, Christianity was well rooted in Egypt, not only in the cosmopolitan city of Alexandria but as far as Nag Hammadi, about 500 miles to the south. Christians constituted the majority of the population in Egypt while Egyptian Christians counted for the largest Christian community in the Roman Empire during the third and fourth centuries.[1]

The Copts Contributions to World Christianity in the Early Centuries of Christianity

Egypt played a remarkable role in the development of early Christianity and its influence continued through the centuries till our modern time. While Egyptian Christianity made its own contribution, most notably in the field of monasticism, it was from Hellenistic Egypt that the most influential church leadership emanated, largely due to the intellectual pre-eminence of Alexandria in the ancient world.

First Christian Theological School

Early Egyptian Christianity is credited with giving the Christian world its first organized theological education. Christian learning and discipleship that started in the cosmopolitan city of Alexandria played a central role in the formation and spread of the Christian faith during that time. Alexandria was home to several philosophical schools centuries before Christianity and by the third century a number of schools dedicated to Christian learning were flourishing in this great city of learning and scholarship. The translation of the Hebrew Scriptures into the Greek language, known as the Septuagint (LXX), was completed in Alexandria by the third century before Christ. The city was also known for its "Great Library," the largest and most significant library in the ancient world, which hosted over 700,000 volumes, according to the Greek historian Aulus Gellius.[2] Demetrius, the bishop of Alexandria (c. 189–232), realized the need for establishing a catechetical school for Christian learning. The head of the catechetical school in about c. 180 was Pantaenus, who was succeeded by Clement (c. 160–215) and Origen (185–254), two of the greatest scholars of Christianity. The model adopted by the Alexandrian catechetical school was one of open dialogue with the culture. The school pioneered new methods of interpreting the biblical text in Hellenistic and philosophical terminologies. This model attracted large number of learners who were able to reconcile their Hellenistic culture with the Christian faith where teaching was done in a friendly intellectual atmosphere. As the number

1. Stark, *The Rise of Christianity*, 13.
2. Worrell, *A Short Account of the Copts*, 20.

of Christian learners grew, Alexandria's position as a center for Christian learning was firmly established across the Roman Empire. Among the great theologians influenced by the School of Alexandria were patriarchs such as Cyril I and Athanasius, who emerged as the key defenders of Christianity against heresies in the Councils of Nicaea and Ephesus.

One of the main reasons that Egyptian Christians were well rooted in their faith is because the scriptures were translated into different Coptic dialects by the third century. This access to scripture in one's own language is a privilege that was lacking in Europe till the fifteenth century.

Spirituality and monasticism

One of the most significant contributions made by Egypt to Christianity was the monastic movement, for it was amongst the Copts that it originated and was developed. Starting from the third century, following a tendency towards asceticism that predated Christian Egypt, Egyptian Christians fathered one of the most influential spiritual movements in the history of Christianity.[3] St. Anthony (c. 251–356), the founder of Christian monasticism, established a monastic tradition where the monks would live alone in total separation from the world in order to devote their lives to prayer and fasting. While St. Pachomius (c. 290–346) established the communal type of monastic life where the monks live separately in their dwellings, but meet together for prayers. In both systems, emphasis was placed on poverty, chastity, and spirituality.[4]

The influence of Egyptian spirituality in the form of monasticism had great impact on Christianity for centuries to come. Athanasius of Alexandria is credited with spreading the movement to the rest of the world during his exile in Rome from 339 to 349. In 357 Athanasius wrote *The Life of Anthony*, a biography that has been read by church leaders and theologians across the Christian world of that time and till today. By the turn of the fourth century the monastic movement influenced many Latin theologians and from the fourth century onwards a large number of church leaders turned to the Nile Valley to spend time in one of the Egyptian monasteries. A long list of church leaders has followed the lead of Egyptian monks and dedicated their

---

3. The life and structure of the church in Egypt was profoundly influenced by the monastic movement, from whose ranks many of its leaders were drawn. To date, there have been 118 patriarchs of the Coptic Orthodox Church. Only twenty-two of them have not been monks; and since 1525 every patriarch has been chosen from within a monastery. Today, both patriarchs and bishops are chosen from monasteries. This is one of the most characteristic features of spiritual leadership in the contemporary church.

4. Watterson, *Coptic Egypt*, 54–61.

lives to the monastic movement, among them are Etherea of Spain, Melania of Rome, Jerome, Rufinus, Basil the Great, Patrick, the first missionary to Ireland, and Radegunde of Gaul (France).[5] Many have adopted the monastic life of Coptic Christianity to their own context. The Celtic Christianity of Ireland for example was primarily monastic. The Irish church was strongly influenced by Egyptian spirituality of the time.[6]

The influence of the monastic movement is reflected in three major areas. First, the monastic movement emphasized a spirituality of self-giving and sacrificial life. Those who joined the movement often gave up materialistic wealth and pursued a life of dedicated prayer and fasting, while being active in serving others, a tradition that continued through the centuries. Meanwhile, monasteries often provided hospitality to strangers and to the community at large. Second, monasteries were great centers of theological education and provided a great wealth of Christian literature. The Egyptian monks often gathered groups of disciples around them and fostered communities of great learners, prayer warriors, and self-disciplined mature Christians. Third, the monastic movement was very instrumental in preserving the Christian faith. Monasteries provided safe havens where worship and prayer could be carried without the interruption usually associated with living in large cosmopolitan cities. Likewise, biblical texts and manuscripts were often kept and protected in monasteries. The monastic movement in Egypt also provided protection from sporadic persecution under the Islamic rule.

Exemplary endurance of persecution

The remarkable spread of the Christian faith was met by severe persecution and opposition from the Roman authorities, who considered Christianity an illegal religion. During the first three centuries of Christianity, Christians in Egypt faced intense times of persecution as elsewhere across the Roman Empire. The first wave of persecution was directed at the leaders of the church, who faced torture and were put to death for preaching the gospel. By the end of the second century ordinary Christians faced sporadic times of persecutions as well. Since Egypt had the largest percentage of Christians in the Roman Empire at the time, Egyptian Christians bore the brunt of the persecution where tens of thousands of Christians in Egypt were massacred by the Roman authorities.[7] A great number of Egyptian

---

5. Irvin and Sunquist, *History of the World Christian Movement*, 209–12.
6. Holt, *Thirsty for God*, 66–68.
7. Stark, *The Rise of Christianity*, 6–13.

martyrs died during the last wave of the Diocletian persecution between c. 300 and 303. The historian Eusebius claimed that he was present in Thebe, Upper Egypt and witnessed many times up to 100 people being put to death in a single day. It is estimated that about 144,000 Egyptian Christians were put to death during this last waive of furious persecution. This period became known in the Coptic Church as "the Era of the Martyrs," a cornerstone of Coptic Christianity's identity. The year 284, the beginning of the reign of Emperor Diocletian is commemorated to this day as the starting point of the Coptic calendar.[8]

Remarkable mission movement

Missionaries were sent from Egypt to eastern Libya, Nubia, the Sudan, and Ethiopia. Egyptian missionaries were also sent to Yemen, India, and Persia. During the fourth and fifth centuries, the missionary outreach of the Copts reached to Gaul (France) and Britain.[9] The Monastery of St. Maurice, named after an Egyptian monk, near modern Geneva is a reminder of these early missionary activities by the Egyptian church.[10]

The Copts under Various Islamic Rules

In the mid-seventh century, Arab armies inspired by Islamic teaching, marched through the Persian and Eastern Roman Empires taking over major territories. Islam entered Egypt in 641. Alexandria was besieged for two years, and its famous library was burned to the ground. Egypt became a province in what was called *Dar-Al-Islam* (the house of Islam). According to the Islamic religio-political system, Muslims and non-Muslims who lived in the house of Islam had to adhere to Islamic religious, social, and political laws and regulations. In the early period of the Islamic dynasty, nothing significant had changed for the average Copts except paying *"jizya,"* the Islamic taxes in exchange of maintaining their religious status. However, such measures started to change gradually wherever the power and authority of the Islamic state were firmly established.

    8. Watterson, *Coptic Egypt*, 16–32.

    9. It must be noted that Christianity reached Gaul (France) in late first and early second century.

    10. Cragg, *The Arab Christians*, 177. St. Maurice was part of a Roman legion serving in Switzerland. The legion included a medical team where people like St. Verena from upper Egypt was sent to attend to the health needs of the Swiss and educate them on new methods of hygiene.

The Copts who formed the majority inhabitants of Egypt during the first centuries of the Islamic rule were given the status of protected people or *Dhimmis*, giving them the choice to either accept Islam or remain Christians, provided that they pay poll tax. On one hand, the *Dhimmi* status protected the Copts as "People of the Book" from being annihilated and gave them the opportunity to practice their faith. On the other hand, it created a context where the Copts became second-class citizens in their own land, paying a poll tax (*jizya*) in order to survive. The conditions governing protected people often involved humiliating provisions based on the Qur'anic instructions in Surah 9:5, 14, and 29. Restrictions were placed on building new churches, Christians were required to wear specifically colored clothes as a form of differentiation. They were banned from carrying arms or riding horses. Such humiliating provisions gradually limited their power and social status.

As the Islamic state started to gain power, the relationship between Muslims and non-Muslims was clearly defined. While Christians were not compelled to embrace Islam; they were encouraged to do so. Meanwhile, they were strictly prohibited from evangelizing Muslims, a practice that continued to our modern time in Egypt and in majority Muslim countries.

By the end of the first Islamic Dynasty, the Umayyad (750s), the Arab rulers started to gain strength from the fact that many indigenous people were converting to Islam. By the time the Abbasid Dynasty was established in 750 majority cities in Egypt were fully controlled by Muslim rulers. Despite the restrictions imposed on the Copts, they managed to survive and even to grow in population. The Copts had endured lengthy periods of persecutions, first under the Romans and then under the Byzantine Empire. The Islamic rule over their land was another form of foreign intervention.

The Copts were able to survive and even to thrive during the Abbasid Dynasty from the eighth to the tenth centuries where they were entrusted with key political positions in the Islamic state. In general, the Copts who had the financial means to pay the taxes as well as useful skills that aided them in finding a means for living were able to survive. Often, however, their skills and wealth (real or perceived) brought trouble for them. They were targets for sporadic attacks and violence, which resulted in either weakening their status or empowering them to become more resilient.[11]

By the eight century a process of Arabization was fully in place along with the process of Islamization. As the Arab rulers became more confident in managing state affairs, they required administrators to use the Arabic language in running state businesses and political systems. For the

---

11. Ye'or, *The Decline of Eastern Christianity under Islam*, 67.

majority of indigenous Copts who spoke Coptic it was clear that Arabic was the language of the day and if they were to succeed in the political and economic sectors of the empire they had to learn the official language of the state. Many Copts saw the advantages of learning Arabic in order to continue serving in their posts. The process of Arabization that started in the eighth century continued through the Abbasid Dynasty and by the eleventh century it had created a climate where the native Coptic language spoken across Egypt started to disappear. The Coptic language survived as the language of church liturgy and with the exception of remote villages in Upper Egypt, the Coptic language ceased to exist as a day-to-day language of the people by the twelfth century. During the Abbasid Golden Era of Islam (eighth and ninth centuries), while the socio-political structure of the state was primarily Islamic, the cultural and religious landscape was still predominantly Christian.

The Abbasid Dynasty was replaced by the Fatimid (921–1171), who ruled from Cairo, Egypt. The Fatimid extended their ruled from Morocco to Syria and were mostly tolerant to Christians. The governor of Syria, Quzman ibn-Nima under the early Fatimid rulers was a Coptic Christian.[12] Unfortunately, the ascending of later caliphs, such as Al-Hakim (996–1021), to power interrupted this tolerant and progressive era. He ordered all Christians to wear only black garments along with 5 pound-wooden crosses on their necks to distinguish them from the rest of society. He tortured and executed his Christian administrators and ordered the destruction of churches and monasteries across the region. In 1009, he destroyed the Church of the Holy Sepulcher in Jerusalem and prevented Christians from entering Jerusalem, a practice that continued for four decades and ultimately resulted in igniting the Crusades. The Crusades that attempted to capture Jerusalem and establish a Latin Christian Kingdom in the Middle East failed. The last attempts at reaching Jerusalem through Egypt also failed. The military encounters of the Crusades, which lasted for almost two centuries, intensified the hostilities between Christians and Muslims. The Fatimid rule over Egypt, which was somewhat tolerant towards Christians, became weary of fighting Europeans in the Crusades and turned against local Christians and started persecuting them. The stories of destruction and persecution were dreadful.[13]

Since Egypt had been the main target of the later Crusades, Egyptian Christians took the brunt of the new intolerance. When the Mameluke[14]

---

12. Atiya, *A History of Eastern Christianity*, 87–88.
13. Riley-Smith, *The Oxford Illustrated History of the Crusades*, 95.
14 The word "Mameluke" means owned or slaved in Arabic. The Mameluke were

rulers established their dynasty in Egypt in 1250, they started a new campaign of persecuting the Copts. The Mamelukes came to power primarily to repel the crusaders and many of their leaders hated Christians. The persecution of Christians in Egypt was due to the fact that the Mamelukes were fighting two major powers right at the doorsteps of Egypt: Western crusaders and Eastern Mongols. As a result, Egyptian Christians endured one of the most vicious and unbearable persecutions in history between the 1290s and 1350s.[15]

By the thirteenth century, Egyptian Christians held one of the most influential statuses among the *dhimmis* living in *Dar-al-Islam*. The fact that Egyptian Christians were wealthy and had great status in a predominantly Muslim society, where many of them held strategic governmental and administrative positions, did not sit well with the Mamelukes. The Mamelukes issued several decrees, from forcing Christians to wear distinctive clothing all the way to dismissing them from their financial and administrative positions. Such measures by the officials enticed the masses to further harass Christians, looting and plundering their properties and businesses. The systematic persecution was further accelerated by the burning and destruction of thousands of churches and properties across Egypt during the fourteenth century. The Muslim historian Al-Maqrizi documented the destruction of churches and monasteries across the land, even in Upper Egypt where Christians still held majority status. He emphasized that the destruction was unprecedented: "In all the provinces of Egypt, both north and south, no church remained that had not been razed; on many of those sites, mosques were constructed." The destruction further intensified by killing and kidnapping Christians and destroying their businesses.[16] The immediate result of these harsh measures and brutal persecution was the conversion of thousands of Christians to Islam.[17]

The unprecedented persecution of the Copts during the thirteenth and fourteenth centuries resulted in reducing their numbers to a minority status by the end of the fourteenth century. The Copts had endured significant persecution under the Romans during the first three centuries,

---

not slaves in the literal meaning, they were cavalrymen recruited as young boys from around the Black Sea and the Caspian Sea to fight the crusaders. While they formed the machine of Jihad that ultimately destroyed the crusaders, they overthrew the dynasty of Saladin who used them to fight the crusaders and established their own rule over Egypt, Palestine, and Syria in 1250. They became the saviors of the Islamic Empire by defeating the Mongols.

15 Ye'or, *The Decline of Eastern Christianity*, 359–60.
16. Little, "Coptic Conversion to Islam under the Bahri Mamelukes," 568.
17. Little, "Coptic Conversion to Islam under the Bahri Mamelukes," 569.

however, the persecution they endured under the Mamelukes was the most devastating. From that time onward, the Copts ceased to form the majority status in Egypt.

By the early sixteenth century, the Ottomans captured the whole Middle East, including Egypt, through bloody wars with other Muslim rulers. The Ottomans were credited with developing a comprehensive judicial system allowing for a creative synthesis between Islamic laws and local customs, including a religious judicial system, *millet*, that governed Christians. The Copts were allowed a limited internal self-governing according to their own laws and traditions, such as family laws that govern marriage, divorce, and inheritance. Each group or *millet* was also directed by its own religious leader who was responsible for civil as well as religious matters. The *millet* system included a host of laws that regulated the process of granting the right of building churches, which was usually granted by the sultan or his representative. The *millet* system guaranteed the continuation of the Islamic tradition where non-Muslims had to pay the poll tax, *jizya*. As in previous centuries, many Copts were not able to pay the heavy taxes and had to convert to Islam.

The Copts in Modern Times

The French presence in Egypt (1798–1801), destroyed the power of the Mamelukes while weakening the Ottoman rule over the country. Archaeological discoveries such as the Rosetta Stone and many others restored to the Copts their sense of Egyptian identity and long prominent history and civilization.[18] The British control over Egypt (1882–1956), serving to protect its interest in the Suez Canal, established civil laws that protected the rights and status of minorities.[19] The presence of European powers and the attempts at modernization by Egyptian rulers during the nineteenth century restored to the Copts their social and political status. The differentiating dress codes for Christians was abolished in 1817 while the poll tax, *jizia*, was abolished in 1855. As a modernized parliamentary system was introduced, many Christians were able to play an active role in the socio-political structure of modern Egypt. In 1908 Boutros Ghali Pasha, a Copt, was named Egypt's prime minister. However, his ascendency to the highest governmental position angered Muslims, resulting in his assassination. In the 1980s, his son Boutros Boutros Ghali held a global influential position as the UN general secretary. Education that suffered

18. Vatikiotis, *The History of Egypt*, 49–69.
19. Vatikiotis, *The History of Egypt*, 169–88.

during the Mamelukes and the Ottomans were restored and flourished while education through major state universities contributed to the transformation of society in general.

Coptic Christian denominations and social and cultural influence

New Christian denominations were introduced to Egypt through the missionary activities of the Catholic and various Protestant churches. Early attempts to introduce Catholicism to Egypt came in the form of forced acknowledgement of the supremacy of Rome, which was rejected by the Copts. By the mid-seventeenth century, Catholic missions focused on converting Copts while building schools and hospitals that served the whole community. Today, an estimated 200,000 worshipers belong to the Coptic Catholic Church, which is one of twenty-three Eastern Rite Catholic Churches in full communion with Rome. The Coptic Catholic Church adopted a modified Coptic liturgy in worship while maintaining a distinctive Eastern tradition. Coptic Catholic priests can marry while bishops are selected from a monastic order like their Coptic Orthodox counterparts. Many Coptic Catholic charity organizations are active in providing social and health care to the larger community. Catholic schools in Egypt are well-known for their outstanding quality education.

The Anglican diocese of Egypt was established in 1840 with an estimated 3,000 worshipers. The Protestant presence in Egypt dates to 1854 when the Coptic Presbyterian Church of Egypt/Synod of the Niles was established. The Presbyterian Church, also known as the Evangelical Church, is the largest Protestant denomination in Egypt with an estimated 300,000 worshipers. The Presbyterian/Evangelical Church was instrumental in establishing various educational schools, including the prestigious American University in Cairo. The Evangelicals introduced education for women in the 1880s, pioneering equal opportunities for women in education and social participation.

By the 1950s other Christian denominations were introduced to Egypt, such as the Free Methodist, Baptist, the Assemblies of God, and various Pentecostal churches, composing sixteen different denominations. The modern translation of the Arabic Bible, completed in 1865, was instrumental in shaping the lives of contemporary Christians in Egypt while supporting the mission of the various churches. The Copts are known for their love of reading the Bible and attending Bible study groups. The weekly Bible study started by Pope Shenouda III, the head of the Coptic Orthodox Church (1970–2010) draw thousands of worshipers. A pattern that continues till today in various Coptic Orthodox, Catholic, and Protestant churches across the country. The Egyptian Bible Society is one the largest producers and distributors of Bibles in the world.

The educational programs that started by the various Egyptian churches led to the formation of several human rights movements in the early twentieth century. Egyptian Christians were active participants in the drafting of the United Nations' Declaration on Human Rights while women were given the opportunity to vote and hold political office, starting from the 1920s.

Several Christian social organizations, such as the Coptic Evangelical Organization for Social Services (CEOSS), are serving the larger community reaching out to an average of 2 million unprivileged people through education, small businesses, and healthcare programs. Meanwhile, hundreds of Christian medical centers and hospitals provide outstanding healthcare for the larger community.

Church-state relations

The relationship between the Copts and the state took different forms in recent times. After the peaceful revolution of 1952, the Copts had limited participation in government, their rule was curbed and restricted, a practice that continued in the following decades. President Nasser (1952–70) was focused on creating and leading a pan-Arab coalition in the Middle East and the Copts had little interest in being involved in such an endeavor. The Copts were interested in a sociopolitical structure that upholds *Egyptian* nationalism and interest, not an Arab one. Nasser's economic policies of nationalizing private sectors impacted the Copts negatively, curbing their economic and social influence. The Copts who excelled in private sectors in previous centuries saw their net wealth disappearing and were denied equality in public services and political positions. However, the overall relationship between church and state remained amicable.

Under president Sadat (1970–82) the relationship between church and state was stormy. Sadat's religious conservatism and his attempts to curb the power of political leftists by empowering the Islamists resulted in constant conflicts and tensions. His attempts to introduce Islamic Sharia laws angered the Christians while the Islamists' campaign of attacking Christian business, churches, and kidnaping Christian girls, forcing them to embrace Islam, further intensified the tension between Christians and Muslims. The conflict between state and church reached the lowest point at the end of

Sadat's regime when he removed the state's recognition of Pope Shenouda III (1970–2010) as the pope of Alexandria.

Under president Mubarak (1982–2011) the church-state relations improved, however tensions between Islamists and Christians continued. The overthrowing of the Muslim Brotherhood-led government (2012–13) by the military in 2013 resulted in the largest attack on Egyptian Christians since the fourteenth century. In August 2013, Muslim extremists massacred hundreds of Christians, burning and looting thousands of Christian homes and businesses while destroying over eighty churches and Christian centers across Egypt. The Christian response by extending forgiveness to those who committed such atrocities won them the respect and support of moderate Muslims.

Discriminatory measures against the Copts range from state and societal discriminations to violent attacks with the purpose of curbing their power and influence. Police absence and the state's failure to prevent such attacks often creates a sense of anxiety and fear among Christians, who are left helpless in the face of such hideous atrocities. Christians who form over 12 percent of the population have very limited rule in governmental positions and near-complete exclusion from high-ranking military and police positions.

The Copts in the Diaspora

Egyptian Christians are known for their attachment to the land. They are aware that one of the oldest and most sophisticated civilizations in world history, which lasted for over five millennia, was developed on the banks of the Nile. A civilization that introduced the first methods of agriculture, writings, mathematics, philosophy, arts, law, medicine, astronomy, and engineering. Christians are also proud of their long Christian history and the significant contributions Egyptian Christianity made to world Christianity.

However, starting from the 1950s a considerable Coptic emigration movement started and accelerated thereafter. Faced with restrictions and nationalization of their lands and business in the 1950s some wealthy Christians decided to leave. In the following decades, the trend continued on a very large scale so that today there are more than 3 million Egyptian Christians living outside of Egypt.

The largest number of Copts living abroad belongs to the Coptic Orthodox Church and they are scattered everywhere on the planet, even in places like Japan and Fiji. Today, there are more than 550 Coptic Orthodox churches outside Egypt led by thirty bishops and hundreds of priests. While these Coptic Orthodox congregations maintain their Coptic liturgy and tradition, many are actively seeking to adapt to the host countries in varies degrees of assimilations. Some see their mission as not simply to survive but to reach out to the new communities they have adopted. In the mid-1970s, Pope Shenouda inaugurated a new mission of the Coptic Orthodox Church to sub-Sahara Africa with the intention of establishing Coptic Orthodox churches for the local communities. Today, the Coptic Orthodox Church has around 100 churches serving half a million African nationals.

Coptic Catholics and Protestants who emigrated to the West and other parts of the world were either absorbed by local Catholic and various Protestant congregations or in some cases establish their own congregations. Despite the trend of large waves of emigration and the continuous persecution of the Copts, the number of Christians in Egypt is significantly higher than any other Middle Easter country. Today, there are over 12 million Copts living in Egypt, comprising 12 percent of the total population of over 100 million.

Looking to the Future

Today, Egypt is witnessing significant cultural and social changes due to the influence of social media and globalization. Traditional religious views and cultural norms are constantly being challenged, especially among the younger generation who form the majority of the population. It is estimated that over 1 million Egyptians have turned to Christianity in the last twenty years. It is also estimated that over 2 million embraced atheistic ideologies as they became disillusioned with violent practices carried by several militant jihadi movements in the region.[20]

Recent attempts to work towards unity among the various Christian denominations in Egypt reflects a new spirit of cooperation and mutual respect. Facing the same sociopolitical challenges, Egyptian churches are coming together, forsaking historical divisions and theological differences, striving towards better ways of collaboration that would strengthen their witness to the larger society. An atmosphere of mutual respect and enduring toleration is needed in order for the Christian and the larger Muslim communities to live in harmony, contributing to the well-being of the whole society.

In a rapidly changing world of social conflicts and political and economic instability, feelings of distress sometimes result in irrational reactions, a reality that sometimes colors the daily encounter between Christians and

20. *Al-Ahram* newspaper, January 15, 2017.

Muslims in Egypt. While Christians and Muslims in Egypt are facing the same sociopolitical problems and economic strains, Christians sometimes become the targets for attacks as Muslims vent their frustrations on them.

Differences in religious beliefs are often perceived as a threat to the very existence of the other. The threat of the other may be real but is most probably imagined. Because of the wealth and prosperity of some Christians, along with their notable role in administration and finance, they become target for attacks and anger that have no legitimate reasons. Such emotions are often undefined, and even the Christians attempt to be public-spirited, assimilable, or apologetic, may only serve to fuel the animosity. In such a context, Christian self-definition and self-fulfillment can only be attained within the limitation of the socio-political framework drawn by the Islamic rule. Shaped by such a cluster of religious, cultural, and political circumstances, a constant theme for the Copts has been their destiny and even survival in coexistence with Islam.

Emphasis on religious differences regrettably creates a sense of mutual isolation between the two communities. Egyptian Christians often resolve to creating their own communities (mainly inside the church) as their way of maintaining their religious beliefs and values against religious criticism and sometimes forced conversion. Such cultural hibernation became a mean for survival while upholding a historical and cultural identity that otherwise will be engulfed by the larger society. The ultimate escape out of this strained social context is leaving the country altogether, and more than half a million Copts have emigrated from Egypt during the last decade alone.

While many Christians struggle between leaving the country or enduring more suffering, the unprecedented Christian response to violent attacks provided an ample opportunity for Christian witness and a renewed sense of mission to the larger community. For Christians did not seek revenge; instead, they extended forgiveness to those who murdered their loved ones, and as they did so a new amicable atmosphere started to emerge. Such extraordinary attitudes of Christian forgiveness were reported by social media, where Christian families who lost loved ones openly spoke about their Christian faith and what it means to extend God's forgiveness. Such powerful Christian testimonies had lasting impact on the larger Muslim community that was stunned by the Christian response. In many instances, Muslims became outraged at the blind and evil hatred of these atrocities, expressing their astonishment with Christians upholding the ethos of love and forgiveness. This powerful Christian testimony of extending God's love and forgiveness amid hatred and violence created a new atmosphere of mutual respect and will have enduring positive impact on the attitudes of the Muslims towards Christianity and Christians. What is happing in Egypt is not a remote event in church history, but a living testimony to the power of the Christian faith. The global church is enriched by the faithful witness of many Egyptian Christians whose living faith exemplifies the true meaning of hope.

For Further Reading

Atiya, Aziz Suryal. *A History of Eastern Christianity*. London: Taylor & Francis, 1968.
Cragg, Kenneth. *The Arab Christians: A History in the Middle East*. Louisville, KY: Westminster/John Knox, 1991.
Guiguis, Magdi, and Nelly Van Doorn-Harder. *The Emergence of the Modern Coptic Papacy*. Cairo: American University in Cairo Press, 2011.
Hassan, S. S. *Christian Versus Muslims in Modern Egypt: The Century-Long Struggle for Coptic Equality*. Oxford: Oxford University Press, 2003.
Kennedy, Hugh. "Egypt as a Province in the Islamic Caliphate." In *The Cambridge History of Egypt*, edited by Karl F. Petry, 62–85. New York: Cambridge University Press, 1998.
Little, Donald P. "Coptic Conversion to Islam under the Bahri Mamelukes, 692–755/1293–1354." *Bulletin of the School of Oriental and African* Studies 39 (1976) 552–69.
Meinardus, Otto F. A. *Two Thousand Years of Coptic Christianity*. Cairo: American University in Cairo Press, 2013.
Sharkey, Heather J. *American Evangelicals in Egypt: Missionary Encounters in an Age of Empire*. Princeton, NJ: Princeton University Press, 2017.
Stark, Rodney. *The Rise of Christianity*. Princeton, NJ: Princeton University Press, 1996.
Tadros, Mariz. *Copts at the Crossroads: The Challenges of Building Inclusive Democracy in Egypt*. Cairo: American University in Cairo Press, 2013.
Tadros, Samuel. *Motherland Lost: The Egyptians and Coptic Quest for Modernity*. Stanford, CA: Hoover Institute, 2013.
Vatikiotis, P. J. *The History of Egypt from Mohammed Ali to Mubarak*. Baltimore, MD: The Johns Hopkins University Press, 1991.
Watterson, Barbara. *Coptic Egypt*. Edinburgh: Scottish Academic Press, 1988.
Worrell, William Worrell. *A Short Account of the Copts*. Lansing, MI: University of Michigan Press, 1945.
Ye'or, Bat. *The Decline of Eastern Christianity under Islam: From Jihad to Dhimmitude*. London: Associated University Presses, 1996.

6

The Syriac Story

GEORGE ANTON KIRAZ

IF YOU STOPPED A Suryānī woman inside of Damascus Gate or Herod's Gate in Jerusalem during the times of the Crusades (in the Quarter which is called today the Muslim Quarter) you may have needed to know Aramaic to communicate with her—in particular, the variety of Aramaic scholars call Christian Palestinian Aramaic. In fact, large portions of today's Muslim Quarter were known during the Crusade period as the Suryānī (or "Syrian/Syriac") Quarter.[1] This is so because most Christians in the Holy Land were called Suryānī, at least by the crusaders.[2] Travel back a few hundred years earlier to southern Iraq and meet Masargawayh, the Physician of Basra. The Muslim author Ibn Abi Uṣaybiʿa (1203–70) defines him as يهودي المذهب سريانياً "a Jew by faith, a Suryānī." Masargawayh was simply an Aramaic-speaker; this was enough to label him as "Suryānī."

Today, no one would call the Jerusalemite woman inside Damascus Gate a Suryānī; rather, she would be labeled as a Christian Arab, more precisely a Rum Orthodox (or Latin, if she had converted to Catholicism). She would most likely be living near New Gate or Jaffa Gate, in today's Christian Quarter. The Physician of Basra would nowadays be called a Jew, definitely not a Suryānī. The modern label "Suryānī"—which I translate here as "Syriac"—strictly applies to adherents of the Syriac Orthodox Church, miaphysite non-Chalcedonians who were scattered by the end of the nineteenth century across a vast area of Syria-Palestine and Upper Mesopotamia numbering less than half a million people at best. It also applies to a much smaller Syriac Catholic counterpart, which has been in union with Rome since the

---

1. For the use of "Suryānī" for non-Syriac Orthodox, see Buck, "Theorising the Religious Borders of the Latin East," 317–31.

2. Boas, *Jerusalem in the Time of the Crusades*, 38, map [xvi]. (Thanks to Maria Thomas for the reference.)

eighteenth century. Today, it is these—and only these—two communities that label themselves "Suryānī" and are labeled as such by others.

Having said that, today's Assyrians and Chaldeans are also rooted in the Syriac heritage. If you were to attend a Church of the East service in Upper Dvin, Armenia, you would hear the congregation recite prayers in Classical Syriac. This is astounding considering that this community left its Aramaic-speaking homeland in Urmia, Iran, around 1820. It is even more astounding when one realizes that for over eighty years during the Soviet era, the community had no priest. The Maronites, even though their current liturgy is mostly in Arabic translation, are also well rooted in the Syriac heritage. And while the Rum Orthodox gradually followed the Byzantine rite in Arabic, they were Syriac-using well into the early second millennium. We know this from a wide range of evidence, for instance, the numerous Syriac manuscripts that they left us. The local artist Basil, for example, who produced many of the beautiful mosaics in the Church of the Nativity in Bethlehem during the times of the Crusades—for sure a Chalcedonian local Christian—signed his name on the walls in Syriac (and Latin). The entire pink area of the following diagram depicts Christianity from Syriac literary and liturgical perspectives.

SECTION TWO: GRAND CHURCH FAMILY MOSAIC

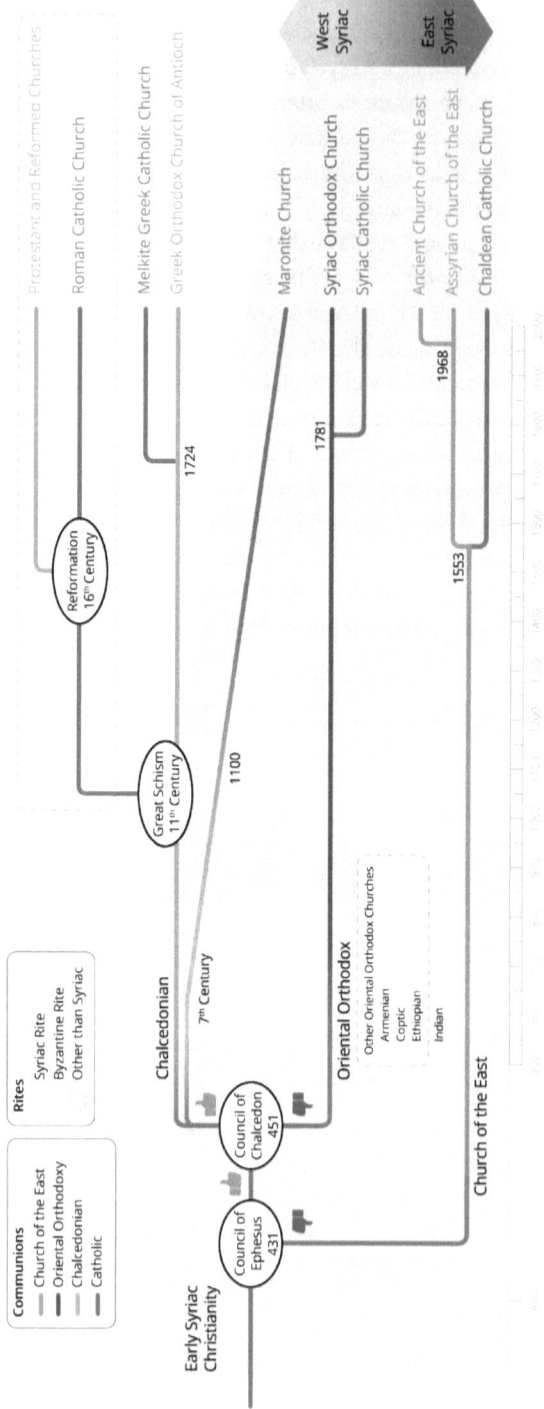

A Map of Syriac Christianity Adapted by George A. Kiraz
Copyright © 2020 (Creative Commons License CC BY-NC 4.0)

But to say that all the members of these (church) communities were "ethnically" (term used very loosely) Syriac or Suryānī is quite misleading. Persian Christians wrote mostly in Syriac. Soon, we will meet Aphrahat, the "Persian sage" in Syriac dress. The large number of Iranian loan words, as well as syntactic borrowings, present in the Syriac language is in itself evidence of this cultural contact. When Christian Persian speakers dipped their quills in ink, what came out on parchment was Syriac, by Late Antiquity a major *lingua franca* for Middle East Christianity. The Christians of Beth Qaṭraye—a vast geographical area covering modern Qatar, Oman, and the entire coast of northeast Arabia—produced their works in Syriac as well.³ Among their writers is Isaac of Nineveh, whose Syriac spiritual works are read in translation by all the Christian denominations of the Middle East and beyond.⁴ These were speakers of *qaṭra' īt*, or Qatarite, a language frequently cited by the tenth-century lexicographer Bar Bahlul that may have been a blend of Aramaic and Arabic.⁵ Arab Christians—Ghassanites, Tanukhites, and others—belonged to Syriac-using churches. Syriac was their liturgical and literary language.

But the opposite is also true. "Ethnic" Syriacs learned Arabic and wrote in it. They include the "Melkite" [=Rum Orthodox] Theodoros Abū Qurra (ca. 755–ca. 830), the "Jacobite" [=Syriac Orthodox] Ḥabīb b. Khidma Abū Rā'iṭa (d. ca. 851), and the "Nestorian" [=Church of the East] ʿAmmār al-Baṣrī (fl. ca. 850).⁶ During the twelfth and thirteenth centuries, Syriac Christians in Cilicia wrote in Armenian. We know about them because the Armenian works referred to them as *Asori*, a term used by Armenians to denote their Syriac-speaking neighbors. One Abu Saʿīd (Busaid) wrote a book on human formation. Another Isaac (Armenian ☐☐☐☐) or Yesu (Armenian ☐☐☐☐) was a prominent representative of the Cilician medical school; he is known as the author of the work "The Book of the Nature of the General and the Private."⁷ The Syriac Orthodox Maphrian⁸

---

3. Van Rompay, "Beth Qaṭraye." In *Gorgias Encyclopedic Dictionary of the Syriac Heritage*. For a recent anthology of Beth Qaṭraye Christian texts, see *An Anthology of Syriac Writers from Qatar in the Seventh Century*, edited by Mario Kozah et al.

4. For the geographic extent of the reception history of Isaac's works, see Brock, "From Qatar to Tokyo, by Way of Mar Saba," 475–84.

5. Kozah, "New Evidence for an Early Islamic Arabic Dialect in Eastern Arabia?"

6. Griffith, "Syriac Interactions with Islam."

7. I am grateful to Vahan Ter-Ghevondian, director of the Matenadaran, for providing me the details of these works.

8. The office of maphrian, sometimes called catholicos, in the Syriac Orthodox ecclesiastical structure is that of a local head of the church above the bishops and under the patriarch.

Basileios Shem'un II (ca. 1670–1740) is well known for his Kurdish song *Lawij* ("lyrical song"), not his numerous literary Syriac works, which included theological treatises, sermons, a collection of poems, and an abridged dictionary. He is said to have recited *Lawij* during an audience with the Kurdish Amir of Jazireh, Muḥammad al-Bakhti, during the time when Muslims were trying to have him killed.[9] While some Syriac Christians have remained Aramaic-speaking until today, many of them have gradually become Arabic-, Armenian-, Turkish-, Persian-, and Kurdish-speaking. I was born into a Syriac Orthodox family. My father's side were Turkish and Armenian speakers, while my mother's side were Arabic and Kurdish speakers. I had to learn Syriac at church! The Syriac story is a story of plurilingualism, a chronicle of linguistic diversity.

Which Syriac story am I to present then? A maximalist approach, covering everything that touches upon Syriac, would require volumes, speaking of not only all the Christian denominations of the Middle East, but also of Jews and Mandaeans. This is not a story that the reader of this volume is expecting. Many chapters already cover one aspect or another of this story. A minimalist approach, strictly limited to the Syriac Orthodox and Catholics, would give a skewed view ignoring modern communities that are well rooted in the Syriac tradition: the Maronites, Assyrians, and Chaldeans. Our modern social constructs of identity, the self, and the other utterly fail us.

Instead, what I plan to do here is to follow the Syriac story as heritage threads (plural intended). Some will be long, others short. These will not be smooth silk threads, but rather thick yarns, coarse and dyed with many colors. Weaving them would result in a vivid carpet—a runner, more precisely—extending from the early days of Christianity until the modern day. The challenge is to do this in fewer than 6,000 words!

From King Abgar to the Bnay Qyāmā

The Syriac story begins with a story, the story of King Abgar of Edessa, which is embedded in a fifth-century text titled the "Teaching of Addai." The story tells of how King Abgar, who ruled the Syriac-speaking city of Edessa, heard of Jesus of Nazareth and all the healings that he performed "without roots." Abgar himself is ill and writes a letter to Jesus, inviting Jesus to come and heal him and to live in Edessa, "a small city but sufficient for both of us to live in it in peace." Jesus, according to the story, writes back that

---

9. Kiraz, "Shem'un II, Basileios," in *Gorgias Encyclopedic Dictionary of the Syriac Heritage*.

he needs first to fulfill what he came for and then to ascend to the Father. But he will send to Abgar one of his disciples to heal him. The disciple is Addai, who is identified as one of the seventy. The story, as we have received it, clearly belongs to the fifth century, but it echoes earlier traditions. The church historian Eusebius of Caesarea, writing around the late third or early fourth century, knows of a document in the archives of Edessa that gives a similar version of the story. Abgar and most of the city end up converting to Christianity. Syriac Christians today pride themselves as being the first nation and first kingdom to adopt Christianity.[10]

While Syriac Christianity during the first three centuries is mired in obscurity—all surviving Syriac inscriptions, numbering over 100, are indeed pagan in nature[11]—a good number of literary works were produced and transmitted by the fourth century. Most of the Old Testament was translated from Hebrew by the end of the second century. The story of Aḥiqar, the "Aramean Sage," circulated in Syriac. It was the source of the later Armenian version (which in turn gave rise to Georgian and Old Turkish versions) and an Arabic version where AḤiqar appears as Luqmān. Bardaiṣan (154–222), who was active at the court of Abgar VIII (177–212)—Julius Africanus met him in 195—is known to have written against Marcion. Aphrahat, the "Persian Sage," wrote twenty-three demonstrations on various spiritual topics in the early fourth century. His descriptions of the Bnay Qyāmā ("Children of the Covenant") and īḤidāye ("solitaries") provide us insights into proto-monasticism and early Christian spirituality in Syria-Palestine and Mesopotamia. The most famous of the early writers is Ephrem (d. 373), whose commentaries and poetic theology survive today, not only in Syriac but also in translation in a variety of languages. Ephrem, in particular, is known for being the first to introduce women choirs.

All this literary production indicates that there was a well-established scribal tradition during this early period. Indeed, the fourth century gives us a few Syriac manuscripts that survived the turbulences of time. The first dated Syriac manuscript was produced in 411 (British Library Add. 12,150); indeed, it is the first dated manuscript in *any* language. The earliest dated Gospel manuscript is a Syriac one, produced in 510 and now preserved at Deir al-Suryān in Egypt (MS Syr 10).[12] The British Library and the Vatican library hold many undated early manuscripts, some of which are quite plausibly products of the fourth century. As the fifth century approached,

10. The Armenians also claim to be the first nation to accept Christianity based on St. Gregory the Illuminator convincing Tiridates III, the king of Armenia, to convert to Christianity in an event traditionally dated to 301.

11. Drijvers and Healey, *The Old Syriac inscriptions of Edessa and Osrhoene*.

12. Kiraz, *Syriac-English New Testament*, 35.

bringing many Christological controversies, Syria-Palestine and Mesopotamia were home to vibrant Christian communities whose literary production and liturgical expression were rooted in Syriac.

Christological Controversies and Theological Diversity

Syriac Christians were scattered across two major empires. The "super powers" of the Late Antique Middle East were Persia and Rome, whose borders were in continuous flux. Ephrem witnessed this himself. He was born in Nisibis (modern Nusaybin on the Turkish-Syrian border), where he spent most of his life. In 363, a peace treaty took place between Rome and Persia according to which Nisibis was handed over to the Persians. The treaty also stipulated that the Christian population had to leave. Ephrem immigrated to Edessa (modern Şanlıurfa), probably via Amid (modern Diyarbakır). He spent the last ten years of his life in Edessa.

Ephrem's journey gives us insight into the wide spread of Syriac Christianity and helps us understand its plurilingual nature. Even though Ephrem travelled from Nisibis to Edessa, 150 miles or so, his literary Syriac did not change at all. In fact, it is the same literary Syriac—morphology and syntax included—of Bardaiṣan "the Aramaean" and Aphrahat "the Persian." It would be the exact same Syriac of Isaac of Nineveh of Qatar—1,300 miles south!—writing 300 years later. Astonishingly, pupils who graduate from a Syriac seminary today, such as Mor Gabriel Monastery in Turkey, will be able to pick up any of these literary works and read them with ease. This, in itself, demonstrates that from these early times, Syriac was virtually fossilized. It is this feature of Syriac that allowed the Christian world around it to be plurilingual in its spoken modality, with Syriac occupying the slot of the literary. It was an ecosystem in equilibrium.

But this would soon change. The Council of Chalcedon, held in 451, came up with a controversial Christological formula, that Christ is "in two natures... concurring into... one hypostasis." Syriac Christianity became trichotomous, doctrinally split into three theological schools. The first accepted Chalcedon. Its adherents were called by their opponents *malkāye*, or Melkites, "followers of the king," as this position was that of the empire. This group morphed into what would become the Syriac-using Maronites and Melkites (or Rum Orthodox).

The two other groups rejected Chalcedon and morphed into the Syriac Orthodox Church and Church of the East. At the heart of their rejection of the Chalcedonian formula lies their understanding of two Greek key terms: "nature" (Greek *physis*) corresponding to Syriac *kyānā* and "hypostasis"

(Greek *hypostasis*) rendered into Syriac as *qnomā*. Usually, technical terms have more than one meaning and this was the case here. Different parties understood these terms differently.[13]

The Syriac Orthodox understood the terms *kyānā* ("nature") and *qnomā* ("hypostasis") to be closely connected semantically. To them, it was illogical for Christ to have one *qnomā*, an ultimate description of singleness, but two natures. Accepting this would imply that Christ had a "split personality." Ironically, Chalcedon's original draft formula, "*out of* two natures" (rather than "*in* two natures"), agreed with them as they had always proclaimed "one nature [= Greek *miaphysite*] *out of* two natures." Their opponents, however, accused them of being monophysite, in Greek meaning "single nature," with the understanding that this single nature expresses only the divinity of Christ, a position the Syriac Orthodox had always rejected.

The Church of the East took no issue with two natures. But "one hypostasis" was problematic for them. The problem is that "hypostasis" was translated into Syriac as *qnomā*. While the Syriac Orthodox (and Chalcedonians) understood *qnomā* ("hypostasis") to mean something close to an "individual" (hence, "one hypostasis" was agreeable), the Church of the East understood the term to mean "set of characteristics." Thus, they professed that Christ is in two *kyāne* ("natures"), with each *kyānā* having its own *qnomā* ("individuating characteristics"). This does not imply that the Church of the East professed two *hypostases* (the Greek term for *qnomā*, as their expression would then be lost in translation), but this is how their opponents took things.

Both the Syriac Orthodox and the Church of the East found the language of Chalcedon too ambiguous. Had the original Chalcedonian draft, "*out of* two natures," been maintained, the three groups would have most likely agreed. The situation is expressed aptly by the Syriac Orthodox thirteenth-century polymath Bar ʿEbroyo (aka Ibn al-ʿIbri):[14]

> When I had given much thought and pondered on the matter, I became convinced that these quarrels among the different Christian Churches are not a matter of factual substance, but of words and terminology; for they all confess Christ our Lord to be perfect God and perfect human, without any commingling, mixing, or confusion of the natures.... Thus, I saw all the Christian communities, with their different Christological positions,

---

13. Brock et al., *The Hidden Pearl*, vol. III, 26ff. and personal communication.

14. Bar ʿEbroyo, *Book of the Dove*, the preamble, trans. by Brock in *The Hidden Pearl*, vol. III, 33.

as possessing a single common ground that is without any difference between them.

To imply that the Syriac Orthodox and the Church of the East were at the heart of this division is quite misleading. The primary protagonists—Nestorius of Constantinople, Dioscorus of Alexandria, and Severus of Antioch, to name three main characters—were all Greek-speaking. The origins of the conflict developed in a Greek milieu, rooted in Greek philosophy. But as the doctrinal positions spread and became sources of contention, Syriac theologians also took positions. The Church of the East translated from Greek into Syriac the works of Theodore of Mopsuestia ("two natures"). The Syriac Orthodox translated Severus of Antioch ("one nature"). As these two figures—and others—became heretics in the eyes of the Greek imperial church, their works disappeared in Greek. It is thanks to Syriac that we have their writings in Syriac translation. While one can see these divisions as weakening Syriac Christianity, one can also look at them as a source of diversity. As it was stated by Sebastian Brock, the Syriac tradition is the only linguistic tradition that represents—and more importantly preserves—all three doctrinal positions.

The Church of the East, being mostly part of the Persian Empire, was not affected much in terms of dealing with the Byzantine imperial church. In a way, they lived outside of the Roman *ecumene*. The councils were imperial in nature and thus did not have any particular relevance outside of the empire. The Church of the East only accepted the Council of Nicaea (held in 325) in 410. The Councils of Ephesus (which deposed Nestorius in 431) and Chalcedon (451) were also irrelevant to them. But as they commemorated Nestorius liturgically, their opponents (including the Syriac Orthodox) began to label them "Nestorian."

In contrast, the Syriac Orthodox lived mostly within Byzantium. Going against the imperial position put them at a disadvantage. Their bishops were deported and imprisoned. Empress Theodora, herself a miaphysite (a believer in "one nature"), used her influence to have two monks consecrated as bishops for the miaphysite cause: the well-known Jacob Burdʿono and Theodore, an Arab, according to John of Ephesus, who was consecrated for Ḥirta of Banu Ghassan covering Palestine and Arabia. With the support of al-Ḥarith, the rule of the Ghassanids, they travelled across Syria, Mesopotamia, and Arabia consecrating bishops to ensure the survival of Syriac Orthodoxy. It is for this reason that their opponents (including the Church of the East) labelled them "Jacobites."

The Ghassanids were not the only Arabs connected to Syriac Christianity. Many tribes adhered to the faith of the Syriac Orthodox Church and the Church of the East. This may explain the ease with which Syriac Christianity came under Islam.

Contact with the Arabs before and after Islam

Syriac writers were aware of the Arabs, whom they called *Ṭayyāye* after the Arab tribe of *Banu Ṭayy*. Bardaiṣan, whom we met above, speaks of them during the second or third century.[15] Contact with the Arabs took a fuller form with the spread of Christianity. By the mid-fourth century, East Syriac Christianity was already present in al-Ḥira (South of Kufah, Iraq), home of the Arab Lakhmid tribe. In fact, al-Ḥira was a diocese within the ecclesiastical structure of the Church of the East. By the fifth century, a large portion of the inhabitants of al-Ḥira had already converted to Christianity and followed the Syriac liturgical rite of the Church of the East. They feature often in Syriac literary sources. We are told in the Acts of Simeon the Stylite how a ban on pilgrims from al-Ḥira visiting Simeon's pillar was lifted by Nuʿman I (506–18). The fascination of the Arabs with Simeon's pillar reappears later in the Arabic poetry of Al-Akhṭal (c. 640–710), arguably the most famous poet of the Umayyad Period, who swears "by the God of the solitaries, walking on the tops of their columns."[16] Al-Ḥira's connection with the Syriac ecclesiastical establishment was not peripheral; rather, al-Ḥira was the residence of the catholicos, the head of the East Syriac Church, on a number of occasions. At least five catholicoi died and were buried in al-Ḥira. The bishops of al-Ḥira were integrated into the Church of the East and attended its Synods. In 424, a bishop of al-Ḥira named Simeon attended the Synod of Markabtha, itself described as the "town of the Ṭayyāye." It was in this synod that a decision was made not to allow the intervention of "Western Fathers" in the disputes of the Church of the East, nor to refer to the patriarch of Antioch against any decisions of the catholicos.[17] This demonstrates further the integration of Arabic-speaking al-Ḥira Christians into the Syriac-speaking church.

The West Syriac church—the Syriac Orthodox—also had its contacts with the Arabs. We know of two attempts to win over the Lakhmids to the miaphysite faith. Severus of Antioch sent emissaries to Mundhir III Dhu Qarnain (r. 506–54) in 513. Philoxenos of Mabbug (d. 523) wrote a letter to Abū Yaʿfūr, the general of al-Ḥira. Jacob of Serug (451–521) wrote a letter

---

15. Cureton, *Spicilegium Syriacum*, 16; Trimingham, *Christianity among the Arabs in Pre-Islamic Times*, 312.

16. Trimingham, *Christianity among the Arabs in Pre-Islamic Times*, 234.

17. Chabot, *Synodicon orientale ou recueil de Synodes nestoriens*, 285.

to the persecuted Christians of Najrān further south in the Arabian Peninsula (now on the Saudi-Yemeni border). The Syriac Orthodox Church also had its own "bishop of Beth ʿArbāye" in the region, the first of which was Ahudemmeh in the sixth century. He was raised to the rank of catholicos, later to be known as the catholicate/maphrianate of Takrit.[18]

This was one factor that helped the Syriac-speaking Christians integrate into the new Islamic realities, at least in the beginning of the Islamic Conquest, or *Futūḥ*. Christian Arabs, who were liturgically Syriac Christians, had a cultural affinity with the new Muslim rules. Al-Balādhurī, in his *Futūḥ*, tells us that when Umar ibn Khattab intended to subjugate Banu Taghlib—Christians of the Syriac Orthodox faith—and make them pay the *jizya* tax imposed on Christians, they refused on account of being Arabs. Umar compromised and allowed them to pay taxes as Muslims with minor modifications.[19]

The proximity of Aramaic and Arabic gave a path to integration. A number of anecdotes illustrate this. When Khalid b. al-Walīd arrived in al-Ḥira, he asked ʿAbd al-Masīḥ ibn Buqaila al-Ghassānī, a Christian Arab of the Syriac Orthodox faith, "What are you, Arabs or Nabaṭ [i.e., Aramaic speakers]?" ʿAbd al-Masīḥ answered, "Arabs who have Nabaṭized; Nabaṭ who have Arabized!"[20] The plurilingual reality continued for centuries. Towards the end of the tenth century, one Abu al-Fatḥ Iskandarī said, "In the evening, I am a Nabīṭ [an Aramaic speaker]; in the morning I am an Arab."[21] It is the survival of Aramaic among the Christians of the Middle East that led the crusaders to call them "Suryānī," both the Chalcedonians [i.e., Rum Orthodox] and the Syriac Orthodox.

The Dawn of a New Millennium

By the end of the first millennium, the majority of the Middle East must have still been Christian. The Syriac Orthodox, whom we will concentrate on going forward (for the Church of the East, see page 19ff., and for the Melkites, see 36ff. in this book), were a major component of this Christian presence.

While Christians became second-class citizens under Islam, with many social and religious restrictions, it wasn't until the rule of Al-Hakim

---

18. Trimingham, *Christianity among the Arabs in Pre-Islamic Times*, 172.

19. Hitti, *The Origins of the Islamic State*, 181–83.

20. This anecdote occurs in a number of Islamic accounts; see Trimingham, *Christianity among the Arabs in Pre-Islamic Times*, 147, citing Shabushti, al-Masʿūi's *Muruj*.

21. Trimingham, *Christianity among the Arabs in Pre-Islamic Times*, 147, citing al-Hamadhānī's *Maqāmāt*.

bi-Amr Allah ("The Ruler by the Order of God") that things really went downhill. The mad caliph, as he has been called, not only resolved to destroy the Christian holy places in the Holy Land, but he also attempted to annihilate the Christian population. The appearance of the crusaders on the stage, partly in response to—in reality, under the pretext of—the persecution of the local Christians, established a new geopolitical reality: the Muslim world against the Christian world. Eastern Christians—who were never part of the crusader movement—became victims of this polarization. It was particularly a double whammy for the Syriac Orthodox. In addition to being persecuted as local Christians, they were now considered heretics by the new crusaders.

But this, as with any other geopolitical development, did not mean that life froze. The first half of the second millennium, especially up to the thirteenth century, was a period of renaissance. Arabic began to have a greater influence on the Syriac literary tradition. Poetic rhyme and prose *saj'* (where every two sentences rhyme in prose), unheard of thus far in Syriac literature, began to appear. While initially the Arab grammarians of early Islam relied on the Syriac grammatical tradition, now the later Syriac grammarians based their grammars on Arabic models. New genres such as wine poetry (*khamriyyāt*) also begin to take shape. One also begins to see Islamic influence on Syriac spirituality and canon law.[22]

But by the middle of the second millennium, Syriac Orthodoxy began to retreat as a result of further persecutions. The Syriac Orthodox patriarch of Antioch, in exile since the days of Severus of Antioch and moving from one place to the next, now settled—more or less—in Deir al-Zaʿfarān outside of Mardin, Turkey. The dioceses, a good indication of faithful settlements, also began to retreat mostly to Upper Mesopotamia. Two centers remained Aramaic-speaking: Tur Abdin in today's southeast Turkey and the Nineveh plains outside of Mosul in today's Iraq. But the rest of the Syriac Orthodox were no longer Aramaic-speaking, though Syriac remained the liturgical language. Arabic was obviously strong, especially with the presence of Islam. But other populations gradually became Turkish-, Armenian-, and Kurdish-speaking.

The following facts from the fifteenth and sixteenth centuries illustrate the status of the community. Widespread diseases were a commonplace; a pandemic took place in Upper Mesopotamia in 1502. (It is such pandemics that caused the faithful not to receive the Eucharistic bread and wine every Sunday but only on major feasts like Christmas and Easter, a custom that

---

22. Teule, "Renaissance, Syriac," in *Gorgias Encyclopedic Dictionary of the Syriac Heritage*.

remained until the end of the twentieth century and is still prevalent in many localities.) Deir al-Zaʿfarān, the seat of the patriarchate, was attacked by local Kurds and ruined on many occasions, starting from 1516.[23] The Syriac Orthodox bishop of Jerusalem, Gregorius al-Kurji, was crucified in front of St. Mark's monastery in 1578. In the Tur Abdin area (today's southeast Turkey), about 500 villages of the MuḤallami tribe converted from Syriac Orthodoxy to Islam.[24] In 1576, the patriarch of the Syriac Orthodox Church, Ignatius Niʿmatallah, was forced to abdicate due to local persecution by Muslims and escaped to Europe. In 1673, the maphrian—or catholicos of Syriac Orthodoxy in the East—was imprisoned in Mosul along with two of his monks. These were the realities of the Early Modern period.

The closest Christian neighbors to the Syriacs were the Armenians, who began to arrive in Cilicia and Anatolia from further East (today's Armenia) by the beginning of the second millennium, when Armenia fell under foreign powers. The great number of Armenian arrivals reshaped the demographics of Anatolia and Upper Mesopotamia. It is for this reason that many Syriac Christians became Armenian speaking in those areas. It is sometimes difficult to distinguish between Armenians and Syriacs. When the Ottomans arrived, they placed the Syriac Orthodox (and Church of the East) under the Armenian *millet*. As a result, the Syriac Orthodox no longer had direct representation with the Ottoman Sultan. Even their taxes had to be paid through the newly established Armenian patriarchate of Istanbul. This had negative effects on the Syriac presence in the Holy Land. Anytime the Syriacs were not able to pay taxes, their rights within the holy places would be diminished in favor of the Armenians. In 1658, St. Mark's Monastery—the center of Syriac Orthodoxy in the Holy Land at the time—was even mortgaged with the Jerusalem Armenian patriarchate for some time. The biggest blow to the Syriac presence during the pre-modern period was the expulsion of the Syriac monks who resided in the Church of Resurrection during the bishopric of George of Sadad (bishop 1877–96). Today, their rooms above the Syriac Chapel above the tomb of Nicodemos remain unoccupied, the key held by the Armenians and handed to the Syriacs only during Holy Week. By the 1890s, Syriac Orthodox from various localities began to petition the Ottoman sultan to give the Syriacs their own *millet* status. Patriarch Peter III even travelled to Istanbul for this purpose, but to no avail.[25]

23. Barsoum, *History of the Zaʿfaraan Monastery*.

24. Barsoum, *The History of Tur Abdin*.

25. The Armenians, in turn, considered the Suryānīs their *Yamaklik* ("assistants, apprentices"; this continues even to the present day in the Status Quo system in Jerusalem). See Cust, *The Status Quo in the Holy Places*; Cohen, *Saving the Holy Sepulcher*, 9.

The Syriac Orthodox were further weakened by internal ecclesiastical divisions. Tur Abdin, an Aramaic-speaking center in today's southeast Turkey, established its own patriarchal line in the fourteenth century, only to be finally united with the main line in 1816. By the turn of the eighteenth century, six individuals claimed the patriarchate and three claimed the maphrianate. But one of these divisions would have lasting effects when a number of Syriac Orthodox bishops placed themselves under the jurisdiction of Rome. This led to the eventual creation of a Syriac Catholic Church. The areas that were mostly affected were Mosul, Aleppo, Homs, and Damascus, along with their respective countryside (especially around Mosul and Homs). Many legal battles and aggravations took place. It was not until the second half of the twentieth century, with the rise of the ecumenical movement, that good relations began to exist again. Today, the Syriac Orthodox and Catholic patriarchs hold many joint events and attend each other's episcopal ordinations.

By the end of the nineteenth century, the Syriac Church was exhausted from all the divisions and local persecutions. The rise of the Turkish Committee of Union and Progress (CUP) and its advocacy for freedom for minorities gave the community a sense of hope. A few newspapers appeared during the early years of the twentieth century. The Intibāh Association, intended for the awakening of the community, was formed with representatives in the various localities of the Ottoman Empire, even in the new American diaspora.

But the CUP would not uphold its promises, and the worst was yet to come.

Sayfo: Sword, Genocide, and Diaspora

Preambles written by Syriacs addressing their patriarchs during the nineteenth century move from describing themselves as a *ṭā' ifa* ("religious community") to a *millet* ("nation"). But, the Syriac Orthodox were unable to obtain millet status within the Ottoman bureaucracy.[26] They remained under the custodianship of the Armenian patriarchates of Istanbul and Jerusalem. The Armenian genocide, perpetrated by the Ottoman and Turkish authorities and carried out with the help of Kurdish tribes, spilled over to affect

---

Twentieth-century historiographers have claimed that Patriarch Peter III (b. 1798, Patr. 1872–94) in fact succeeded in obtaining an independent millet status for the Suryānīs, freeing them from the control of the Armenians.

26. Kiraz, "Negotiating Identity with the Homeland," 66.

all the Christians of the Ottoman domain, especially in Anatolia. Today, the Syriacs refer to this suffering as the Sayfo genocide.

While it is difficult to come up with exact numbers—or even estimates—entire Syriac Orthodox villages, towns, even dioceses were obliterated. Take, for example, Kharput, where there was a vibrant Syriac presence: the first newspaper in West Syriac letters (the language was Turkish) was established there. Today, the town no longer exists, and only St. Mary's Church remains as a witness to yesteryear. Apart from the Syriacs of the Mosul and Homs regions, all the Syriacs of Upper Mesopotamia were affected by the atrocities. Those who survived began to move south to what later became Arab countries: Syria, Iraq, Lebanon, Palestine and Jordan. Except for in the Homs and Mosul regions, all Syriacs today—whether they live in the Middle East or the diaspora—can trace their roots to a town or village in Upper Mesopotamia.

Syriacs began to arrive in the United States during the 1880s, and they formed communities on the East Coast (and by the 1910s in California as well). But continuous wars in the Middle East kept feeding the diaspora with more immigrants. It began with the Palestinian tragedies of 1948 and 1967, then these were followed by the Lebanese Civil War, and finally the most recent wars in Iraq and Syria. During the 1970s and 1980s, Syriacs began to immigrate into Europe in large numbers. With the beginning of the Syrian civil war, I personally began to say that we were witnessing the beginning of the end of Syriac Christianity. As immigrants tend to survive only for three generations in the United States—maybe a bit longer in Europe; only time will tell—it is difficult to see how Syriac Christianity can go on in the long term. At some point, there will no longer be communities in the Middle East to feed immigration. Today, less than a quarter of the members of the Syriac Orthodox Holy Synod manage dioceses within the homeland. The rest are in the diaspora. The patriarch himself is a Syriac-American, a phenomenon that is becoming widespread. In September 2021, I posted on Facebook that six of the Eastern patriarchs are in fact American, at least by citizenship.[27]

Alas, the colorful carpet is beginning to fade away. The next to write the story of Syriac Christianity will be writing a story of a diaspora.

---

27. The six patriarchs are 1. Mor Ignatius Joseph III Yonan, Syriac Catholic Church (installed 2009), formerly served in NJ. 2. Abune Mathias, Ethiopian Orthodox Tewahedo Church (2013), formerly served in DC. 3. Mor Ignatius Ephrem II, Syriac Orthodox Church (2014), formerly served in NJ. 4. Youssef Absi, Melkite Greek Catholic Church, a US citizen. 5. Mar Awa III, Assyrian Church of the East (2021), former bishop of CA (and born in Chicago). 6. Archbishop Raphaël François Minassian, Armenian Catholic Church (2021), formerly a pastor in the US.

For Further Reading

Barsoum, Afram. *History of the Zaʻfaraan Monastery*. Translated by Matti Moosa. Piscataway, NJ: Gorgias, 2009.

———. *The History of Tur Abdin*. Translated by Matti Moosa (2008). In the series Publications of the Archdiocese of the Syriac Orthodox Church. https://doi.org/10.31826/9781463213336

Boas, Adrian J. *Jerusalem in the Time of the Crusades*. London: Routledge, 2001.

Brock, Sebastian P. "From Qatar to Tokyo, by Way of Mar Saba: The Translations of Isaac of Beth Qatraye (Isaac the Syrian)." *Aram* 11–12 (1999–2000) 475–84.

Brock, Sebastian P., et al. *The Hidden Pearl*, vol. III. Piscataway, NJ: Gorgias, 2001.

Buck, Andrew. "Theorising the Religious Borders of the Latin East: Some Reflections on the Inter-Christian Landscape of Frankish Northern Syria." *Journal of Medieval History* 47.3 (2021) 317–31.

Chabot, Jean Baptiste, ed. *Synodicon orientale ou recueil de Synodes nestoriens*. Washington, DC: The Catholic University of America Press, 1902.

Cohen, R. *Saving the Holy Sepulcher*. Oxford: Oxford University Press, 2008.

Cureton, William. *Spicilegium Syriacum*. Whitefish, MT: Kessinger, 1855.

Cust, L. *The Status Quo in the Holy Places* (1980). https://en.wikisource.org/wiki/The_Status_Quo_in_the_Holy_Places

Dinno, Khalid. *The Syrian Orthodox Christians in the Late Ottoman Period and Beyond: Crisis Then Revival*. Piscataway, NJ: Gorgias, 2017.

Drijvers, Han J. W., and John F. Healey. *The Old Syriac Inscriptions of Edessa and Osrhoene*. Leiden: Brill, 1999.

Gorgias Encyclopedic Dictionary of the Syriac Heritage, available online at gedsh.bethmardutho.org.

Hitti, Philip. *The Origins of the Islamic State: Being a Translation from the Arabic Accompanied with Annotations, Geographic and Historic Notes of the Kitāb Futūḥ Al-buldān of Al-imām Abu-l'abbās Aḥmad Ibn-Jābir Al-balādhuri*. New York: Cosmimo, 1966.

Kiraz, George A. "Negotiating Identity with the Homeland: The 'Syriac Orthodox' of North America in the Early Twentieth Century." In *From Polarization to Cohabitation in the New Middle East*, edited by Catalin-Stefan Popa and Adrian Mladinoiu, 77–93. Wiesbaden: Harrassowitz Verlag, 2020.

———. *Syriac-English New Testament*. Piscataway, NJ: Gorgias, 2020.

———. *The Syriac Orthodox in North America (1895–1995): A Short History*. Piscataway, NJ: Gorgias, 2019.

Kozah, Mario. "New Evidence for an Early Islamic Arabic Dialect in Eastern Arabia? A Literary and Historical Survey of Qaṭrāyīth ('in Qatari') Spoken in Beth Qaṭraye." *Journal of Near Eastern Studies* (forthcoming 2022).

Menze, Volker L. *Justinian and the Making of the Syrian Orthodox Church*. Oxford: Oxford University Press, 2008.

Murray, Robert. *Symbols of Church and Kingdom: A Study in Early Syriac Tradition*. Piscataway, NJ: Gorgias, 2006.

Teule, Herman G. B. "Renaissance, Syriac." In *Gorgias Encyclopedic Dictionary of the Syriac Heritage: Electronic Edition*, edited by Sebastian P. Brock, Aaron M. Butts, George A. Kiraz, and Lucas Van Rompay. Digital edition prepared by David Michelson, Ute Possekel, and Daniel L. Schwartz. Gorgias, 2011; online ed. Beth Mardutho, 2018. https://gedsh.bethmardutho.org/Renaissance-Syriac.

Trimingham, John Spencer. *Christianity among the Arabs in Pre-Islamic Times.* Boston: Addison-Wesley Longman, 1978.

Van Rompay, Lucas. "Beth Qaṭraye." In *Gorgias Encyclopedic Dictionary of the Syriac Heritage: Electronic Edition*, edited by Sebastian P. Brock, Aaron M. Butts, George A. Kiraz and Lucas Van Rompay. Digital edition prepared by David Michelson, Ute Possekel, and Daniel L. Schwartz. Gorgias, 2011; online ed. Beth Mardutho, 2018. https://gedsh.bethmardutho.org/Beth-Qatraye.

Wood, Philip. *The Imam of the Christians: The World of Dionysius of Tel-Mahre, ca. 750–850.* Princeton, NJ: Princeton University Press, 2021.

7

The Armenian Story

HRAYR JEBEJIAN

ARMENIANS HAVE A HISTORY that extends over three thousand years. They have excelled in agriculture and trade and created a culture in arts and crafts. The Armenian architectural monuments, sculptures, illuminated manuscripts, literature, and philosophical and legal tracts are unique. Many important and international philosophical and scientific works have been translated into Armenian. Some of these international works have been lost in their original language, but the Armenian translations still remain. The geographical location of Armenia has contributed not only to international trade but also to cultural and scientific exchanges and developments between east and west. Yet, in spite of its great contribution to the world's civilization, college graduates and even teachers know very little about the Armenians and their history. As Bournoutian attests, "Thus, despite their accomplishments, the Armenians have been given less space in general history texts than any other nations with much less contribution to the world civilization."[1]

The Armenian alphabet was invented in fifth century AD. Before the invention of the Armenian alphabet, Aramaic, Greek, modern Persian, and Syriac dominated the intellectual scene. Later, knowledge of Arabic, French, German, Georgian, Latin, Modern Persian, Mongolian, Russian, Turkish, as well as classical and modern Armenian were paramount.

Due to its geographical location, Armenia experienced many earthquakes and invasions, which eventually led to the destruction of much historical information and data. Armenia was often divided between its modern-day neighboring states, mainly Iran and Turkey, rendering the archival and archeological research a sensitive, difficult, and often an impossible task. Today,

---

1. Bournoutian, *A Concise History of the Armenian People*, 5.

modern historical research techniques have been applied to the study of the Armenian history, but this is only a recent phenomenon.

Armenia is a small nation but has managed to survive repeated invasions, destructions, and persecutions, including the massacres perpetuated by Ottoman Turkey in the 1890s, 1909, and the ethnic cleansing of one-and-a-half million in 1915. The Armenians have been described through centuries as adaptable, enterprising, resilient, and steadfast. Rightly, "How they managed to survive while larger and more powerful states disappeared, and how, at the same time, they were able to make significant contributions to world civilization, is the amazing history of the Armenian people."[2]

Armenia is a landlocked, mountainous plateau that rises to an average of 3,000 to 7,000 feet above sea level. It extends to the Anatolian plateau in the west, the Iranian plateau in the southwest, the plains of the south Caucasus in the north, and the Karadagh Mountains and the Moghan Steppe in the south and the southeast. The Armenian highlands stretch roughly between 38 degrees and 48 degrees longitude, and 37 degrees and 41 degrees north, with a total area of over 120,000 square miles. In present day terms, historic Armenia comprises most of eastern Turkey (occupied after the ethnic cleansing of 1915), the northeastern corner of Iran (Nakhichivan), parts of Azerbaijan (Nagorono Karapagh), and the Georgian Republic (Abkhazia). As for the present status of the Republic of Armenia, which is an independent state with its own local Armenian government, it is 11,484 square miles in total.

The Armenian Diaspora

The massacres of 1895–96 and the anti-Armenian policies of Sultan Abdul-Hamid forced many Armenians to emigrate from Anatolia. The Armenian Genocide in 1915, where one-and-a-half million people were killed, also urged thousands of refugees to leave their hometowns and seek refuge all over the world. The Armenian diaspora, to a great extent, is the result of the Armenian Genocide. In one single year, 1915, the Armenians lost their 3,000 years of historical legacy. Churches were destroyed, libraries were burnt, and towns and villages were robbed and turned to ruins. "The Armenians saved only that which formed part of their collective memory," writes Adalian.[3] Armenians managed to rebuild this very same "collective memory" in their new diaspora communities, namely, "little armenias," but in foreign lands.

2. Bournoutian, *A Concise History of the Armenian People*, 5.
3. Adalian, *The Armenian Genocide*, 10.

The exodus of the Armenians from their homeland continued during the years following the Genocide. Some also went to the Armenian Republic in 1918–19 and in the early 1930s, and still Stalin exiled others in the years 1936–39. There was a second big attempt of repatriation to Soviet Armenia, around 100,000, from different diaspora countries during 1945–48 and 1953–65. Civil wars, political unrest, and economic depression in the Middle East over the last several decades resulted in the decrease of the Armenian communities there and the growth of Armenian diaspora in Europe, Australia, and the Americas. The Republic of Armenia became an independent state in 1991 after the collapse of the Soviet Union. The economic hardship following the collapse of the Soviet Union urged many Armenians to leave their homeland and settle in different parts of the world, thus creating a new diaspora next to the existing one that was formed after 1915. It is estimated that out of the 10 million Armenians, around 2.5 million live in Armenia. Like the Jews, Armenians are found almost in every country of the globe.

The Armenian presence in the Middle East-Levant region, by and large, is also the result of the Armenian Genocide. Having said that, the records also indicate the presence of Armenians in the Middle East from early historical times, which will be highlighted in brief in the section below.

Iraq

Armenia-Iraq relationships started from the ancient times. According to Greek historian Herodotus, Armenian businessmen sailed through Euphrates and Tigris rivers and reached Babylon and Nineveh. In 83 BC, King Tigran (Tigranes) II, conquered Iraq and enhanced the migration of Armenians there. The Armenian community was formed later during the Abbasid Caliphate between the seventh and thirteenth centuries, in particular, in Basra and Baghdad. In 1640, the first Armenian church was built in Baghdad. The Armenian community developed further in the nineteenth and twentieth centuries, after the 1890 pogroms and 1915 Genocide. Armenians also reached Iraq from Iran because of political upheavals there. In 1920, the Armenian community in Iraq counted 30,000 but decreased to 20,000 in the 1970s. During the Iraq Iran war (1980–88), 104 Armenian soldiers were martyred within the ranks of the Iraqi army. The Armenian community decreased further because of the war and the severe international sanctions imposed on Iraq. Presently, around 10,000 Armenians live in Iraq, primarily in Baghdad, Basra, and Zakho. The Armenian Prelacy governs the Armenian community life, which is part of the holy site of Catolicosate of Etchmiadzin in Armenia.

There are Armenian educational, cultural, sports, and other committees that organize the community life. Armenian Catholic and Evangelical churches also exist in Iraq and render their spiritual and social services to the community. Due to political instabilities in Iraq, the Armenian Evangelical community was diminished. It was only in 2004 that the church in Baghdad was re-established and during the critical times of the country "to inspire hope and inner peace in the hearts of its believers."[4]

Jordan

The Armenian presence in Jordan started very early, during the Crusades in the eleventh and thirteenth centuries. However, the community was mainly formed after the Armenian Genocide in 1915, when Armenian refugees settled in the capital Amman and other cities. In 1948, the number Armenians reached 6,000. During the 1948–49 Arab-Israeli war, many Armenians left their homes in Palestine and settled in the old district of Jerusalem, which was then under the control of the Jordanian authorities. After the Arab-Israeli war in 1967, many Armenians left Jordan for the US and Canada. Today, around three thousand Armenians live in Jordan.

Armenians in Jordan have the reputation for being skilled in professions like watchmaking. Many are also successful business people, who contribute to the economy of the country. Some renowned photographers in Jordan are also Armenians. The Armenian community has a church, Sourp Tateos (St. Thaddeus), located on the hills of Al Ashrafieh district in Amman. The church is under the jurisdiction of the patriarchate of Jerusalem. The Armenian Catholic community consecrated its church building in 1952. The Armenian elementary school Yuzbashian-Gulbenkian, founded in 1932, ceased its operation a couple of years ago because of the decrease in the number of Armenian students. The Armenian community in Jordan, in spite of its small number, tries to organize its community life through social, cultural, and sports functions with the aim of preserving the Armenian language and identity.

Lebanon

The Armenian presence in Lebanon started during the early years of history and in particular during the reign of King Tigran II. King Tigran encouraged many Armenians to come and live in Assyria and the provinces of

---

4. Alemian, "Union of the Armenian Evangelical Churches in the Near East," 22.

Phoenicia. In the twelfth and up to thirteenth century, Armenian communities were formed in the port cities of Sidon and Tripoli. The Armenian community grew in number during the seventeenth century, when the Maronite feudal lords, aiming to create an autonomous region, encouraged the Christian communities fleeing the Ottoman rule to seek refuge in the country. In 1721, the Armenian Catholic Andonian friars established monasteries in Ghosta and Ghazir. These monasteries remained active until the nineteenth century. The Armenian Catholic monastery of Bzoumar was established in 1749. More Armenians arrived after the 1894–96 and 1909 massacres of Armenians by Ottoman Turkey. Mount Lebanon had two Armenian governors—Daoud Basha and Hovhannes Basha Kouyoumjian.

In the nineteenth century, the three Christian denominations within the Armenian community were very well established in Lebanon. The Armenian Orthodox community, governed by the patriarchate of Jerusalem, built Sourp Nishan church in 1851. The Armenian Catholic Church, affiliated with the monastery in Bzoumar, built Sourp Yeghia church in 1890.

The community developed in the 1920s when Armenian refugees from Western Armenia and Cilicia arrived. In 1923–24, around 40,000 Armenians lived in Lebanon. According to a 1945 census, 50,000 Armenian Orthodox were registered, 10,000 Armenian Catholics, and 3,000 Armenian Evangelicals. The Armenian Catholic patriarchate moved to Lebanon from Constantinople in 1925. In 1929, the Armenian patriarchate in Jerusalem transferred its administrative jurisdictions, including ownership of land, to the Catholicosate of Cilicia. The Armenian Catholicosate of Cilicia was transferred to Antelias in 1930.

In early 1975, before the civil war, the Armenian community counted approximately 200,000. This number also includes around 60,000 Syrian and Palestinian Armenians who have no Lebanese citizenship. Many Armenians emigrated to the US, Europe, Australia, Canada, and other countries during the civil war, which started in 1975 and lasted till 1990. It should be noted that the last official census in Lebanon was made in 1932. In this respect, precise statistics are hard to obtain. The numbers are all estimates and are obtained through the prelacy, social committees, and observation. Today, the number of Armenians varies between 60,000 and 80,000.

Lebanon is governed by religious denominations. The Armenian Orthodox community is the seventh largest denomination in the country. The Armenian Orthodox and Catholic communities have their representatives in the Lebanese parliament. Armenian Evangelicals compete for the parliament seat they share with the local Evangelical community.

The Armenian community has many social, sports, and cultural organizations, political parties, and media (press, radio, Armenian program in local TV stations) affiliated with the three denominations. The first long-lasting Armenian-language daily, *Aztag*, was established in 1927 by the Armenian Revolutionary Federation (Tashnagtsoutyoun) that was established in 1904. *Zartonk*, another daily, dates from 1934 as an organ of the Ramgavar Liberal Party, established in 1921. *Ararad*, a daily, was established in 1937 by the Social Democrat Henchag Party, which was established in 1912. Armenians founded the Armenian Relief Red Cross in 1930, the Karaguezian Center in 1940, and the Jinishian Center in 1966. These charitable organizations were established with the sole purpose of supporting the spiritual, intellectual, health, and economic development of Armenians. The Armenian community has a university—Haigazian University, established in 1955, through the joint efforts of the Union of the Armenian Evangelical Churches in the Near East and the Armenian Missionary Association of America. Haigazian University is the only Armenian university in the diaspora.

The Armenian community established many schools after WWI. In the 1920s, there were ten orphanages with around 7,000 orphans. The city of Byblos was known for two main orphanages. The first orphanage was initiated and run by the American Board between 1920–25 and had 1,500 orphans. The second one—Birds' Nest, was established by the Danish Mission in 1928. The latter is still a school which caters to the needs of children from broken families. It is run and administered by the Catholicosate of Cilicia in Antelias.

By 1926, the Armenian Orthodox Church had fifteen schools, the Armenian Catholic Church had eight, and the Armenian Evangelical Church had six. In 1975, there were around sixty schools with around 21,000 pupils. The Armenian schools in Lebanon follow the Lebanese government curriculum and also teach Armenian language, literature, history, Bible lessons, and Armenian geography.

The civil war affected negatively on the community's life, including the schools. In 1991, there were forty-two schools—sixteen elementary, ten intermediate, and sixteen high schools. There were also five technical schools and three seminaries. In 2003, there were thirty schools—eight elementary, nine intermediate, and twelve high schools. The total number of students enrolled in Armenian schools was 8,400. There were also five technical schools with 534 students, two schools for pupils with special needs, and three seminaries. Today, there are twenty-one schools in all.

The Armenian Orthodox and Evangelical churches together run a hospital, which first began as a refuge for people suffering from Tuberculosis. Today, Azounieh, established in 1923, provides various medical services to the Armenian and non-Armenian communities. The

Swiss-Armenian Friendship Organization, established in 1896, started its mission activities in Lebanon in the 1920s. They established a school for the blind in 1927. Today, this institution—CAHL, Center for the Armenian Handicapped people in Lebanon, has expanded its services and caters to the needs of the elderly and people with special needs. This institution is run by a board that includes representatives from the Orthodox, Evangelical, and Catholic Churches.

Almost most of the above-mentioned institutions were first located in Bourj Hamoud, an area on the eastern banks of the Beirut River. It is one of Lebanon's most dynamic and vibrant areas, with residential apartments, commercial centers, shops, restaurants, churches, schools, social relief centers, and other facilities. It also connects the capital to Mount Lebanon. What makes Bourj Hamoud special to Armenians is that it is the "manifestation of the collective memory of a people uprooted from its ancestral homeland, . . . a place of memory, product of refugees and a city in exile."[5]

The Armenian community has been a vibrant community throughout the years and is considered to be the "heart of the Armenian diaspora."

Palestine/Israel

Armenia-Palestine relationships started during the reign of King Tigran II. The main exodus of Armenians to Palestine started with the spread of Christianity in the early centuries. In the fourth century, Armenians built churches and monasteries in Jerusalem. This was soon followed by the formation of Armenian business communities in the various districts of Palestine and Jerusalem. Historical records indicate that there were around seventy Armenian monasteries and churches in Jerusalem in the seventh century. During the Arab and Muslim invasion and occupation of Jerusalem between seventh and eleventh centuries, the Armenian community obtained official recognition and was given access to some of its church buildings. In the eleventh century, the Armenian community in Jerusalem had its district, called the Armenian quarter, in the old town, along with three other religious families, each having its own share. The Armenian community preserves this district until today. The Armenian community in Jerusalem developed further during the Armenian Cilicia Kingdom and later when the crusaders arrived in the late eleventh century. The influx of Armenians increased in the twelfth century.

The Armenian community in Palestine shrank, however, during the Ottoman rule in 1517. It later increased after the 1894–96 and 1909

---

5. Avedanian, *Bourj Hammoud*, 1.

massacres of Armenians, and after the 1915 Genocide. In 1918, the Armenian community was around 10,000 and in the 1920s around 20,000. It shrank after the 1948–49 Arab-Israeli wars and when the Palestinian territory was divided between the newly established government of Israel and Jordan. In 2003, they counted a mere 3,000. Around 700 lived in the old Armenian quarter, and 600 held Israeli citizenship. However, in the 1990s, around 13,000 Armenians from Armenia migrated to Israel. The Armenian community in Israel has churches, schools, social, and cultural organizations, and press.

The Armenian patriarchate in Jerusalem was established in the seventh century. The headquarter was in the Saint Hagopiantz monastery, built in the early years of the start of Christianity. During the Ottoman rule, the patriarchate of Jerusalem had its jurisdiction on the Armenian communities in Syria, Lebanon, and Cyprus, and in 1839 it extended over Egypt as well. Today, the Armenian patriarchate in Jerusalem is responsible for the Armenian community's affairs in Jordan and Israel.

Syria

The relations between Armenia and Syria started in the early years of history. It developed mainly during king Tigran II, when Assyria fell under the reign of Armenia. Many Armenians, including businessmen and laborers, settled in Antioch and its surrounding regions. The Armenian and Assyrian communities lived together, and their relationship flourished between the third and the fourth centuries. It was during this era that political, economic, cultural, and social networking and cooperation were enhanced. Many Assyrian evangelists visited Armenia for mission work in the early years of Christianity. Many Armenians, including Mesrob Mashdotz the inventor of the Armenian alphabet, received their education in Assyrian cities.

In the seventh century, the Arabs conquered Armenia, and many Armenians held high positions within the Arab communities. In 1016, an Armenian by the name of Aziz El Towlen, was appointed as governor of the Citadel of Aleppo. The number of the Armenian community in Syria increased between the ninth and eleventh centuries, especially after the fall of the two Armenian kingdoms of Pakradouniatz and Cilicia in 1375. Many Armenians fled to Syria in those days. Armenians settled in Aleppo, Alexandretta (Iskenderun), Damascus, and other cities.

The Armenian Prelacy in Syria was formed in the late tenth century. Sourp Asdvadsazin Church was built in 1329. In the fifteenth century, Armenian businessmen started to come to Aleppo for trade and also those who continued their journey to Jerusalem for pilgrimage. The Armenian Prelacy in Aleppo, which is the second biggest and oldest prelacy within the Catholicosate of Cilicia, was established in the thirteenth century. The patriarchate of Jerusalem formed the Prelacy in Damascus in the fifteenth century. Today, the Prelacy of Damascus is under the jurisdiction of the Catholicosate of Holy Etchmiadzin in Armenia.

The Armenian Sourp Manoug Church was built in the fifteenth century along with the prelacy. The Armenians in Syria were known as goldsmiths, painters, tailors, and other similar skilled professions. In the nineteenth century, the Armenian community in Syria decreased in number because of the legal restrictions imposed by the Ottoman rule. Between 1880 and 1890, the Armenian community in Syria counted 77,000 people.

In 1871, Mazloumian brothers from Anatolia, had the idea to build the first hotel in Aleppo, which came to existence in 1909 and was named Hotel Baron. The brothers were passing through Aleppo on their way to Jerusalem for pilgrimage. They saw how poor accommodation facilities in Aleppo were for foreigners and visitors. Hotel Baron remained a historical icon in Aleppo until 2014.

The Armenian community in Syria enjoyed the warm welcome and hospitality of the native Arabs, who welcomed and supported them in their endeavors. The Armenian community flourished after 1920, when many Armenians fled to Syria because of the Genocide. There they built many churches, schools, and established cultural, sports, and social organizations that function until today. More than 100 schools existed in Syria after the 1915 Genocide and when Armenian refugees settled in the country. The first Armenian school was founded in 1848 in the village of Kessab, in the north-western part of Syria. In Aleppo, Haigazian school was founded in 1850, next to the Armenian Sourp Karasoun Manoug Church. In Damascus, the National Tarkmanchatz school was founded in 1898. In 2003, the number of Armenian schools in Syria was twenty-six, as many left for better opportunities abroad, and more recently because of the civil unrest in the country.

The Armenian community in Syria has Catholic and Evangelical churches as well. The civil war and the political upheavals that started in 2011 urged many Syrians, including Armenians, to leave for the West and Armenia. According to non-confirmed statistics, the number of Armenians in Syria today is around 10,000.

The Armenian Church

Around 90 percent of the 10 million Armenians in the world belong to the Armenian Orthodox Church.[6] Most of the Armenians live in the diaspora, whose number changes because of migration due to civil unrest, economic, and social challenges. In many ways, the Armenian Church "has permeated all spheres, aspects, and dimensions of Armenian life and witness has been strongly affected by the circumstances and developments of the Armenian people's history."[7] His Holiness Aram I believes that the Armenian Church is the "people's church par excellence."[8]

The Armenian Church, besides its ethnic and cultural identity, is characterized by its geographical locality. The Christian faith was first started in Armenia when the gospel was preached and the church was founded. This is also why the church is called "Church of Armenia." With the growing number of Armenian diaspora communities due to emigration and in the present era of global world context, the Armenian Church is now the "Church of Armenians; a global reality."[9]

The Armenian Orthodox Church is part of the Oriental Orthodox Church family, together with Coptic, Syriac, Ethiopian, Indian-Malabar, and Eritrean Churches. "They are autocephalous churches. Although they display a large variety of cultural and liturgical differences, they confess the same faith, share common doctrinal teachings, and are in full sacramental communion with each other."[10] The second large Orthodox Church families are named as the Eastern Orthodox. The Oriental and Eastern Orthodox churches have many common liturgical and theological teachings, but "they are not in Eucharistic communion with each other."[11] The main reason for this division is the Council of Chalcedon in 451, whose resolutions were not endorsed by the Oriental Orthodox Church family.

The rejections of the resolutions of the Council of Chalcedon had its consequences on the Armenian people and its church. The Byzantine Empire considered this a political act against both the empire and the church of Constantinople. The Greeks wanted the Armenian Church to accept the Council of Chalcedon, so that they will be subjugated to them. The Armenian fear remained dominant, and they determined not to accept the Council of

---

6. Aram I. *The Armenian Church*, 20.
7. Aram I. *The Armenian Church*, 21.
8. Aram I. *The Armenian Church*, 197.
9. Aram I. *The Armenian Church*, 20.
10. Aram I, *The Armenian Church*, 16.
11. Aram I, *The Armenian Church*, 16.

Chalcedon. The Armenian Church could foresee that if they accepted the Council's resolutions, they would be assimilated by the Byzantine Empire. The Armenian Church officially severed ties with Rome and Constantinople in 554, during the Second Council of Dvin. In recent times, however, both Chalcedonian and non-Chalcedonian churches have developed a deeper understanding for each other's positions, recognizing their substantial agreement while maintaining their respective positions.

The Armenian Apostolic Church is the central religious authority for the Armenian Orthodox population in Armenia as well as for Armenian Orthodox communities worldwide. It is headed by a catholicos. The Armenian Apostolic Church presently has two catholicoi—Karekin II, supreme patriarch and catholicos of all Armenians, and Aram I, catholicos of the Great House of Cilicia—two patriarchs, primates, archbishops, bishops, clergy, and laity. Both clergy and laity are involved in the administrative structure of the Church.

The following three sees have their own jurisdictions:

- The Catholicosate of the Great House of Cilicia located in Antelias, Lebanon, is led by Catholicos Aram I, and it has dioceses in the countries of the Middle East, Europe, and North and South America.

- The Armenian patriarchate of Jerusalem, which has jurisdiction over the Holy Lands and the diocese of Jordan, is led by Patriarch Archbishop Nourhan Manougian.

- The Armenian patriarchate of Constantinople and All of Turkey, which has jurisdiction in the modern day Republic of Turkey, is led by Patriarch Archbishop Sahak II Mashalian.

On July 1, 1846, thirty-seven Armenian men and three women established the Armenian Evangelical Church in Istanbul (then Constantinople). Four years later, on November 21, 1850, Sultan Abdul Mejid granted formal recognition to the newly established church—"Protestant millet." The Armenian Renaissance in the nineteenth century had a direct impact on the great upsurge of the Armenian intellectual spirit, as "there was a revival of thinking in the social, economic and religious realm."[12]

The first ethnic cleansing of the twentieth century—the Armenian Genocide, perpetrated by the Ottoman regime—devastated the vibrant Evangelical community which had 137 churches, 179 pastors, 14,000 communicant members, about fifty-one adherents, hundreds of elementary schools, thirty-four secondary schools, seven colleges, and three seminaries.

---

12. Tootkian, "Armenian Evangelical Church," 4.

The Armenian Evangelical church had and still has its share in organizing the lives of the Armenian diaspora.

The Union of the Armenian Evangelical Churches in the Near East is an autonomous body of Armenian Evangelical churches comprising twenty-five congregations in nine countries, including Lebanon, Syria, and Iraq. It is the continuation of the Union of the Armenian Evangelical Churches in Cilicia. Those who survived the Genocide formed the timber around which the Armenian Evangelical community was founded in the Near East. The Union's first general assembly was held in Aleppo from April 30 to May 3, 1924. The Armenian Evangelical communities started to take shape in the Middle East as early as 1922, when churches, schools, charitable organization, and publications were founded.

The Armenian Evangelical churches in the Middle East belong to the Reformed tradition and are congregational in structure. It is a very ecumenical church with active involvement in inter-church relations. The Armenian Evangelical Church in the Near East is one of the founding members of the Middle East Council of Churches and the World Council of Churches. July 1, 2021, marks the 175th anniversary of the founding of the Armenian Evangelical Church. Tchillingirian says: "One of the most impressive characteristics of the Armenian Evangelical church is the fact, despite being small in numbers among Armenians worldwide, this 175-year-old church is one of the most active, visible, and organized institutions in the Armenian world."[13]

The crusaders had very close relations with the Armenians and the Latin in Cilicia, which gave birth to "Latinophile tendencies in the political and ecclesiastical sphere."[14] Missionary activities by Dominican friars and Franciscans and Jesuits continued among Armenians in Armenia and Cilicia in the thirteenth century. Mkhitar of Sebastia (1676–1749) established the Mkhitarist order first in Constantinople then in Morea, Greece, and Venice, Italy. After his death, his followers established a separate Mkhitarist order, first in Trieste and then in Vienna. These orders, both in Vienna and Venice, have rendered remarkable services to Armenian culture and scholarship. The Mkhitarist order has also been instrumental in the field of education and has established schools in Lebanon and Syria. These schools still function until today.

In 1740, Abraham Arzivian was elected as patriarch, and he received confirmation from Pope Benedict XIV. This was followed by the establishment of the Armenian Catholic Church in the monastery of Bzoumar,

---

13. Tchillingirian, *Fidelity to the Mission of Renewal*, 8.
14. Aram I, *The Armenian Church*, 192.

Lebanon, as a separate ecclesiastical entity. In 1830, the Ottoman authorities legally recognized the Armenian Catholic community as "millet." In 1867, the patriarchate was united with the Armenian Catholic diocese of Constantinople and moved there. In 1925, the patriarchate was relocated to Bzoumar. Today, the Armenian Catholic patriarchate is located in Beirut.

In spite of the association of the Armenian Catholic Church with the Vatican and the close relationship of the Armenian Evangelical churches with the Western mission agencies, "the Armenian Catholic church was not Latinized and the Armenian Evangelical church was not westernized."[15] The two churches are an integral part of the Armenian nation and are strongly attached to the national identity and culture. In today's challenges, it is imperative that the three churches develop a renewed collaboration with a wider scope and perspective, as "such an effort will contribute powerfully to the internal unity of the Armenian nation."[16]

Conclusion

Armenia adopted Christianity in 301 AD and became the first nation in the world to accept Christianity as state religion. The Armenian alphabet was invented after the adoption of Christianity as state religion in 405 AD by St. Mesrob and St. Sahak. This was followed by the translation of the Bible into Armenian, referred as the "Queen of all translations." The fifth century is described by historians as the Golden Age. Many religious texts were translated into Armenian, and countless liturgical texts, hymns, and theological writings were produced. "The conversion of Armenia to Christianity altered the destiny of the Armenian people, putting Armenia on a new historical track," writes Aram I.[17]

The history of the Armenian nation, in particular its post-Genocide era, cannot be appreciated without a thorough analysis and understanding of the ethnic cleansing that they went through. The lives of the Armenians, in particular in the diaspora, including the Middle East, can be grasped if and when the notion of the Genocide and its impact are well observed. The Genocide has brought all Armenians together in spite of their differences in national, regional, religious, ideological, political, socioeconomic, and generational domains. The Genocide has challenged Armenians to come together to preserve their national identity. According to Richard Hovannisian, the Genocide has given the Armenians the motivation and the passion

15. Aram I, *The Armenian Church*, 194.
16. Aram I, *The Armenian Church*, 195.
17. Aram I, *The Armenian Church*, 32.

for peoplehood, cultural rebirth, and historical continuity. This sense of peoplehood has engaged the Armenians in "creative interplay and dialogical interaction with other cultures and context."[18]

And as one follows Armenians' stories in the Middle East, it is important to observe how Armenians are eager to build/rebuild their culture, also the culture of the communities in which they live. This Armenian-Lebanese, Armenian-Syrian, Armenian-Iraqi, Armenian-Israeli, Armenian-Palestinian, and Armenian-Jordanian identity has many challenges. Balancing these two identities has helped Armenians to endure and thrive. The inter-relation, inter-action, and the aim to create a balanced relationship between the two identities contribute both to the preservation and continuation of the Armenian national spirit and the building of socio-economic and cultural values in their adopted countries. To live with two identities and homelands is neither a conflict nor an obstacle. It is a richness that adds to the life of the person—the Armenians' in this case, who in turn capitalize this legacy in the effort to build communities with values and norms in a more meaningful way.

His Holiness Aram I rightly says that Middle East will lose its unique character without the Christians. And the Armenian story in the Middle East, which is a Christian story, plays a crucial role in creating and preserving this unique character. To achieve this, it is important for the nation to survive.

This is the story of the Armenian nation. It is a story of survival—survival against all odds.

Bibliography

Adalian, Roupen. "The Armenian Genocide: Context and Legacy." *Social Education* 55 (1991) 99–104.

Alemian, Rosette. "Union of the Armenian Evangelical Churches in the Near East." *AMAA News*, April-June 2021, 21–25.

Aram I. *The Armenian Church*. Beirut: Armenian Catholicosate of Cilicia, 2017.

Avedanian, Hrag. "Bourj Hammoud: An Armenian City in Exile." *The Armenian Weekly*, August 31, 2021. https://armenianweekly.com/2021/08/04/bourj-hammoud-an-armenian-city-in-exile/

Bakalian, Anny. *Armenian-Americans: From Being Armenian to Feeling Armenian*. New Brunswick: Transaction, 1994.

Bournoutian, George. *A Concise History of the Armenian People*. Costa Mesa, CA: Mazda, 2006.

Hovannisian, Richard. *The Armenian People: From Ancient to Modern Time*. New York: St. Martin's, 1997.

---

18. Aram I, *The Armenian Church*, 5.

Sanjian, Ara. "Armenians in Lebanon." In *Encyclopedia of Diasporas: Immigrant and Refugee Cultures Around the World: Overviews and Topics*, edited by Melvin Ember et al., 291–328. New York: Springer, 2003.

———. "Armenians in Jordan." In *Encyclopedia of Diasporas: Immigrant and Refugee Cultures Around the World: Overviews and Topics*, edited by Melvin Ember et al., 368–69. New York: Springer, 2003.

Sarksian, Aram, and Bedrossian Amalya. "Armenians in Iraq." In *Encyclopedia of Diasporas: Immigrant and Refugee Cultures Around the World: Overviews and Topics*, edited by Melvin Ember et al., 268–73. New York: Springer, 2003.

Tchillingirian, Hratch. "Fidelity to the Mission of Renewal." *AMAA News*, April-June 2021, 8–9.

Tootkian, Vahan. "Armenian Evangelical Church: A Brief History." *AMAA News*, April-June 2021, 4–6.

———. "Armenians in Israel." In *Encyclopedia of Diasporas: Immigrant and Refugee Cultures Around the World: Overviews and Topics*, edited by Melvin Ember et al., 213–19. New York: Springer, 2003.

———. "Armenians in Syria." *Encyclopedia of Diasporas: Immigrant and Refugee Cultures Around the World: Overviews and Topics*, edited by Melvin Ember et al., 508–34. New York: Springer, 2003.

8

The Greek Story

Nicolas Abou Mrad

Historical Overview

The "Greek Orthodox" family of churches in the Middle East comprises the three patriarchates of Alexandria, Antioch, and Jerusalem, which together with Rome and Constantinople constitute the so-called Pentarchy (*lit.* the five heads), or the five oldest churches of Christendom. As far back as the fourth century AD, these Churches played a crucial role in defining the main theological trends of the Christian faith, as well as in establishing its liturgical practices with all their diversity and wealth.

Following the administrative and political order of the Roman Empire, the Pentarchy was given formal recognition by the Roman emperors, starting with Justin I (527–65) and the Churches were ranked in order of preeminence: Rome as the first, given that it was the capital, followed by Alexandria and Antioch. Constantinople came to the fore only after it had become the imperial residence in the fourth century, ranking second after Rome. Jerusalem, however, received the fifth rank, not because of its political and administrative value, but rather for its symbolic status as the cradle of the Christian faith. It is to be noted that this order of preeminence was solely an administrative one, with no theological or ecclesial implications. In fact, the notion of the "local" church as the embodiment of its universal dimension has had prevalence in ecclesiology over the administrative universality, and therefore the supremacy of one Church over the others.

In its canons, the First Council of Nicaea, known also as the First Ecumenical Council, in 325, recognized and specified the extent of the authority of Rome, Alexandria, and Antioch; the authority of the Church of Rome extended over most of central and Western Europe, that of Antioch covered the southeastern part of Asia Minor (Turkey today), Syria, Lebanon, and parts of Mesopotamia (Iraq today) and Jordan. Alexandria covered Egypt,

Ethiopia, and most of Northern Africa, while Jerusalem's authority was limited, as determined later, to Palestine and Sinai.

Today, the Greek Orthodox Churches of the Middle East have maintained the main lines of their geographical extent and jurisdiction, with important developments associated with demographic changes, such as the establishment of new parishes outside the historical realm of each of these Churches, due to emigration as in the case of Antioch and Jerusalem, or expansion through missionary activity, as in the case of Alexandria.

The historical course of the Churches of Alexandria, Antioch, and Jerusalem, to which this chapter shall be limited, was marked not only by a wide contribution to the formulation of faith, and to the elaboration and crystallization of liturgical forms and traditions, but also by Christological controversies associated with the debate over the relationship between the divine and human natures in Christ, which led to the first great schisms, as a result of the doctrinal resolutions of the Third and Fourth Ecumenical Councils, held respectively in Ephesus (431 AD) and Chalcedon (451 AD). These controversies led to the emergence of parallel Churches in Alexandria and Antioch: Churches that recognized the teaching of Chalcedon on the two natures of Christ and churches that have rejected Chalcedon (Copts, Syriacs, and the Armenian Church).

In fact, one can assume that the two schools of theology, known as the school of Alexandria and that of Antioch, have prepared the fertile ground for these eventual disagreements by producing opposing approaches to biblical interpretation. The School of Alexandria was the first Christian institution of higher learning. Founded in Alexandria, in the mid-second century AD, it became a leading center of the so-called "allegorical method" of biblical interpretation, espousing a rapprochement between Greek philosophy and Christian faith and attempting to assert "orthodox" teachings against heterodox views in an era of doctrinal proliferation, by stressing the full divinity of Christ. On the other hand, the School of Antioch, traditionally thought to have been founded in Syria in 200 AD, stressed the literal interpretation of the Bible and the fullness of Christ's humanity. The divergent approaches of these two schools fostered the estrangement between them to the extent of a total disunion—nurtured by competition and tensions between Byzantium on one hand and the churches of the provinces on the other, in which nationalistic assertiveness played a remarkable role.

The Greek Orthodox churches of the East are those churches that have accepted Chalcedon and took the side of Constantinople and the emperor. Historically, they were called Romans, whose Arabic demonym, "ar-rum," is still used by the adherents of these churches to this day to describe themselves. In their self-perception, the Orthodox Churches of the East are the continuation of the historical churches of the Roman Empire, and the direct heirs of the early churches established through early apostolic mission in the areas which witnessed the birth of Christianity.

Indeed, in Jerusalem, Antioch, and Alexandria, the first encounter of the nascent Christian faith with cultural diversity and ethnic plurality has taken place, as testified in the book of Acts. This early encounter, though often not without tension and confrontation, has shaped, not only the course of life of the early communities in the East, their worship and their mission, but had contributed even to the formation of the New Testament writings, in which the interaction between Jews and gentiles (mainly Greeks and Romans) is not less than a normative feature. Hence, it is not fortuitous that the followers of Jesus were first called "Christians" in Antioch (Acts 11:26). For it was only natural for a city that gathered believers from both Jewish and gentile backgrounds in one eucharistic community to be linked to the very nature of Christianity. By extension, the same can be said about Alexandria, especially that this city had already witnessed an intense cross-acculturation between the Greco-Roman and Jewish worlds, centuries before the rise of Christianity, as testified in numberless literary works, including the monumental translation into Greek of the Old Testament writings, known as the Septuagint (third or second century BC).

This "pluralistic dimension" has always characterized the Orthodox Church of the East and shaped its theological discourse. From the very first years, Alexandria, Antioch, and Palestine have had a unique experience of multiplicity and diversity; they have always represented a rich human and cultural tapestry, resulting from the encounter of the civilizations of the East with the Graeco-Roman culture. Later in their history, Alexandria, Antioch, and Palestine co-existed with Islam, experiencing both the tolerant openness of the early Islamic rulers and the strict control of the Mamluks and the Ottomans. Due to cultural and historical circumstances, the Christians of the East did not experience the triumphant dominance of an established Christianity such as in both the Byzantine world and medieval Western Europe. This fact forever shapes their worldview, as well as their understanding of co-existence with other cultures, denominations, and religions.

Current Situation

The Greek Orthodox Church of Alexandria

As mentioned above, the Church of Alexandria appeared together with the Coptic Church as parallel Churches as a result of the split following the

Council of Chalcedon in 451. In Egypt itself, it has always been a rather small community compared to the Coptic Church. It witnessed some growth in the nineteenth century, due to migration of people from Greece, Syria, and Lebanon who established communities in Egypt and other African countries under the jurisdiction of the Church of Alexandria.

This Church has experienced a drastic decrease in the number of its adherents in the mid-twentieth century with the departure of Greeks from Egypt. Yet, the twentieth century has also witnessed an intensive missionary movement in sub-Saharan Africa, in which the Church of Alexandria played a leading role. Communities were established in most of the African countries, with high concentration in Kenya, Uganda, and Madagascar. These communities were given the status of dioceses and were received into the Church of Alexandria.

More recently, a considerable missionary effort was conducted throughout the African Continent, encouraging the rise of local clergy and the use of local languages, customs, and traditions in the liturgical life of the Church. Moreover, as a Church in co-existence with Islam, Alexandria worked on promoting dialogue with the Muslims based on mutual respect and understanding. On the ecumenical level, Alexandria works towards improving relations with other Churches, especially with the Coptic Church.

Nowadays it comprises more than 300,000 Orthodox Christians, a striking number, giving the fact that this Church has always been a small community since the schism in 451.

The Greek Orthodox Church of Jerusalem

The Church of the Holy Land, as it calls itself. The adherents of the Orthodox Church of Jerusalem, the actual jurisdiction of which covers historic Palestine and Jordan, perceive themselves as the inheritors of the first church. In the modern history, the Church of Jerusalem was not spared from the repercussions of the Arab-Israeli conflict. The constant changes in the balance of power, as well as the establishment of the State of Israel on the territories of historic Palestine, have all contributed to the weakening of the Church of Jerusalem, and the decrease of the numbers of its adherents, due to a massive emigration towards Europe and the Americas.

Comprising around 80,000 believers in historic Palestine, the Orthodox Church of Jerusalem is struggling to maintain its pastoral work in rather difficult circumstances due to ongoing tensions between Israelis and Palestinians and the quest for a clear identity and the increased politicization of religion. The distribution of its parishes in both Israel and the territories under the

Palestinian authority presents another pastoral challenge for this Church. An even more critical challenge is the dominance of ethnic Greeks in the Church's hierarchy over against the Arabic speaking majority among the believers. The exclusion of the Arab majority from its upper ranks, has always been a point of tension between the leadership and the believers.

The situation is remarkably better in Jordan, where around 80,000 believers are distributed to different parishes across the country. Enjoying a great deal of freedom and respect, the Orthodox Christians have always been a prominent component of the Jordanian society.

It is to be noted that the Church of Jerusalem, in both its Palestinian and Jordanian wings, has witnessed a revival among the youth, mostly influenced by the youth movement in the Church of Antioch in the mid-twentieth century. This revival has led to the intensification of the involvement of the youth in the life of the Church, despite the huge challenges.

The Greek Orthodox Church of Antioch

By far the largest Church among the Greek Orthodox are the Antiochian Orthodox—or the Rum (Roman) Orthodox Christians. They consider themselves the direct continuation of the apostolic church of Antioch, where the followers of Jesus were first called Christians.

Unlike the Churches of Jerusalem and Alexandria, where the higher clergy are predominantly ethnically Greek, Antioch has been led, since 1899, by local bishops, after it had experienced an intensive involvement by the patriarchate of Constantinople in its affairs after the Uniat schism of 1724. For well over a century, patriarchs and several bishops were chosen from the ranks of Greek-speaking clergy from Constantinople, Jerusalem, or Cyprus. In the second half of the nineteenth century, however, the Antiochian Church experienced an educational revival, which, coupled with the rise of Arab nationalism and the rivalry represented by extensive Roman Catholic and Protestant missionary activity, led to the emergence of Antioch from Greek domination. At the end of the nineteenth century, Meletius Al-Doumani (*sed.* 1899–1906) was elected as the first Arab patriarch since 1724.

This emergence coincided with the increasing weakness of the Ottoman state, and the rise, towards the end of the nineteenth century, of the Arab renaissance movement as a reaction to Turkish hegemony, within which Antiochian Christians played a leading role. Many of these Christians were prominent advocates of a secular state, secularists with important cultural ideas, who were active in the fields of literature, poetry, and journalism, championed the Arab cause, and resisted Western forms of colonization. Once Antioch was free to elect its own hierarchs, religious life witnessed a remarkable and unequaled flowering. Church leaders saw the need for an educational movement to make believers more aware of their religious and cultural identity. Several institutions for theological education were opened in monasteries and publications have been issued in forms of magazines and newspapers, which were edited by some of the most prominent theologians of the Antiochian Church.

The Church of Antioch suffered immensely during World War II and in its aftermath, as the re-drawing of national boundaries in the Middle East divided its flock between Syria, Lebanon, and Turkey. However, the emergence of the Orthodox Youth Movement in 1942 breathed fresh life into the Church, bringing a serious commitment to ecclesial life and openness towards the challenges of the modern age, not only for the Church of Antioch, but also for Orthodox Churches in Jerusalem and Alexandria.

The Church of Antioch is today the largest among the Greek Orthodox Churches of the East. In Syria and Lebanon, it comprises more than 1 million believers distributed in twelve dioceses and hundreds of parishes. Yet, the overwhelming majority of Antiochian Christians live in the diaspora, in Europe, the Americas, and Australia. Very active in adapting to new contexts, the Church of Antioch has established parishes and dioceses across the world to provide pastoral care for its emigrating adherents. These communities, established as early as the late nineteenth century, are very active in the life of the Church, and are still attached to their "mother" Church within the new cultures and contexts they have embraced.

Worship Practices

Liturgy and the Church

Liturgy is where the Church appears in its fullness as community of believers gathered around the Table of the Lord. Eucharistic liturgy is, therefore, the center of Christian life in Orthodoxy, where all aspects of the Church receive their full meaning and utmost expression. Drawn from the meaning and function of the story of the exodus from Egypt, where the people of God, freed from the hegemony of worldly powers, finds its way to the Mountain of the Lord to worship him and hear his words, the Eucharistic liturgy, in the understanding of the Orthodox Church, is nothing less than the activation of the same exodus, here and now, for those who are called, at all times, to abandon worldly matters and gather around the word of God.

Hence, it is around the table of the Lord that everything takes shape: the community as the Church, and the ministries of the clergy as functions in the service of the word of God and the community. One of the aspects of this liturgical understanding of the Church that has defined Orthodox ecclesiology, is the centrality of the notion of local church versus the universal Church. In Orthodox theology, the local church is the full and undiminished expression of the "Church," in the sense that the community gathered around the table of the Lord represents the fullness as well as the universality of the Church.

This understanding has shaped the organizational aspect of the Church in Orthodoxy, at the center of which stands the local parish, constituted of believers pertaining to a local community. Following a concentric model, a group of local parishes form a diocese, headed by a bishop, and a group of dioceses form the local synod, headed either by an archbishop or a patriarch, depending on the canonical status of the local church. In other words, the organization of the Orthodox Churches does not follow a pyramidal scheme, following which everything culminates in the primacy of the head, but rather the model of concentric circles, revolving around the local parish, their very center. The more the local church grows the wider the circles become, without, however, ceasing to depart for the "local" as their epicenter. In other words, the universality of the Church has much less to do with geographic extent of presence and jurisdiction than with liturgical expression and realization of the universal Church of God in a particular location.

It is precisely this understanding of the Church that is at the root of the disagreement between the ecclesiology of the Orthodox Churches and that of the Roman Catholic Church. Whereas universality, in the latter, came to be viewed from the perspective of the primacy of the bishop of Rome over the universal Church, the nature of the Church, in the Orthodox view, is local while universality remains a theological notion rather than an organizational model. For this reason, there is no hierarchy among the Orthodox Churches, except for the order of preeminence mentioned above, with no effects on ecclesiology.

In his letters, Ignatius of Antioch speaks of the bishop as representing God while celebrating the Eucharistic liturgy with the community of believers, the deacons as Christ himself, and the presbyters as the apostles (*Letter to the Trallians*, 3). With this model, Ignatius meant to stress the fact that the Church appears, in the Eucharist, in its fullness as a paradigm for the world; the bishop, as supervisor of the teaching of the word, represents God, from whom the word has emanated. The presbyters are the apostles who have carried the word to the world, and the deacons, as servants, represent Christ, the Servant of the Lord and the Word of God. This understanding remains the basis for the Orthodox understanding of the relationship between Eucharistic liturgy and the Church.

The bishop, hence, is the head of the local church, in the liturgical sense of the word. There is no authority over the bishop, in the sense that he is the one who holds on his shoulders the responsibility of teaching and preaching. The local bishop is the highest authority, in as much as he presides at the Eucharistic liturgy as teacher, preacher, and caretaker of the "flock of Christ." The local bishops in the different regions of a geographical area form the synod headed by a patriarch, in the case of the historical Churches, or by an archbishop, such as in Greece, for example, or Cyprus or Albania, etc. Titles such as patriarch, archbishop, metropolitan, have no bearing on the theological understanding of the role and function of the bishop, but are rather associated with the administrative aspect of the organization and administration of Church matters. For example, a patriarch is a bishop like any other local bishop, yet, he assumes administrative functions as head of the synod of bishops, without any special prerogatives such as the right to interfere, for example, in the administration of the local churches, or to impose certain views or practices without the consent of the local churches.

The synodal organization of the Orthodox Churches echoes the centrality of the local church, and is expected to implement, in the everyday life of the Church, in a given geographical area, the Eucharistic model of the Church as the community of those who are faithful to God and to his word in Jesus Christ.

Liturgical traditions

The Orthodox Church is known for the richness of its liturgical traditions, a fact that reflects the central role of liturgy as described above. Considered both as the source and expression of theology, liturgy has been associated with the Church's identity and presence. The Greek Orthodox Churches of today have inherited the wealth of the liturgical heritage of ancient Jerusalem, Antioch, and Alexandria, which is the product of influences that overlapped and mixed at different times and in different places and molded into a plethora of liturgical practices. The ancient Antiochian realm, for example, is known for its rich collection of anaphoras, which are preserved to us in various euchologies, compilations and patristic monographs. Yet, this plethora of forms and traditions was boiled down at a later stage to a homogenized practice and is now universally adopted by the Orthodox Churches around the globe.

Out of a wide range of anaphoras, the Orthodox Churches chose the liturgy known as the anaphora of Saint John Chrysostom—a relatively late text ascribed to the renowned father of the Church—to be the form of the Eucharistic celebration on Sundays and feast days throughout the year, with the exception of a few occasions, where the Chrysostom liturgy is replaced by one ascribed to Basil the Great. Substantially longer, the anaphora of Basil the Great is rooted in the ancient Syrian liturgies of the Apostolic Constitutions and Saint James (no longer in use).

The uniformity of the Eucharistic liturgical practice is the result of the universal adoption of Byzantine traditions after the Seventh and last Ecumenical Council, in which Constantinople played a leading role in the so-called struggle against iconoclasm. Aiming at defining the Orthodox faith, once and for all, over against heterodox practices and teachings, all the Eastern Churches convened in Nicaea (787 AD) opted for a uniform liturgical practice following the compilation of former traditions as it took shape in the practice of the Byzantine capital. Royal in its character, the Byzantine liturgical tradition is marked by its sumptuousness and majesty, when compared to traditions still preserved in other oriental Churches.

Yet, despite their uniformity and apparent complexity, the Greek Orthodox liturgy shares with liturgies of the other families of Churches, as well as with the ancient liturgical forms, a certain understanding of time, space, and the material word that has clearly marked the worship of the Churches and their notion of it.

Like in other Churches, the worship in the Greek Orthodox tradition is defined by three cycles of time: daily, weekly, and yearly. The daily cycle consists of daily prayers, such as Vespers, Matins, the office of the hours, Compline, and Midnight services. The structure and the main features of these services remain unchanged, yet the feast of the day as well as its themes define the content of the hymns, as well as the readings from the Bible.

There are certain constants in these services, usually related to the understanding of time from a biblical point of view. In the Orthodox Church the liturgical day begins in the evening, with the setting of the sun. This practice follows the biblical account of creation, "and there was evening and there was morning, one day" (Gen 1:5). The connection with creation sets the time, as viewed liturgically, as a dimension of God's salvation. This is expressed through the reading of Psalm 104, which revolves around the themes of the good creation and salvation. Yet, since man has filled the time with sins, the theme of sin and the fall of man follow, expressed in the reading of psalms of repentance and prayers of forgiveness. The vespers then proceed to emphasize on the theme of salvation and the coming into the world of the Son of God, as Light from the Father, to abolish the forces of darkness in the same way as the Light created by God in Genesis 1 transformed the darkness into a component of time.

The theme of light as an expression of God's salvation is also taken up in the service of Matins, which contains the same themes of sin, repentance, and light as the vespers. It is centered in thanksgiving for the coming of the true light of Christ and calls to repentance by uniting the elements of morning psalmody and prayer with meditation on biblical canticles, the Gospel reading, and the particular theme of the day in the given verses and hymns. Whereas all readings in the Vespers are taken from the Old Testament, the readings in the Matins derive from both Old and New Testaments. This can be explained as follows: Vespers talk about the new creation and salvation by pointing to the coming of Light, while Matins bring to the fore the same themes from the point of view that the Light of God has come in Jesus Christ.

The four services of the hours revolve around the coming of the true Light (first hour), the descent of the Holy Spirit on Pentecost (third hour), the crucifixion and the passion of the Lord (sixth hour/midday), and the death and burial of our Lord (ninth hour).

The Compline and Midnight services focus on thanksgiving for the day that has passed, protection for the ensuing night, and forgiveness of wrongs committed during the day, the resurrection of the Lord and his second coming.

The weekly cycle revolves around the Sunday Eucharistic liturgy, dedicated to the theme of resurrection. Every Sunday, the Orthodox Churches celebrate a "minor" Pascha. Sunday is the day of the Lord, the day of his resurrection which he had ordered his disciples, at the Last Supper, to commemorate until his second coming. The week, the set of seven days, is viewed as one unit of time. Every week throughout the year is a liturgical commemoration of the seven days of creation. However, it is worth noting, that in the Orthodox Church the seventh day, the day of the Lord, is not the last day of the week, but the *first* day. The week begins with God defeating the adverse powers of darkness through the resurrection of his Son from death. This is the day of the coming of Light to the world; the day on which the Word of God, the true Light that gives light to everyone came to world (John 1:9). While the day of the Lord is fully dedicated to God and his salvation, the remaining days of the week are dedicated to the creation. So, Monday is dedicated to the holy bodiless powers, the angels and archangels; Tuesday to the prophets of the Old Testament and to the culmination of prophecy in John the Baptist; Wednesday to the crucifixion; Thursday to the apostles and holy bishops of the Church; Friday to the cross; Saturday to all saints, martyrs, and to the memory of those who have departed this life in the hope of resurrection and eternal life. The theme of Saturday prepares to the resurrection on Sunday, with which a new weekly cycle begins.

The annual cycle includes three parts. The first, which begins on September 1st, includes the fixed feats, fasts, and commemoration of saints. The second part is the liturgy of the period of the Great Lent, which includes three preparatory Lenten weeks, six weeks of Lent and the Passion Week culminating in Pascha. This part does not fall on a precise calendar day but is rather defined according to the yearly calculation of Easter. The third is the liturgy of the Paschal period, consisting of the services of Easter, Easter Week, and the period between Easter and Pentecost. The liturgy of the yearly cycle includes both biblical and hymnographical material, which is inserted into the structure of the daily and weekly cycles.

The Eucharist

Besides the remarks mentioned above about the interaction between Eucharistic liturgy and Church organization, I would like to stress other aspects of the Orthodox Eucharist that are of importance. The most important of these aspects is the inseparability between the proclamation of the word and the Eucharistic table. The "liturgy of the word" and the "liturgy of communion" are not, in Orthodoxy, two juxtaposed units, but constitute one and the same gathering in which the community hears the word of God in the readings from the Bible and the sermon and partakes in the Eucharistic communion.

The Eucharistic liturgy is viewed as a replication of the story of exodus, both theologically and formally; it is an "exodus" from the world governed by human desires, and an "entrance" to the kingdom of heaven represented by the symbolism of the church building, icons, and hymnology. The liturgy of the word proper begins with a procession headed by the deacons carrying the Bible. Originally, this procession, called "the entrance," was the movement of all believers from outside into the church. The elements of this "entrance" suggest a *mimesis* of the exodus to the wilderness: the golden Bible adorned with figures of the cherubim stands for the ark of the covenant (Exod 37:1–9); the table in the midst of the "holy of holies" stands for the table in the center of the tabernacle (Exod 37:10–16); the veil usually covering the table is reminiscent of the tabernacle itself; the priestly garments mimic the garments of Aaron and his sons (Exod 39); the light, the incense, and the covers are all elements pertaining to the exodus scenery. "Blessed is the entrance of your saints" is the sentence uttered by the celebrant, reflecting the understanding of this movement, not only as procession into the church, but as movement towards the presence of the Lord in his word in the Bible as the "ark of the covenant." The "entrance" culminates in the Lord's ceremonial appearance in the readings from the Bible, preceded by the *trisagion* (three-times holy) chanted in the book of Isaiah to the Lord who appeared in his glory in the temple (Isa 6:1–4), as he appeared on Mount Horeb, allowing only those who are purified to approach it (Exod 19; Isa 6:5–7).

Called an "entrance," this movement towards the proclamation of the word is understood as the final goal of an exodus. The theme of exodus is developed in the *anaphora*, or the Eucharistic prayer, which, in the liturgy of Saint Basil the Great, recapitulates the biblical story from creation to the Last Supper. Starting with the fall of the man God "*honored with his own image*," through the disobedience of the commandments, the theme of exodus is brought up in the following sentence: "*Releasing us from the delusions of idolatry, He guided us to the sure knowledge of You, the true God and Father. He acquired us for Himself, as His chosen people, a royal priesthood, a holy nation.*" The place from which the celebrants are released is "the delusions of idolatry." Further, Basil refers to this place as "*death in which we were held captive, sold under sin.*" In his abridged version of the much longer *anaphora* of the Apostolic Constitutions, Basil omits the detailed mention of the exodus from Egypt, in order to highlight the universal bondage of all nations under the sin, expressed in the form of "delusions of idolatry." Not only Israel, but "the whole lost race of the men" broke "the natural law" and, through this, suffered its captivity. Besides the universal character of the exodus, Basil stresses that it was the act of Jesus, who "released us" and "guided us," pointing to the ultimate act of salvation, namely his death and resurrection. The place towards which the path of exodus leads is "the knowledge of God." There, the people consisting of "all nations" is sanctified and appointed as "a royal priesthood and a holy nation" (Exod 19:6), precisely in the gathering around the presence of the Lord in his word.

The act of exodus reaches its culmination in the Last Supper, the table at which Jesus offers his flesh and blood as food for "all" those who were guided by him, as the ultimate expression of the knowledge of God. Hence, the cross becomes the final goal of the biblical story and the "location" to which the exodus path leads. There the Lord appears in his glory and reveals his commandment that all be "*united to one another in partaking of the one bread and the one cup in the communion of the Holy Spirit*" (epiclesis). What is worth pointing to, in this context, is that the *anaphora* ends with an *anamnesis* (remembrance) of a long list of "suffering" groups of human beings: the sick, travelers, widows, orphans, captives, exiled, prisoners, afflicted needy, distressed, etc. The remembrance of the marginalized between the cross and the breaking of bread concretizes the knowledge of God the people was guided to through the cross. There can be no passage from cross to "table fellowship" without "remembering" the afflicted and the needy, that is, without the Church's full awareness that standing before the cross as the ultimate knowledge of God entails carrying the cross of others, so that the table fellowship be completed.

Recent Developments

Renewal movement in the Church of Antioch

The rise of the Orthodox Youth Movement (called MJO) in 1942 was one of the most obvious signs of revival in Antioch's modern history. The founders of this movement, led by Georges Khodr (former Metropolitan of Mount Lebanon), were disturbed by the state of their Church, which was riven by inner tensions and dominated by confessional and sectarian ambitions fomented by Western powers. Inspired by religious zeal and the discovery of Orthodox spirituality, these young people called for a revival based on a "rediscovery" of the richness of the Bible and the Orthodox tradition. They were convinced that a genuine Christian life is distinguished by a true commitment to prayer and a conscious participation in the sacraments, which went hand in hand with a deep desire to strengthen theological education, with the aim of crystallizing a committed Orthodox awareness, caring for the poor and the needy, rejecting sectarianism, and opening up to other Churches and to Islam.

After its recognition by the Antiochian Synod, the movement spread rapidly. Youth groups were formed in the dioceses of Lebanon and Syria. Sunday Schools were established almost everywhere to teach children of all ages the basics of the Orthodox faith. The MJO has created an incomparable dynamic in Church involvement and ecclesial awareness that has touched almost every active member of the Antiochian Church. Under the influence of the MJO, and with a growing awareness of the importance of monasticism in the life of the Church, several monasteries were reopened in Lebanon and Syria to welcome new brotherhoods of monks and nuns. These monasteries have since played a crucial role in counselling and spiritual guidance.

Within the circles of committed and educated youth, the MJO has triggered a large-scale re-thinking of the Church's witness and its role in society, and of the interaction between the Church and the challenges of modern trends and thoughts. The MJO has produced a number of authors who, in their turn, have enriched it with their insights.

Ecumenism

The twentieth century has seen a process of mutual openness on the part of the Churches, and the ecumenical movement has emerged as one of the principal dimensions of the Christian presence in the world. Churches became aware that their encounter can make a great contribution to the realization of world peace, as it increases the credibility of Christians' witness to their crucified and risen Lord in a rapidly changing and fluid world. At the beginning of the twentieth century, the Ecumenical patriarchate played a crucial role in urging "the Churches of Christ everywhere" to live out the "fellowship" (*koinonia*) that exists between them. The Church of Antioch was one of the first Orthodox Churches to join the WCC. It was followed by the Church of Alexandria. The late Patriarch Ignatius (+ 2012), gave the opening speech at the fourth general assembly held in Uppsala (1967), and later became one of the WCC's presidents.

Antioch and Alexandria have also participated in the official dialogue between the Catholic and Orthodox Churches since its foundation in the early 1980s. The Church of Antioch hosted the 1993 meeting of the dialogue, which issued the well-known Balamand document rejecting proselytism and calling for the abandonment of uniatism as a way of achieving unity between the Orthodox and Roman Catholic Churches.

On the local and regional level, the Middle East Council of Churches (MECC) was founded in Nicosia (1974). The MECC is an independent regional structure which concentrates on facilitating unity and allowing the Churches to work together. The Church of Antioch has been a member of MECC since its foundation. Some of its members, particularly Patriarch Ignatius IV, played an important role in leading the MECC and orientating it. Achievements within the context of the MECC include work on common textbooks for religious education to be used in schools in Lebanon, agreements between Orthodox and local Catholic Churches on mixed marriages, religious education in schools and first communion, and the important agreements on pastoral matters between the Antiochian Orthodox Church and the Syriac (non-Chalcedonian) Orthodox Church in 1991.

Interaction with Islam

The Orthodox Churches of the East encountered Islam just a few years after the appearance of that religion in the Arabian Peninsula. In the course of the Middle Ages, representatives of the two religions would confront one another, as Christian theologians attempted to defend the basic dogmas of the faith and to refute Islamic beliefs. However, many Christian apologists tried to expound their faith more positively, in order to assert themselves as monotheists.

In its modern theological discourse, the Eastern Orthodox Church has always insisted on the importance of both a dialogue of life and one of thought with the Muslims. This conviction is rooted in the experience of common history and in the necessity for understanding the other more deeply. In the Christian–Muslim dialogue in the East, emphasis has been put on the faith in the same one God and also the common values and virtues shared by the two religions. In both, caring for the poor and for suffering persons and "bearing one another's burdens" are the utmost expressions of religious piety. Moreover, in both Christianity and Islam the human being is the highest value; he is God's "image and likeness" in Christianity, and God's "representative on earth" in the Qur'an. Both religions call for an expectation of "blessings to come" (Heb 9:11) and their realization in the present world through genuine service.

Conclusion

Orthodox Christians in the Middle East, like all their fellow citizens, are experiencing difficult times in a region trapped in an ongoing turmoil. However, with their long experience of historical difficulties and challenges, as well as with a deep understanding of the value of pluralism, they have always expressed and lived the conviction that the Church is the conscience of the world, and that its role lies in proclaiming, prophetically, the will of God for human life and dignity. With loving openness, they have a word to say in today's rapidly changing world.

For Further Reading

Coniaris, Anthony. *Introducing the Orthodox Church: Its Faith and Life*. Minneapolis, MN: Light and Life, 1982.
Lossky, Vladimir. *The Mystical Theology of the Eastern Church*. Crestwood, NY: St. Vladimir's Seminary Press, 1998.
Ware, Timothy. *The Orthodox Church: An Introduction to Eastern Christianity*. London: Penguin, 2015.

9

The Assyrian Church

KARL PINGGÉRA

The Beginnings of Christianity in Mesopotamia

IN THE FIRST CENTURIES of Church history, the Christian message fell on fertile ground, and not only in the Roman Empire. East of the imperial borders, in the Empire of the Persians, congregations arose from which an independent Church was to emerge. In historical continuity with these beginnings is the Church that today calls itself "The Apostolic Catholic Church of the East of the Assyrians." The abbreviations "Assyrian Church" or "Apostolic Church of the East" are also in use. Geographically, one can also speak of the "East Syrian Church." Because of its theological character, this Church often was called "Nestorian." This use of language should be a thing of the past, since it is avowedly contrary to the Church's self-understanding. The Church traces its origins back to apostolic times and not to the Byzantine patriarch Nestorius, who lived in the fifth century. Recent research has led to the realization that the East Syrian confession of Christ has nothing in common with the doctrine usually labeled "Nestorianism" (in the sense of a heretical doctrine of two sons).

We have only legendary reports about the origins of Persian Christianity. The apostle Thomas is mentioned as the first messenger of faith. A certain Mari is said to have come to the Persian capital Seleucia-Ctesiphon around the year 100 and first worshipped in a place called *Kokhe* ("huts"). In any case, the "Book of Laws and Lands," a treatise written in Edessa between 196 and 226, mentions Christian communities in almost all areas of the Persian Empire. On both sides of the border, the majority of the population was Aramaic-speaking. Edessa may be assumed as the starting point of evangelization. The Aramaic dialect of this city, called "Syriac," became the liturgical and theological language of the Christians in Mesopotamia.

The Church in the Persian Empire

Christianity in Persia seems to have developed unhindered under the Arsacid dynasty. The Church also had a firm place in Persian society in the Sasanid Empire, which came to power in 224. Christians were resettled from the west when the troops of Shapur I advanced far into Roman territory in 260 and even temporarily captured Antioch. In this process, parts of the population, including Christians, were deported to various cities in Persia. Many of them were settled in Gundishapur. The city became the center of Christians in Khuzistan and in later times was to become one of the most important episcopal sees of the Church of the East. In an inscription of the Zoroastrian priest Kartir, "Nazoreans" and "Christians" are mentioned. Although no final certainty can be gained here, the pair of terms seems to refer to different groups of Christians: the native Aramaic Christians of Mesopotamia and the Christians of Greek tongue who were carried off from the Roman Empire.

Kartir mentions these Christian groups in the context of repressions of other religions. Nevertheless, the situation of the Christians at the beginning of the fourth century seems to have been consolidated to such an extent that the bishop of the imperial capital Seleucia-Ctesiphon, Papa bar Aggai (310–17), could attempt to extend his sovereignty over the other bishops of Persia. Papa's request, however, met with the resistance of several bishops. An internal consolidation of the Church was then prevented by the systematic persecutions of Christians under King Shapur II (309–79). Growing tensions between Persia and the Roman Empire may have been in the background. Didn't the Christians of Persia have to appear as partisans of the enemy after the emperor of the Roman Empire had turned to Christianity? After all, Eusebius of Caesarea records a letter that Emperor Constantine wrote to Shapur II shortly before his death in 337 (*Vita Constantini* IV,9–13). With his request to the Persian ruler to take care of the Christians, Constantine had presented himself as a patron for the Christians also outside the Roman Empire.

The persecutions were triggered by the Christians' refusal to pay a doubled tribute to finance the campaigns against Rome. Bishop Simon bar Sabbae of Seleucia-Ctesiphon was found guilty of collaboration with the enemy and executed on Good Friday of 341. This was the prelude to a chain of anti-Christian violence that continued until the end of the reign of Shapur II in 379. Numerous records of martyrs have been preserved. They bear witness to the courage of many Christians to confess their faith. Even after the era of Shapur II, persecutions flared up again and again, but they were no longer carried out systematically and remained locally limited. Only after the persecutions had ceased could the church organize its hierarchical structure.

A first signal of ecclesiastical reconstruction was the Synod of Seleucia-Ctesiphon, which met in 410 under the patronage of King Yazdgird I. In a period of relative détente between Persia and Rome, the king was keen to involve Christians in imperial politics. Now, and also in later centuries, Persian monarchs frequently considered it advantageous to send Christian bishops on diplomatic missions to the neighboring Roman Empire. The way to the synod of 410 was paved by a bishop from the Roman Empire, Marutha of Maypherkat. At the synod, he presented the Persians a letter from the "bishops of the West" asking them to adopt the Nicene Creed. The bishops complied with the request and adapted the Nicene symbol on the basis of an own Persian confession. The hierarchical structure of the East Syrian Church was then determined by the stipulation that the bishop of the imperial capital was to be considered the "head of all Christians of the East." Subordinate to him were five metropolitan sees, from which further bishops depended: Bet Lapat (the Syriac name of Gundishapur in present-day Iran), Nisibis (Nusaybin, in Turkey), Prat de Maishan (Basra), Arbela (Erbil), and Karka de Bet Selok (Kirkuk, in Iraq). In the fifth and sixth centuries, these metropolitan sees were joined by Rev Ardashir (in the province of "Persis") and Merw (in present-day Turkmenistan). Further synods in 420 and 424 underlined the independence of the East Syrian Church. The ruling bishop was called "catholicos" (later extended to "catholicos-patriarch").

Christology

The dogmatic break with the Roman imperial Church occurred when the East Syrian Church adopted the Antiochian Christology during the fifth century. This Christology was officially adopted by the East Syrian Synod of 486. Antiochian doctrine had penetrated into Persia via the theological School of Edessa, the so-called "School of the Persians." The legacy of the preeminent Antiochian theologian Theodore of Mopsuestia (d. 428) had been cultivated there. His works had been translated into Syriac. After Theodore fell into disrepute in the imperial church of the fifth century, the Edessa school faced increasing hostility and was closed by Emperor Zeno in 489. Some of its theologians had already left for Persia, where they were received by Metropolitan Barsauma in neighboring Nisibis. From Nisibis, Antiochian theology began its triumphal march through the East Syrian Church. Soon Theodore of Mopsuestia was regarded as its norm theologian.

When East Syrian authors speak of "the interpreter" of the Holy Scripture, it is Theodore they speak of.

The formative figure of the "School of the Persians" in the fifth century was Narsai (c. 399–502), whom posterity honored as the "Harp of the Holy Spirit." Nestorius did not play a decisive role in his thought, but as Theodore's disciple, Narsai nevertheless counted him among the authoritative Greek theologians. Along with Diodorus of Tarsus and Theodore of Mopsuestia, Nestorius appears in Narsai's praise poem of the three "Greek fathers." Like Theodore, Narsai strictly distinguished between two natures and a single "person" of Christ (Syriac *parsopa*, derived from Greek *prosopon*). Therefore, it is impossible to ascribe the properties of human nature to the nature of God, the Word. The suffering and death on the cross must be attributed exclusively to the person of Jesus. For the same reason, Antiochian Christology refuses to call Mary the "Mother of God." For the Almighty could not possibly dwell in the womb of a woman. In adopting this doctrine, the East Syrian Church clearly differed from the Chalcedonian Church of the empire as well as from the Miaphysites.

With Babai the Great (d. 628), an important monastic father and theologian, the Christological terminology was expanded, in order to clarify the distance to the other denominations. If God, the Word, assumed a human nature, then it did not assume human nature in general, but that of the concrete man Jesus. This concretion is designated by the Syriac term *qnoma*. Since God, the Word, is also a concretion of the Trinity, the East Syrian Church professes the doctrine of the two *qnome*. It is useful not to translate the term immediately. In Greek it corresponds to *hypostasis*. This word *hypostasis* carries also the meaning of "person." But this broader notion is not intended in Syriac. The East Syrian theologians did *not* want to divide Christ into "two sons." Later East Syrian authors have pointed to the difference meaning of Syriac *qnoma* and Greek *hypostasis*. This distinction would become the starting point for the ecumenical dialogues in the recent past.

The Church under the Caliphs

The Persian Empire was conquered by the Muslim Arabs within a few years. The last Sasanid King Yazdgird III fled to Merv, where he was assassinated in 651. According to the Arab historian al-Tabari, it was the East Syrian bishop of the city who laid the king to rest. The Church of the East seems to have soon established good relations with the new rulers. This was helped by the experience of having always lived under non-Christian kings. Patriarch Ishoyahb III (650–58) reported in a letter that the priests were respected by the Muslims, and churches and monasteries were protected. For Ishoyahb III, God himself had given to the Muslims the dominion over the world.

At the same time, however, the patriarch's body of letters also reveals that quite a lot of members of his church had already converted to Islam. Ishoyahb III claims purely material reasons for this. Probably, he was alluding to the special tax for non-Muslims. The Muslims' conviction of the superiority of their religion also contributed to the increasing number of conversions. From the 720s, we have a Syriac text that exemplifies how ecclesiastical writers responded to the challenge of the Muslim claims of truth: the (fictitious) conversation of a high Muslim dignitary with a monk of the monastery Bet Hale (near al-Hira). The conversation revolved around questions of faith. In the end, the Muslim is said to have been convinced of Christianity. Only out of fear and shame in front of his co-religionists, he kept this insight to himself. A number of such reports were intended to strengthen Christians in their faith. In many cases, one has to doubt whether these conversations really took place.

When the caliphate passed from the Umayyads to the Abbasids in 750, the center of gravity of the Muslim empire shifted from Damascus to Mesopotamia. Caliph al-Mansur founded his new capital Baghdad not far from Seleucia-Ctesiphon in 762. Catholicos Timotheos I (780–823) moved his residence to Baghdad. This gave him access to the Caliphs al-Mahdi (775–85) and Harun al-Rashid (786–809). Timotheos reports of an extensive religious disputation with al-Mahdi in 782/83 in one of his letters. Possibilities and limits of a religious discussion within the framework of Muslim rule become visible here: The catholicos was able to express his Christian convictions, but without making any criticism of Islam. Although he does not recognize Muhammad as a prophet in the sense of Islam, he concedes that he walked "on the path of the prophets" and did much good for the people of the Arabs. The catholicos attributes the victory of the Arabs over the Christian Byzantines to the fact that the Greeks had incurred God's wrath with their heretical creed.

Catholicos Timotheos I reports elsewhere that he was asked by al-Mahdi to translate the Topics of Aristotle into Arabic. Thus, the East Syrians were also involved in the translation of numerous works of classical Greek. Through their knowledge of Greek and Syriac, educated Christians were well equipped for this task. Hunain ibn Ishaq (808–73) in particular stood out as a translator into Arabic. He contributed decisively to the creation of an Arabic scientific language in the field of medicine. His text-critical studies as well as his theory of translation meet the highest standards.

In the course of time, Arabic was increasingly used among East Syrian authors. Ammar al-Basri (ninth century) was the first systematic theologian of his church writing in Arabic. In his *Book of Questions and Answers* he makes an attempt to defend the incarnation of the Son of God exclusively on the ground of reason. From Elias of Nisibis (975–1046) the transcript of seven meetings with a Muslim vizier is preserved, which revolve around religious topics, but also around questions of language and culture. Elias was aware that Christians had to be part of both the Syrian and the Arabic culture. Therefore, he created an Arabic-Syrian dictionary and a world chronicle in both languages. Later theologians of the Church of the East were also familiar with this form of bilingualism.

Monasticism and Mysticism

East Syrian monasticism was inspired by Abraham of Kashkar, who built his monastery on Mount Izla in Northern Mesopotamia (now Southeastern Turkey) in 571. From Mount Izla, the monastic movement spread throughout the Church. A rich spiritual life flourished in these monasteries. The monastic fathers of the early Church were translated into Syriac and influenced the East Syrian spirituality. Evagrius Ponticus, Pseudo-Macarius, and John of Apameia (fourth/fifth century) deserve special mention. Hard asceticism and constant meditation were practiced to reach the inner vision of God.

East Syrian mysticism experienced its heyday in the seventh/eighth century. The spiritual writings of the hermit Isaac of Nineveh (seventh century) were made known beyond the East Syrian Church by Greek translations as early as the ninth century. Today, the works of Isaac have been translated into many languages of the world. They are among the basic texts of Christian spirituality. Isaac devoted his special attention to the so-called "non-prayer," a state of inner contemplation in which all words and discursive intellectual activities are silenced. In this inner space of silence, mystical union can be experienced. Recent textual discoveries show that Isaac further advocated the notion of the redemption of all creatures. The tracts of Joseph Hazzaya (eighth century) show a mature systematic of mystical theology. For him, the ascent to God starts from the contemplation of the humanity of Jesus, which passes into the vision of the light of the Trinity. Similar ideas are encountered in John of Dalyatha (eighth century), whose epistolary corpus contains precious descriptions of his own mystical experience. This form of mysticism, however, was opposed by Catholicos Timotheos I. At a synod in 786/87, the catholicos patriarch condemned the mystics. The condemnation did not last long. It was already revoked by the successor of Timotheos.

The Missionary Church

Christians in the state of Kerala in South India trace themselves back to the mission of the apostle Thomas. Since the sixth century Christian communities in this region are historically verifiable. They belonged to the East Syrian Church and were initially subject to the Metropolitan of Rev Ardashir. There are only a few sources for this period of time. At least cross-stones of the seventh to the ninth centuries in some of Kerala's churches testify to the connection with the East Syrian Church. They are cross reliefs with Persian inscriptions. Under the rule of the Portuguese in sixteenth century, this connection broke down and the Christians of Kerala joined other churches. It was not until the beginning of the twentieth century that a small congregation was re-established. It is under the jurisdiction of the bishop of Thrissur and has about 30,000 members.

Although missionary activities inside the Islamic empire were strictly forbidden, the East Syrian Church became the largest missionary church of the pre-modern era. It became the first "universal church" in the history of Christianity, taking the Christian message as far as to Central Asia, China, and Mongolia. It was Persian merchants who carried the Christian faith to these regions on the trade routes, especially on the famous Silk Road. They were followed by the establishment of monasteries and bishoprics, which formed an ecclesiastical organization spanning almost all of Asia. People of different languages and nations came together in the Apostolic Church of the East. They were held together by a communication network with the catholicos-patriarch at its head and by the unifying bond of the Syriac liturgical language (although parts of the service could be held in the vernacular). A training school for the missionaries was established by Catholicos Timotheos I at the monastery of Bet Abe, where monks were instructed in the languages of the mission areas.

The starting point of the long journey to Central Asia was the bishopric of Merv, located on the Silk Road. From there, the mission led to Transoxania in the sixth century and reached members of Turkish tribes as well as the Soghdians. On the southern route of the Silk Road through the Tarim Basin, Christianity found its way also to the Tibetans in the eighth century. On the northern route of the Silk Road, the oasis of Turfan developed into a center of the Church of the East. The spiritual life of the Christians there is documented by texts found in Dunhuang and Bulayïq.

How East Syrian Christianity found its way into China, we learn from the famous stele of Xi'an. This stele had been erected in 781 in the capital of China under the Tang Dynasty (618–907) and probably belonged to a Christian monastery. It reviews the beginnings of Christianity in China and gives an outline of the Christian doctrine. Thus, we learn that a Syrian monk with the name "Aluoben" had reached China already in 635. The stele continues with an imperial edict that allowed the construction of a monastery in the capital. In its external design, the stele can be described as a document of inculturation. The monument, carved from stone, stands like many other Chinese stelae on the back of a turtle, the symbol of stable world order. At the top, one sees three intertwined pairs of dragons with a pearl as a symbol of the sun. Below, a shield with nine large Chinese characters states the heading: "Stele for the Propagation of the Luminous Religion of Da Qin [the Near East] in the Middle Kingdom." Above the characters a cross is recognizable, which rests between clouds and tree branches on a lotus blossom. Christianity appears here in the garb of symbols from Chinese culture. But also in terms of content, inculturation processes have taken place, as far as we can gather from the few remnants of a Chinese-Christian literature. Besides the inscription of Xi'an, six other texts from the seventh–tenth centuries have survived.

Nevertheless, Christianity does not seem to have succeeded in casting off the character of a foreign religion. Thus, the Church of the East became a victim of the measures taken by Emperor Wuzong (841–46), a convinced Taoist, against the "foreign" religions of his empire. After the banishment of Manichaeism in 843, the emperor issued an edict against Buddhism two years later, which also affected Christians. The first attempt at a Christian mission to China thus failed in 845. The Apostolic Church of the East, however, came back to China when the Mongols under Genghis Khan and his successors conquered the Middle Kingdom in the course of the thirteenth century. This was preceded by missionary successes among a number of Turco-Tatar peoples. There were Christian women even in the family of Genghis Khan. Under him and his successors, we also know of some ministers and army commanders who belonged to the Church of the East.

Mongol armies advanced to Mesopotamia and the Middle East in the middle of the thirteenth century under Hulagu Khan. Baghdad was conquered in 1258. The last caliph from the Abbasid dynasty was assassinated. The conquered territories came under the rule of a Mongol "Ilkhan" (vice king). The Christians of the city were spared during the violent conquest. Under the Mongol rulers, who were initially benevolent towards Christians, the second half of the thirteenth century was to become the—admittedly last—heyday of the Church of the East. The contemporary Syrian Orthodox historian Bar Hebraeus (d. 1286) compared Hulagu, who was a Buddhist, and his Christian wife Doquz Khatun to Constantine and Helena.

The Mongol advance was brought to a halt by the resistance of the Muslim Mamluk rulers of Egypt. In the Battle of Ain Jalut in Galilee in 1260, the Emir Baibars inflicted a decisive defeat on the Mongol armies led by Kitbuqa, an East Syrian Christian.

The Mongols in the Middle East now sought to join forces with the Christian powers of the West. Ilkhan Arghun (1284–91) sent the monk Rabban Sauma (d. 1294) to Europe in 1287. Rabban Sauma belonged to the Uighur people and had lived as a hermit in the mountains north of Beijing before setting out on a pilgrimage to Jerusalem and being taken into service by the Ilkhan of Persia. Rabban Sauma wrote a detailed report in Syriac about his journey to the papal court, to Paris to Philip the Fair of France and to Bordeaux to Edward I of England. Although Rabban Sauma found friendly reception everywhere, his mission brought no concrete political or military results.

It was fateful that Ilkhan Ghazan (1295–1304) converted to Islam and promoted his new religion in every way. Now the Muslims' resentment was vented against the previously favored Christians (as well as against Jews, Zoroastrians, and Buddhists). The catholicos was temporarily imprisoned and tortured, churches were destroyed, and discriminatory regulations against non-Muslims were reintroduced. The now strictly Islamic orientation of the Mongol rulers did not change under Ghazan's successors. The fanatical Timur Lenk (1386–1405), who had set up his residence in Samarkand, devastated the lands from Central Asia to the Middle East and destroyed almost all remnants of East Syrian Christianity during his cruel campaigns.

Meanwhile, in China, Mongol rule had collapsed. The conquest of Khanbaliq and the establishment of the Chinese dynasty of the Ming in 1368 led to the expulsion of all foreign traders and monks. East Syrian Christianity was thus banished from the Middle Kingdom for a second time—and would never return there.

Within only one century, the Apostolic Church of the East had shrunk from a church spanning the vastness of Asia to a few Aramaic-speaking congregations, which essentially retreated to the area around Persian Urmia and to the inaccessible mountains of Kurdistan (the Hakkari Mountains in what is now Southeastern Turkey). Under these highly restricted living and working conditions, the East Syrian Church soon took on the character of a kind of tribal religion. Around the middle of the fifteenth century, the office of the catholicos-patriarch became hereditary in a family and has been passed down from uncle to nephew until the twentieth century. In such a modest form, the Church of the East entered into modern times.

Union with Rome, Western Missionaries, and the Assyrian Nation

In the sixteenth century, a part of the Church entered into a union with Rome. The reason for this was dissatisfaction with the hereditary nature of the patriarchal office. Thus, in 1552, John Sulaqa, the abbot of Rabban Hormizd monastery in the north of the Nineveh Plains, was elected by some bishops as a counter catholicos. The following year, he was formally recognized in Rome by Pope Julius III. After his return to the Middle East, his opponent Shimun VII managed to influence the Ottoman authorities to have John Sulaqa arrested. He died (murdered?) in prison in 1555. Before that, however, he was able to consecrate a couple of bishops. From this point onwards—with interruptions—the Chaldean Church emerged. Its head is based in Baghdad and until recently held the title of a patriarch "of Babylon." In August 2021, the Synod of the Chaldean Church decided to remove this title. The reason given is that Babylon was the capital of the Babylonian Empire, and it never has been an episcopal or patriarchal seat. By the time Christianity came to Mesopotamia, Babylon was already in ruins.

The catholicos-patriarch of the Apostolic Church of the East had taken his seat at the beginning of the nineteenth century in Qudshanis in the Hakkari Mountains. After Protestant missionaries from America encountered Eastern Syrians in Urmia, they also contacted the catholicos. The "discovery" of these last representatives of an independent church of apostolic origin spread rapidly throughout Europe and North America. They were followed by other representatives of Protestant churches, the Anglican Archbishop of Canterbury, and also the Russian Orthodox Church. The Russian mission to the Church of the East was successful in 1897, when some Eastern Syrians converted to the Russian Orthodox Church, not without first renouncing the "Nestorian" heresy. Descendants of these converts still live today in various places in Russia and still cherish the memory of their East Syrian origins.

For the self-image of the East Syrians, the encounter with representatives of the West was not without consequences. The missionaries brought the modern concept of nation to the Middle East. This discourse gave rise to the idea that the members of the Church of the East were descendants of the Assyrians of the ancient Near East. The sensational excavations of Assyrian buildings in northern Iraq had aroused a lively interest in the peoples of the ancient Near East. In the late nineteenth century, leading East Syrian intellectuals adopted this interpretation and began to develop an "Assyrian" national consciousness. It is not incomprehensible that a small and ever-threatened minority should have embraced the past of a powerful people who once dominated the Middle East. The Apostolic Church of the East has incorporated the term "Assyrian" into its self-designation. The Chaldean Church is more restrained in this regard and cultivates a greater awareness of also being part of the Arab cultural world.

Surviving in Difficult Times

At the outbreak of World War I, the Russian Empire declared war on the Ottomans. When the Russian troops had to evacuate northwest Persia for a short time in January 1915, the Christians were considered traitors by the invading Turks. Massacres and looting occurred in Christian villages, with the Turkish army supported by Kurdish volunteers. Some 10,000 Eastern Syrians were killed. When the Russians advanced as far as Van, Patriarch Shimun XIX Benjamin (1903–18) hoped for their support and—as the spiritual and temporal head of his nation—declared war on the Ottoman Empire on May 10, 1915. As the situation in Hakkari became more and more uncertain, the patriarch and the people decided to leave the mountains to seek shelter in Urmia. However, after the October Revolution of 1917, the Russian troops were abruptly withdrawn. In a desperate situation, surrounded by Turkish army units, the Assyrians decided to break through to English-occupied Iraq. There were 70,000 people who went on a forced march of about 500 km to Baghdad. About a third of them were swept away by hunger, epidemics, and Kurdish raids. Thousands more succumbed to the hardships in the Baqubah refugee camp near Baghdad.

Catholicos-Patriarch Shimun XIX Benjamin had already been shot in March 1918 by a Kurdish leader. His brother held the patriarchal office as Shimun XX Paulos until 1920. He died of tuberculosis in the Baqubah camp. Now his nephew, only eleven years old, was installed as Shimun XXI Eshai (1920–75). It was the sister of the two deceased patriarchs, Surma, who safeguarded the rights of the patriarchal family against rival clans. Contrary to all promises made by the British, plans to establish an autonomous area for the Assyrians fell through in the post-war period. Turkey, founded in 1923, forbade the Assyrians to return to Hakkari.

In Iraq, the situation of the fled Assyrians worsened when it became clear that the nascent independent Iraq was unwilling to grant autonomous status to their ethnic group. The government was only willing to recognize the catholicos-patriarch as the spiritual head, but not as the secular leader of his people. However, Shimun XXI Eshai refused to relinquish his civil office powers stemming from the Ottoman period. When Iraq became independent in 1933, a group of Assyrians decided to emigrate to the safer French mandated territory of Syria. On their way to Syria, thousands of Assyrians were massacred by Iraqi troops near Semile. Assyrian settlements in other areas of Iraq were also burned and many of their inhabitants killed. The hatred for the Assyrians that broke out here also had to do with the fact that their people were considered an ally of the British Mandate power. Assyrian combatants had been used by the British to suppress Arab and Kurdish insurgents. Nevertheless, starting in 1934, some Assyrians managed to settle along the Khabur River in northeastern Syria. In memory of the victims of the persecution, August 7, on which the Semile massacre took place in 1933, is celebrated today as a national holiday by Assyrians all over the world.

The catholicos lost his Iraqi citizenship and was expelled from the country. He arrived in the USA via Cyprus. The approximately 20,000 Assyrians who remained in Iraq were settled at the beginning of World War II mainly in the north of the country. Catholicos-Patriarch Shimun XXI Eshai settled in San Francisco in 1954. From there he tried to keep contact with his scattered faithful. Several had followed him into emigration. Assyrians live today in the USA, but also in some European countries. Besides the communities in Iraq, Syria, and Lebanon, there is also a bishopric in Iran. Smaller groups can be found in other countries of the Middle East.

The metropolitan of Trichur in Southern India, Thomas Darmo, spoke out strongly against the hereditary succession of the patriarchal office. He was supported by a group of Assyrians in Iraq who did not want to approve the reforms of the catholicos. Shimun XXI had in fact decreed in 1964 that the Gregorian calendar be introduced in place of the old Julian calendar. He had also ordered a shortening of the fasting periods and liturgical reforms. What seemed to make sense in the West as an adaptation to modern living was regarded as an unauthorized innovation by some Middle Eastern Christians. In addition, there was general discontent that the catholicos did not return to Iraq. Thomas Darmo placed himself at the head of the inner-church opposition and consecrated three bishops in Baghdad in 1968, from whom he was elected as counter catholicos. This schism within the Apostolic Church of the East continues to this day. Thomas Darmo's successor, Addai II, has been in office since 1972 and resides in Baghdad. His old-calendar church includes some 50–70,000 believers in Iraq, Syria, and the United States. Shimun XXI Eshai again caused turmoil when he married an Assyrian woman in 1973. An assembly of bishops in Beirut deposed the catholicos-patriarch. The quarrels ended tragically when a young Assyrian shot the catholicos in his San Francisco home in 1975.

The hereditary nature of the patriarchal dignity, which had endured for five centuries, was thus extinguished. In 1976, six bishops met in London and elected a new head of the church. Mar Dinhka IV (1976–2015) did much to renew his church and opened it to ecumenical dialogue. With Thomas Darmo's successor in Thrissur, Metropolitan Mar Aprem, the reconciliation of the divided Church succeeded at least in India. The dialogue with the Roman Catholic Church led to a first success in 1994, when Mar Dinkha IV and Pope John Paul II signed a Common Christological Declaration. Both sides recognized the legitimacy of the other's theological terminology. This also applies to the titles "Mother of God" and "Mother of Christ," which in substance express the same faith. In 1996, an official process of pastoral and practical cooperation was established between Mar Dinkha IV and the patriarch of the Chaldean Church, Mar Raphael I Bidawid. In July 2001, this rapprochement between the two Churches from the East Syriac tradition led to a major ecumenical breakthrough: an officially permitted limited Eucharistic communion between a Church in communion with Rome and a Church separated from Rome.

The successor of Mar Dinkha IV, Catholicos-Patriarch Gewargis III (2015–20) had been metropolitan of Baghdad since 1981. After his election in 2015, he remained in Iraq and established the patriarchal seat in Ankawa, a suburb of Erbil in northern Iraq. Due to the numerous difficulties in Iraq, many Christians had fled to the north or emigrated altogether. Christians from Mosul were also forced to flee after the Islamic State captured the city in 2014 and also managed to capture parts of the Nineveh Plains. Numerous churches were destroyed or desecrated during this time. Even with the victory over ISIS, the situation in Iraq remains uncertain. The resettlement of Christians to the Nineveh Plains is making slow progress. It is the biggest problem for the Church, that more and more people no longer see a future in Iraq.

On September 8, 2021, a new catholicos-patriarch was elected. He is Mar Awa Royel, who was previously bishop of the diocese of California. He was born in Chicago in 1975, making him the first bishop of the Assyrian Church to be born in the United States. He had obtained a licentiate in sacred theology and a doctorate from the Pontifical Oriental Institute in Rome. His ecumenical openness and direct involvement in fraternal relations with the Catholic Church are well known, which he also took care of his capacity as president of the Commission for Inter-Ecclesial Relations of the Assyrian Church of the East. It is a sign of hope for the Assyrians in Iraq that Mar Awa Royel decided to keep the patriarchal seat in Ankawa.

From there, the catholicos-patriarch leads a Church of about 350,000 members scattered throughout the world. Parishes exist in Iraq, Iran, India, Syria, and other countries of the Middle East, Europe, Caucasus, Northern America, and Australia. This Church has contributed a lot to the Christian heritage of the Middle East. For Christian-Islamic dialogue today, it would still be important to study the theological works of East Syrian authors on Islam. Works of East Syrian monks enrich the spiritual life of many people to this day. The Church remains a model of the spirit of mission and the ability to adapt the Christian faith to other cultures. East Syrian scholars have contributed to the emergence of Arabic sciences. Finally, throughout its history, the East Syrian Church has witnessed the faith even in the most adverse circumstances. Perhaps it is fitting to conclude with the following words of the apostle Paul: "My grace is sufficient for you, for my power is made perfect in weakness." (2 Cor 12:9)

For Further Reading

Becker, Adam H. *Revival and Awakening: American Evangelical Missionaries in Iran and the Origins of Assyrian Nationalism*. Chicago: University of Chicago Press, 2015.

Deeg, Max. *Die strahlende Lehre. Die Stele von Xi'an*. Orientalia-Patristica-Oecumenica 12. Münster: Lit-Verlag, 2018.

Hunter, Erica. "The Holy Apostolic Catholic Assyrian Church of the East." In *Eastern Christianity and Politics in the Twenty-First Century*, edited by Lucian N. Leustean, 601–20. London: Routledge, 2014.

Jenkins, Philip. *The Lost History of Christianity: The Thousand-Year Golden Age of the Church in the Middle East, Africa, and Asia—and How It Died*. New York: Harper One, 2008.

Li Tang. *East Syriac Christianity in Mongol-Yuan China*. Orientalia Biblica et Christiana 18. Wiesbaden: Harrassowitz, 2011.

Wilmshurst, David. *The Martyred Church. A History of the Church of the East*. London: East & West, 2011.

Winkler, Dietmar W., and Wilhelm Baum. *The Church of the East: A Concise History*. London: Routledge, 2003.

10

The Catholic Story

David Bertaina

The Catholic story in the Middle East is seldom investigated. While Middle Eastern Catholics make up a diverse fabric of languages, worship styles, theological traditions, and traditions of fine arts, few Eastern Catholic Churches are known outside of their homelands. Catholics in the Middle East can be better understood through their history, political voice, enduring persecution, dialogue with Muslims, leadership, intellectual and physical contributions to society, and charity in the midst of crises.

There are six Middle Eastern Catholic Churches that have their own patriarchates, whose leaders are elected by their respective synods of bishops: Maronite, Melkite, Armenian, Chaldean, Syriac, and Coptic. Their origins came out of a desire to restore the union of the early Church: "that they may all be one" (John 17:21). Eastern Catholic Churches have their origins in the apostolic churches, although most of them came into communion with Rome during the sixteenth through the eighteenth centuries. During this period the Catholic Church promoted a policy of reintegration through the concepts of reform, return, and reunion (so-called "uniatism"). An Eastern Catholic Church has its origins in an Eastern Church counterpart, except for the Maronites. They are full communion with the Catholic Church, having a dual fidelity to the bishop of Rome and to their own Eastern traditions.

The Catholic Church is made up of particular Churches *sui iuris* ("Churches of their own laws") which are autonomous Churches with discrete liturgical, spiritual, theological, and canonical traditions. Middle Eastern Catholic Churches consist of a community of faithful, with their own hierarchy, and are recognized by the Catholic Church as autonomous and part of the wider communion. According to the two-lungs model advocated by Pope John Paul II (*Orientale Lumen*, 1995), Eastern Catholic Churches help the Catholic Church embody a fuller likeness of catholicity, that is, the universality of the whole Church, united in a common faith, sacraments, and governance as particular Churches equal in dignity. Each particular Church also has its own doctrine, history, sacred space, language(s), and lived experience.

The process to reach this understanding had a difficult history. Initially, during the thirteenth to the fifteenth centuries, the Catholic Church sought to achieve reunion through a conciliar approach. But the proclaimed unions that were achieved at the Council of Florence from 1438–45 between Catholics and various Eastern delegations were not received in the Christian East. The results gave rise to a different approach to ecclesiastical union by the Roman Catholic Church after the Council of Trent. (The Maronites, who had been in official union with the Latin Church since 1182, were a model for this approach.) By the sixteenth century, policies were enacted to allow individual Eastern Churches to "return" to Rome, while retaining their rites and traditions. These discussions of cooperation and communion went in both directions and were often started on the initiative of pro-Catholic Middle Eastern Christians.

By 1834, the Ottoman Empire gave recognition to some Eastern Catholic Churches in their realm, constituting their own millet, or autonomous grouping. In 1862, Pope Pius IX established the Congregation of Oriental Rites. Pope Leo XIII emphasized better relations through his encyclical *Orientalium Dignitas* (1894), although Latinization endured in some cases. Pope Benedict XV established the Congregation for the Eastern Churches in 1917. Pope Pius XI published *Rerum Orientalium* (1928) to promote the study of the Eastern Churches, and reinvigorated the Pontifical Oriental Institute in Rome, perhaps the most important center for Eastern Catholic studies. *Orientalium Ecclesiarum* from Vatican II emphasized the historic rights, privileges, disciplines, and spiritual heritage of the Eastern Churches. More recently, Eastern Catholics have been left in an awkward position in relation to their Roman Catholic brethren and Orthodox counterparts. Middle Eastern Catholics are a resource for ecumenical dialogue and engagement with Islam, but they are also perceived as a historical anomaly and problematic for relations with Orthodox Christians. No longer a model for reunion or a bridge for communion in the twenty-first century, Eastern Catholics have sometimes felt an identity crisis in a new ecumenical world. Eastern Catholic theologians such as Antoine Audo emphasize that they should refuse to be considered strangers in their own land, or second-class citizens under Islam, or succumb to an ideology of victimhood.[1] Middle Eastern Catholics remain a sign of visible unity between the Catholic and Eastern Churches. Their identity as a people of spiritual ecumenism, holiness, service, dialogue,

---

1. Audo, "Eastern Christian Identity," 19–35.

and immigration were key themes of Pope Benedict's apostolic exhortation *Ecclesia in Medio Oriente* (2012).

Middle Eastern Catholics sometimes share daily practices with their Orthodox counterparts as well as other Eastern Catholic communities. These activities include liturgical celebrations, requests for sacraments, mixed marriages, processions, festivals, the veneration of saints and relics, and other activities that suggest ecclesiastical boundaries are more porous in practice than in theory. Today, Middle Eastern Catholics have special charisms that focus on understanding and appreciating their Eastern heritage, developing models of intercultural openness, and working as facilitators of ecumenical dialogue. There are also pastoral challenges facing the Middle Eastern Catholic Churches, such as assimilation to other cultures, geo-political controversies, and emigration—50 percent of all "Middle Eastern" Catholics live in the global diaspora. In response, Middle Eastern Catholics are focusing on their liturgical worship, educational formation, synodal autonomy, care for immigrants/emigrants, and ecumenism as the main areas where they can positively contribute to the life of the Catholic Church.

There are four rites represented by Middle Eastern Catholics:

1. the Armenian liturgy celebrated in classical Armenian,
2. the Byzantine liturgy used in Arabic by the Melkites,
3. the Coptic liturgy celebrated in the Bohairic dialect of Coptic and Arabic, and
4. the Syriac liturgies practiced by the Chaldeans, the Syriac Catholics, and Maronites.

The Chaldean liturgy is of Edessan origin and utilizes East Syriac, while the Syriac Catholics and Maronites use West Syriac in their liturgies of Antiochene origin, along with Arabic.

The Maronite Church

The origins of the Syriac-speaking Maronites, who are predominant in Lebanon, are traced to Saint Maron (d. 410) and the monastery named after him.[2] Founded in the fifth century, the monastery supported Chalcedonian theology among Syriac speakers. These Syriac Christians were in contact with Pope Hormisdas (514–32) regarding violence against their

---

2. For all data in this section, including bibliography and statistics, see the Congregation for the Eastern Churches publication in Farrugia, et al., *The Catholic East*, 215–51.

monasteries. Later during the Acacian schism, Syriac Chalcedonians supported the bishop of Rome. They received letters of solidarity from the pope in 518 and again in 535 from Pope Agapetus I. By the sixth century, the monastery of Saint Maron was the governing center of Syriac-speaking Chalcedonian Christians in the region. After the Council of Constantinople (680–81), the Syriac Chalcedonians of Saint Maron monastery accepted Heraclius' proposal to unify the empire with a monothelite (one will) doctrine of Jesus Christ in contrast to the dyothelite (two wills) position held by other Syriac Chalcedonians (Melkites). In the mid-eighth century, the Umayyad Caliph Marwan II permitted the Syriac Chalcedonians to select their own Maronite patriarch. During the period from the eighth to eleventh centuries, Maronites emigrated from parts of the Middle East to the regions of Lebanon, Antioch, and Aleppo. By 939, the Maronite patriarchate was relocated in Lebanon and Saint Maron monastery was abandoned due to repeated raids. When the crusaders arrived at Tripoli, they encountered these Maronite Christians. The Maronite Patriarch Youssif al-Jurjissi sent envoys to Rome in 1100, and in 1131 the Maronite leadership affirmed their communion with the Latin Church. Although they did not participate in the excommunications of the Byzantine Orthodox in 1054, the Maronites formalized their communion with the Latin Church in 1182. Patriarch Jeremiah al-Amshiti (d. 1230) attended the Fourth Lateran Council of 1215. The Lateran Council determined the Eastern patriarchs would receive the pallium from the bishop of Rome, who would recognize his jurisdiction in the Middle East.

Frankish-Maronite relations continued in the thirteenth century through the Franciscans. Many of the final crusader holdouts were in Maronite lands in Lebanon, and so they were often the victims of violence and persecution. During this period, the Maronites became more concentrated in Lebanon, and contact with Rome was discouraged by Mamluk Muslim rulers. In 1439 at the Council of Florence, the Maronite Patriarch John al-Jaji reaffirmed their communion with Rome but the patriarchate was forced to move to Our Lady of Qannubin monastery in 1440. In the sixteenth century, the French signed an agreement with the Ottomans promising safety for Roman Catholics in Ottoman lands, which was extended to Maronites. The Counter Reformation Council of Trent also led to the founding of the Maronite College in Rome in 1584. The Maronite College led to the formation of an educated and multilingual clergy in Lebanon who were influential in many fields pertaining to the study of the Bible and Eastern Christianity. This group introduced the first Arabic printing press in the Middle East. They taught Arabic and Syriac at Western universities, and they helped to develop collections of Eastern Christian manuscripts at libraries across Europe. The most famous products of the Maronite College included patriarch and historian Stephen al-Duwayli (d. 1704), and Joseph Simon Assemani (d. 1768), author of the *Bibliotheca Orientalis* on Syriac literature.

In 1736, the Lebanese synod reorganized Maronite canon law, liturgy, and the jurisdiction of its bishops and patriarch. They also set up a strategic plan for the establishment of schools in cities, villages, and monasteries. Lebanon became an educational hub with Ain Warqa College and Seminary as a major center. Maronite religious orders were instrumental in this success. Maronites even gained converts from Sunni and Druze members who were impressed by the educational and financial success of the Maronites. A disastrous setback occurred, however, when Druze and Sunni Muslims killed nearly 8,000 Maronites and destroyed hundreds of villages, churches, and schools between 1859–61. The following year, European powers stepped in and established Mount Lebanon as a semi-autonomous region.

After the First World War, the Maronites advocated for an independent Lebanon, which would include its historic borders and not just the mountainous Christian-majority area. This was agreed upon and set up by the French Mandate established in 1920. Greater Lebanon added many Muslims and Druze to its population, making it a religiously plural nation. Lebanon gained independence in 1943, and the democracy required a Christian president. During Vatican II, the Maronite Church was encouraged to remove Latinizations from its liturgy and rediscover its ancient Syriac Antiochene traditions and heritage. Lebanese Christianity was paralyzed by political conflict, however, due to the Lebanese civil war from 1975–89. In 1997, John Paul II made the first official papal visit to Lebanon. Beginning in 2005, the Maronite patriarchate initiated a comprehensive plan for emphasizing worship service in line with the Syriac heritage.

The Maronite patriarchate has led the Assembly of the Catholic Patriarchs and Bishops in Lebanon. The Maronites are also a member of the Middle Eastern Council of Churches (all Eastern Catholic Churches joined in 1990). The Council of Catholic Patriarchs of the Orient, including all six Eastern Catholic patriarchs and the Latin patriarch of Jerusalem, is an important group that addresses wider pastoral issues. Its headquarters are at the Maronite patriarchate in Bkerke. The Maronites are organized into eparchies in Lebanon (ten), Syria (three), Israel, Cyprus, and Cairo. There are another ten eparchies around the world.

There are three Maronite religious orders for men: the Maronite Lebanese Order, the Maronite Order of the Blessed Virgin Mary (Mariamite), and the Antonine Maronite Order. Religious sisters have their own Lebanese and Antonine counterparts along with three other orders. Maronite spirituality is devoted to the monastic tradition, the study of scripture, the Syriac tradition,

Marian devotions, and the veneration of holy saints, including Maron and Sharbel Makhlouf (d. 1878), whose intercession is widely sought for miracles. Maronites are also devoted to Mary's assumption at a shrine in Harissa. Maronites have four seminaries, with three in Lebanon and one in Washington, DC. Maronites have established several important universities, the most famous being Holy Spirit University in Kaslik, and Notre Dame University in Louaize. They also run 325 schools for more than 200,000 students and have six hospitals in Lebanon. Maronites are estimated to have 1.3 million members in the Middle East (3.5 million total).[3]

The Melkite Greek Catholic Church

Melkites are the Chalcedonian Christians of the patriarchates of Antioch, Jerusalem, and Alexandria.[4] Their support for Chalcedon in 451 later resulted in their community being named as those who were faithful to the emperor, hence the Aramaic *malka* (Arabic *malik*) became their title: Melkite, or royalists. While primarily using Syriac until the Arab conquest, this group adopted Arabic and retained some Greek in medieval times. In origin their liturgy came from Antioch, but due to Byzantine Orthodox connections and Jerusalem liturgies, it became hybridized. The Church of Antioch held communion with the Byzantine Orthodox and the Roman Catholic Church. Melkites such as Theodore Abu Qurra (d. after 830) even wrote a defense of the bishops of Rome as guarantors of the Church councils and apostolic faith. When the Schism of 1054 occurred between Roman papal and Constantinopolitan Orthodox parties, Patriarch Peter III confirmed dual communion with both. During the Crusades, Melkites retained their jurisdictions and shared churches with Latin-rite Catholics. By the sixteenth century, there began to be a closer connection between the Arab Orthodox and the Catholics of the Middle East, resulting in a double association that renewed the affirmation of the Council of Florence for union. Patriarchs were known to send their election confirmations to Rome in this period.

By the 1720s, double communion by the Melkites of the patriarchate of Antioch had come to an end, forbidden by the Orthodox (1722) and Catholics (1729). A pro-Catholic party emerged among these Orthodox Christians. In 1724, the synod elected Cyril VI, who supported the Catholic party. Another synod then met and selected the pro-Greek Antiochene Orthodox

---

3. All demographic data in this chapter is taken from the 2019 *Annuario Pontificio* as reported in Farrugia, et al., *The Catholic East*, xv.

4. For all data in this section, see the Congregation for the Eastern Churches publication in Farrugia, et al., *The Catholic East*, 187–214.

Sylvester as patriarch, resulting in a split of the Church. Consequently, the Melkite Greek Catholic Church traces it origins back to apostolic times but became an official particular Catholic Church in 1724.

Cyril VI Tanas served 1724–59 and Melkites maintained their liturgical practices while acknowledging communion with Rome. However, the Ottomans would not recognize the Melkites. The patriarchs had to govern from the mountainous regions of Lebanon at Holy Savior, St. John, and Chouer and later at Ain Traz in the nineteenth century. In 1838, the cities of Alexandria and Jerusalem were added to the patriarch's title along with Antioch, in order to reflect Melkite jurisdiction throughout the Middle East. By the mid-nineteenth century, European diplomats were able to coerce the Ottomans into recognizing the Melkites, and they continued to stay close to Orthodox practice under Maximos III Mazloum (d. 1855). Melkite Patriarch Gregory II Youssef (d. 1897) was an important contributor at Vatican I, calling for nothing new to be introduced contravening Eastern Church doctrine and preserving their patriarchal prerogatives, rights, and liturgical practices. By the time of Vatican II, Melkite Patriarch Maximos IV Sayegh (d. 1967) was an influential speaker for episcopal collegiality, ecumenism, and explaining how the Eastern Churches reflected the catholicity of the Church. In the twenty-first century, Melkites such as Patriarch Gregory III Laham have continued to promote ecumenical relations among Middle Eastern Christians.

Melkites are not identified with a specific homeland and are found throughout the Middle East, including Syria, Lebanon, Jordan, Israel-Palestine, and many other emigrant communities in the world. In the Middle East, they have eparchies in Lebanon (seven), Syria (five), Israel, Jordan, Iraq/Kuwait, and Africa, along with several in the diaspora. Their bishops are all united by a synod. The patriarch resides in Damascus and the Archeparchy is the location for the annual Melkite synod, which addresses issues of liturgy, ecumenism, and policy matters. They have close relations with their counterpart, the Orthodox Church of Antioch. In some cases, the two communities have issued joint ecumenical statements and shared religious spaces. The Melkites have created youth organizations, as well as catechetical centers for religious instruction at parishes. In terms of media, the Melkite Church publishes a journal, *Le Lien*, and *al-Maçarrat* is published by the Missionary Society of Saint Paul.

Melkites have diaspora communities in the Americas (USA, Canada, Brazil, Argentina, Venezuela, and Mexico) and in Australia and New Zealand, making up nearly 900,000 members. The Melkite clergy have also translated many texts from Arabic into English to make the tradition more accessible to emigrants. The Seminary of St. Anne is located in Rabouè,

Lebanon. Religious orders include the Basilian Order of the Most Holy Savior (Salvatorians), the Chouerite Basilians, and the Aleppan Basilians. Their main vocations include parish work, ecumenical relations, homes for the needy, including orphans, technical schools, and educational publishing. The Missionary Society of Saint Paul began in 1902 and focuses on preaching evangelization, and ecumenism and has a seminary and headquarters at Harissa, Lebanon. They have a counterpart in the Missionaries of Our Lady of Perpetual Help, founded in 1936. The Chouerite Sisters, Basilian Salvatorian Sisters, and the Aleppian Sisters focus on education, hospitals, and other charitable works. The Melkite Greek Catholic Church is a member of the Council of the Catholic Patriarchs of the Orient and the Middle East Council of Churches. Melkites number around 630,000 in the Middle East and 1.56 million worldwide.

The Armenian Catholic Church

The Armenian Catholic Church is descended from the Armenian Apostolic Church of Cilicia.[5] Armenians are an anomaly in the Middle East, since they are not Arab (nor even Semitic), nor Muslim, and their Christian practices differ from others as well. Along with the genocide perpetrated against the Armenians, these differences have made their history one of minority status and martyrdom.

The first contact between the Armenian Church and Catholics after their doctrinal differences in the late antique period came during the Crusades with the Armenians of the Kingdom of Cilicia. Pope Nicholas I probably exchanged messages with the Armenian leader Ashot I. At the Council of Florence in 1439, the Armenian delegation and Catholic Church announced a reunion, although it was not widely received. However, while there was no patriarchate to formalize this action, some Armenian bishops joined in communion with the Latin-rite Church, especially in Eastern Europe and in Mardin. Rome and Venice had Armenian Catholic communities. In 1740, the patriarchate of Cilicia elected the Armenian bishop of Aleppo, Abraham Ardzivian as catholicos-patriarch. He went to Rome and was acknowledged by Pope Benedict XIV as patriarch and Armenian Catholics officially established their Catholicosate of Cilicia in 1742. Since the Armenian Apostolic Church held sway in the Ottoman Empire, Patriarch Bedros I Ardzivian made Lebanon the spiritual center for Armenian Catholics with jurisdiction in Cilicia, Syria, and Lebanon.

---

5. For all data in this section, see the Congregation for the Eastern Churches publication in Farrugia, et al., *The Catholic East*, 283–319.

Armenian Catholics in the diocese of Constantinople were under a Latin vicariate until 1829 when they were granted status as a recognized religious community. In 1866, the Armenian Catholic patriarchate of Cilicia united with the Apostolic patriarchate of Constantinople, and the patriarchate was moved there. They remained there until the Armenian massacres, which led to the deaths of perhaps 100,000 Armenian Catholics (out of 1–1.5 million total). At this point the patriarchate moved back to Lebanon. In 1883, the Pontifical Armenian College was created in Rome at the behest of Patriarch Andon Hassoun. Among the most famous Armenian Catholic leaders was Patriarch Krikor Bedros XV, who was made a cardinal and supported the construction of many churches and schools and was named the first delegate of Vatican II in 1962. Due to the civil war in Lebanon from 1975–90, many Armenian Catholics left for the diaspora and their numbers in the Middle East declined. Some went to the Republic of Armenia, and others to Eastern Europe and to the West. Armenian Catholics now have formalized relations with the Catholicosate of Etchmiadzin.

The Armenian Catholic Church has Middle Eastern eparchies in Syria (three), Egypt, Iran, Iraq, Lebanon, Palestine-Jordan, Turkey, and Armenia. Armenian Catholics have held regular synods in recent decades focused on Church law and updating liturgical texts. They have a Patriarchal Institute and Seminary in Lebanon dating to 1759 and the Pontifical Armenian College in Rome (1885) has been a key center for leadership in the Church. Armenian monasticism is preserved by the Mekhitarists. Named after Mekhitar, he founded a religious institute in 1700 dedicated to education and the publication of books. Forced to flee Constantinople, he gathered disciples near Venice and organized his order in 1711. They have two centers at the Monastery of San Lazzaro in Venice and a monastery in Vienna. There is also a group of Armenian Catholic Sisters of the Immaculate Conception focused on education of youth and care for the needy. There are around 600,000 Armenian Catholics in the Middle East if one includes Armenian territory, and 757,000 globally.

The Chaldean Catholic Church

The Chaldean Catholic Church has its origins in the Eastern Syriac Christianity of Iraq, known as the Church of the East, which was first evangelized by the apostles Thomas and Thaddeus (Addai).[6] Chaldeans use Syriac, a dialect of Aramaic, in their liturgies and some individuals still speak modern

---

6. For all data in this section, see the Congregation for the Eastern Churches publication in Farrugia, et al., *The Catholic East*, 253–82.

neo-Aramaic. The term "Chaldean" is somewhat anachronistic as it refers to an ancient biblical group of the region. It was applied to East Syriac Christians in the fifteenth century, identifying them as the heirs of the Magi who came from the East to worship the birth of Jesus Christ. By the eighteenth century, "Chaldean" came to be used to refer to the Syriac Christians who were united to Rome, and it became the official title in 1818.

The emergence of the Chaldean Catholic Church is complex. The Church of the East first encountered Catholic missionaries traveling eastward including William of Rubruck (d. 1270), Riccoldo da Monte di Croce (d. 1320), and John of Montecorvino (d. 1328). John even brought a letter from Pope Nicholas IV to Catholicos Yaballaha III to establish relations. In 1340, a group from the Church of the East came into communion with Rome, as well as the group from Cyprus in 1445, but serious discussion only developed after the massacres by Tamerlane and the refugee communities which remained in northern Mesopotamia, Mosul, and Urmia. In this period, the patriarch came to be determined through a line of succession kept to a single family, passing from the patriarch to one of his nephews. Due to the policies of a hereditary patriarch, a protest group selected their own leader, Patriarch Yohannon Sulaqa. He went to Rome with a delegation, and confirmed communion with Pope Julius III in 1553. His successor Abdisho IV Maron (d. 1570) also traveled to Rome and their Chaldean Church continued until the seventeenth century, when Shimun XIII Dinkha (d. 1700) moved the patriarchate to the mountains of Hakkari and lost contact with Rome. The modern Assyrian Church of the East descends from this patriarchal line. Interestingly, the hereditary line of patriarchs held a synod in 1616 affirming Catholic Christology after sending two delegations to Rome. Then in 1672, Metropolitan Joseph of Amid affirmed the Catholic faith and was confirmed in 1681 as patriarch of the Chaldeans. Thus, there were three East Syriac communities. When Joseph V of Amid died, he was not replaced and instead united with the Mosul patriarchate centered at Rabban Hormizd monastery. Yohanon Hormizd, who was the metropolitan of Mosul and a self-professed Catholic, was confirmed as patriarch of Babylon for the Chaldeans by Pope Pius VIII in 1830, and this patriarchal line has remained in communion with the Catholic Church.

In 1844, the Chaldean Catholic Church received recognition as a religious community by the Ottoman Empire. Among its most important figures were Joseph VI Audo (d. 1878), who supported Eastern Church rights and privileges at Vatican I. He established a seminary in Mosul. His successor Emmanuel II Thomas was patriarch for forty-seven years (1900–1947) as the Chaldeans became the largest East Syriac group in Iraq. However, the Chaldeans (like the Armenians) suffered through the massacres committed during the First World War that resulted in the deaths of around 20,000 people. In the second half of the twentieth century, many Chaldeans moved from Mosul to Baghdad and major cities in Iraq, although violence due to ethnic, religious, and political factors meant there was no area with lasting stability. Due to the Iraq wars and the Islamic State, the Christian population in Iraq has dropped from 20 percent to less than 5 percent as many Christians have emigrated for other places in the Middle East, Europe, and the United States.

The Chaldeans have had close connections with their counterparts in the Church of the East. In 1994, they signed a common Christological Agreement with the Catholic Church and both patriarchs signed a joint statement in 1996 for further cooperation. In some cases, communion between Chaldeans and Assyrians is considered acceptable. Most Chaldeans live in northern Iraq in the Mosul region and in Baghdad. They have dioceses in Iraq (eight), Iran, Lebanon, Syria, Egypt, Turkey, and the United States (two). Chaldeans run St. Peter's Patriarchal Seminary in Baghdad and Babel College since 1990. The Chaldeans have a longstanding monastic tradition. The Antonine Order of St. Hormisdas of the Chaldeans was founded by Gabriel Dembo, although he was martyred in 1834 prior to its recognition. The monks have the monastery of St. Anthony in Baghdad and publish on East Syriac monasticism. The Chaldean Congregation of the Daughters of Mary Immaculate serve in education, orphanages, and charitable service areas. The Congregation of the Daughters of the Sacred Heart of Jesus focus on the education of women and have seven houses in Iraq. Statistics for Chaldean Catholics are difficult to project accurately due to recent conflicts and emigration from Iraq, but it is estimated that there are 300,000 members in the Middle East and 628,000 worldwide.

The Syriac Catholic Church

The Syriac Catholic Church has its origins in Antioch and the local Semitic peoples who spoke Syriac.[7] During the Crusader era, relations between the Syriac Orthodox Church and Latin-rite Catholics were cordial, although they held different Christological positions. For instance, the famous polymath Gregory Bar Hebraeus (Abu al-Faraj) communicated with Catholics, while the historian Patriarch Michael I was even invited to the Third Lateran Council in 1179. In 1183, the Syriac Orthodox Christians living in Jerusalem came into communion with the Latin Church and in 1237, the Syriac

---

7. For all data in this section, see the Congregation for the Eastern Churches publication in Farrugia, et al., *The Catholic East*, 163–86.

Orthodox Patriarch Ignatius III (d. 1252) negotiated union with Rome, although it was mostly rejected by Syriac Orthodox communities. When the crusader presence in the Middle East was extinguished, the era of close contact paused. In 1444, a Syriac Orthodox delegation signed papers of union with Rome at the Council of Florence, but the decree did not result in a Syriac Catholic hierarchy or community. Diplomatic negotiations continued, with an attempted agreement between Patriarch Nemet Aloho and Pope Pius IV, but Ottoman fears of collaboration nixed the effort. Western religious orders continued to develop amenable relations, and by the seventeenth century, some Syriac Orthodox had formed a pro-Catholic party within the Church. The Syriac Orthodox Church even selected a Syriac Catholic, Andrew Akhijan, as archbishop of Aleppo, but his consecration was carried out by the Maronite patriarch, technically making him a Maronite archbishop. Through French diplomatic influence and missionaries, Andrew was eventually installed with Ottoman acknowledgment in 1662. The Syriac pro-Catholic sentiment in the Orthodox Church led to disputes over his successor and the Syriac Orthodox were able to displace the pro-Catholic party after his death. But in 1782, Michael Jarweh, the Syriac Orthodox archbishop of Aleppo, was nominated and elected as Syriac patriarch of Antioch. Michael publicly accepted Catholicism, and so with his election, he and four other bishops joined in communion with Rome. Thus, the Syriac Catholic patriarchate of Antioch was established. However, the Ottomans rejected this election which forced Patriarch Michael to take refuge in Sharfeh, Lebanon, where he led Syriac Catholics until 1801. The patriarchate continued, and eventually the Ottomans were forced to recognize Syriac Catholics in 1830. During the First World War, many Syriac Catholics, like their fellow Armenian and Chaldean Christians, were massacred and had their churches and possessions destroyed. These events led Ignatius Ephrem II Rahman (d. 1929) to move the patriarchate to Beirut. He was a famous scholar who founded a number of schools as well as the Order of Sisters of St. Ephrem. Ignatius Gabriel I Tappouni guided Syriac Catholics from 1929 to 1965 by building up infrastructure in Sharfeh and Beirut. Due to mass emigration from the Middle East in the twentieth century, many Syriac Catholic concerns are centered on the global community.

Syriac Catholics use the Syriac liturgy of Antioch, the West Syriac script for texts (Serto), and Arabic for daily use in the Middle East. Some speak modern Syriac (Sureth). Due to violence, Syriac Catholics continue to be displaced. They have a Seminary in Sharfeh that is affiliated with the University of the Holy Spirit in Kaslik. As for religious life, there is the Syriac Catholic monastery of Dayr Mar Musa al-Habashi in Syria. The Ephremite Sisters are active in Lebanon and Syria, including running an orphanage.

Syriac Catholics have dioceses in Iraq (four), Syria (four), Lebanon, and Palestine/Jordan. They number around 120,000 in the Middle East, although this number may be difficult to ascertain due to violence and emigration. There are an estimated 195,000 Syriac Catholics globally.

The Coptic Catholic Church

The Copts are Egyptians descended from the native population.[8] As a Miaphysite Oriental Orthodox Church, the Coptic Orthodox renewed encounters with Catholics during the Crusades, including Saint Francis and the Franciscans during the thirteenth century. The first attempts at reunion between the Coptic Orthodox Church and the Roman Catholic Church began at the Council of Florence when a Coptic delegation signed an agreement in 1442, although this decree of union was not accepted in Egypt. In 1739, the Coptic bishop of Jerusalem, who was living in Cairo, became Catholic and was put in charge of Coptic Catholics living in the area. Afterwards, Saleh Maraghi was named apostolic administrator for this group. Bishop Raphael Tuki was given the right to ordain Coptic Catholic priests in 1761, and in the same year Antonios Fleifel, a convert from Coptic Orthodoxy, was named as apostolic vicar. The Ottomans did not recognize the Catholic Copts as a religious community and they could not build or worship in their own churches until 1829. This line of Coptic Catholics was under the care of the Franciscans until the First World War.

While there were Coptic Catholics who were part of the Catholic Church from 1741, the official establishment of a patriarchate of Alexandria in communion with Rome only appeared in 1895–1908. During this period, several Latin-rite churches were turned over to Coptic Catholics. George Makarios was named apostolic vicar as Cyril II and traveled to Rome where Leo XIII consented to a Coptic Catholic patriarchate of Alexandria in 1895. An official synod was held promoting him to the position in 1899, although he resigned at the behest of Rome in 1908 and the patriarchate was to remain vacant until 1947. During the twentieth century, Coptic Catholics emigrated from Egypt across the globe. There are eleven Coptic Catholic communities outside the Middle East.

Coptic Catholics have a seminary in Maadi, near Cairo, and they make use of the Pontifical Oriental Institute in Rome for clergy formation. Coptic religious orders include the Egyptian Franciscan Province, the Egyptian Sisters of the Sacred Heart, which has founded thirteen schools, the Coptic

---

8. For all data in this section, see the Congregation for the Eastern Churches publication in Farrugia, et al., *The Catholic East*, 149–62.

Sisters of Jesus & Mary, and the Fraternity of the Little Sisters of Jesus. The Coptic Catholic Church has seven eparchies, all located in Egypt: Alexandria, Ismailia, Giza, Minya, Asyut, Sohag, and Luxor. Data for the Coptic Catholics indicates they have approximately 187,000 members in Egypt.

The Latin-Rite Roman Catholic Church in the Middle East

The Roman Catholic Church of the Latin-rite has always had a presence in the Middle East. This connection goes back to the founding of the first churches and care for Western pilgrims traveling to holy sites. Connections were enhanced by the crusader states and continue under the custodianship of the Franciscans of the Holy Land.[9] The patriarchate of Jerusalem remained in communion with the bishop of Rome over the first millennium until a Latin patriarch was named in 1099. In 1342, Pope Clement VI named the Franciscans as the Custodians of the Holy Land for Catholic sacred sites. In later times, Roman Catholic communities were cared for by the Franciscans, Dominicans, Jesuits, Capuchins, Lazarists (Vincentians), Theatines, Passionists, Redemptorists, and other religious orders. While these Roman Catholic missionary orders were catalysts in the formation of Catholicism in the Middle East, it is also important to note that Middle Easterners themselves played the decisive role in the formation, development, growth, and endurance of the Eastern Catholic Churches and that most Latin-rite Catholics were of Middle Eastern origin.

In 1622, Pope Gregory XV put all Latin-rite Catholics in the Middle East under the care of the Congregation for the Propagation of the Faith, which was to coordinate missionary activities by the religious orders and work with Eastern Catholics. The Roman Catholic leadership in the East was coordinated by the patriarchal apostolic vicar in Constantinople. In general, Roman Catholics were administered by religious orders already active in these regions. These orders were dedicated to establishing parishes, schools, and hospitals to help the infrastructure of the Christian East. One feature of Roman Catholicism by the early modern era was that it was pluralistic in terms of languages, ethnicities, and social statuses. Even Constantinople was home to colonies of Genoese, Venetians, and French Catholics, while converts from Syriacs, Arabs, and other groups also joined the Roman Catholic communities. During the nineteenth century, the disintegration of Ottoman hegemony over the Middle East and Eastern Europe led to Catholic reliance on vicars for guidance. These administrative centers were located in Constantinople, Asia

---

9. For all data in this section, see the Congregation for the Eastern Churches publication in Farrugia, et al., *The Catholic East*, 693–782.

Minor, Syria, Egypt, Persia, and Mesopotamia. In 1847, the Latin Catholic patriarchate of Jerusalem was restored to organize educational and spiritual affairs for Roman Catholics in the Middle East.

Catholic religious orders continued to be a driving force for Latin-rite parishes, monasteries, schools, and hospitals in the Middle East. Women's missionary orders also demonstrated agency in connecting Roman Catholics and Eastern Christians. Some key orders were the Jesuits in Syria and Lebanon, as well as the Carmelites, Lazarists, Capuchins, and Trappists. In the Holy Land, in addition to the Franciscans of the Custody of the Holy Land, there were Carmelites, Dominicans, Assumptionists, Missionaries of the Sacred Heart, the Salesians, and the Christian Brothers. Female orders serving included the Poor Clares, Congregation of Our Lady of Sion, Scalabrinians, Sisters of Charity, Sisters of Mary Reparatrix, and several others. In short, members of Catholic religious orders from the era of the Crusades until the present have exerted a decisive role in Catholic life in the Middle East. At the same time, the zeal of Western religious orders and their institutions (parishes, schools, hospitals, orphanages) also brought Latinization and controversy with other Eastern Catholic groups, and suspicion among Orthodox, Oriental Orthodox, and Muslim groups. But they also helped gain concessions and protections for Catholics.

The events of the First World War and the massacres committed against Eastern Christians also depopulated Constantinople (renamed Istanbul) and Asia Minor of its Catholic communities. Turkish policies resulted in the closure of schools, the removal of autonomy for religious orders, and the Latin-rite Catholic presence has declined since that time. In the Middle East, the Sykes-Picot Agreement of 1916 put Lebanon and Syria under the French Mandate while the British Mandate encompassed Palestine, Transjordan, and Iraq. The Congregation for the Eastern Churches became the primary link between the Vatican and the Middle Eastern Roman Catholics, along with the other Eastern Catholic Churches. With the nationalist declarations of independence after the Second World War, Latin-rite Catholics were in a precarious situation as minorities who were perceived as foreign others. The rise of anti-Western rhetoric, birthrate declines, and emigration all led to challenges for Roman Catholics in the Middle East over the course of the latter half of the twentieth century.

The Latin patriarchate of Jerusalem has a complicated relationship with Israel, since its faithful are largely Arabs. The patriarch, papal nuncios, and Franciscan custodian are the main figures representing the Roman Catholic Church's interests in the region. Roman Catholics promoted educational initiatives through the Franciscan Biblical Institute, the Dominican École Biblique, the Jesuit Pontifical Biblical Institute, the St.

Anne Center, and the Tantur Ecumenical Institute. Many religious orders remain active and cultivate education and study in the region. In Lebanon, Roman Catholics have tended to be associated with higher social status and French culture. Their main agency comes through education, such as at the Université Saint-Joseph and Notre Dame de Jamhour. In Syria, Roman Catholics are concentrated in Aleppo, Damascus, and Latakia. In Iraq, most reside in Baghdad. In Egypt, Roman Catholics have three dioceses and in Cairo there is the Franciscan Center of Eastern Christian Studies and the Dominican Institute of Eastern Studies (IDEO). In addition to the patriarchal diocese of Jerusalem, the Roman Catholic Church has apostolic vicariates (Lebanon, Syria, Turkey, Egypt, Jordan), and archdioceses (Iraq, Turkey) in the Middle East. The Latin-rite liturgies tend to be in Arabic (although many global languages are used for pilgrims).

Middle Eastern Catholics are active in charitable works, including education, healthcare, social services, and spiritual care. There are approximately 400 institutions, many of which draw support from local Catholics, not foreign missionaries. Many of them are organized under the Assembly of Organizations for Aid to the Oriental Churches (https://www.orientchurch.va/roaco). Some of these charitable institutions include the Catholic Near East Welfare Association, Pontifical Mission for Palestine, Caritas International, Aid to the Church in Need, the Equestrian Order of the Holy Sepulchre of Jerusalem, and more than a dozen other groups from the United States, Germany, France, Belgium, Netherlands, Switzerland, and the Vatican. There are a number of educational institutions run by the Roman Catholic Church in the Middle East, from primary and secondary schools to universities and professional programs. Two of the most notable include Bethlehem University run by the Christian Brothers and the Jesuit Université Saint-Joseph in Beirut.

Middle Eastern Catholics help the Catholic Church express more clearly the greater Truth of Jesus Christ through their living traditions, connections to sacred spaces, and clearly articulated identities. Yet they face many challenges, including political conflicts and extremist violence, discrimination, matters of freedom of religion and conscience, interreligious relations, demographic shifts resulting in declining vocations and birth rates, emigration, assimilation, and the global culture of secularism. Middle Eastern Catholics have a clear mission to live as faithful disciples of Jesus Christ, preserving and transmitting their cultural traditions and church identities to future believers. Using the 2010 synod of the Catholic Church in the Middle East as a guide, Eastern Catholics have committed to developing vocations, the family, young people, the word of God as a source of communion and witness, liturgy and sacramental life, prayer and pilgrimages, evangelization and charity, and catechesis and Christian formation.

For Further Reading

Audo, Antoine. "Eastern Christian Identity: A Catholic Perspective." In *The Catholic Church in the Contemporary Middle East: Studies for The Synod of the Middle East*, edited by Anthony O'Mahony and John Flannery, 19–35. London: Melisende, 2010.

Badr, Habib, Suad Abou el Rouss Slim, and Joseph Abou Nohra, eds. *Christianity: A History in the Middle East*. Beirut: Middle East Council of Churches, Studies & Research Program, 2006.

Farrugia, Edward, Gianpaolo Rigotti, and Michel Van Parys, eds. *The Catholic East*. Rome: Valore Italiano, 2019.

O'Mahony, Anthony, and Emma Loosely, eds. *Eastern Christianity in the Modern Middle East*. London: Routledge, 2010.

O'Mahony, Anthony, and John Flannery, eds. *The Catholic Church in the Contemporary Middle East: Studies for the Synod for the Middle East*. London: Melisende, 2010.

Winkler, Dietmar, ed. *Middle Eastern Christians Facing Challenges: Reflections on the Special Synod for the Middle East*. Piscataway, NJ: Gorgias, 2019.

11

The Protestant Story

Mitri Raheb

The impetus for the Protestant mission was triggered by major changes that took place within the Protestant landscape in Europe and the United States. Following a series of religious revivals in Germany and England in the eighteenth century, a second religious revival, known as the Second Great Awakening, started in New England and swept through the US (ca. 1790–1850). The nineteenth century was to become the century of Christian mission and the largest mission expansion in history. The arrival of Protestant missionaries in the Middle East coincided with major political developments.

The year that Napoleon landed in Egypt, 1798, conventionally marks the beginning of the end of the Ottoman Empire. However, the major change to the empire did not come from Napoleon but internally, triggered by Muhammad Ali Pasha (1769–1849), an Ottoman Albanian who seized power over Egypt after the withdrawal of Napoleon. Ali's dream was to create a modern megastate on a European model that would cover the area between the Nile and the Euphrates. This move presented a threat not only to the Ottoman rulers but also to Europeans with vital interests in the Middle East, particularly England and Austria. To ensure control of trade routes and resources, these countries mobilized their forces and brought about the withdrawal of Ibrahim Pasha from the territory of Greater Syria. In return for the European powers forcing Muhammad Ali and his son Ibrahim Pasha to leave Syria and Palestine, and to modernize their empire, the Ottomans introduced major political and administrative reforms: the Edict of Gühane in 1839 and the Hatti Humayun in 1856. The latter edict initiated further reforms that included freedom of worship, the possibility to maintain and repair church properties, the right to open schools, and the right of foreigners and foreign missions to acquire land.

The establishment of "mission stations" went hand in hand with the opening of foreign embassies in major cities of the Middle East such as Alexandria, Damascus, Beirut, and Jerusalem. European intervention in the Middle East in the mid-nineteenth century was not only political and military in nature, but also socio-cultural, economic, and religious, through the missionary agencies. In colonial fashion, the mission agencies divided the region up between them: Presbyterians became active in Syria, Lebanon, and Egypt; Congregationalists mainly in Anatolia, Turkey, and Lebanon; the Dutch Reformed Church in the Gulf; Anglicans in the north of Palestine, Egypt, Sudan, and Iran; and Lutherans in southern Palestine.

The Mission Rationale

The rationale behind this Protestant movement was that every Christian has an obligation to actively participate in the conversion of "heathens," those not yet touched in any way by the gospel or Christian civilization. It was in this context that the Protestant mission arrived in the Middle East, although there were no heathens in the eras of occupation by the Ottoman Empire. On the contrary, Palestine and Greater Syria are the cradle of Christianity. The population of the Ottoman Empire was majority Muslim, a good percentage of Middle Eastern Christians, and a Jewish minority, all members of the three monotheistic religions.

The rationale for the mission to the Middle East region was best expressed in two sermons given by the first two missionaries recruited by the American Board of Commissioners for Foreign Missions, a congregational mission agency established in Massachusetts in 1810. Pliny Fisk and Levi Parsons were recruited to go to Palestine and establish a mission station, preferably in Jerusalem or in Bethlehem. Both missionaries were aware that their mission there was different than others to the "heathens" and Pliny Fisk made that very clear in his sermon:

> All the inhabitants of the country believe in one God, and the leading facts recorded in the Old Testament. Here are no gods of brass or wood; no temples to Juggernaut, or the Grand Lama; no funeral piles; no altars stained with the blood of human victims. Everywhere you see a faint glimmering of light, through the gross and almost impenetrable darkness.

Then he adds:

> These people are not sunk in such entire stupidity and such brutal ignorance, as are the Hindoos of India, and the Hottentots of

Africa. Here is intellect, enterprise, and some degree of literature and science. Here several classes of men are among the most interesting that dwell on earth and are worthy of the prayers and the attentions of all those who desire to see influence, learning, talent, and strength of character consecrated to Christ.[1]

Yet, all these attributes were not good enough. Pliny Fisk and Levi Parsons were convinced that they were called for a much more important and noble task. They shared the millennialist conviction that four developments were necessary for the second coming of Christ: the revival of the Oriental Churches, the conversion of Muslims to Christ, the defeat of the pope, and the restoration of the Jews.[2] Thus, their mission was clear: to revive the churches of the Orient, to convert Jews and Muslims, and to do this before and better than the Roman Catholics. These four features were, to varying degrees, the main characteristics of Protestant missions to the early nineteenth-century Ottoman Empire. It was from these missionary efforts that several indigenous Protestant churches grew in the twentieth century.

The Established Protestant Churches in the Middle East

Protestant Churches in Syria and Lebanon[3]

The American Board of Commissioners of Foreign Missions, a joint body of Presbyterians and New England Congregationalists, decided in 1818 to start a mission in the Middle East. In 1827, they formed a nucleus for the first Protestant congregation in Beirut and Middle Eastern Protestantism was born. It took twenty years for the first Protestant church in the region, the National Evangelical Church of Beirut, to be officially established on March 31, 1848. In the second half of the nineteenth century, more Protestant churches were established throughout Lebanon and Syria, forming in 1920 a single synod called the National Evangelical Synod of Syria and Lebanon. In the wake of Arab nationalism, the National Evangelical Synod of Syria and Lebanon became fully independent from the US Board of Foreign Missions of the Presbyterian Church in 1959. The Synod follows Reformed theology and the Presbyterian form of government.

The National Evangelical Church of Beirut did not join this Synod but joined with nine other congregational churches to form the National Evangelical Union of Lebanon in the early 1960s. The highest governing

---

1. Hubers and Makari, *I Am a Pilgrim*, 116.
2. Raheb, *Das reformatorische Erbe*, 24.
3. Raheb, *Protestants*, 259–61.

body within the Union is its General Assembly, which is formed of both clergy and laity. The presiding senior pastor of the Beirut Church is traditionally the president of the Union.

The ministry of both Presbyterian Church bodies, the National Evangelical Union of Lebanon and the National Evangelical Synod of Syria and Lebanon, was negatively affected by the civil war in Lebanon from 1975–90. Most of the churches of the National Evangelical Union of Lebanon were destroyed or deserted, including the main church building and congregation of the National Evangelical Church of Beirut. A new church building was built and rededicated in 1998. Four (out of twenty-three) churches of the National Evangelical Synod of Syria and Lebanon in south Lebanon were deserted, their members displaced as a result of the civil war and the Israeli invasion of south Lebanon. More painful for the Synod was the war in Syria that started in the wake of the so-called "Arab Spring." Five of the twenty Presbyterian churches in Syria were destroyed. As a result of the two wars in Lebanon and Syria, a majority of Protestants were internally displaced, fled to Lebanon, or emigrated to other countries. Serious efforts were made in recent years to rehabilitate these churches and their members.

Of importance is the Near East School of Theology (NEST) that dates back to 1932. Today NEST is jointly sponsored and managed by the National Evangelical Synod of Syria and Lebanon, the Union of the Armenian Evangelical Churches in the Near East, the Episcopal diocese of Jerusalem, and the Evangelical Lutheran Church in Jordan and the Holy Land. A new campus for NEST was inaugurated in 1971. The civil war in Lebanon took its toll on NEST as it lost teachers through emigration and its student body was reduced to one third of its pre-war size. In 2010 NEST launched its Centre for Middle Eastern Christian Heritage. The Centre preserves, catalogues, and publishes important documents, most of which are stored in the school library's rare books section.

The Protestant Church in Lebanon played an important role in shaping the music of the Protestant churches in the Middle East. In 1878 the first Evangelical hymnal was printed. While the tunes were Western, the lyrics were crafted in classical Arabic by some of the earlier and prominent Protestant converts. The Fellowship of Middle East Evangelical Churches sponsored its latest revision in 1990. This hymnal is used by all mainline Protestant churches in the Middle East, thus shaping Protestant worship identity and providing an important intra-Protestant platform that glues these churches together.

The Union of the Armenian Evangelical Churches[4]

In 2021 the Union of the Armenian Evangelical Churches in the Near East celebrated its 175th anniversary, dating its beginnings from 1846 in Istanbul. Armenians were among the earliest Protestant converts in Turkey, Lebanon, and Egypt. Following the Armenian Genocide around World War I, tens of thousands of Armenians, many of whom were Protestants, had to escape from Turkey and were scattered throughout the Middle East. A majority of the Armenian Evangelicals fled to Syria and Lebanon. In 1924 several Armenian Protestant churches formed the Union of the Evangelical Churches in the Near East. The location of the twenty-five Armenian Protestant churches that form the Union is an expression of this history of displacement. Eleven churches are in Syria (mainly in Aleppo, Kassab, and one in Damascus); six are in Lebanon; three are in Tehran, Iran; two in Greece; two in Istanbul, Turkey; one in Alexandria, Egypt; one in Bagdad, Iraq; and one in Sydney, Australia. In the wake of the so-called Arab Spring, and especially from summer 2012 onwards when Aleppo became a major conflict zone with fierce military activity and Kassab was isolated from the outside world, a new wave of Armenian emigration took place. It is estimated that about one-third (10 thousand) of the Armenian Protestant community fled from Syria to Lebanon, and another third to Armenia in 2013. A second displacement at a time when Armenians were commemorating the 100th anniversary of the Genocide made many Protestants question their future in the region. They consider Lebanon as an interim station on the way to the ultimate diaspora in the US, Canada, or Australia.

The Union of the Armenian Evangelical Churches in the Near East is organized according to the congregational governing system and doctrinally subscribes to Reformed theology based on the Heidelberg Catechism. The official language of the Union is Armenian and the denomination's headquarters are located in Beirut. Strong ties exist between the Union and other Armenian Protestant bodies in the Armenian motherland and the diaspora.

The Evangelical Lutheran Church in Jordan and the Holy Land (ELCJHL)[5]

The roots of the Lutheran presence in Palestine date from German Protestant involvement in the region. On December 7, 1841, Frederic Wilhelm IV,

---

4. Raheb, *Protestants*, 261–62.
5. Raheb, *Sailing through Troubled Waters*, 77–92.

who had become king of Prussia in 1840, signed an agreement with Queen Victoria of England to establish in Jerusalem a "Bishopric of the United Church of England and Ireland." By 1879 there were twelve Protestant congregations in the Holy Land. Among the German missions, three were important for the development of the Lutheran Church: the Kaiserswerther Deaconesses, who founded, among other things, the first Protestant female school, Talitha Kumi; Schneller who started the first Protestant orphanage combined with a vocational school in Palestine; and the Jerusalem Society, which took over the congregations and school in Bethlehem in 1860 to found new four new congregations. In 1886 following the establishment of a united Germany under Bismarck, the German Protestants separated from the Anglican Church and created their own structure under a German propst. The Lutheran identity of the Protestant congregations coming out of the German mission work was crystallized only after the direct involvement of the Lutheran World Federation (LWF) in Palestine in 1947. With the help of the LWF, a Lutheran Church was established and officially recognized by the Jordanian government in May 1959. It was called the Evangelical Lutheran Church in Jordan (ELCJ). In 1979 the first Arab bishop was elected to succeed the German propst as the head of the church. To adjust to the changing political realities, in 2005 the Lutheran synod adopted a new name for the church: the Evangelical Lutheran Church in Jordan and the Holy Land. Today the church runs six congregations: five in the West Bank of which three are in the Bethlehem area, one in East Jerusalem, and one in Ramallah, plus a sixth in Amman, Jordan.

The Evangelical Presbyterian Church of Egypt[6]

The first Presbyterian missionary arrived in Egypt with his wife in November 1850. They started their work in Lower Egypt, in Cairo, Alexandria, and the Nile Delta. On April 13, 1860, the first Egyptian Presbyterian Synod was organized. In 1899 it was expanded to include the Sudan, thus forming the Synod of the Nile. The Church experienced continuing maturity and growth with the establishment of schools, hospitals, development programs for self-governance, and social service projects.

The Nasser Revolution of 1952 that overthrew the monarchy and quickly ended British occupation, brought major transformations to Egyptian society through land reform laws and the nationalization of most private companies and institutions, including the Suez Canal. Following the Suez Crisis of 1956, most missionaries had to leave and the church

6. For a detailed story, see Sharkey, *American Evangelicals in Egypt*.

exercised full autonomy. Those events were an important turning point in the life of the Church. Celebrating its centennial in 1958, the Evangelical Church of Egypt gained its independence and committed to full self-governance and self-support. Acknowledging its Coptic (i.e. Egyptian) heritage, the Church became known as the Coptic Evangelical Church. Under the leadership of its general secretary, the late Rev. Dr. Samuel Habib, the Church joined the WCC and WARC, participated in forming what is now the MECC, and started new outreach programs to combat poverty and foster self-development. The entity that undertook to carry out those programs was registered with the Ministry of Social Affairs in 1960 under the name of the Coptic Evangelical Organization for Social Services (CEOSS). In the course of its fifty-five years of experience, CEOSS became a leading national agency, spawning and training numerous local organizations that focus on sustainable development.

With the proliferation of other Evangelical denominations, the official name of the Church became the Evangelical Presbyterian Church of Egypt in 2004. It is now the largest Protestant Church in the Middle East and consists of eight regional presbyteries, about 270 congregations, 300 pastors and twenty-five schools, while local congregations operate fifty-five others. The Synod also manages a number of conference centers and two major medical centers. Several clinics are affiliated with local congregations.

In 2013, the Evangelical Theological Seminary in Cairo (ETSC) celebrated its 150th anniversary. Besides studies that equip students to become pastors, the seminary offers evening courses for its Lay Academy and special short-term courses in women's studies. On the occasion of its sesquicentennial, ETSC inaugurated a new Centre for the Study of Middle Eastern Christianity. Behind this center is a shift toward a more contextualized approach to theology and biblical interpretation.

The Anglican Church in the Middle East[7]

The Anglican presence in the Middle East is closely connected to the British Empire of the nineteenth century and covered two distinct regions. The first region of Palestine and Egypt dates from the establishment of the "Bishopric of the United Church of England and Ireland" in Jerusalem in 1841; the second focus on Iran and the Gulf dates from the Act of Parliament of 1877.

The aim of the Bishopric in Jerusalem was to convert Jews. Accordingly, Professor Dr. Michael Solomon Alexander (1799–1845), a Jewish convert, was chosen as the first Anglican bishop of Jerusalem; he arrived in January

---

7. For a summary of the Anglican Church, see Said, *Anglicans*.

1842. By 1847 only fifty-seven Jews there had converted to Anglicanism. On November 26, 1845, Bishop Alexander died and the king of Prussia nominated Samuel Gobat (1799–1879) to succeed him. Soon after his arrival in Jerusalem on December 30, 1846, Bishop Gobat shifted the emphasis from conversion of Jews to reformation of the Oriental churches. Gobat entrusted the Church Missionary Society with this mission. By the time of his death in 1879, Bishop Gobat had established twelve Protestant congregations in the Holy Land. The polity of these congregations was in accord with Anglican structures where the bishop had final authority.

It took the Anglicans almost twenty years, from 1886–1905, to establish their own Synod of the Episcopal Evangelical Church and to achieve some independence from the English episcopate. In the interwar period, this quest for independence grew stronger. The Synod of the Evangelical Episcopal Church fought for its independence throughout the Mandate years (1920–48) without success. Not only were the British authorities opposed to recognition, but so too was the British Anglican bishop in Jerusalem. Episcopalian Christians in Palestine consequently felt betrayed by both the British Mandate and their own British hierarchy. While the British Mandate government was not ready to recognize the Anglican Church in Palestine, the Jordanian government recognized the Protestant Anglican millet and published its name in the official list of recognized churches for 1938. On October 29, 1947, the Jordanian Cabinet accepted the new name of the Arab Evangelical Episcopal Church, adding it to the official list.[8] This process, led by the Synod, failed to gain the approval of the British Anglican bishop in Jerusalem. The Anglican Church wanted to keep the Jerusalem diocese directly under Canterbury. For that reason, the Anglican bishop in Jerusalem was elevated to be an archbishop with jurisdiction over Jerusalem, Iran, Egypt, Libya, Sudan, Cyprus, the Gulf, and Iraq. This change allowed Canterbury to consecrate the first Arab Anglican bishop for Jordan, Lebanon, and Syria in East Jerusalem in 1958. Almost all the Anglicans in Lebanon and Syria are former Palestinian refugees from 1948. In 1976 a new structure was developed with the region being seen as one province with four dioceses: Jerusalem, Egypt, Iran, and Cyprus and the Gulf. Recently, the bishops in Jerusalem and Egypt were elevated to become archbishops. The province runs around 200 congregations with several schools, hospitals, and St. George's College in Jerusalem.

---

8. Raheb, *The Politics of Persecution*, 99.

Protestant Churches in Sudan

The first Protestant missionaries arrived in Sudan in the 1890s following the defeat of the Mahdist movement and the beginning of Anglo-Egyptian rule. While American missionaries started the Presbyterian mission in South Sudan, Coptic Evangelical missionaries were sent to the north of Sudan to pastor the many Arab Christians, who were hired by the new government in public administration, commerce, and education. The division between North and South Sudan is not only geographical but also religious and racial. While the population in the south is exclusively Black African and followers of African traditional religions, the majority of those in North Sudan are Arabs and mainly Muslims. Several tribal languages dominated the south, while Arabic was the official language spoken in the north. Today there are fourteen congregations in the Sudan Presbyterian Evangelical Church, which also runs several Protestant schools.

Most of the Protestant Churches in Sudan were established in the mid-twentieth century and belong to the Reformed tradition: the Sudan Interior Church, which stands in the Baptist tradition; the Sudanese Reformed Presbyterian Church; the Sudanese Church of Christ; and the Pentecostal Church of Sudan. The latter is considered the fastest growing Church in Sudan. All of these churches are members of the Sudan Council of Churches, and have congregations in Khartoum and in the Republic of Sudan. However, most of their congregations and members are found today in the independent Republic of South Sudan.

Protestant Churches in Iraq and the Gulf Region

The first Protestant communities were established in Iraq as early as the first half of the nineteenth century. Armenian Presbyterians established churches in Baghdad, Mosul, Kirkuk, and Basra. The Protestant church in Iraq, however, was not able to grow to the same extent as in other regions. The Iran-Iraq war 1980–88, followed by the invasion of Kuwait in 1991 and the war to liberate Kuwait, the sanctions imposed on Iraq, and the invasion of Iraq by the US in 2003 took a major toll on Christians in that country. Of the five Presbyterian churches, only three survived this turmoil while the other two lost many of their members. In addition to the Presbyterian churches in Iraq, other Protestant Churches of the Reformed tradition exist today in the Gulf region. The National Evangelical Church in Bahrain dates from 1889 and the National Evangelical Church in Kuwait was founded in 1931. From the 1950s, these churches experienced immense growth due to the discovery of oil in that region and the influx of migrant workers from Syria, Lebanon, Egypt, and Palestine. In the late twentieth century with the mega construction projects that took place in the United Arab Emirates, Qatar, and Oman, hundreds of thousands of Asian migrant workers came to work in the Gulf, many of whom were Christian.

The Gulf is now the only place in the Middle East where the number and percentage of Christians is on the increase. Almost all churches in the Gulf developed into multi-lingual, multinational, and multiethnic churches where services are held by the hour in diverse languages to cater for the different communities. In all these countries, except for Saudi Arabia, the governments provided land to build churches and to enjoy freedom of worship as long as the laws of the country are respected.

Newer Protestant Churches[9]

Several other Protestant Churches exist in the Middle East. The Baptists came to the region in late nineteenth century, followed by the Church of God, the Church of the Nazarene, the Christian Missionary Alliance, and others. In the second half of the twentieth century, several Pentecostal and charismatic churches like the Assemblies of God started mushrooming in the region. They claim to have thousands of converts from Islam in underground churches in North Africa and they are very active among migrant workers in the Gulf region. Starting in the late 1970s, an influx of Evangelical theological seminaries resulted in the training of hundreds of young Evangelical leaders in the region. With the spread of satellite television in the 1990s, Evangelicals used the opportunity to reach out to Christians, but mainly to Muslims. Today, over fifteen Christian satellite television stations broadcast in several languages. In recent years, other Evangelical proselytizing groups such as Koreans, Africans, and Australians have become active in the region. The diverse brands of Anabaptist churches and the fact that most of these churches are not organized on a regional level makes it difficult to cover them in any detail within the scope of this chapter.

Messianic Jews[10]

Messianic Jews are Jews who believe in Christ as the Jewish Messiah. Their history in the region dates back to the early nineteenth century and the work

---

9. For more by Newberg, *Pentecostals/Charismatics*.
10. For a good summary, see Rucks, *Messianic Jews*.

of the London Society in promoting Christianity among the Jews. Throughout the twentieth century, the work of Messianic Jews was concentrated mainly among a few charismatic individuals and very small congregations. The 1967 War and the decisive victory of Israel gave wind to the Christian Zionist movement and the movement came under the influence of American Messianic Jewish leaders. Two major developments were significant in the current Messianic Jewish movement: the immigration of Ethiopian Jews to Israel in the 1980s and of Russian Jews in the 1990s. Seventy percent of the Messianic congregations in the region worship in the Russian language. Many of these are not necessarily Jews but are of Russian Orthodox heritage.

The Protestant Presence Today

The Protestant presence in the Middle East is now 200 years old. During these two centuries, Protestantism underwent several transformations.

From Colonialism to Liberation

Over the course of the years there has been strenuous debate about the role of Christian missions in the context of European colonialism. Christian missionaries in the Middle East were often portrayed as "cultural imperialists" or as "agents of the empire." It is not possible to conclude that the European Christian mission to the Middle East was unambiguously a colonialist enterprise, nor is it possible clearly to distinguish between the two. What the two had in common was a desire for the expansion of Western Christian and European influence beyond national or geographic borders. The case can surely be made that both phenomena, "mission" and "colonialism," stem from a common European expansionist culture that felt itself superior and powerful enough to bring others who were at a great distance under their military or religious control. Both groups were convinced that they had "products" to offer and that there were "markets" abroad awaiting fulfillment. Without doubt, there were links between the rise of imperialist domination in the Middle East and the spread of the missionary enterprise.

In general, religious identity in the Middle East was linked to national identity: Protestant missions were mainly British, American, and to some extent German; Catholic missions were mainly French, Austrian, and Italian; while the Orthodox mission was exclusively Russian. This meant that intra-European national rivalries and competition in religious missions were two sides of the same coin. This rivalry and competition planted the seeds for sectarian identities that were not previously known in such a form or intensity. The Christian mission schools became tools to not only educate local Christians but to instill in them an allegiance to the "motherland" of the missionaries, and a strong loyalty to a specific religious denomination, often even within the same denomination to a specific country (Russian versus Greek for Orthodox) or even order (Jesuits versus Dominicans). A culture of sectarianism was thereby magnified, leading later to a weakening of social cohesion and the fragmentation of the social fabric in the Middle East.

While missions and colonialism are no longer connected, one particular form of colonialism is still in place. Support from Christian Zionism[11] for Israeli settler colonial practices continues to constitute a major problem for indigenous Christian communities, particularly Middle Eastern Protestant communities. Protestant Christian Zionist ideology undoubtedly played a role in the creation of the State of Israel from Shaftesbury to Balfour, and constitutes an essential element in Anglo-Saxon Evangelicalism and the American Christian Right. Blind support for Israeli politics based on a narrow "Evangelical" reading of biblical passages constitutes nothing less than heresy for Protestants in the Middle East. Unfortunately, some theological concepts of Christian Zionism are found today within a number of the Evangelical congregations in the region.

From early on, indigenous Protestant leaders became aware of the colonial web of the missions and opposed it. The best example was Butrus al-Bustani in the mid-nineteenth century. Many Protestant church leaders became known for their struggles for the independence of their countries from colonial rule. Protestant theologians like Naim Ateek and Mitri Raheb developed liberation and de-colonial theologies against the Israeli occupation and settler colonialism, while the Anglican Bishop Elia Khoury served on the executive committee of the Palestinian Liberation Organization (PLO). The Presbyterian theologian Najib Awad has been very engaged in Syrian politics and calls for democratic change in Syria. Andrea Zaki, the head of the Protestant Churches in Egypt, has been articulate about his concept of "dynamic citizenship."

From Conversion to Coexistence

Protestants came to the Middle East with the aim of converting Jews and Muslims, but this mission failed. Very few Jews were open to conversion. Today, there are a few Messianic Jewish congregations in Israel, run either by Lutheran, Baptist, or Latin churches. Following World War II,

11. Raheb, *The Politics of Persecution*, 57–64.

Protestants who had seen the Holocaust pioneered the establishment of Christian-Jewish dialogue forums in both the US and Western Europe. This dialogue remained a Western phenomenon of white European Christians and a few Ashkenazi Jews. Christian-Jewish dialogue in the Middle East was not possible due to the Israeli occupation of Palestinian, Egyptian, and Syrian land. Some isolated attempts to do so in the Jerusalem or Galilee area remained of limited impact.

The conversion of Muslims by Protestants was also unsuccessful as Muslim communities in the Middle East proved to be resilient to Western Christian missions. Only a small number of Muslim individuals converted, yet the impact of Protestantism on society as a whole cannot be underestimated. While religious conversion failed, Protestant education proved successful on several levels. The schools established by the Protestant mission provided an important tool in the development of local communities. Political leaders, middle-class intelligentsia, and many successful businesspeople were products of Protestant education. Although Protestants were as engaged as the Catholics and Orthodox in Christian-Muslim dialogue, it took a Palestinian Christian Protestant like Edward Said to defend Islam when stereotyped by Western orientalists.

The Protestants were more successful in their endeavor to reform the national churches in the Middle East. Their mission triggered a series of substantial changes in some of these churches, including the Coptic Church and the Latin Church in Jerusalem. It forced Catholic missions to emulate them in a fierce competition for the souls of the native Christians. Many locals, mainly Orthodox Christians who interacted closely with Protestant missions or were educated by Protestant churches, decided to join these missions. This led to the creation of local Protestant churches. The Orthodox churches view these activities as proselytism, and this remains a difficult issue in Orthodox-Protestant dialogue. Protestants in the nineteenth century portrayed the native churches as dead, yet it was these churches that triggered the ecumenical movement in the region that led to the establishment of the Middle East Council of Churches and who continue to support its work up to the present day.

From Preaching to Teaching

Protestants made an important contribution to the Middle East in the realm of education as Protestant missions established hundreds of Protestant schools. Although many of these schools were intended originally as Bible schools, with time they proved to be dynamic and adapted to the context. Their role became more and more secular, as is evident in higher education. The Syrian Protestant College established in Beirut in 1866 following the civil war became the American University of Beirut in 1920. Instead of training leaders for the church and its missions, the college's aim became the education of professional people for the larger region and its needs. The American University of Cairo was established in 1919 as a pan-Presbyterian project by the son of a Presbyterian missionary. Following anti-missionary sentiments in the 1930s, a process of secularization was triggered and led in 1956 to morning prayers being halted.

In Palestine, Bir Zeit University was originally founded in 1924 by the daughter of an Anglican pastor. In 1953 it developed into a college, and in 1973 it became a Palestinian public university and a center for the Palestinian national movement. The same is true of the Haigazian University established in Beirut in 1955 jointly by the Armenian Missionary Association of America (AMAA) and the Union of the Armenian Evangelical Churches in the Near East (UAECNE). This university continues to provide quality education to all the Lebanese society. The Lebanese American University was started in 1835 by Sarah Smith, wife of the Protestant missionary Eli Smith, as the American School for Girls. In the 1920s it became the American Junior College for Women and by the early 1990s, the college became the Lebanese American University. Although the ties to the church still exist, the university is a secular institution today.

Finally, Dar al-Kalima University was started in 2006 by the Rev. Dr. Mitri Raheb as a program within the facility of the Christmas Lutheran Church in Bethlehem, Palestine. In 2013 it became a university college and in 2021 a fully fledged university. Dar al-Kalima is the first and only university in Palestine with a focus on arts and culture. Although some of these universities were opened as mission schools to serve the church, they are now all national institutions in service of the larger community and society. To use the words of Samir Khalaf, these institutions of higher education decided to "civilize" rather than "Christianize," to "teach" rather than "preach," and to focus on "culture" rather than on "Christ."[12]

From patriarchy to gender justice

Another important Protestant contribution was in female education.[13] The Protestant missions started some of the earliest girls' schools in Egypt,

---

12. Khalaf, *Protestant Missionaries in the Levant*, xvi.

13. For the early Protestant contribution to gender, see Womack, *Protestants, Gender, and the Arab Renaissance*.

Palestine, Lebanon, and Syria. As explained earlier, some of these schools became the first women's colleges in the region. In January 2010, the Sixth General Assembly of the FMEEC adopted a proposal that "supports the ordination of the women in our churches in the position of ordained pastor and her partnership with men as an equal partner in decision making." In 2016 the Synod of the Evangelical Lutheran Church in Jordan and the Holy Land adopted the first personal status law giving full equality to women in terms of inheritance, divorce, etc. In 2017 Rola Sleiman was ordained as the first female pastor in the entire Middle East to serve Tripoli Evangelical Church that belongs to the Synod of Syria and Lebanon. Many Protestant women occupied key positions in the Church structures: Mary Mikhael was the first female president of the Near East School of Theology (NEST); Viola Raheb served for seven years as the superintendent of all Lutheran schools in Palestine; Rose Jarjour has been the general secretary of the Fellowship of the Middle East Evangelical Churches (FMEEC) for many years; and Rev. Najla Kassab serves as president of the World Communion of Reformed Churches (WCRC).

Conclusion

The Protestants of the Middle East are small in number but reject any minority complex that might isolate them from their neighbors. With the exception of the Armenians and Sudanese Africans, these Protestants see themselves as Arabs who must contribute to their society. As founders of the ecumenical movement in the Middle East, they were eager to work together with other Churches in the region and beyond. Although their influence today is much weaker than it was in the nineteenth century, Protestants continue to play a much bigger role than their numbers imply. Together with Christians of other denominations, they face several challenges. The first relates to the prevailing political realities in the aftermath of the Arab Spring, the rise of political Islam, and the ongoing Israeli occupation of Palestinian land. Their response to these challenges takes on different forms that range from developing diverse forms of contextual theologies to becoming more engaged in ecumenical and interfaith dialogue. A major focus in the early twenty-first century was on exploring new ways of looking at faith and citizenship.

The second challenge is that of demographic decline due to displacement, emigration, and a lower birth rate. It is foreseeable that several Protestant Churches may not survive in certain areas of the Middle East. Nevertheless, Protestants continue to introduce new thinking into the region, as the ordination of women demonstrates. Their calling is to continue to push the envelope towards more inclusive societies based on equality, freedom, and grace.

For Further Reading

Awad, Najib. "Where Is the Gospel, What Happened to Culture? The Reformed Church in Syria and Lebanon." *Journal of Reformed Theology.* Accessed May 3, 2021. https://www.academia.edu/6848552/Where_is_the_Gospel_What_Happened_to_Culture_The_Reformed_Church_in_Syria_and_Lebanon.

Badr, Habib, ed. "Christianity: A History in the Middle East." In *Christianity: A History in the Middle East*, 687–713. Beirut: World Council of Churches, 2005.

Grafton, David. "Protestants." In *The Rowman & Littlefield Handbook of Christianity in the Middle East*, edited by Mitri Raheb and Mark A. Lamport, 316–30. Lanham, MD: Rowman & Littlefield, 2020.

Hubers, John, and Makari, Peter E. *I Am a Pilgrim, a Traveler, a Stranger: Exploring the Life and Mind of the First American Missionary to the Middle East, the Rev. Pliny Fisk.* Eugene, OR: Pickwick, 2016.

Khalaf, Samir. *Protestant Missionaries in the Levant: Ungodly Puritans, 1820–1860.* London: Routledge, 2017.

Loeffler, Roland. "Aggravating Circumstances: On the Processes of National and Religious Identity within the Arab Lutheran and Anglican Congregations of Palestine during the Mandate Years." In *Christian Witness between Continuity and New Beginnings: Modern Historical Missions in the Middle East*, edited by Martin Tamcke and Michael Marten, 99–123. Münster, Germany: LIT Verlag, 2006.

Meinardus, Otto F. A. *Christians in Egypt: Orthodox, Catholic, and Protestant Communities—Past and Present.* Cairo: The American University in Cairo, 2006.

Newberg, Eric. "Pentecostals/Charismatics." In *Christianity in North Africa & West Asia*, edited by Kenneth Ross, Mariz Tadros, and Todd Johnson, 293–302. Peabody. MA: Hendrickson, 2020.

Raheb, Mitri, ed. *Middle Eastern Women: The Intersection of Law, Culture and Religion.* Bethlehem: Diyar, 2020.

———. "Protestants." In *Christianity in North Africa and West Asia*, edited by Kenneth R. Ross, Mariz Tadros, and Todd M. Johnson, 259–70. Edinburgh: Edinburgh University Press, 2018.

———. *The Politics of Persecution: Middle Eastern Christians in an Age of Empire.* Waco, TX: Baylor University Press, 2021.

———. *Das reformatorische Erbe unter den Palästinensern. Zur Entstehung der Evangelisch-Lutherischen Kirche in Jordanien, Bd 11.* Reihe: Die Lutherische Kirche. Geschichte und . . . edition. Gütersloh: Gütersloher Verlagshaus, Gerd Mohn, 1990.

———. *Sailing through Troubled Waters: Christianity in the Middle East.* Bethlehem: Diyar, 2013.

Ross, Kenneth R., Tadros Mariz, and Todd M. Johnson, eds. *Christianity in North Africa and West Asia.* Edinburgh: Edinburgh University Press, 2018.

Rucks, Hanna. "Messianic Jews." In *The Rowman & Littlefield Handbook of Christianity in the Middle East*, edited by Mitri Raheb and Mark A. Lamport, 331–40. Lanham, MD: Rowman & Littlefield, 2020.

Said, Yazid. "Anglicans." In *Christianity in North Africa & West Asia*, edited by Kenneth Ross, Mariz Tadros, and Todd Johnson, 219–26. Peabody, MA: Hendrickson, 2020.

Sharkey, Heather J. *American Evangelicals in Egypt: Missionary Encounters in an Age of Empire*. Princeton; NJ: Princeton University Press, 2015.

Tamcke, Martin, and Michael Marten, eds. *Christian Witness between Continuity and New Beginnings: Modern Historical Missions in the Middle East*. Münster: LIT Verlag, 2006.

Trexler, Melanie E. *Evangelizing Lebanon: Baptists, Missions, and the Question of Cultures*. Waco, TX: Baylor University Press, 2016.

Womack, Deanna Ferree. *Protestants, Gender and the Arab Renaissance in Late Ottoman Syria*. Edinburgh: Edinburgh University Press, 2020.

— Section Three —

The Story of Christianity Encounters Twenty-First-Century Issues

12

Diaspora and Middle Eastern Christianity

Mariam Youssef

Middle Eastern Christianities, as diverse as they come, are marked with one similarity—their complicated positioning amidst global conflict. The twentieth century saw the emergence of global Middle Eastern Christian communities, as Christians in Lebanon, Egypt, Palestine, and elsewhere led diasporic movements to secure their survival.

In this chapter, I will discuss the complications of diaspora in the expansion of Middle Eastern Christian communities using the global Coptic Orthodox Church as a case study. I will explore how these churches make their homes in diaspora, and the politics of Coptic diaspora from a neocolonial lens. We can use this example to consider how trends of diaspora affect other Middle Eastern Christian communities.

Diaspora Case Study: Coptic Orthodoxy

The Coptic Church is one of the oldest Christian Churches in the world. Founded in the first century, the Coptic Church is based in Egypt and is today categorized as an Oriental Orthodox Church. Since the ninth century, Copts have been a minority group in Egypt and have held varying (but always precarious) political and economic power. Best estimates suggest that there are about 10 million Copts in Egypt. In the diaspora, there are approximately 500,000 Copts. Since Copts are a minority both in Egypt and in the diaspora, the global Coptic community (under the leadership of a patriarch based in Egypt) has always had to carefully consider its position in the world and in society.[1]

---

1. Yefet, "The Coptic Diaspora and the Status of the Coptic Minority in Egypt," 1211.

The Coptic Church has been a survival community virtually since its inception. Copts in Egypt have always suffered persecution and discrimination, whether from dominant pagan, Byzantine, or Islamic forces.[2] This sense of survival has shaped the culture and theology of the Coptic Church. Currently, Copts make up about 15 percent of the Egyptian population.[3] As a marginalized minority, the Coptic community has had to develop paradigms that encourage their survival and promote a strong sense of Coptic identity. Importantly, although the term *Copt* has both religious and ethnic implications, across the board it is typically used to refer to Egyptian Christians.[4]

Therefore, while Coptic communities have ethnic and national commonalities, it is their identity as Christians that ties them together and forms their identity. There is virtually no separation between religious and ethnic identities, and as a result, there exists no secular culture that is unique to the Coptic community. Since the common ground for Coptic identity lies entirely in the church, survival paradigms are necessarily couched in theological rhetoric. The cultural and socio-historical contributors to Coptic survival will always come back to the Coptic church.

In the last fifty years, the Coptic community has expanded globally through diaspora. Diaspora has created interesting conditions for Coptic survival.[5] In some ways, diaspora has aided Coptic survival by providing alternative communities where Copts can live in relative peace. In other ways, diaspora has produced identity anxiety in the global Coptic community, since so much of Coptic identity is tied to national and ethnic expression.[6]

Development of Diasporic Coptic Theology

Since Copts in Egypt experience discrimination and marginalization and do not have a secular culture to call their own—only that of secular Muslim-majority Egypt—one of the major roles of Coptic theology has been to affirm Coptic identity within their religious context. Coptic theology has long reflected the marginal experience of the Copts. In writing, liturgy, and from the pulpit, diasporic Coptic leaders acknowledge the difficulty of sustaining Coptic community in Egypt.

2. Meinardus, *Two Thousand Years of Coptic Christianity*, 38.
3. Ibrahim and Ibrahim, "Building a Diaspora."
4. Tadros, *Copts at the Crossroads*, 23.
5. Ibrahim and Ibrahim, "Building a Diaspora," 252.
6. Ibrahim and Ibrahim, "Building a Diaspora," 254.

In the diaspora, Copts continue to ask questions about identity through theology as they have again found themselves occupying a marginal identity. The question of how to translate Coptic theology into a new place has been a challenging one. Much of this initial energy was spent building community and reinterpreting Coptic ritual and practice in American culture.[7] Therefore, I am using the term "Coptic diasporic theology" to distinguish Coptic theology as it develops and is interpreted in the context of the diaspora.

Eventually, the Coptic Church in the diaspora became increasingly established. Churches were built and clergy were brought over to serve in them. While these clergy were held in high esteem by diasporic congregants, who went to them for teaching and guidance, many Copts also continued to look to well-known clergy in Egypt for their spiritual direction. The writings and sermons of Pope Shenouda III were held in especially high regard. During his enthronement as patriarch, Pope Shenouda III was particularly vocal about the plight of Copts in Egypt, becoming one of the most politically involved clergy in modern Coptic history.[8] Pope Shenouda III refused to identify Copts as a minority in Egypt, arguing instead that Copts should be seen as indigenous, "true" Egyptians, for whom Egypt was their rightful home.[9] At the same time, he encouraged the Coptic diaspora as a necessary means for Coptic survival. Under his supervision, the number of diasporic churches in North America expanded from four at the beginning of his papacy to over 200 at the end. In his writings and weekly sermons, he often considered Copts in the diaspora and the implications of a global Coptic Church.[10]

Coptic hymnology and liturgical rite also give us some clues about survival paradigms in recent Coptic thought. Copts take pride in their liturgical traditions, many of which are more than a thousand years old, and equate the preservation of Coptic liturgy and hymns with the preservation of Coptic heritage and identity, which take on cultural significance as well.[11] Diasporic Coptic communities often find themselves divided in their stances on the role of Coptic liturgy and hymns. Many want to make changes, advocating for linguistic and tonal shifts that will better reflect the influence of American culture on the Coptic church. They want to revisit parts of the liturgy that are seen as outdated or culturally irrelevant in the diaspora, arguing that this will help Copts born in the diaspora and

7. Boulos, *The History of the Early Coptic Community*, 26.
8. Saad, "The Modern Period (1952–2011)," 91.
9. Mahmood, *Religious Difference in a Secular Age*, 79.
10. Iskander, *Sectarian Conflict in Egypt*, 150.
11. Ramzy, "Music: Performing Coptic Expressive Culture," 161.

non-Copts who marry into the Church to make a deeper connection to the community. Others argue that in doing so, diasporic Copts show disrespect to their heritage and those who suffered to preserve it.[12] They argue that Coptic spirituality cannot be separated from Coptic cultural expression and that Copts in the diaspora have a responsibility to remember their history and maintain Coptic language and culture for future generations. Despite differing views on the role of Coptic liturgy and hymnology, these remain pervasive parts of Coptic theology and identity. As reflections of Coptic heritage, they contain meaningful examples of the survival paradigms held dear by Copts both inside and outside of the diaspora.

Some of the most major shifts for Coptic theology in the diaspora have been structural. Individual churches began to emerge in somewhat scattered patterns, wherever there were enough Copts to sustain them. Frequently they rented space from a school, office building, or another church. This was a significant shift from the churches in Egypt, some of which were centuries or millennia old and carried with them the history that gave Copts pride in their heritage. Many Copts questioned the significance of the liturgy in this new environment, asking what changes needed to be made to adapt liturgical practice in the diaspora. Many churches began translating prayers into English and incorporating concepts borrowed from local Catholic and Protestant churches.

The introduction of American and European cultures into Coptic praxis raised the question of which traditions were flexible and which were worth keeping. Although Pope Shenouda III lived in Egypt, he took the issues of the diaspora into deep consideration and his writings and teachings were incredibly influential to Copts in the diaspora. He was ordained to the patriarchate in 1971, but even prior to this Pope Shenouda III had begun to think seriously about the effects of the diaspora on Coptic identity.[13]

Goals and Ideals of Coptic Diasporic Theology

One of the major goals of Coptic theology, both in Egypt and in the diaspora, is the preservation of Coptic culture and language.[14] Copts represent a religious and ethno-cultural minority in Egypt and the United States. Since there is no secular culture unique to the Coptic community, the church has taken on the responsibility of preserving and expressing Coptic culture. This has

12. Brinkerhoff, "Assimilation and Heritage Identity: Lessons from the Coptic Diaspora" 472–73.

13. Saad, "The Modern Period (1952–2011)," 91.

14. Farag, "Theology: Defending Orthodoxy," 113–14.

become a major focus of Coptic religious practice, since Copts in Egypt find themselves not only unable to preserve their culture outside the Church but also find their very existence constantly under threat. For so much of Coptic existence, Copts have felt the pressure that comes with being a persecuted minority, ultimately compromising their sense of self-definition.

Therefore, many elements of Coptic culture that would otherwise have become irrelevant—using languages that the vast majority of Copts no longer speak (both in Egypt and the diaspora), or using hymns set to tunes that are no longer musically intuitive to most Copts—are viewed by many as still vitally important to the survival of the Coptic community. Many Copts argue that it is crucial to continue praying in Coptic, even though virtually no Copts speak it, because if it were not used in worship it would completely die out. The remaining elements of Coptic life—holidays, the Coptic calendar, and rituals for birth and death, for example—continue to be used in the diaspora for the primary reason that there is no other way for them to remain known and present in Coptic culture, despite their lack of meaning in the lives of many diasporic Copts. Copts in the diaspora find themselves mixing these elements of Coptic living with the more practical elements of assimilation in Coptic culture.[15] For example, Coptic Christmas is celebrated on January 7. Many Copts in the diaspora observe some form of dual celebration—perhaps exchanging presents on December 25 and then going to church and meeting with extended family on January 7—in order to feel like they are functioning as "good" Americans while remaining true to their heritage.

The Coptic diaspora has triggered an increased interest in defining and supporting Coptic families—displaying rhetoric that can often be seen in communities anxious to maintain their populations. Pope Shenouda was known to frequently remark that "the Coptic family unit is the rock on which the community stands."[16] The diaspora coincided with the increased Islamization of Egypt, during which Coptic leaders viewed the family as the most important place of refuge for Copts. They began to speak of the responsibility that parents, especially mothers, bore towards their children to raise them with the knowledge of their faith and identity. In a world where they were increasingly marginalized, the family became more and more important as a safe haven from violence and discrimination.

For diasporic Copts, survival revolves around building the foundations necessary to maintain community in America. This meant that most of the efforts of early Coptic American communities were dedicated to growing

15. Brinkerhoff, "Assimilation and Heritage Identity," 471.
16. Armanios and Amstutz. "Emerging Christian Media in Egypt," 515.

their numbers and securing the loyalty of their congregants. Without sufficient numbers, Copts could not financially support a priest, pay rent for a building, or find other Copts to socialize with and marry.[17] Therefore, most of the time, energy, and charitable giving of Copts in the diaspora was and continues to be focused on building and maintaining foundations, as well as helping Copts in Egypt.[18] This meant that one of the major goals of diasporic Coptic theology has been to secure the loyalty of Copts in the diaspora, although it would be more convenient for many of them to simply pray and find community in other churches.

The Martyr Paradigm

Martyrdom lies at the heart of Coptic identity. Since its very beginnings, Copts have been persecuted for their faith. This has been a point of pride for many Copts, who see their heritage as one of survival against all odds.[19] Even for Copts in the diaspora, who do not directly experience religious persecution, martyrdom is an important element of their faith, since it is the driving force behind the diaspora.

Indeed, in its own way, the diaspora has become a form of martyrdom. Immigration is an ordeal, often an emotionally, physically, and financially fraught process. Most Copts find themselves in America in a state of social, political, and financial duress.[20] Therefore, Copts begin their lives in the diaspora with a strong sense of their identity as martyrs, carrying with them the stories of discrimination they suffered—or perhaps that their parents or grandparents suffered—under an unjust regime. As a Copt born in the United States, I have never experienced this injustice firsthand. However, the stories are real to me. Much of my upbringing is marked by stories of the job discrimination, incarceration, and physical violence suffered by my relatives and family friends. I was raised on their experiences. My earliest memories are hearing these stories from my parents, and so from my very beginnings it was imprinted on me that the suffering of Copts in Egypt was my legacy, even in the diaspora. Over time, the diaspora has become a way for Copts to identify with the ordeals of Copts remaining in Egypt.[21]

---

17. Boulos, *The History of the Early Coptic Community in the U.S.A. (1955–1970)*, 43.
18. Brinkerhoff, "Diaspora Philanthropy," 978.
19. Papaconstantinou, "Historiography, Hagiography, and the Making," 65–66.
20. Hanna, "With Friends Like These" 31.
21. Yefet, "The Coptic Diaspora and the Status of the Coptic Minority in Egypt," 1207.

Copts in the diaspora have formed global communities outside Egypt at a cost. They sometimes see their sacrifice as an alternative contribution to the larger identity of martyrdom. In this way, the Coptic Church in the diaspora is both foreign to and commensurate with the paradigmatic martyr identity that defines the Coptic Church in Egypt.

For Copts in the diaspora, the martyr paradigm helps to secure the loyalty needed to establish its foundations. The martyr paradigm gives Copts the sense that their community is one worth fighting for, even dying for. Copts in the first wave of the diaspora who prayed in other Orthodox churches still felt like something was missing, even if those churches were theologically and ritually consistent with their own religious heritage.[22] They wanted a religious community that was truly Coptic, because they knew themselves to be a community that would survive in the face of any form of persecution or hardship. To not establish a strong community in the diaspora would be read as a betrayal to those who endured discrimination, violence, and death to maintain the Coptic community in Egypt.[23] As a child growing up in the Coptic church, my priests, Sunday school teachers, and mentors all imparted on me the sacrifice made by the martyrs for my sake. For thousands of years, I was taught, my ancestors underwent unspeakable hardship so that their faith could be passed down to me. Therefore, a rejection of that faith or the Coptic community was a rejection of this gift that came at such a cost. Only an ungrateful person would do this; therefore, the only acceptable alternative is to enthusiastically embrace Coptic community in the diaspora.

Martyrs feature prominently in Coptic ritual and worship.[24] The Synaxarium, the record of the lives of the saints, has an overwhelming number of martyrs.[25] It is rare to find a day recorded in the Synaxarium without the commemoration of a martyr. Matins, liturgies, and midnight praises are not complete without the commemoration of martyrs. Much of Coptic hymnology is dedicated to revering martyrs and recounting their stories.[26] These hymns paint stories of courage and strength. They are meant to honor

---

22. Boulos, *The History of the Early Coptic Community in the U.S.A. (1955–1970)*, 26–28.

23. Khalil, *The Making of a Diocese*, 4.

24. For example, doxologies for specific martyrs are often sung during Matins, and they are commemorated in the Morning Doxologies. In the Liturgy of St. Basil, martyrs are mentioned in the Hymn of the Intercessions, the Commemoration of the Saints, and often sung about during communion hymns. Vespers typically features several references to martyrs.

25. *Coptic Synaxarium*.

26. Baumeister, "Martyrology," in *Claremont Coptic Encyclopedia*, 2–3.

the sacrifices made by the martyrs, and also to encourage contemporary Copts to see the martyrs as role models, demonstrating the same loyalty. For example, the doxology of St. Mina presents him as a brave warrior and encourages the Copts who sing it to follow his example:

> What will it profit a man
> If he gains the whole world
> And loses his soul
> This would be the life of vanity.
>
> The saint Abba Mina
> Heard the Divine voice
> And has forsaken the whole world
> And its corrupt glory.
>
> He gave his soul unto death
> And his flesh to the fire
> And received great sufferings
> For the Son of the Living God.
>
> Therefore our Savior
> Lifted him to His kingdom
> And granted him the good things
> Which an eye has not seen.
>
> Hail to you O martyr
> Hail to the courageous hero
> Hail to the struggle-mantled
> The saint Abba Mina.
>
> Pray to the Lord on our behalf
> O struggle-mantled martyr
> The saint Abba Mina
> That He may forgive us our sins.

This doxology, and others like it, center on the martyr's courage and loyalty. These hymns also place a strong emphasis on the reward that the martyr receives for her/his sacrifice. As they hear and sing hymns like these, Copts in the diaspora are exhorted to also demonstrate courage in the face of persecution and hardship.

In his teachings, Pope Shenouda III frequently drew on martyrdom as a survival paradigm for Copts. In a sermon delivered on Nayrouz,[27] the Coptic New Year, he spoke about the importance of martyrs in Coptic heritage:

> The martyrs in their martyrdom demonstrated the deepest form of love towards God. Our Lord Jesus Christ said, "Greater love has no one than this, than to lay down one's life for his friends." The martyrs loved God more than their personal lives, and they laid down that life for Him. In their martyrdom they not only displayed the depth of their love to God, but it also contains the depth of their courage. . . . Furthermore, they were an incredible example to all the generations in witnessing to the faith and being steadfast despite all the torture and persecutions. They are the ones who preserved the faith for us with their blood until it was given to us intact. This is why we consider the martyrs to be the seeds of faith, and the foundation of faith in the church. . . . What do we benefit from the Feast of the Nayrouz? Its spiritual lesson is not just that we have a fascination for the faith, courage, and steadfastness of the martyrs and we become proud that we are the children of the martyrs. The spiritual lesson is that we must walk in their ways.[28]

He emphasizes the courage of the martyrs, who were willing to put their commitment to the church before all else, and speaks about the rewards that martyrs receive for their sacrifice. Ultimately, he argues that the martyrs are role models for Copts everywhere, who should strive to have the same level of loyalty. The prevalence of martyrs reminds Copts that their loyalty should first and foremost be to the tenets of the church, and that in doing so they will receive significant rewards in the afterlife. For example, the Coptic Church commemorates the deaths of martyrs as their "birthdays," the days on which their real lives begin.[29] Therefore, Copts look to the martyrs as the ultimate examples of what they too can earn if they are faithful to the Church and its teachings.

Both in Egypt and in the diaspora, churches and children are often named after martyrs as a way of continuing their legacy. For example, in the diocese of Los Angeles, Southern California, and Hawaii, twenty-one

---

27. One of the major themes of Nayrouz is martyrdom, and most churches place a high emphasis on the commemoration and remembrance of martyrs. For more information, see Miyokawa, "The Struggle over Egyptianness," 126.

28. From a sermon delivered on September 11, 2013 in St. Mark's Cathedral, Cairo, Egypt.

29. Meinardus, *Two Thousand Years of Coptic Christianity*, 97.

of the forty-one churches are named after martyrs.[30] Stories of the martyrs are shared with children born in the diaspora in order to link them to their heritage and remind them that they are expected to display the same commitment to the Coptic community and faith through their loyalty. Much of my own childhood was spent watching movies telling the lives of martyrs, all of which were portrayed in the maximum graphic detail. The moral at the end of each of these gruesome tales was one of loyalty. As he would put in the VHS tape with the movie of the life of St. Demiana[31]—for whom I was given my middle name—my father would remind me that, like St. Demiana, I was called to a life of virtue and loyalty, and that I bore that calling in my very name.

The martyr paradigm continues to be relevant in the Coptic diaspora because Copts still face religious persecution in Egypt. Sometimes this persecution results in extreme violence or death. Contemporary victims, like those of the kidnapping and beheading of Copts in Libya in February 2015,[32] the Botroseya Church bombing in December 2016,[33] and the Palm Sunday bombings in Tanta and Alexandria in April 2017,[34] are honored as martyrs. Their narratives, however, are markedly different. They are not brought before the emperor, or asked to offer incense to pagan gods;[35] rather, their religious identity alone makes them targets for the violence of political ideologues. It is still a risk to attend services and participate in Church life, but the narrative of modern martyrdom is marked by a different kind of confrontation.

Copts in the diaspora are typically experiencing these attacks from a distance, but they worry for family and friends still living in Egypt, they mourn destruction of cities and churches that they love, and they feel the weight of marginalized Coptic existence. With every news story, I mourn. Even though I don't personally know the victims of these attacks, and I am as far removed from this kind of danger as is geographically possible, I feel deeply for these Copts, whom I have never met, because they are still a part of me. I have been raised to consider them part of my own heritage, and their suffering is my legacy, even if I never experience it myself. Identifying

---

30. For the complete list, see http://lacopts.org/the-diocese/parishes/directory/.

31. St. Demiana is one of the most popular female Coptic martyrs.

32. Hammill, "Martyrs in Orange."

33. Rothwell and Samaan, "The Dead Were Everywhere."

34. Gaball and Tolba, "Palm Sunday Bombings of Egyptian Coptic Churches Kill," 44.

35. This is the most common trope in the narratives of canonized martyrs, such as St. Maurice, St. Demiana, St. George, and St. Mina, who all follow this trope.

as martyrs, and honoring those who died as martyrs, is an important way for Copts both inside and outside of Egypt to cope with these tragedies.

The Obedience Paradigm

Another major paradigm on which Coptic survival is founded is the emphasis on obedience. Coptic communities are structured on a strict hierarchy, and those on lower rungs of it are expected to unquestioningly obey those on the higher rungs. This can be seen clearly in the early development of Coptic diasporic communities. The first intentional Coptic-American community, formed in New Jersey in 1962, involved the efforts of a number of Coptic immigrants who worked tirelessly to form the foundations necessary for a thriving Coptic Church in the diaspora.[36] However, despite their hard work, the final say on all decisions involving the formation of the Church rested on the clerical hierarchy in Egypt.[37] This rigid hierarchical structure has been important for Coptic survival because it allows for strong community foundations. Pope Shenouda III argues that the hierarchy of clergy, especially the authority of priests, is crucial to the maintenance of Coptic survival.[38]

The Coptic community in the diaspora is not a democracy. In some ways, it mimics a democracy, often having laypeople vote on various issues, but these votes are mere suggestions. Ultimately, decision-making power lies in the hands of the clergy, and they have the final word.[39] In my conversations with clergy, I know that we do not hold the same power. I cannot make any meaningful decisions that will affect that Coptic Church on any level—not even in my own parish. Any structural changes that I might want would have to go through clergy, and if they do not agree, that is the end of the conversation.

The origins of the obedience paradigm can be found in the Coptic Church's rich history of monasticism. Coptic monasticism developed in the third century and flourished in the fourth century.[40] It has been a deeply influential and constant contributor to Coptic spirituality. Monasticism is arguably the Coptic Church's greatest contribution to world civilization.

36. Boulos, *The History of the Early Coptic Community in the U.S.A. (1955–1970)*, 27.

37. Boulos, *The History of the Early Coptic Community in the U.S.A. (1955–1970)*, 43.

38. Pope Shenouda III. *The Priesthood*, 67.

39. Ibrahim and Ibrahim, "Building a Diaspora, Adopting a New Nationality," 258.

40. Farag, "Monasticism: Living Scripture and Theological Orthodoxy," 116–17.

Monasteries were, and continue to be, geographically isolated from the rest of the Coptic Church.[41] Because of this they experience some degree of separation from secular Egyptian culture, politics, and the persecution that the rest of the Coptic Church experiences.[42]

Under Islamic rule, monasteries were often seen as a safe haven in which Coptic Christianity could flourish.[43] Although there were periods during which monasteries suffered attacks, many monasteries were able to survive as viable and relatively safe spaces to maintain Church life. In many respects, it was easier to preserve Coptic culture and spirituality in monasteries because of their isolation and distance from persecution.[44] However, this has resulted in a complicated relationship between monasteries and laypeople, especially when it comes to monastic influence over the Church.

Due to their unique status during periods of persecution, monasteries were held in high regard. As they unintentionally took on the task of preserving Coptic religious practice, they were seen as more authentic versions of Coptic Christianity, unsullied by persecution and Islamic influence. Farag writes:

> Monasticism is a spiritual force in Coptic society. From its inception it attracted thousands of Christians who aspired to live a life that would bring them closer to God. The faithful sought advice from monastics, not only in spiritual matters but in most matters of life, and returned to their homes transformed. . . . As for the Coptic Church, monastic spirituality has influenced lay spirituality in may ways, including fasting, the centrality of Scripture, the use of the monastic prayers of the hours (*Agbeya*) as the daily prayers of the faithful, just to mention a few. In addition, may laypeople have monastics as their spiritual guides.[45]

Therefore, in their own way, monasteries became hubs of Coptic survival. Because bishops and patriarchs were taken from monasteries, their spiritual guidance was influenced by their monastic lives. Ascetic practices like fasting, prostrations, and praying the hours were encouraged and incorporated into lay Church life.

Initially, monasteries functioned somewhat outside of the ecclesiastical structure of the Coptic Church. While they ascribed to Coptic theology, ritual, and practice, they were not held accountable as members of the

---

41. Farag, "Monasticism," 125.
42. Farag, "Monasticism," 126.
43. Farag, "Monasticism," 129.
44. Swanson, *The Coptic Papacy in Islamic Egypt*, 11.
45. Farag, "Monasticism," 127–28.

hierarchy. However, as monastic communities formalized, it became important for them to have a stronger connection to Church hierarchy. This connection came from St. Athanasius, who under his time as patriarch in the fourth century, selected bishops from among the monks.[46] This practice is still held today. Selecting church leadership from the monasteries has had a significant effect on Coptic spirituality, as ascetic practices are incorporated and encouraged by bishops. St. Athanasius' *Life of Antony* also brought widespread recognition to monasticism.[47]

Obedience is one of the highest virtues in the monastic life. It is only through obedience to a spiritual father that one can truly count oneself as an ascetic. Stories of obedience are not uncommon in the narratives of the lives of Coptic monks.[48] It is the virtue from which all of his other virtues emerge. Monasticism presents a strong sense of hierarchy and an understanding that spiritual growth can only be experienced through complete obedience to a spiritual father.

Pope Shenouda III also writes about the importance of obedience in the spiritual life of a Copt:

> So then simply listening to the words of a teacher, does not mean that one is his disciple. One has to be firmly grounded in his teaching. This means converting the teacher's words into a life, so that they become principles that are firmly established in the one who is learning.[49]

Pope Shenouda III also argues that one must have a teacher or mentor to look to for spiritual guidance. The teacher experiences some level of authority over the disciple. The disciple is responsible for taking the teachings of the teacher and turning them into a complete way of life. Central to this model is the paradigm of total obedience. This obedience is manifested through an absolute surrender to one's mentor, taking their words and actions as a guide to proper spiritual living:

> In your discipleship you do not learn from the words of your teachers, but from their behavior and way of life. Even when they say nothing, you still absorb their way of living, by absorbing the good qualities, standards and patterns which they demonstrate in their life.[50]

46. Davis, *The Early Coptic Papacy*, 61–62.
47. Davis, *The Early Coptic Papacy*, 60.
48. Russell, *The Lives of the Desert Fathers*, 114–15.
49. Pope Shenouda III. *Discipleship*, 10.
50. Pope Shenouda III, *Discipleship*, 20.

It is important to recognize that, in the model of obedience and discipleship that Pope Shenouda III outlines here, one is called to not only listen and obey her spiritual guide, but to also meet her guide with attentiveness, paying attention to the actions and ethos of the guide and seeking to mimic them to the best of her ability. Good obedience, then, requires the mentee to actively observe the mentor and to explicitly identify the mentor as a person she seeks to emulate.

Pope Shenouda also argues that the role of the priests and bishops should parallel that of Christ. Christ, taken to be the ultimate authority, teacher, and mentor, manifests his authority through the clergy.[51] Therefore, disobeying the clergy is interpreted as disobedience (and disrespect) of Christ himself.

Additionally, hymnology and liturgy reinforce the paradigm of obedience by frequently referencing Coptic hierarchy. At several points in the liturgy, past and present patriarchs are commemorated. Clergy are prayed for, and the congregation asks God to strengthen priests, bishops, and patriarchs as those who "rightly define the word of truth."[52] These prayers identify clergy as spiritual fathers who possess ultimate decision-making power. By participating in these prayers, laypeople acknowledge the authority of the clergy and agree to respond with obedience. The structure of the liturgy itself reflects the authority of the clergy, who are the only ones allowed to enter the altar and touch sacred vessels and utensils.[53] The vast majority of the liturgy consists of words spoken only by the priest. Even the congregation's responses are led by chanters who are specially ordained for the task and who hold a place in the hierarchy. In short, Coptic liturgical rite revolves around the clerical hierarchy and reflects the authority held by the clergy.

Since the struggle for Coptic survival centers on the struggle to establish and maintain foundations, and since Coptic civilization finds its foundation in a strict hierarchy, obedience is a crucial paradigm. The obedience paradigm reinforces the authority of the clergy and makes the recognition of clerical authority a condition of Coptic survival. To disobey, therefore, is not simply a disregard for an individual or a small group but can instead be interpreted as a lack of commitment to Coptic survival.

---

51. Pope Shenouda III, *The Priesthood*, 194–95

52. Litany of the Fathers, Litany of the Priests and Deacons, and the Diptych (Liturgy of St. Basil).

53. Pope Shenouda III, *The Priesthood*, 215.

Conclusion

The Coptic Church, like so many other Middle Eastern Christian Churches, has learned to adapt and survive through diaspora. This has produced many challenges and opportunities as churches try to figure out how to preserve their identities while adjusting to new environments. Churches respond to this struggle by embedding paradigms of survival into their theologies that encourage participants to stay loyal to their church community and to pass down culture to future generations. The Coptic Church as done this by promoting paradigms of martyrdom and obedience. It will be interesting to see how our paradigms shift to support the continued spread of Middle Eastern Christianity throughout the world.

For Further Reading

Armanios, Febe, and Andrew Amstutz. "Emerging Christian Media in Egypt: Clerical Authority and the Visualization of Women in Coptic Video Films." *International Journal of Middle East Studies* 45.3 (2013) 513–33.

Baumeister, Theofried. "Martyrology." *Claremont Coptic Encyclopedia*, 2–3. Claremont, CA: Claremont Graduate University, School of Religion, 1991.

Boulos, Sami. *The History of the Early Coptic Community in the U.S.A. (1955–1970)*. Coptic Orthodox Patriarchate, 2006.

Brinkerhoff, Jennifer. "Assimilation and Heritage Identity: Lessons from the Coptic Diaspora." *Journal of International Migration and Integration* 17.2 (2015) 467–85.

———. "Diaspora Philanthropy: Lessons from a Demographic Analysis of the Coptic Diaspora." *Nonprofit and Voluntary Sector Quarterly* 43.6 (2013) 969–92.

Coptic Synaxarium. Hindsdale, IL: St. Mark and St. Pishoy Coptic Orthodox Church, 1987.

Davis, Stephen. *The Early Coptic Papacy: The Egyptian Church and Its Leadership in Late Antiquity, The Popes of Egypt, Volume 1*. Cairo: American University in Cairo Press in Cairo, 2004.

Farag, Lois. "Monasticism: Living Scripture and Theological Orthodoxy." In *The Coptic Christian Heritage: History, Faith and Culture*, edited by Lois Farag, 116–31. London: Routledge, 2014.

———. "Theology: Defending Orthodoxy." In *The Coptic Christian Heritage: History, Faith, and Culture*, edited by Lois Farag, 105–15. London: Routledge, 2014.

Gaball, Arwa, and Ahmed Tolba. "Palm Sunday Bombings of Egyptian Coptic Churches Kill 44." *Reuters*. Thomson Reuters, April 2017.

Hammill, Ryan. "Martyrs in Orange: One Year Later, the Coptic Orthodox Church Observes Feast Day of 21 Christians." *Sojourners*, March 2016.

Hanna, Michael Wahid. "With Friends Like These: Coptic Activism in the Diaspora." *Middle East Report* 267 (2013) 28–31.

Ibrahim, Fouad, and Barbara Ibrahim. "Building a Diaspora, Adopting a New Nationality: Egyptian Copts in the United States." *Imagined Identities: Identity Formation in the Age of Globalization*, edited by Gonul Pultar, 249–66. Syracuse: Syracuse University Press, 2014.

Iskander, Elizabeth. *Sectarian Conflict in Egypt: Coptic Media, Identity and Representation*. London: Routledge, 2012.

Khalil, Elhamy. *The Making of a Diocese: The Early Years of the Coptic Orthodox Diocese of Los Angeles, Southern California, and Hawaii*. Los Angeles: Coptic Orthodox Diocese of Los Angeles, Southern California and Hawaii, 2008.

Mahmood, Saba. *Religious Difference in a Secular Age: A Minority Report*. Princeton, NJ: Princeton University Press, 2016.

Meinardus, Otto F. A. *Two Thousand Years of Coptic Christianity*. Cairo: American University in Cairo Press in Cairo, 1999.

Miyokawa, Hiroko. "The Struggle over Egyptianness: A Case Study of the Nayruz Festival." *Minorities and the Modern Arab World: New Perspectives*, edited by Laura Robson, 122–39. New York: Syracuse University, 2016.

Papaconstantinou, Arietta. "Historiography, Hagiography, and the Making of the Coptic 'Church of Martyrs' in Early Islamic Egypt." *Dumbarton Oaks Papers 60* (2006) 65–86.

Pope Shenouda III. *Discipleship*. Alexandria: Coptic Orthodox Patriarchate, 1990.

———. *The Priesthood*. Cairo: Dar El Tebaa El Kawmia, 1990.

Ramzy, Carolyn M. "Music: Performing Coptic Expressive Culture." *The Coptic Christian Heritage: History, Faith, and Culture*, edited by Lois Farag, 160–76. London: Routledge, 2014.

Rothwell, James, and Magdy Samaan. "The Dead Were Everywhere: 23 Coptic Christians Killed in Bomb Attack on Chapter Complex." *The Telegraph*, December 2016.

Russell, Norman, trans. *The Lives of the Desert Fathers: The Historia Monachorum in Aegypto*. London: Mowbray, 1981.

Saad, Michael. "The Modern Period (1952–2011): An Era of Trials, Tribulations, and Triumphs." In *The Coptic Christian Heritage: History, Faith, and Culture*, edited by Lois Farag, 87–102. London: Routledge, 2014.

Swanson, Mark. *The Coptic Papacy in Islamic Egypt: The Popes of Egypt, Volume 2*. Cairo: American University in Cairo Press, 2010, 11.

Tadros, Mariz. *Copts at the Crossroads: The Challenges of Building Inclusive Democracy in Egypt*. Cairo: American University in Cairo Press, 2013.

Yefet, Bosmat. "The Coptic Diaspora and the Status of the Coptic Minority in Egypt." *Journal of Ethnic and Migration Studies* 43.7 (2017) 1205–21.

13

Women in Middle Eastern Christianity

Pamela Chrabieh

The story of Christians in the Middle East, i.e., Southwestern Asia and North Africa, has seldom been told in terms that highlight their major contributions to local/regional cultures, their traditions and popular cultures, their denominational identities, their demographic states, their legal standing, their encounters with diverse local religious communities, their minoritization, their emigration, and even their disappearance. Numerous first-rate studies of and about Christians of this part of the world have been published in the last two to three decades, but most have not been so much concerned with Christian women's situations, narratives, struggles, and achievements, specifically those of contemporary Christian women. This is a facet that deserves attention, as it has often been neglected by both "Westerners" and "Easterners." In that sense, two of the many current issues about Christian women in this part of the world are addressed in this chapter—women and the scriptures, and religious authority—by focusing on a number of narratives and initiatives for change produced by contemporary scholars, such as Syrian Mary Mikhael, Viola Raheb, Maria Kabara, Anne Zaki, Hosn Abboud, Therese Farra, Johnny Awwad, Nancy Jabra, Lise Galal, Gihane Tabet, and Claudia Mende.

Tackling these issues is more than needed nowadays given the fact that women in Southwestern Asia and North Africa are still facing a patriarchal environment/system and mentality in varying degrees. This environment/system enshrines the assumptions that heads of institutions must be male, male voices rightfully dominate public and private spaces, and female position is subordinate, although necessary. As Suad Joseph defines it, patriarchy in the Arab context is the prioritizing of the rights of males and elders, and the justification of those rights within kinship values, which are usually supported by religion.¹ According to Joseph, the persistence of patriarchy is an obstacle for women, and it affects health, education, labor, human rights, and democracy. A similar insight is shared by numerous scholars and activists, such as Nahla Yassine-Hamdan,² who asserts that gender inequality is visible in the Arab world with cross-national differences in gender inequality that reflect cross-national differences in patriarchy, in particular differences in how men use their power over women (including by instrumentalizing religions) to limit their agency or ability to make decisions for themselves. Several feminists who have been part of the "Red Lips High Heels" online movement from 2012 to 2017 also share the same observations/conclusions.³ In addition, they offer a sample of the extended debate about the best method to fight patriarchy within local societies, ranging from views that define patriarchy as a "Western" concept not applicable to local Christianity and to Islam, through to secularist views that hold that Christianity and Islam are intrinsically patriarchal. Some Christian and Muslim contributors to the Red Lips High Heels movement argue for the emergence of a subjective turn that would eclipse traditional religions and open the door to an expressive selfhood in a post-religious society. Others argue for a progressive reform of institutionalized religions and the integration of women in decision-making processes. And there are a few who seek to offer alternative experiences of self, body, and spirituality that challenge dominant representations of women.⁴ These feminist views/currents, along with many others, are found at the basis of contemporary narratives,

---

1. Joseph, "Patriarchy and Development in the Arab World."

2. Yassine-Hamdan, "Gender Inequality in the Arab World: A Comparative Perspective."

3. I founded this movement in 2012, an online network and a platform for feminist voices/narratives in the region. From 2012 to 2017, authors, artists, and activists wrote about their experiences and observations of gender-based discrimination in Southwestern Asia and North Africa, including about gender and religions. https://redlipshighheels.com/.

4. Usual characteristic descriptors sometimes portray women in this region to be oppressed, weak, and needing rescue. In that perspective, one of the main goals of this book was to deconstruct positivist or essentialist views while digging the past. Thus, it was designed to give its readers an understanding of the often-forgotten foundations of many contemporary cultures and religions in this region concerning womanhood, especially as they apply to the status and relationships of men and women today. Investigating the past and examining the development of gender norms, identities, and roles, contribute to understanding ideas, practices, customs, and trends that have shaped regional cultures. However, this understanding ought to be considered as limited and continuously in process. There will always be a difficulty to come up with the general past and present "truths." I therefore chose to only focus on a few issues that can hopefully provide some sort of insight into the matter at hand.

perceptions, and positions about women and Christianity in Southwestern Asia and North Africa. Characteristics of some of these currents are highlighted in the following sections of this chapter.

Women and Scriptures

Although feminist (and gender equality) views, acts, and narratives existed long before the nineteenth century, as argued in *Womanhood in Western Asia*, feminist consciousness developed in the last 100 years alongside a sense of nationalism based on the idea of liberation from oppression.[5] Numerous feminist groups, associations, journals, and magazines were established in Southwestern Asia and North Africa in the 1800s and 1900s, and women struggled to liberate themselves from prescribed gender roles and from what hindered their emancipation. Many also stood against the exploitation of feminist rhetoric by patriarchal institutions and proved that local feminisms are much more than a "Western import" or "a tool to fight Western imperialism/patriarchy." And since the 1970s, with rising literacy and awareness of women's rights, and an increasing access to scriptural knowledge by women, local feminisms diversified and started to include religious-centered currents. In a substantial issue of *Al-Raida* (*The Pioneer*, issue 129, spring 2009), published by The Institute for Women's Studies in the Arab World at the Lebanese American University, scholar on Qur'anic Mary and literary critic Hosn Abboud states that since the 1970s, "Jewish, Christian, and Muslim women, including scholars, historians, literary critics, psychologists, feminist theologians, activists, and devout women attending to their rituals in the synagogue, the church, or the mosque, have studied the Old Testament, the New Testament, and the Qur'an throughout the Arab world."[6] However, one will find only a few names of women scholars at schools of theology, and institutes of religious studies continue to either exclude women, belittle their scholarly contributions, silence their voices, or "to rely on male leadership and traditional methods of education."

Among these few names is a noted authority, Syrian Mary Mikhael, who was the president of the Near East School of Theology in Beirut-Lebanon from 1994 to 2011, and the first woman seminary president in the region.[7] As a fellow founding-member of the Christian Academic Forum for Citizenship in the Arab World (CAFCAW), Mikhael co-organized with her colleagues at Dar al-Kalima University College of Arts and Culture

5. El Bachiri. "Féminisme Historique."
6. Abboud, "Women and Scriptures," 2.
7. The Outreach Foundation, *Near East School*.

(Bethlehem) several conferences and workshops on Christians of Southwestern Asia and North Africa, gender issues, state and religion, youth, identity, and inclusive societies. Mikhael's publications include: "St. Paul and the Place of Women in that Church" (*Theological Review*, 2002); "Women in Middle Eastern Societies and Churches" (*The Ecumenical Review* 64.1, March 2012); "The Christian Woman" (in *Arabic Christian Theology: A Contemporary Global Evangelical Perspective*, ed. A. Z. Stephanous, 2019), etc. We should also note that Mikhael served on the Executive Committee of the Women's World Day of Prayer and directed the Women's Program for the Middle East Council of Churches for nine years.[8]

Another notable Christian scholar is Viola Raheb. Born in Bethlehem, Raheb gained her master's degree in education and Evangelical theology from the Ruprecht-Karls-University in Germany and her PhD in advanced theological studies from the University of Vienna. She is currently a researcher at the University of Vienna, Faculty of Protestant Theology, Department of the Studies of Religions. According to Raheb, Christian women "are faced with obstacles within their own religious communities, [especially] patriarchal traditions, exclusion from church hierarchies, lack of recognition of their contribution to the advancement of their respective religious communities and their leadership both in ordained and lay levels, religious-based Family Status Laws (Personal Status Laws) . . . ."[9] Raheb has published several articles and book chapters focusing on reading the Bible through the eyes of Christian Palestinian women.[10] For instance, in "Women in Contemporary Palestinian Society: A Contextual Reading of the Book of Ruth,"[11] she explains the situation of women in Palestine through the window of the story of the Moabite woman Ruth. "Upon arrival in Palestine, Ruth had to search for a source of living. Women worked for food and lodging. The Palestinian society is no longer a peasant society and agriculture is no longer the main source of income. Accordingly, the areas of work for women have become more diverse. Although some Palestinian women have made their way into previously male-dominated professions, the majority [including Christians] are still working in the traditionally accepted female professions such as nursing, teaching, or secretarial work." Raheb also compares the contemporary remarriage of widows—with the current Palestinian reality showing "schizophrenia": men ought to remarry, but women should remain

---

8. Arteen and Hill, "18 Arab Females."
9. Interview conducted by email on April 7, 2021.
10. Among her publications: "In Conflict" and "Reading Micah."
11. Schroer and Bietenhard, *Feminist Interpretation*, 89.

faithful to their late husbands[12]—with being a widow in the story of Ruth, where women work securing each other's futures. Furthermore, she tackles the issue of interreligious marriages, by comparing once again Ruth's decision to marry a Jew—a decision either based on openness to the "other" or a matter of survival—with current marriages of Palestinian Christian women to Muslim men, and the diverse causes explaining this growing development within the Palestinian society.[13]

A further example of women Christian scholars is Syrian Greek-Orthodox Maria Kabara, whose texts in Arabic are published on the telosmagazine.org blog.[14] Kabara is writing a PhD thesis at the Aristotle University of Thessaloniki-Greece entitled "The Woman and Social Justice in the Works of Bishop George Khoder: Contemporary Theological Approach." She challenges taboos within the Orthodox Church, which, as she states, is governed today by a traditional, inherited mentality that negatively affects contemporary pastoral life. She also tries to face through her writings the limitations imposed by both civil laws and personal-status laws. For Kabara, religious texts and laws emerged from the extreme traditionalism of religious institutions and from patriarchal societies, which imposed and still impose obedience of various forms on women. Thus, the need to promote a moderate and open-minded mentality to overcome the traditional/conservative religious thoughts that hinder women.

In her article "Martha or Mary: The Woman's Position and Role in the Orthodox Church" (in Arabic), Kabara argues that Jesus Christ accepts the role of Mary, "a charismatic role based on gift/spiritual gift" (thus a woman is a disciple equal to a male disciple), while the Church prefers that of Martha—i.e., "a traditional institutional role, a woman who takes care of house chores and family matters" (Luke 10:38–42).[15] According to Kabara, despite Jesus praising Mary's role and teaching the equal status of men and women in terms of salvation, holiness, and sanctification, Martha's role has gained increasing importance over the centuries, following a parallel process of Church institutionalization. Kabara continues to argue while using an often-cited biblical passage cited in Christian discussions about gender equality, in which Paul states: "There is neither Jew nor Greek, slave nor free, male nor female, for you are all one in Christ Jesus" (Gal 3:28). According to her, Christ's attitude towards women and this Pauline passage led women

12. Schroer and Bietenhard, *Feminist Interpretation*, 91.
13. Schroer and Bietenhard, *Feminist Interpretation*, 91.
14. An interview with Kabara was conducted by email on April 6, 2021.
15. Published by *Telos Magazine*, February 28, 2021, https://www.telosmagazine.org/blog_arabic/9268646 (last retrieved April 7, 2021).

to play an effective role in the early Church, such as taking on the roles of evangelists, teachers, and deaconesses (Rom 16:1–16).

Yet the apostle Paul, according to Kabara, did not avoid institutionalization. His first attempts at organizing the church revealed another attitude towards women within society. He presented the hierarchical, patriarchal structure of the dominant social organization either through the subordination of the woman to the man in the family (Eph 5:21–33) or through a prohibition on women speaking in general and commending the passive presence of women in the ecclesiastical community (1 Cor 11:1–16; 1 Tim 2:9–14). In Kabara's view, although women competed with men in spiritual and ascetic life during the Byzantine era, the Church accepted the differentiated roles of men and women, thus reducing and limiting the role of women in society at the time. Furthermore, women's roles gradually decreased with the abolition of the deaconesses' roles.

As Kabara explains, the existing distinction between men and women became entrenched, and their role and position further declined during the Ottoman Empire, for many reasons, including "well-known political and social ones." After the establishment of the modern Greek state at the beginning of the nineteenth century, the religious institution separated men and women within churches, considering this act as "traditional" and "sacred." According to Kabara, today's situations of women within the Greek Orthodox Church in particular and in the Arab world in general is not better, as the distribution of different roles for men and women still prevail—men manage the public space, and women take care of the private space. The ecclesiastical community legalized/institutionalized these roles, thus reinforcing the historical-traditional attribute of men's supremacy over women. In that sense, there is an urgent need to put into practice Galatians 3:28 and what Saint John the Merciful stated in the sixth century: "We are all equal, and we must become equal."

The work of the Darb Maryam (Mary's Path) movement in Lebanon is also worth mentioning here. This movement encourages Christian-Muslim encounters through pilgrimages on the path of Mary. It was founded by Therese Farra, and co-headed by Farra and Hosn Abboud, who both work on promoting a renewed perspective of Mary as a bridge between Christianity and Islam by going back to the scriptures, beyond the traditional patriarchal-centered perspective. In a recent report published by Adyan NGO in Lebanon, Abboud said that although their movement was founded by women, and that there is growing support for the participation of women within interreligious activities (such as for the Annunciation Day on March 25, which became a national Christian-Muslim celebration in Lebanon), and that there are women who hold positions of leadership (such as at the

Adyan Foundation and the Middle East Council of Churches), women are still absent from most of the scripture-interpreting circles, theology commissions, and decision-making tables of dialogue organizations in Southwestern Asia and North Africa.[16] "People have to understand and acknowledge that women have different perspectives regarding theological and religious matters. It is time to give women and youth space to speak about religions and a chance to modernize certain ideas and concepts."[17]

It is important to note here that when it comes to the issue of gender and scriptures, in Lebanon special attention has been given to the study of Mary, both in the New Testament and in the Qur'an. This can be seen in *Al-Raida* (*The Pioneer*, issue 129, spring 2009) with an article by Abboud, "Is Mary Important for Herself or for Being the Mother of Christ in the Holy Qur'an?" Abboud adopts a feminist approach by criticizing religious discourse that emphasizes and values the role of the female in family relationships only. Another article in the same issue is "Liberation and Universality: Women in Luke's Gospel," by Johnny Awwad, who invites readers to read Luke using a gendered perspective and to understand how Luke classified the women mentioned in his gospel—a classification using "the technique of pairing." There is also an interesting article by Nancy Jabra, "Women's Marian Devotions in a Melkite Greek Catholic Village in Lebanon," focusing on devotions to Mary as celebrated in a village in the Beqaa Valley of Lebanon. As the author argues, these devotions, while not commanded in Christian scripture, have enabled women to carve out a spiritual place for themselves in a patriarchal Church. Last but not least, from the same issue, is "Sacred Women in Coptic Cinema" by Lise Galal. Although it is not concentrated only on Mary, it is worth mentioning. Galal tackles the subject of Coptic saints and martyrs in the context of Egyptian Coptic revivalism using an anthropological approach, while analyzing movies that have been produced since the late 1980s.

These are only samples of scholarly work on women and the scriptures in Southwestern Asia and North Africa that present some of the contemporary feminist approaches within Christian communities. These scholars are usually broadly categorized as *rejectionists* (meaning those who reject religious traditions altogether), *traditionalists* (who keep the patriarchal framework of Christianity as it is, although they work through a methodology of reinterpretation of sacred scriptures and traditions), and *reformists/moderates* (who adopt a more dynamic approach and dare to reinterpret some of the elements of this framework). The examples of women scholars who

---

16. Adyan Foundation Report, *Interreligious Dialogue*.
17. Abboud in the Adyan Foundation Report, *Interreligious Dialogue*, 43.

were previously mentioned could belong to the third category (noting that Viola Rehab simply identifies herself as "feminist Christian theologian"[18] and Mary Mikhael sees herself as "a Christian woman who has always been concerned about women in the Church as well as in society").[19] This "category" faces numerous obstacles when it comes to promoting its framework and content—mainly from traditionalists and conservatives within their communities, but also from secular feminists or rejectionists who ask fundamental questions, i.e., is it necessary to have religious legitimacy to establish gender equality today? Can't a secularization of personal-status laws, for instance, allow full equality of rights?

These are questions worth tackling in Middle Eastern regions as local communities still exercise enormous control over the lives of women. Claudia Mende explains it well in "Arab Christian Women Take a Stand against Church Paternalism," when she states that "this [oppositional stance] is because the state has allocated them [religious communities/institutions] jurisdiction over matters concerning marriage, divorce, custody rights, and inheritance. As such, Islamic or church dignitaries decide upon important questions in the lives of individuals."[20] The same statement is shared by Gihane Tabet in "Women in Personal Status Laws: Iraq, Jordan, Lebanon, Palestine, Syria," as she explains the legal system pertaining to women's rights in Southwestern Asia and North Africa by focusing on inequalities in marriage, inheritance, and nationality, "which have in common a traditional and patriarchal system in which family law is based on interpretations of Sharia (Islamic religious) law [and Christian laws]. Obviously, beyond being different, these legal regimes are never egalitarian. This inequality, which is not only legal but also political and social, is also the case for women."[21] She notes, however, that Jordan has launched a reform of personal-status laws that currently penalize Christian women in Greek Orthodox and Latin Catholic Churches.[22] That is a positive change. Nonetheless, obstacles to changing inheritance laws still mark the Jordanian society as there are Christians who prefer the application of the Islamic inheritance provisions. As for Syria, local

---

18. Interview conducted by e-mail on April 7, 2021. According to Raheb, her theological work is inspired by "contextual, liberation, and feminist theological thought and personalities from around the globe, who have been struggling to do theology from the perspective of the experience of those on the margin as well as from women's experiences. A theology that is emphasizing religion as a source of and a motivation for an emancipatory endeavor for justice and equality for all."

19. Interview conducted by e-mail on April 11, 2021.

20. Mende, "Arab Christian."

21. Tabet, "Women in Personal."

22. "ASIA/JORDAN" and Engelcke, "Jordanian Christians."

Churches, such as the Roman Catholic Church (2006) and the Armenian Orthodox Church (2012), issued their own egalitarian inheritance laws.[23] And in Egypt, a rather egalitarian ruling was obtained by a lawyer in 2018 in an inheritance case within the Coptic Orthodox Church.[24] Nonetheless, the rules for divorce are still in need of urgent change—a cause that has been promoted by prominent women journalists, such as Karima Kamal, and groups such as "Copts 38" and "Right for Life."

Religious Authority

In "Against the Current: Rethinking Gender, Religious Authority and Interreligious Dialogue,"[25] it is argued that most religious institutions and grassroots interfaith initiatives in Southwestern Asia and North Africa are attributed to men, leadership continues to be predominantly male, and it is to be expected that women appear absent or underrepresented in official dialogues between religions. Indeed, although there are many women and feminists who are actively engaged in making changes in their religious communities, the mainstream patriarchal orientation of religious and theological discourses and practices, and the challenges of contemporary forms of religious fundamentalism and conservatism, impose numerous limitations on women's visibility, credibility, and agency. Other causes include the fact that any authority figure

> owes its allegiance to the boundaries and structures created by tradition, and to written laws that codify tradition: for example, many Christian churches are today episcopal which means that the principal authority figures known as bishops control the functioning and direction of the churches, and this authority is traced back to Jesus Christ. This means that the inheritance is itself a function of tradition and that the characteristics of the office of bishop, such as the requirement to be male, are also dependent upon religious tradition. [But it also means that] this relation between religious authority and tradition can be rethought as tradition itself is not a fixed atemporal entity.[26]

One example is that of women in the Maronite Church. Indeed, as argued in the above-mentioned article, "Maronite feminist theologians are

---

23. "Syrian Law Allows."
24. "A Lawyer" and Engelcke, "Jordanian Christians."
25. Wardeh and Chrabieh, "Against the Current," 159.
26. Wardeh and Chrabieh, "Against the Current," 159.

considered a rare breed in Lebanon, and Maronite feminists either do not openly tackle religious authority and gender issues as they are still considered taboo, and/or focus on the legal framework and socio-political issues." Nevertheless, here are a few reasons for the possibility of rethinking the Maronite theology of gender relations: The first reason is that not all Maronites/Catholics agree with the official religious discourses and practices. A second reason is that the process of rethinking tradition and developing theologies of gender equality is already ongoing on a global level, therefore, the local deconstruction of official normative traditional narratives and construction of counter-narratives could be both inspired and backed up by the global conversations. A third reason is that issues of women's rights have been further debated in Lebanese society in particular and in Southwestern Asia [and North Africa] in general in the last few years, and gender equality is not seen any more as an alien concept/praxis by all. In that sense, even the Maronite patriarch, Cardinal Bechara Boutros Rai, stated in 2014 during a celebration on the occasion of the 25th anniversary of the message of Pope John Paul II to Lebanon that he supports "full gender equality," noting that the Church highlights the importance of preserving the dignity of women, and calling on the Lebanese parliament to end all violations against women.[27] "Full gender equality" of course, still does not encompass the religious leadership realm, welcoming women into positions of official religious authority, nor the production and acknowledgment of authoritative religious discourse by women, but one ought to be optimistic, as now and more than ever, there is an urgent need for a shift from complementarianism to egalitarianism—this shift is also being promoted in Egypt by assistant professor in the Department of Practical Theology at the Evangelical Theological Seminary in Cairo (ETSC), Anne E. Zaki.

As explained in her paper entitled "Diversity and Inclusion: Gender Justice in the Evangelical Church in Egypt,"[28] Zaki applied to the Evangelical Presbyterian Church of Egypt (EPCE) to be ordained as a minister of word and sacrament, "which would have made her the first woman ordained to the ministry in Egypt. However, the Church's Synod at its 2016 meeting decided to delay its decision and place a 10-year moratorium on discussing the issues."[29] Zaki's paper highlights the main issues related to religious authority and gender inclusivity in her Church, and starts it by identifying

---

27. "Maronite Patriarch."

28. Presented as an address to the Christian Academic Forum for Citizenship in the Arab World (CAFCAW), at a conference held in Cyprus on November 1, 2019.

29. Zaki, "Diversity and Inclusion," 1.

two dimensions to most conversations around these issues, the biblical-theological and the socio-cultural. According to Zaki:

> Proponents of gender inclusion and justice emphasize eight prominent scriptural texts to validate their position along with a plethora of examples for women as teachers, prophets and preachers, evangelists, and leaders of God's people. They also point to the grand narrative of God's design and desire for gender inclusion proceeding from creation and the fall to redemption, and from the sign of the new covenant to giftedness through the Holy Spirit for all ministry roles. Additionally, opponents of gender inclusion and justice cite eight scriptural texts to validate their stance. As well, they emphasize both the absence of women priests in the Bible and of women among the disciples of Jesus. I have examined both sides, and while I think that each has valid arguments, I am convinced that the proponents of gender inclusion and justice hold the stronger arguments, both biblically and theologically as well as socio-culturally.[30]

Zaki then presents socio-cultural arguments supporting gender justice in the Evangelical Church in Egypt:

1. the migration of men from their villages to cities and other countries, leaving vacant positions that women can easily fill;
2. the presence of several "gifted women" who are "called";
3. the historical support of the Evangelical Church in Egypt for women's ministry;
4. the rise in visibility and prominence of women in Egyptian society.

According to Zaki,

> in 2017 the Ministry of Mosque Affairs appointed 144 female preachers and teachers in local mosques as official employees of the Ministry. They also licensed women maathoonas, a specific category of Muslim clergy who are authorized to officiate at weddings. Since women in recent years have been assuming leading roles in business, government, and mosque, why hasn't the church been part of this movement? Indeed, shouldn't the church of Jesus Christ be leading this movement?[31]

Although, for Zaki, proponents of gender inclusion and justice have been developing and proposing a middle-ground approach, where

30. Zaki, "Diversity and Inclusion," 3–4.
31. Zaki, "Diversity and Inclusion," 9–10.

progressive and conservative can meet "as a first step towards fuller gender inclusivity"—such as proposing that women "be ordained for specific ministries: pastors for children, women, youth, and congregational care; chaplains in hospitals and schools; professors in seminaries and other religious institutions"—opposition to the middle-ground is still prevailing, and change will need time to take place.

Zaki concludes her valuable paper by reiterating the fact that she is among those who seek to make changes within the Presbyterian Church in Egypt, by promoting and applying gender inclusion and justice based on a "distinct theology of the priesthood of all believers" and the removal of "discrepancy between doctrine and deeds." According to Zaki, women should not keep silent when it comes to religious authority and gender roles, she calls for not losing hope, and she still has faith in a Church that "must remain the prophetic voice, challenging cultural norms that counter the gospel. Courageous challenges facilitate healthy growth."[32]

The same belief is shared by Mary Mikhael:

> As a Christian woman, I believe that men and women are one in Christ. My committed faith in Christ is what defines my identity. This gives me the freedom to respond to the call of God for any role or position God has for me. Throughout history, the Church, unfortunately, instead of creating positive changes in the society's rules regarding women's equality with men in the decision-making processes, had identified with the society in all matters. The Church has imposed on women limited participation in its ministries and has ignored what women felt called by God to do. Thus, sadly I say that society is far ahead of the Church. We need to be more vocal and courageous to request equal rights in leadership positions. Surely matters that remain in the dark cannot change. I believe that women from all Church traditions must work together, study together and cooperate, planning with love and care to avoid misunderstanding, and show faith at work. . . . Our request for change and/or renewing traditional practices, all but to serve and enrich the ministry of the Church. The Church must be convinced that women must be helped to become part of God's movement to heal and to save. If God calls women for God's mission, no one must have the right to stop women responding to God.[33]

---

32. Zaki, "Diversity and Inclusion," 23.
33. Interview conducted by email, April 11, 2021.

Conclusion

This preliminary overview of two main current issues addressed by contemporary Christian women from the Middle East ought to push scholars who are interested in the religious and cultural phenomena to further highlight the richness, diversity, and impact of these voices within their communities, societies, and beyond, and to think/rethink the common and different challenges/obstacles that need to be faced, but without referring to Christian women as a never-changing, objective entity. Indeed, womanhood in this region cannot be summarized in "clichés." It is a complex notion, undergoing construction over a period of thousands of years and covering a multiplicity of roles, situations, status, characteristics, values, visions, and practices.

In Middle Eastern societies, laws against marital rape and spousal abuse are largely absent, the so-called "honor" killings persist in some areas, and discriminations prevail in most public and private institutions. Many are the women, including Christians, who are suffering from deficits in human rights. Societal norms that relegate women to subordinate status continue to impede progress. Governments remain resistant to addressing inequalities through progressive policy or legislation, except for a few recent legislative changes, such as in the Maghreb region with new laws including provisions combating violence against women, in Palestine with the repellent of a provision that had allowed individuals suspected of rape to avoid prosecution and imprisonment if they married their victims (as well as in Jordan, Lebanon, and Tunisia in 2017), and the adoption of measures by Jordan and Qatar that allow the children of female nationals married to foreign fathers to acquire permanent residency.[34] Certainly, women throughout the region are still struggling to be able to fully participate in the religious, cultural, economic, and political life of their countries by sitting at the decision-making tables. Not to mention the fact that since 2010, women have been facing the risks of forfeiture of revolutions that were also theirs.

Several issues still need to be addressed, such as the importance of pursuing studies of the past gender roles; conducting more comprehensive research and mapping of the present situation regarding gender roles; better understanding of the situations and praxis of women working against the traditional/conservative currents within their communities or seeking middle grounds; deconstructing orientalist discourses but also some postcolonial discourses that claim to be going beyond stereotypes of Middle Eastern societies, and of gender roles and relations—a first step towards

---

34. Amnesty International, *Human Rights*.

the production of inclusive knowledge; creating networks of feminist organizations, both secular and religious, to demand local governments implement the CEDAW Convention by reviewing national laws, including personal-status laws; supporting academic work in the fields of theology and sciences of religions/religious studies that challenges those theological approaches that exclude or downplay women. In that sense, women are called to do theology while embarking on a pilgrimage towards gender equality/inclusion and the affirmation of the validity of women's perception of religious reality, definition of the world, reading of history, and interpretation of human experience.

Furthermore, on one hand, the experiences of women ought to be integrated within the teachings of Christianity in order to advance the empowerment of women within local Christian communities, and on another hand, there is a need to address Christian women's issues and experiences with a kaleidoscopic prism, as various forms of inequality operate together and exacerbate each other. In "Women in Middle Eastern Societies and Churches," Mikhael's perspective is:

> We are accustomed to marginalize and push women's issues to the corner when the discussion deals with big questions such as the political ones with which we are struggling for over half a century, or the situation of the Christians in general. As we all know, women's issues are not separate from all other human issues, be these political, religious, or societal. They are at the heart of all human rights together. Naturally, I am deeply concerned about women in the Churches of the Middle East. However, speaking about Christian women's place in the Church, while neglecting the situation of women in general and how the political, religious and societal issues affect them, would be presenting an incomplete picture.[35]

Thus the importance of adopting an intersectional approach, which focuses on overlapping experiences of oppression and inequalities. In other words, one should not try to tackle the situations, rights, roles, and opportunities of Christian women without also taking into consideration the interplay between different kinds of discrimination, such as those based on gender in different domains—ethnicity, age, socioeconomic class, physical and mental ability, sexual identity, etc.—and the different historical pathways, cultural heritage, post-colonialist coping mechanisms, and reforms implementation in the region. Christian women's pasts, presents, and futures are indeed part of complex gender cultures in Southwestern Asia and

---

35. Mikhael, "Women in Middle Eastern Societies and Churches."

North Africa, and this complexity ought to be acknowledged, along with the multiple opportunities that lie ahead to continue fighting the internalization of powerlessness we notice every day around us, and to recognize at the same time the fact that many women are not simply passively socialized by religion, but also have agency within their religiosity.

For Further Reading

Abboud, Hosn. "Women and Scriptures in the Arab World." *Al-Raida* (*The Pioneer*) 129 (Spring 2009). Lebanese American University. https://bit.ly/2TYmDKQ/.

Adyan Foundation Report. *Interreligious Dialogue Mapping of the Middle East, 2020.* https://bit.ly/3gxJ8xS/.

"A Lawyer in Alexandria Obtains Hereditary Notices according to Christian Law, Which Equates Men and Women" (in Arabic). Coptstoday.com, March 24, 2019. https://bit.ly/3q2uL9i/.

Amnesty International. *Human Rights in the Middle East and North Africa, 2018 Report.* https://bit.ly/35nwSe8/.

Arteen, Grace Al-Zoughbi, and Graham Joseph Hill. "18 Arab Female Theologians and Christian Leaders You Should Know About." *The Global Church Project*, October 8, 2019. https://bit.ly/3gn4Rts/.

"ASIA/JORDAN—New Rules on the Personal Status of Christians, to Eliminate the Rules That Penalize Women." *Agenzia Fides*, April 4, 2019. https://bit.ly/2RYorD6

Chrabieh, Pamela. "Contemporary Feminisms in Lebanon: Lights in the Tunnel." In *Shifting Identities: Changes in the Social, Political and Religious Structures in the Arab World*, edited by Mitri Raheb, 155–72. Bethlehem: Diyar, 2016.

El Bachiri, Leila. "Féminisme historique et féminisme islamique émergent au Maroc. Quels enjeux pour l'égalité de genre?" In *Femmes, printemps arabes et revendications citoyennes*, edited by Gaëlle Gillot and Andrea Martinez, 73–93. Paris: IRD Editions, 2016.

El Khoury, J. Peter. *Aramaic Catholicism, Maronite History and Identity: A Journey from the Ancient Middle East to the Modern West.* Cleveland, Australia: Connor Court, 2017.

Joseph, Suad. "Patriarchy and Development in the Arab World." *Gender and Development* 4.2 (1996) 14–19. https://bit.ly/2TuY7Bo/.

"Maronite Patriarch Bechara Rai: Church Supports Gender Equality." *Lebanon News*, April 4, 2014. https://bit.ly/2TuYop4/.

Mende, Claudia. "Arab Christian Women Take a Stand Against Church Paternalism." *qantara.de*, May 4, 2020. https://bit.ly/2Ubthhb/.

Mikhael, Mary. "Women in Middle Eastern Societies and Churches." *The Ecumenical Review, World Council of Churches*, March 2012. https://bit.ly/3gCWmt8/.

Moosa, Matti. *The Maronites in History*. Piscataway, NJ: Gorgias, 2005.

Naaman, Paul. *The Maronites*. Collegeville, MN: Cistercian, 2011.

Raheb, Viola. "In Conflict with the Old Testament about the Land." In *Christian Theology in the Palestinian Context*, edited by Rafiq Khoury and Rainer Zimmer-Winkel, 297–311. Berlin: Aphorism, 2019.

———. "Reading Micah 5 in Modern Bethlehem." In *Micah (Wisdom Commentary)*, edited by J. O'Brien, 65–67. Collegeville, MN: Cistercian, 2016.

Schroer, Silvia, and Sophia Bietenhard, eds. *Feminist Interpretation of the Bible and the Hermeneutics of Liberation.* London: Sheffield Academic, 2003.

"Syrian Law Allows Women to Be Equal with Men in Inheritance and Wills" (in Arabic). addustour.com, January 15, 2011. https://bit.ly/3pSngSe/.

Tabet, Gihane. "Women in Personal Status Laws: Iraq, Jordan, Lebanon, Palestine, Syria." *UNESCO,* July 2005. https://bit.ly/3zsQf3h/.

Wardeh, Nadia, and Pamela Chrabieh. "Against the Current: Rethinking Gender, Religious Authority and Interreligious Dialogue." In *Middle Eastern Women: The Intersection of Law, Culture and Religion,* edited by Mitri Raheb, 153–92. Bethlehem: Diyar & Dar al Kalima University College of Arts and Culture, 2020.

Yassine-Hamdan, Nahla, and John Strate. "Gender Inequality in the Arab World: A Comparative Perspective." *Contemporary Arab Affairs* 13.2 (2020) 25–50.

Zaki, Anne E. "Diversity and Inclusion: Gender Justice in the Evangelical Church in Egypt." Paper presented at the Christian Academic Forum for Citizenship in the Arab World (CAFCAW), Cyprus, November 1, 2019.

14

Interfaith Relations and Middle East Christianity
Beyond Dialogue, Toward Interrelationality

NAJIB GEORGE AWAD

IN THE BEGINNING WAS not dialogue, but the discovering of inevitable interrelationality. History teaches us how naïve one would be if one thought that people opt for dialoguing with the different, or even similar, other for the sheer sake of it or out of purely instinctive human desire or curiosity. The realization of the *inevitability* of the involvement in a form of interrelational co-existence with someone else is the "big-bang," the primary *ex-nihilo* moment that generates a dialoguing orientation; that impregnates an interlocution event. The interrelationality that breeds such realization, therefore, is principally more essential, more fundamentally significant, than the dialogical moment this breeding source births. In the experiential and intellectual zone of interreligious presence or plural religious communities' co-existence, this interrelationality is the *logos* by means of which every dialogue or interconnection is made, and without which none will truly be. It is the *logos*, whose becoming a spatio-temporal reality and whose dwelling among the religious people is what makes dialogue a destiny, not just a necessity; an inevitability that is created by more basic inevitability, and not just a favorability.

Starting this chapter on Christian-Muslim relations with the above prologue aims to propose the following: Discerning the interreligious affairs between the Christians and the Muslims in the Middle East requires traveling beyond the boundaries of narrating the story of inter*locution* between the Christians and Muslims. It demands pondering, instead, these Christians' and Muslims' inter*relationality* and their perception of it, which eventually generates their awareness of the inevitability of engaging in continuous interreligious dialogue. This chapter will first start with an argument on the basicality and *a priori* necessity of constructing the perception of dialogue and its nature on a primary conception of "interrelationality." If this proposed premise is the needed one, a re-consideration of the nature of relationality is required. In the second section, I will suggest that the interreligious relationality that is productive of the needed interfaith dialogue is one that is shaped after "symbiotic interaction" rather than dialectic one. Next, we dedicate the remaining space to a diagnosis of how Christians and Muslims in the Middle East personally view an interfaith co-existence and interreligious relationality, and their stances on it. The chapter ends with concluding assessments on what kind of interfaith dialogical interrelation is needed in the present and the future of that region.

Interrelationality as the Ground of Dialogue

In 2012, I published monograph, *And Freedom Became a Public Square*. I called for the development of an Arab contextual theology as a Christian contribution to, but also on, the *Sitz im Leben* of the Arab Middle East. There I admit that the public scene in that context "may not be ready [or even no more willing] to realize the necessity of a *theology*, or any theological discourse, at this very moment."[1] I also emphatically argue in support of the inescapable necessity of such a theological approach. I stress that calling for developing a Christian theology on the multi-religious context of the Arab Middle East should not be dubbed "a religious agenda for evangelizing and proselytizing the Arab societies or for making [non-Christians] the followers of Christ."[2] What I meant with my call is shaping the Christians' life in the societies of that context, and then relating to the Muslim majority of their living spaces, in qualitative and particularity-centered perspectives that are "derived from, and inspired by, the values of truth, love, reconciliation, other-acceptance, altruism, relationality, hope and peace . . . ."[3]

It is these values that are derived from the Christian faith, which would invite the Christians in the Middle East (or anywhere else, for that matter) to ground their stance(s) on, and practice of, dialogue with Muslims or non-Christians in a more foundational and *apriori* perception of interrelationality. Before the a posteriori incarnation, stands the a priori *Logos*. Before the empirical interreligious dialogue, stands the conceptual probing

---

1. Awad, *And Freedom Became a Public-Square*, 123. In this call for an Arab contextual theology, I share a common concern with my Arab-Lutheran Palestinian theologian, Mitri Raheb. See his *I Am a Palestinian Christian* and "Palestinian Christians in the Holy Land," 97–102.
2. Awad, *And Freedom Became a Public-Square*, 124.
3. Awad, *And Freedom Became a Public-Square*, 124.

of the interrelational perception of, and stance on, other religions and co-existence with them. More than the occupation with dialogue, "the question of the *relationship* of Christianity to Islam . . .occupies the center-stage"[4] of the Middle Eastern realistic *Sitz im Leben*.

I am proposing that the core-issue of the Christians' life and co-existence with Muslims in the Middle East is not necessarily or primarily centered around *dialogue*. The inquiry, that is, is not necessarily "how can the Arab World's Christianity and Islam launch a dialogue of mutual understanding that leads to co-existence between each other?"[5] The beginning point is the belief in the ability of the Christians and Muslims to *interrelate* to each other in peace, reconciliation, mutual-acceptance, and tolerance. It is the belief in their ability to interrelate without

> the prosperous and more educated and cultured side among them secludes [or alleviates] itself by virtue of a societal ranking and elitist boarders within the society; or even without the side that once ruled the region in the name of its religious identity and heritage attempts to invoke this authoritarian past and drive the ruled minority into a serious fear from experiencing persecution and religiously-driven discrimination, which are reminiscent of what was once called "the status of *dhimmitude*."[6]

Interrelationality as the foundation of religious co-existence not only liberates both the Christians and the Muslims in the Middle East from religious discrimination. It also emancipates them from the delusion of cultural otherness and superiority. Gone is the time when the modernist sociology and anthropology of ontological and cultural ranking dominated the intellectual scene and shaped the worldview of theologians and religious hermeneutes, who divided religions upon preconceived hierarchical structuring of faiths and cultures—a hierarchy that placed Christianity at the top of the religious and cultural pyramid of worth and authenticity. We live today in a new intellectual era, when such discriminative and superiority-centered theories are seriously questioned and deconstructed in the academic world. Today's social theories, as Kenneth Rose correctly points out, "begun to employ notions such as syncretism, hybridization, and creolization" to analyze human existence on various levels, including primarily the religious and cultural ones. This new paradigm-shift not only weakens the plausibility of the notion of "cultural purity." It questions the notion of "religious purity" as well. Rose is right in noticing that "if we

4. Awad, *And Freedom Became a Public-Square*, 156.
5. Awad, "Ab'ad min al-Ḥiwār?" (Beyond Mere Dialogue?), 4–9.
6. Awad, *And Freedom Became a Public-Square*, 157.

grant the premise that there are no pure cultures, then we are led to suppose that there are no pure religious traditions either."[7]

In the context of the Middle East, Christians and Muslims might not be intellectually aware of the syncretistic co-existence situation they live in. They may tend instead to drag their interreligious and intercultural reality into a psychological "state-of-denial" and almost imaginary sentimentally tensional situation. The needed remedy from this imaginary state is to re-probe seriously the state of interrelationality, which Christians and Muslims in the Middle East have existed in for one-and-a-half millennium. This interrelationality is what will not only make them realize that they have never been living in a state of "pure culture" or "cultural parallelism," but also their religious traditions have never been developed in seclusion and self-sufficiency at any time of their history. Without discerning this "beyond-purity" state of interrelationality, interreligious dialogue will be a-historical, a-contextual, and far from an activity rooted in reality, i.e., something pursued in the mind, and not practice in life. The real historically grounded interreligious dialogue in the Middle East is not between two religious communities that are culturally and religiously pure and self-contained. It is rather a dialogue between two sides that come evenly from, and share existentially, the very same constitutive role and status in relation the creation of the Middle Eastern cultural and religious imaginations.

I question the most common modern understanding of Christian-Muslim interaction in the twentieth and twenty-first centuries, which presents this interaction as overarchingly "an oppositional clash between two totally antagonistic, separate entities who try to survive by reciprocally excluding and banishing each other."[8] My support of interrelational religious co-existence as the foundational epistemological means for assessing interreligious dialogue in the Middle East is grounded in recent scholarly attention to the "cross-pollinating" or "intertwining" symbiotic relation that characterized the *Sitz im Leben* of the early Islamicate world.[9] The cross-communal interaction between the members of the Christian and Muslim communities in the Middle East is something no one can deny in the light of the treasure of historical and textual data scholars

---

7. Rose, *Pluralism, The Future of Religion*, 75. See also Stewart, "Syncretism and Its Synonyms," 40–62.

8. See Awad, "Is 'Post-Christendom' a Relevant Hermeneutical Framework?" 39–49). See also Penn, *Envisioning Islam Syriac Christians and the Early Muslim World*.

9. On the implications of "cross-pollination" and "intertwinement," see Goodman, *Jewish and Islamic Philosophy*; Montgomery, "Islamic Crosspollinations," in *Islamic Crosspollinations*," 148–93; Lazarus-Yafeh, *Intertwined Worlds*; and Ben-Shammai, Shaked, and Stroumsa, eds., *Exchange and Transmission across Cultural Boundaries*.

now have after the discovery of beyond-valuable extant manuscripts and data, for example, the Cairo Genizah documents that were found during the second half of the last century. The realization of the predominance of interrelationality in the early Islamicate world is derived from these documents' content on the Jews, Christians, and Muslims as members of a pluralistic society.[10] The profound passion of that era's intellectuals toward knowledge drove them into making their intellectual concerns trespass the dividing confessional boundaries that distinguished them as followers of three different religions. The interrelation between these knowledge-seekers was not just shaped after a "borrowing" strategy, where one group of scholars who represent one religion would borrow its knowledge to the other two and influence them one-sidedly. Far from that, the influence and borrowing were both reciprocally experienced between the three religions, beyond one-sidedness and in symbiotic interactivity.[11]

It is this attention to "interrelation," and its treatment as the starter, or the foundation, of the review and assessment of Christian-Muslim dialogue in the Middle East, that makes me, in the ensuing section, make the following two claim: The best medium to glean from data on the interrelational dimension of Christian-Muslim existence are the stances and views of the Middle Eastern Christians and Muslims on each other, as well as their appraisal of interfaith relations in the Middle Eastern context.

Interfaith Relationships in Arab Middle Eastern Eyes

Following are various stances on interreligious relations in the Middle East as they are presented by Christian and Muslim scholars. From Muslims include stances from a Sunnite, Raḍwān al-Sayyīd; from a Shi'ite, Mahmoud Ayoub; from the historically Eastern tradition of Christianity, George Khodr; and from the historically Western (missionary-rooted) tradition of Christianity, Martin Accad.

---

10. Goitein, *A Mediterranean Society*, and Tannous, *The Making of the Medieval Middle East*.

11. On the support of "borrowing" and one-sided influence language, see, Freindreich and Goldstein, eds., *Beyond Religious Borders*; Salaymeh, "Between Scholarship and Polemic," 407–18. I do support a symbiotic, crosspollinating approach between Christian and Muslim intellectuals, particularly *mutakallims*, in my forthcoming, "Christian Muʿtazilism? Tracing Features of Muʿtazilite *Habitus* in Christian *Kalām* in Early Islam," in press for 2022.

A Sunnite Voice: Raḍwān al-Sayyīd

One of the texts Al-Sayyīd produced to touch upon the interfaith relations and dialogue was in 2015. Al-Sayyīd starts his argument in this text by the following words: "in the beginning was communication (*tadāwūl*)."[12] Elsewhere, al-Sayyīd relates his conviction that this centralization of communicative relationality is direly missing in the Arab societies and culture, where the culture of dialogue is either weak or totally absent.[13] Conceding that the present situation of the Middle East is quite different from its content in the past centuries, al-Sayyīd tries to connect the present "no-communication" state to the Islamic theological and Qurʾānic teaching. Reading the history of the interreligious existence in the Middle East from the perspective of the Qurʾānic attestation, al-Sayyīd points to moments in the history of the Middle East when a communication based on reciprocal freedom and equality was experienced.

Al-Sayyīd suggests that the religious people of the Middle East do co-exist today and they intermingle normally. However, what one witnesses in this context is far from the communicative reciprocation the Qurʾān speaks about. What this interreligious communication seriously lacks are the elements of "equality" and "freedom," in the absence of which "the communicative dialogue remains . . .a problem by itself, since it requires many prerequisites and broadly satisfactory environments that are often unavailable."[14] The core-abstract before interreligious communication or dialogue in the Arab context, according to al-Sayyīd, is the fact that contrariety and tension have become "culture" or defining cultural components, if not even becoming, for some people, absolute and referential "traditions" or "legacies."[15] What makes contrariety and tension cultural in dimensions today, according to al-Sayyīd, is the fact that vast segments of the public in Middle Eastern societies tend to believe in them and manifest them in their daily life.[16]

---

12. Al-Sayyīd, "Ishkāliyyāt al-Ḥiwār fī Mujtamʿātinā wa-muʿauwiqātih" (The Problem and Obstacles of Dialogue in Our Societies).

13. Al-Sayyīd, "Ishkāliyyāt al-Ḥiwār fī Mujtamʿātinā wa-muʿauwiqātih" (The Problem and Obstacles of Dialogue in Our Societies).

14. Al-Sayyīd, "Ishkāliyyāt al-Ḥiwār fī Mujtamʿātinā wa-muʿauwiqātih" (The Problem and Obstacles of Dialogue in Our Societies).

15. Al-Sayyīd, "Ishkāliyyāt al-Ḥiwār fī Mujtamʿātinā wa-muʿauwiqātih" (The Problem and Obstacles of Dialogue in Our Societies).

16. Al-Sayyīd, "Ishkāliyyāt al-Ḥiwār fī Mujtamʿātinā wa-muʿauwiqātih" (The Problem and Obstacles of Dialogue in Our Societies).

Be that as it may, al-Sayyīd opines that a cultural phenomenon, like the one diagnosed above, cannot be overcome except by means of a counter-culturalization of reciprocal relatedness that is based on freedom and equality. He, then, suggests that turning free and equal communicative reciprocity as such into a culture in the present *Sitz im Leben* happens when people disallow their negative appraisal of the belief of the other and degradation of her religiosity to control their view of the other as equal and free human being.[17] Al-Sayyīd argues that a true communicative symbiosis that is rooted in equality and freedom lies in equal recognition of the others and their belief narratives freely and volitionally, rather than opting for such recognition due to coerced or forced circumstantial necessities.[18] The prerequisite of every dialogue, al-Sayyīd stresses, is *equality*: equality in terms of mutual recognition and equality in terms of interests.[19]

What al-Sayyīd ultimately concludes from his attention to the historiological process of the Muslims' involvement in interreligious communication with the Christians is that the Muslims' stance is consistently characterized with evident and manifested strong need for gaining the Christians' recognition of them as equally true religion.[20] "The issue of recognition (*al-i'tirāf*)," al-Sayyīd states, "remains strongly present in the Muslims' conscience and sub-conscience [alike]."[21] This excessive thirst for recognition from the Christians and the failure in gaining it is the main reason behind the Muslims' disbelief today in the usefulness of interreligious communication. Al-Sayyīd goes farther to state that in the context of the Middle East, the level of disappointment from interreligious communication is periled by an impasse. The local Eastern Christians (Orthodox or Syriac) and Muslims (Sunnites or Shi'ites) in the Arab world, he opines, failed until today in co-creating their own special cultural and intellectual communication environment, and followed instead the initiatives and rules of engagement that are created by the Western-generated Christian sides in the region, the Catholics and the Protestants.[22] For al-Sayyīd, a more useful and relevant dialogue between the Muslims and the Christians in the Middle East is one that is created by the local Eastern Christians and

---

17. Al-Sayyīd, "At-Tafakkur al-Islāmī fīl-Masīḥiyyah" (The Muslim Thinking about Christianity), 16.

18. Al-Sayyīd, "Ishkāliyyāt al-Ḥiwār fī Mujtam'ātinā wa-mu'auwiqātih" (The Problem and Obstacles of Dialogue in Our Societies), 18.

19. Al-Sayyīd, "Al-Ḥiwār al-Islāmī al-Masīḥī" (The Muslim-Christian Dialogue), 1.

20. Al-Sayyīd, "Al-Ḥiwār al-Islāmī al-Masīḥī" (The Muslim-Christian Dialogue), 5.

21. Al-Sayyīd, "Al-Ḥiwār al-Islāmī al-Masīḥī" (The Muslim-Christian Dialogue), 6.

22. Al-Sayyīd, "Al-Ḥiwār al-Islāmī al-Masīḥī" (The Muslim-Christian Dialogue), 11.

Arab Muslims, who belong evenly to the soil of the region's *Sitz im Leben*.[23] The Christians and Muslims manifest this interrelationality and generate dialogical communication on its basis by means of "recognizing the other by conversing with her and perceiving her problems and intentions and by appreciating her on even ground and never targeting her by any discrimination or degradation or abolition."[24] This is how dialogical communication, or communicative dialogue, becomes a *"culture"* or "environment of change" (*bī' at taghiyyr*); a culture of reciprocal change.[25]

A Shi'ite Voice: Mahmoud Ayoub:

Like his Muslim Sunnite colleague, Ayoub departs in his understanding of interreligious relations from the Qur'ānic attestation. He builds the understanding of interreligious relation in the Qur'ān on the text's use of the term "*Ahl al-Kitāb.*" He, then, proposes deeming "*Ahl al-Kitāb*" to mean "family of the book" and to imply that all the people of Abrahamic faiths are one united *family* descended from the monotheistic faith of Abraham.[26] This familial nature of unity, Ayoub proceeds, does not impose on religious people one hegemonic identity and monolithic religiosity. It, rather, respects and maintains their differences and particularities and calls them all to discern the inclusivist care and providence of the family's father, or head, God.[27]

In his understanding of interreligiosity, Mahmoud Ayoub believes Christian-Muslim communication in the Middle East must be scrutinized on the more fundamental level of their interreligious relationality within the Middle East's particular frameworks of socio-political identity that makes Christianity and Islam alike "a culture and way of life."[28] The moments of mutual acceptance and tolerance in the history of the Christian-Muslim interrelations must prevail over the moments of "polemical debate, repudiation and subjugation" that characterized their dialogues at some occasions. They must prevail, so that the theological disagreement will not detain the Christians

---

23. Al-Sayyīd, "Al-Ḥiwār al-Islāmī al-Masīḥī" (The Muslim-Christian Dialogue), 14.

24. Al-Sayyīd, "Al-Ḥiwār al-Islāmī al-Masīḥī" (The Muslim-Christian Dialogue), 16.

25. Al-Sayyīd, "Al-Ḥiwār al-Islāmī al-Masīḥī" (The Muslim-Christian Dialogue), 17.

26. Omar (ed.), *A Muslim View of Christianity*, 13.

27. Al-Sayyīd, "Al-Ḥiwār al-Islāmī al-Masīḥī" (The Muslim-Christian Dialogue), 14.

28. Ayoub, "Islam and Christianity between Tolerance and Acceptance," 172.

and Muslims from working out mutually acceptable relationships.[29] Interreligious dialogue in the particular Middle Eastern *Sitz im Leben*, Ayoub opines, images "a neighborly relationship of sharing; sharing in each other's festivals and other joyous celebrations, and in sad occasions of death and calamity."[30] Unless we perceive this and realize that the practice of Christian-Muslim dialogue as it is pursued in the West is "too foreign to the whole culture and mentality of the people"[31] in the Middle East, we will misread the Christian-Muslim relations in context.

What does dialogue among Christians and Muslims, then, requires to successfully reflect the contextual Middle Eastern interreligious relation and communication between Christians and Muslims? Ayoub suggests that, for this to happen, "Muslims and Christians must accept each other as friends and partners in the quest for social and political justice, theological harmony and spiritual progress on the way to God, who is their ultimate goal."[32] In the Middle East, interreligious dialogue that is based on the symbiotic interreligious relationality will express "a genuine and creative intercultural dialogue," apart from which, Ayoub emphasizes, mutual understanding and respect are impossible.[33] Within the framework of intercultural communication, "the ultimate purpose of dialogue is to create fellowship of faith among the followers of Islam and Christianity."[34]

Eastern Orthodox Voice: George Khodr

We now move to an Eastern Orthodox stance from the Lebanese *Rūm Orthodox*, George Khodr. Khodr constructs his assessment of the Christian-Muslim dialogue on a hermeneutical appraisal of how the Christians and Muslims view each other in life, and what kind of interrelationality this mutual viewing generates. According to Khodr, the problem between human beings in general lies in the fact that each one of us synthesizes (*yaṣṭaniʿ*) the other and then reads her from the perspective of the image he carved her according to (*naḥataha ʿanhu*).[35] This synthesization of the other, instead of relating to her in her self-distinction, requires from us a critical anatomization

---

29. Ayoub, "Islam and Christianity between Tolerance and Acceptance," 174–75.
30. Ayoub, "Islam and Christianity between Tolerance and Acceptance," 178.
31. Ayoub, "Islam and Christianity between Tolerance and Acceptance," 178.
32. Ayoub, "Christian-Muslim Dialogue," 315.
33. Ayoub, "Christian-Muslim Dialogue," 318.
34. Ayoub, "Christian-Muslim Dialogue," 318.
35. Khodr, "Madkhal ilā al-Naḍrāt al-Mutabādalah" (An Introduction to the Reciprocal Views), 107.

of our other-view and a realization of the unfairness that could linger within it. This view of the other creates in society a state of injustice, the roots of which is nothing external but rather intrinsic to our perception of the other.[36] This is what drives Muslims to view Christianity from the history of colonialism and Christians to view Islam from the history of the Mamlukides' persecuting policies.[37] What colors the perspective of our view of each other is our condition and realistic status in relation to the other in life-setting; "Whether we are rulers or ruled, in the position of minority or the position of majority."[38] If the interreligious relation is injured, the interreligious dialogue that is pursued on its basis would turn into a demonstration of violence, generated from a conglomeration of pragmatist interests, political hauteur, and religious inspiration that are all implemented in the service of beneficiary agendas.[39] In the light of this, the noble and positively relational values and lessons found in the religious holy scripture, do not really lay any tangible impact on the dialogue's process, content, or consequences. What would actually communicate in the dialogue are not the texts, but the minds and sentiments of their readers.[40]

Proper interrelational dialogue, Khodr opines, is one that results from the Christians' and Muslims' cooperation and co-creation of the contextual and social setting (or "city/*madīnah*," in Khodr terms) that will be the ground of their interreligious communication. It is a true setting of social coalition (*i' tilāf ijtimā'ī*), wherein "I can say 'I' and I can say 'you,' but also we can together say 'us'"; an 'us,' that is, which Christians and Muslims co-create upon their common geography, history, and destiny.[41] True "us-ness" is possible only in democratic venues, where freedom and equality are foundational and not subjected to or pre-conditioned by interpretations that are dictated by the tolerance or intolerance extent of the powerful and dominating side.[42]

The needed dialogue, Khodr opines, is the dialogue of life, wherein there is no disregard or subordination, where there is no "original" (*aṣīl*)

---

36. Khodr, "Madkhal ilā al-Naḍrāt al-Mutabādalah" (An Introduction to the Reciprocal Views), 108.

37. Khodr, "Madkhal ilā al-Naḍrāt al-Mutabādalah" (An Introduction to the Reciprocal Views), 108–9.

38. Khodr, "Madkhal ilā al-Naḍrāt al-Mutabādalah" (An Introduction to the Reciprocal Views), 109.

39. Khodr, "al-Ḥiwār al-Islāmī al-Masīḥī" (The Muslim-Christian Dialogue), 59.

40. Khodr, "al-Ḥiwār al-Islāmī al-Masīḥī" (The Muslim-Christian Dialogue), 62.

41. Khodr, "al-Ḥiwār al-Islāmī al-Masīḥī" (The Muslim-Christian Dialogue), 63.

42. Khodr, "al-Ḥiwār al-Islāmī al-Masīḥī" (The Muslim-Christian Dialogue), 67–68.

versus "alien" (*dakhīl*) and no one is under the state of *dhimmitude* in relation to the other, but all religious groups are equal.[43] Here, Khodr stresses that this dialogue of life is not really different from the dialogue of ideas.[44] The dialogue of ideas is another form of the central and ultimate dialogue of life. He says: "the dialogue of life is the one we taste and experience every day. It is the good common life between the people of the two religions, especially the spiritual unity between the Arab Muslims and Christians."[45] The interreligious life of the Arab Muslims and Christians fuel their dialogue with the common aspirations they share about the renaissance of the Arab world, as much as with the fear and questions they hold on the challenges that threaten their common destiny.[46] After all, the essence of dialogue for George Khodr is the pre-dialogue relationship that paves the way for conversations, "social intercourse (*muʿāsharah*) is the secret of convergence in actions."[47] A Christian-Muslim dialogue born from an interreligious life would be a venue for dissipating the misunderstanding between the two sides and perceiving that the distance between them is far shorter than what many imagine. Dialogue departs from interrelation and aims at creating symbiosis (*muʿāyashah*) at all levels of existence.[48]

Protestant Voice: Martin Accad

In 2019, Martin Accad published *Sacred Misinterpretation*, about Christian-Muslim dialogue. He reveals the primary motivation of his discourse on Christian-Muslim dialogue is "the idea that religious discourse can also contribute significantly in working toward peaceful relations between populations with rival ideologies."[49] How can religions become part of the remedy's prescription instead of one of the conflict's ingredients? The transformation of the role of religious interrelations and communication in our living context, Accad suggests, lies in re-viewing the Christians' and Muslims' theological

---

43. Khodr, "al-Ḥiwār al-Islāmī al-Masīḥī" (The Muslim-Christian Dialogue), 69.

44. Khodr, "al-Ḥiwār al-Islāmī al-Masīḥī" (The Muslim-Christian Dialogue), 78ff.

45. Khodr, "Maʿrifatnā Baʿḍunā li-baʿḍ" (Our Knowledge of Each Other), 90.

46. Khodr, "Maʿrifatnā Baʿḍunā li-baʿḍ" (Our Knowledge of Each Other), 93.

47. Khodr, "Maʿ baʿḍ al-Muslimīn" (With Some Muslims), in *Afkār wa-Arāʾ fī al-Ḥiwār al-Masīḥī al-Islāmī wal-ʿAiysh al-Mushtarak* (Ideas and Opinions on Christian-Muslim Dialogue and Co-existence), 215–20.

48. Khodr, "Maʿ baʿḍ al-Muslimīn" (With Some Muslims), in *Afkār wa-Arāʾ fī al-Ḥiwār al-Masīḥī al-Islāmī wal-ʿAiysh al-Mushtarak* (Ideas and Opinions on Christian-Muslim Dialogue and Co-Existence), 156.

49. Accad, *Sacred Misinterpretation*, 6.

reasoning about each other.⁵⁰ It is this essential role of theologization in the history of interreligious relation between Christianity and Islam that makes theology "a foundation of dialogue," Accad believes.⁵¹

Based on this, Accad creates what he calls "the SEKAP spectrum of Christian-Muslim interaction."⁵² SEKAP stands for "syncretistic, existential, kerygmatic, apologetic, and polemical." From all these trends of interaction between the Christians and Muslims, Accad leaves those that resonate with interrelationality and focuses on the one that centers around theology: the "kerygamtic interaction" option. According to him, this option more than any other enables the exploration and the finding of the most "Christ-like" symptoms in Islam and the Muslims.⁵³ Accad opines that such an evangelistic stance is not conflictual but peaceful, because it maintains the distinction between "kerygma" and "apologia," which, for him, merely lies in the communicational *attitude* or *manner* each delineates or pertains to.⁵⁴

Accad promotes a Christian-Muslim interaction wherein the Christian seems to be expected to treat dialogue as a chance for evangelism and faith-promoting. Does this kerygmatic approach to the other allow for any recognition of some values to be found in the other's religiosity as such? Accad suggests that the value of Islam's religiosity, from this kerygmatic perspective, lies in the fact that "Islam preserved many important and positive elements from the Judaeo-Christian tradition."⁵⁵ Whichever value one bestows upon Islam or detects in the Muslim message or religious texts is decided and appreciated by virtue of its closeness to, or remoteness from, the divine revelation in Jesus Christ and to Christ's life and ministry's value-system.⁵⁶ What is, then, Christian-Muslim dialogue within the framework of Accad's thesis? It is that venue of theological correspondence, the success of which is determined by the Christian interlocutor's ability to be a smart and successful evangelizer.

Accad parts ways with the three other Middle Eastern voices discussed above when he argues that what drags Christians and Muslims into a vicious circle of interaction is their opting for "dialogue of life" and their avoiding of dialogues on theological issues. Accad opines that, without theological dialogue, co-existence and friendship will not change the Muslims'

50. Accad, *Sacred Misinterpretation*, 7.
51. Accad, *Sacred Misinterpretation*, 7.
52. Accad, *Sacred Misinterpretation*, 8.
53. Accad, *Sacred Misinterpretation*, 7.
54. Accad, *Sacred Misinterpretation*, 9.
55. Accad, *Sacred Misinterpretation*, 11.
56. Accad, *Sacred Misinterpretation*, 11ff.

theological-rejecting views against the Christians.⁵⁷ Accad is convinced that mere dialogue of life will be a moment of meeting at the mercy of "fluctuating feelings and moods, which tend to swing between highs and lows depending on the latest representations of Islam in the news media."⁵⁸ Only a theological perception of Islam in its reality and faith, on the basis of "a biblical understanding of divine revelation,"⁵⁹ can grant the Evangelicals, Accad says, the chance of having "profound and balanced comprehension of Islam" and can breed an interfaith that goes beyond exposing Islam to either "slanderous caricaturing" or "idealized representation" tendencies.⁶⁰

Overall, Accad's monograph seems to be a manifesto written for Evangelical Christian audiences to guide them into becoming successful kerygma-conveyers in the occasions of dialogue that can occur between them and Muslims.

Toward an Assessment and a Suggestion: Interrelationality or Dialogue?

The above reveals how the people of that region view interreligious dialogues and relations. What one extracts from these voices is a primary realization of the particularity of the interreligious experience in that part of the world. One cannot just apply to the Christian-Muslim relations in this context a ready-made or preconceived static understanding of interreligiosity that is developed in the Western context of scholarship or any other intellectual centers of idea-creation around the globe.

It is this point that makes me principally sympathetic with the three approaches of the Sunnite, Shi'ite, and Eastern Orthodox voices on interreligious dialogue and critical of the fourth approach of the Protestant voice (despite the fact that I have a Protestant background). It is my belief that Martin Accad's kerygmatic approach will be appealing to Christians, Evangelical or not, in Western circles of theological reasoning, because it begins from what professional academic work in the West drives me to describe as a "Euro-Americano-centric essentializing and dialectic stance on Christianity over-against Islam." I do not believe that the kerygmatic approach to dialogue with Islam is the most needed option for Christian-Muslim relations in the Middle East. This kerygmatic approach was the driving force of the American

---

57. Accad, *Sacred Misinterpretation*, 67–68.
58. Accad, *Sacred Misinterpretation*, 323.
59. Accad, *Sacred Misinterpretation*, 323.
60. Accad, *Sacred Misinterpretation*, 342.

missionary work in the region, and it did not leave positive results on the broader contextual scene of interreligious connections.

A careful reading of Accad's thesis reveals that what he offers is a strategic recipe on the *modus operandi* of converting, not on the relational and interrelational preconceptions of the relatedness to the other. For him, the dialogue event is a call from one side of the supposedly dialoguing partners to the other side to concede the truth and embrace belief in single revelation, namely Jesus Christ. This means what is expected to happen in the dialogue is not truly "*dia*-logia," not truly interrelation, inter-communion between two equally other-recognizing theological discourses. It seems, rather, to still be an example of an "action-reception" and "call-response" encounter. Within the framework of such a one-way kerygmatic approach to dialogue, it is hard to find any logical chance for allowing an interrelational reciprocity even on the theological level of interaction. It is not clear in this approach whether Islam is looked at as having any theological or religious value and truth by itself. If this is the case, dialogue then is not a chance for the Christian evangelizer to encounter any truly transforming impact from knowing Islam or to gain anything from Islam that can invite reforming Christian faith. Such a chance seems to rather be available strictly to the Muslim, whereas the only thing interesting for the Christian in the dialogue is to *give*, to *convey* something to the Muslim.

Rather than founding dialogue on an a priori interreligious relationality, Accad seems to be ontologically essentializing Islam and Christianity alike in a phenomenological comparativist manner that is reminiscent of the phenomenological Hegelian-dialectic methodology, which ends up ordering religions on a hierarchical structure of value and appraisal, the ultimate purpose of which is demonstrating the superiority of one religion over the rest.[61] Such an understanding of the nature of dialogue like the one proposed by Accad is the Achilles-heel of his attention to interfaith relations. Such an understanding is questionable from a *dialogical* perspective.

The difference between Accad's approach and the approaches of the other three examples is difficult to be missed. The similar concerns of the other three Sunnite, Shi'ite, and Eastern Orthodox voices invite us to glean that the concern about interreligious relationality is more (rightly so, I believe) fundamental and essential than necessarily the interest in interreligious dialogue and its proselytizing subtleness. Except for Accad's enthusiastic call for pursuing dialogue of theologization, the other three Middle Eastern voices seem to believe that if (and only if) the interreligious relation between the Christians and Muslims was based on, and is expressive

---

61. Developed further in my *After Mission, Beyond Evangelicalism*.

of, a symbiotic reciprocation of equality, recognition, and freedom, it does not matter much whether they, then, dialogue on life-affairs, or theological convictions: Either way will be just reflective of the interrelational nature of the life they live together as two communities within one single human overarching state of existence or *Sitz im Leben*. This was eloquently articulated in relation to interreligious life in general by Perry Schmidt-Leukel, but his view is applicable to the Middle Eastern context and its rootedness in a focus on interrelationality. He says:

> Christianity's relation to the religious other is no longer understood along the lines of a "we-they" paradigm, but as a relationship within an overarching human community, in which "*some of us* are Christians, *some of us* are Muslims, *some of us* are Hindus, *some of us* are Jews, *Some of us* are sceptics," which would indeed constitute a ground-breaking change in understanding Christianity's relation to other religions.[62]

The track of the mentioned groundbreaking change is already paved in the interreligious context of the Middle East. For the Christians and Muslims are both the indigenous people of the land and their co-existence has originated (whether deliberately or accidentally, positively or negatively) the historical narrative of that region on all levels of being. The Christians and Muslims in the Middle East do not need, in my opinion, to pursue dialogues in order to create possible interrelation and life-based symbiotic togetherness under an overarching human communion between each other. The Christians and Muslims in the Middle East can pursue dialogues on everything and anything *because* they are interrelated and *because* they are sociologically, anthropologically, culturally, and experientially already from one overarching human reality. They need to dialogue to *remember* this when they tend to forget it. They need to dialogue to *implement* this in their theological and religious communication. Dialogue in this sense is not a "creation" venue, but a "confirming" and "realifying" one.

The common goal, which the Christians and Muslims in the Middle East need to invest their interreligious relation in the service of, is how to make this interrelation between their religions, and between their religions and the public sphere alike, fruitful and constructive in the Arab societies. This common concern would enable the religious Christians and Muslims alike to realize that what might torment human life in the Middle East at the present is not the clash between Christians and Muslims. It is rather a clash of worldviews between religious Christians and Muslims on one side, over-against the secular Christians and Muslims on the other. A dialogue

62. Schmidt-Leukel, "Christianity and the Religious Other," 101.

based on interreligious relationality over societal, cultural, and political challenges may generate a symbiotic relationality that will transform religiosity *per se* from a clash-breeding and backwardness-causing ingredient into a positive and constructive factor in the public sphere. Is this an invitation for pursuing a non-theological dialogue? Not necessarily if we broaden the perspectives of our understanding of the term "theology." It is rather a call for developing a contextualized theological reasoning and hermeneutic shaped by, and based on, interreligious reconciliation and symbiotic existence. This will produce a theological perception of the reconciliation between the religions themselves, as well as between religiosity and secularity or non-religiosity in the public sphere. It is, nevertheless, a call that does not make theology exhaustively definitive of the interreligious communication. It just deems it as one among many other equally constitutive levels of reasoning that are procreated by interrelationality.

Bibliography

Accad, Martin. *Sacred Misinterpretation: Reaching across the Christian-Muslim Divide*. Grand Rapids: Eerdmans, 2019.

Al-Sayyīd, Raḍwān. "At-Tafakkur al-Islāmī fīl-Masīḥiyyah: al-Jidāl wal-Ḥiwār wal-Fahm al-Mukhtalif fīl-'Uṣūr al-Wusṭā" (The Muslim Thinking about Christianity: Debating, Dialoguing, and Differentiation in Understanding in the Middle East), 1–20 in www.radwanalsiyyed.com/cms/assets/pdf/9820f49e0c11413d8414096b2 1dd5cb9.pdf.

———. "Ishkāliyyāt al-Ḥiwār fī Mujtam'ātinā wa-mu'auwiqātih" (The Problem and Obstacles of Dialogue in Our Societies). www.ridwanalsayyid.com/contentpage. aspx?id=27567F.XOIMtYhkhPZ.

Awad, Najib George. "Ab'ad min al-Ḥiwār: Hal Yakfī Ḥiwār al-Ta'āyūsh bayn al-Adiyān?" (Beyond Mere Dialogue: Is the Dialogue of Co-Existence among Religions Enough?). *Al-Nashra of the Royal Institute for Religious Studies* 35 (2005) 4–9.

———. *After Mission, Beyond Evangelicalism: The Indigenous 'Injīliyyūn' in the Arab-Muslim Context of Syria-Lebanon*. Leiden; Brill, 2020.

———. *And Freedom Became a Public-Square: Political, Sociological and Religious Overviews on the Arab Christians and the Arabic Spring*. Berlin: LIT Verlag, 2012.

———. "Is 'Post-Christendom' a Relevant Hermeneutical Framework to the Situation of the Christians in Greater Syria? Towards a Critical Appraisal." *Post-Christendom Studies* 1 (2016) 31–76.

Ben-Shammai, Haggi, Saul Shaked, and Sarah Stroumsa, eds. *Exchange and Transmission across Cultural Boundaries: Philosophy, Mysticism and Science in the Mediterranean World*. Jerusalem: Israel Academy of Sciences and Humanities, 2013.

Goodman, Lenn Evan. *Jewish and Islamic Philosophy: Crosspollinations in the Classical Age*. Edinburgh: Edinburgh University Press, 1999.

Khodr, George. "Al-Ḥiwār al-Islāmī al-Masīḥī" (The Muslim-Christian Dialogue). In *Afkār wa-Arā' fī al-Ḥiwār al-Masīḥī al-Islāmī wal-ʿAiysh al-Mushtarak* (Ideas and

Opinions on Christian-Muslim Dialogue and Co-existence), by George Khodr, 59–86. Jounieh, Lebanon: Bouluṣiyyah Bookshop, 2000.

———. "Ma' ba'ḍ al-Muslimīn" (With Some Muslims). In *Afkār wa-Arā' fī al-Ḥiwār al-Masīḥī al-Islāmī wal-◻Aiysh al-Mushtarak* (Ideas and Opinions on Christian-Muslim Dialogue and Co-existence), by George Khodr, 215–20. Jounieh, Lebanon: Bouluṣiyyah Bookshop, 2000.

———. "Madkhal ilā al-Naḍrāt al-Mutabādalah" (An Introduction to the Reciprocal Views). In *Afkār wa-Arā' fī al-Ḥiwār al-Masīḥī al-Islāmī wal-◻Aiysh al-Mushtarak* (Ideas and Opinions on Christian-Muslim Dialogue and Co-existence), by George Khodr, 107–23. Jounieh, Lebanon: Bouluṣiyyah Bookshop, 2000.

Lazarus-Yafeh, Hava. *Intertwined Worlds*. Princeton, NJ: Princeton University Press, 1992.

Montgomery, James E. "Islamic Crosspollinations." In *Islamic Crosspollinations: Interactions in the Medieval Middle East*, edited by A. Akasoy, P. Pormann, and J. Montgomery, 148–94. Oxford: Gibb Memorial Trust, 2007.

Omar, Irfan, ed. *A Muslim View of Christianity: Essays on Dialogue by Mahmoud Ayoub*. Maryknoll, NY: Orbis, 2007.

Penn, Michael Philip. *Envisioning Islam Syriac Christians and the Early Muslim World*. Philadelphia: University of Pennsylvania Press, 2015.

Raheb, Mitri. *I Am a Palestinian Christian*. Minneapolis: Fortress, 1995.

———. "Palestinian Christians in the Holy Land." *Dialog: A Journal of Theology* 2.41 (2002) 97–102.

Rose, Pluralism. *The Future of Religion*. London: Bloomsbury Academic, 2013.

Salaymeh, Lena. "Between Scholarship and Polemic in Judeo-Christian Studies." *Islam and Christian-Muslim Relations* 24 (2013) 407–18.

Stewart, Charles. "Syncretism and Its Synonyms: Reflection on Culture Mixture." *Diacritics* 29.3 (1999) 40–62.

15

Public Theology and Middle Eastern Christianity

Anne E. Zaki

Throughout history, the Middle Eastern church has overcome many challenges by developing a compelling theology that secured and spread its presence and witness. At this season of her life, a constructive public theology is necessary in order for the church to talk *with* society, not just *to* society.[1] I am convinced that our region needs a Christian theology that helps the church engage in contemporary discourse, which seeks the welfare of the state and the common good of all people. Given our current Islamic context, which regularly forbids her to *speak* out loud, public theology will catalyze the church to alternatively *live* out loud through social witness and cultural engagement, building peace and pursuing justice for all.

Brief Description of Our Context

Since Egypt has the unique geography of sitting on two continents, Africa and Asia, in this chapter I will refer to the Church in nations across the MENA region, i.e., Middle East-North Africa region. However, since Egypt is the context I am most familiar with, the majority of my examples come from there.

The MENA region is comprised of twenty-one countries. Starting from the Atlantic Ocean moving eastward: Western Sahara, Morocco, Algeria, Tunisia, Libya, Egypt, Sudan, Israel, Palestine, Jordan, Syria, Lebanon, Iraq, Iran, Kuwait, Bahrain, Qatar, United Arab Emirates, Oman, Yemen, and Saudi Arabia.

In most of these countries, especially in North Africa, the Church under the shadow of Islam is extremely small—with the exception of Egypt. It is noteworthy that it was not always the case that the Church in MENA was

---

1. Day and Kim, "Introduction," *A Companion to Public Theology*, 1–21.

small as it is today under the shadow of Islam. In fact, this whole region was one of the first places to be evangelized by the apostles and early followers of Christ before Islam came into being in the seventh century. Through a series of world events, Islam spread across the MENA region leading to the situation in which the Church finds herself today.

This small Church, by God's grace, has endured and stood strong. It weathered not only the storm of the Islamic Conquest, but also other major historic events: the Crusades, World War I & II, the Holocaust, the Armenian Genocide, the aftermath of the establishment of the State of Israel, the 6-Day War, the civil wars in Lebanon, the Iraq War, the Arab Spring, the chaos following the Egyptian revolution, and today, the ongoing tragic crises facing Lebanon, Syria, and Yemen.

The health of the Church in a few Middle Eastern countries (Egypt, Jordan, Palestine, Israel, Syria, Lebanon, and Iraq) fared better historically than in countries of North Africa and the Gulf. Yet, this strong Church has recently experienced a dwindling presence, as it lost many of its members in recent decades, to death, to the mass Christian exodus resulting from forced displacements, as believers fled war or persecution, or perhaps even to seek out better opportunities for their children. These things have happened over and over . . .

- In Palestine, after the establishment of the State of Israel, the Christian presence fell from 10 percent in the 1940s to 2 percent nowadays.
- In Lebanon, which was once a majority Christian country, with 62 percent Christians in the 1970s, now only 39 percent of its population is Christian.
- In Iraq, where Christians were once 8 percent of the population in the 1980s, now they represent less than 1.5 percent of the people.[2]
- And of course, the tragedy in Syria is ongoing, and predictions are dim concerning her pre-war 10 percent Christian population.

Yet small does not mean insignificant. In each of these contexts, no matter how small the Church is quantitatively, it has left a qualitative impact through a variety of subversive and creative tools advocated by a public theology of hope, and it was through these tools that it has kept an uninterrupted presence in the region since the day of Pentecost.

Through all of this, the word of God is still proclaimed week after week, from active desert monasteries that date back to the fourth century to church plants sprouting in new suburbs; and from house churches that meet

---

2. See *Cradle of Our Faith*.

underground to mega churches in major metropolitan cities. And the name of Jesus is still praised, from the lips of those who faithfully passed down the gospel from generation to generation, as well as from the lips of former terrorists, our modern-day versions of Paul of Tarsus.

Today, Christ's followers in the MENA region exceed 15 million, approximately 10 million of them live in Egypt, of which 2 million are Protestants, the second largest Christian community after the Coptic Orthodox. Over the past decade, the Arab Spring and consequent Egyptian revolutions of 2011 and 2013, have had a negative impact on the Christian population of Egypt—a story to which we now turn our attention for a brief analysis of its challenges and opportunities.

The Challenges of Our Context

With this familiarly with the context, we now turn to a systematic categorization of some of the challenges the Egyptian Church had to face in recent years. I have arranged the challenges in the order of concentric circles, starting from the core with the most immediate internal *theological* challenges, then moving outward to the intermediate challenges presented by *regional and international* crises, and finally concluding with the external pressures the Egyptian Church faces from *political and socio-economic* challenges.

Internal theological challenges

The top theological challenge related to the Christian community's understanding of the kingdom of God, which inevitably impacts her understanding of ecclesiology—particularly the identity and mission of the Church in the world. Everyone agrees that since its inception the Church lives in the tension of being "in" yet "not of" the world, but not everyone agrees to the dimensions and boundaries of the *in* and the *not of*.

Some have tried to resolve the tension by leaning towards the *in* side of it, where the Church is seen as an integral part of society, affected by its crises and celebrations, and even more so, a contributing partner to its crises and celebrations. I describe this as *Integrated Ecclesiology*. Thus, when a crisis occurs, the Church is united to its surrounding context, sharing in its suffering with a clear call to engagement, participation, and partnership with the world to alleviate such suffering. The principle dogma behind such ecclesiology is an understanding of the kingdom of God as *already and not yet*, where the reign of Christ has already begun here and now and will reach completion in the future. It is also formed by the doctrine of creation with its emphasis on humanity being created in the image of God (imago Dei), and God's concern with the spiritual as well as the material created order. Proponents believe that Christ is concerned not just with individual salvation, but also with the redemption of the whole creation.

Others have tried to resolve the tension by leaning towards the *not of* side of it, where the Church is seen as separate from society, excluded from its crises and celebrations. I describe this as *Isolated Ecclesiology*. Thus, when a crisis occurs, the Church examines the reasons behind and impact of it, evaluating how these affect the Church, and thus, directs its efforts to responses that aim at alleviating the suffering of the Christian community, while more urgently evangelizing new members into this community through the salvation of their souls. The principle dogma behind such ecclesiology is an understanding of the kingdom of God as an apocalyptic event, where the reign of Christ is a future reality. It is also formed by an eschatology that strives to free as many as possible from the bondage of sin and from clinging to a world that is doomed to eternal damnation. Proponents *ultimately diminish the value of the Church's social and political involvement based on this logic:* "If politics and culture are not truly part of God's vision of salvation and contribute nothing to our ultimate relationship with God, (then) they are optional rather than necessary aspects of the Christian's vocation."[3]

Although, the Protestant Church in Egypt has swung back and forth between both sides of this tension, depending on the political, social, and economic milieu of the time, I am convinced that her default tends more towards Isolated Ecclesiology. There are two reasons for this. First is the prominent prevailing theology and practice of monasticism that was birthed in the Egyptian desserts in the fourth century and is still actively practiced to this day. This movement was partially in response to severe persecution of the Church by the governing rulers of the time, which created an enmity and suspicion between Church and state politics. The second reason is the influence of puritanism which characterized many of the early Protestant missionaries to Egypt in the middle of the nineteenth century.[4] Upon their arrival on Egyptian soil, they defined the mission of the Church quite narrowly to concern itself only with personal piety and churchly revival.

However, some early missionaries, whose views clearly advocated for more corporate activism and cultural renewal, elevated social action and the incarnational model of the great commission to new heights. By doing so, they enlarged the view of God's authority, and thus, gained a more

---

3. Epperly, *Wisdom & Wonder*, 2.
4. Zaki, *The Copts and The Revolution*, 102.

comprehensive perspective on evangelism and worship. They saw the implications of the redemption found in Christ as infiltrating all spheres of society, and they taught that the Church's role in society is to equip believers for their comprehensive vocations.

But even the line between these two groups, with their differing views of the Church's mission, is not that clear cut. It is certainly not clear in the case of Kasr El Dobarah Evangelical Church (KDEC), a church located within walking distance of Tahrir Square, the central hub of the 2011 Egyptian Revolution. Members of this church successfully bridged the gap between the two groups by pointing to a complex relationship between piety and politics.

Anna Dowell, an anthropology researcher at Duke University, investigated what it meant to the KDEC community that the prayers and practices of the faithful might not only transform the inner thoughts and outward behaviors of practitioners, but that it could also effect change in the power structures of the state. This is a vision of political power, exercised through prayer, and sustained in corporate worship.[5] When interviewing a young person in the congregation about his reason for not joining the revolution in the public square, he answered: "I do not need to go to Tahrir Square to change my country because I am already in the spiritual square."[6] Dowell thus concludes:

> It is not just the overtly political actions that shape the kinds of *citizens* at KDEC, but also practices like prayer, fasting, and corporate worship. These affective practices create particular enemies, distributions of power, and sites of resistance. For example, one's allegiances are oriented differently if one is in a supernatural war between good and evil than if "power" is negotiated and regulated exclusively between activist collectives, political parties, and state institutions.[7]

Intermediate challenges: regional-international crises

The second set of challenges concerns regional-international crises. While we try to engage in public theology and help build our nations on democratic values and ethics through the Church's involvement in the public square, we

---

5. This is similar to how some South Korean Christians saw the coming together of their leader with the North Korean leader as a direct answer to their prayers.

6. Dowell, *The Church in the Square*, 35.

7. Dowell, *The Church in the Square*, 40.

are constantly bombarded by regional and international crises. Examples include the Israeli-Palestinian conflict, wars, cultural colonialism, terrorism, and the refugee crisis (5 million in Egypt alone from Sudan, Palestine, Iraq, Somalia, Ethiopia, Eretria, Yemen, and finally Syria). These are the same basic crises that the West also struggles with, except that the Middle East deals with them at close range. We try to listen well to current regional and world affairs, however, our witness in this volatile region is often ignored, even discredited, by divisive politics inside the Church in the West. This predicament manifests itself in our region in two major ways.

First, there is a toxic understanding of the eschaton in ways that favor the Israeli State, while dehumanizing the Palestinian people. In 2009, following the example of South Africa, a group of Palestinian Church leaders produced a well-written Kairos Statement, in which they stated: "We declare that any use of the Bible to legitimize or support political options and positions that are based upon injustice, imposed by one person on another, or by one people on another, transform religion into human ideology and strip the Word of God of its holiness, its universality and truth."[8]

Second, our witness is harmed when the Church in the West aligns herself with political powers that are racist, misogynistic, and materialistic. Mark Labberton, the president of Fuller Theological Seminary, spoke prophetic words to a gathering of Evangelical leaders at Wheaton in 2018 that are most pertinent to us here:

> For white evangelicals to embrace a platform and advocacy that primarily promotes, prioritizes, and defends America above all and over all, is to embrace an idolatry that has only ever proven disastrous. However, identification with the use of demeaning rhetoric toward other nations, not least nations of color that are facing the challenges of poverty and war, is not only confusing but violating to the dignity, value, and truth of the gospel. It is, as well, violating to the people we otherwise claim to see, serve, join, and love—nations to which, ironically, American evangelicals annually send millions of dollars for mission and evangelism.[9]

---

8. Kairos Palestine, *A Moment of Truth*, section 2.4.
9. Labberton, "Political Dealing: The Crisis of Evangelicalism."

External challenges: political and socio-economic pressures

As to political pressures in the MENA region, apart from the exceptions of countries like Tunisia and Lebanon, where Christians experience relatively high degrees of freedom,[10] most of the countries in the MENA region exhibit a number of common inequalities under their current regimes. These include, but are not limited to, government restrictions imposed on the Christian community, poor representation in the executive, legislative, and judicial branches of government, and treatment of Christians as second-class citizens, resulting in an invasive glass-ceiling effect in all public spheres, and resulting in a minority-victim mentality.

Moreover, Christians in the MENA region have also suffered the effects of socio-economic pressures, which are deeply connected to the rise of Islamic fundamentalism. In our region, the root cause of Islamic fundamentalism is actually economic, not religious. With a decline of economy and a rise in unemployment rates in many of our nation states, a large number of our citizens (mainly men) migrate to oil-rich countries within our region to seek employment. To give you an idea of the size of this phenomenon in Egypt, for example, the private transfers from these Egyptian foreign workers represented the third source of our national income, only passed by revenues from tourism (pre the Arab Spring) and the Suez Canal.

Many of these migrant workers, after spending a number of years in these Islamist countries, return to their homelands, saturated with a Wahabi form of Islam that is more extreme, less tolerant of Christianity, and often demanding the implementation of Sharia law and the inferior treatment of non-Muslim citizens. Many MENA countries, historically known for their doctrine and practice of moderate Islam, have suffered this fate. Their governments are torn between restrictively protecting its citizens on the one hand and pleasing the rising fundamentalist voice, which has not only become a political and economic force but has also been prone to violence, on the other. In several of these nations today, when you enter a local church, you will pass by armed police, and possibly even a metal detector set up to catch suicidal bombers.

This rise in fundamentalism has resulted in two negative practices that have harmed the Christian community in Egypt greatly. The first is the establishment of "Community Reconciliation Sessions" in towns across Egypt, under the disguise of a desire to restore peaceful community relations between Christians and Muslims, by resolving community conflicts without resorting to the police or law-enforcement officials. These sessions

---

10. This list used to include Syria under Bashar Al-Assad's pre-war regime.

have stripped the law of its sovereignty, and many Christians are frequently pressured to drop their complaints for the sake of communal peace, allowing the Muslim perpetrators to go unpunished.

The second harmful practice has been an intentional effort to erase Christian history in the land. Islamic fundamentalists spread rumors about Christianity as a Western colonial import, rather than the native religion of the region. Such lies inevitably lead to suspicion of the patriotism and loyalty of native Christians to their homelands. In this environment of distortion and suspicion, citizenship is a daily struggle to prove the Christians' worthiness of equal rights, of pluralism, of freedom of expression, and of worship. It is a constant burden on Christians to prove that they have no trouble both being loyal to the Triune God, and still being loyal to their homeland. In fact, good Christian theology asserts that Jesus' teaching actually compels them to be good citizens of whatever homeland they are in, even though they are citizens of every land, and at the same time of a completely different spiritual land.[11] This quote by a Church leader writing to a Roman official while trying to explain this new faith called Christianity summarizes this idea well: "For a Christian every homeland is a foreign country, and every foreign country is a homeland."[12]

Given the internal, intermediate, and external challenges mentioned above, Christians in the MENA region do not have the luxury not to be involved in the public square, because our silence will confirm the prevailing distorted view of our apathetic patriotism. Our lack of action will simply prove the lie to be true, that we have no interest in this land and its welfare. Nonetheless, we also do not have the luxury of engaging the public square, both state and civil society, with less than utmost care and wisdom, because one misstep, or poor expression of where we stand can actually jeopardize not only an individual's life, but the state of the whole Church.

Now, how that looks and in what ways and what forms it takes place, is what I would like to turn to in the second half of this chapter.

The Opportunities of Our Context

In the MENA context, God has offered us many insights and opportunities for political participation, interfaith engagement, and social services through development and education.

---

11. John 19:11, Rom 13:1–5; Phil 3:20; 1 Pet 2:13–25.

12. From *The Epistle of Diognetus*. This is one of the earliest documents after the New Testament.

Political participation

There are many strong and inspiring initiatives on the *regional* level. One example of such a Christian initiative is "The Arab Group," headquartered in Beirut under the leadership of Rev. Dr. Riad Jarjour. Founded in 1995 to help resolve conflicts in the Arab world, this organization demonstrates that there is an important role for religious leaders in peacemaking. The group is comprised of Christian and Muslim intellectuals, clergy, and other public leaders from Lebanon, Syria, Egypt, Jordan, Palestine, Sudan, and the UAE, who work together to launch initiatives to promote coexistence and mutual understanding between Muslims and Christians in the Arab world and elsewhere. Notably, members of this group have participated in peacemaking efforts in northern and southern Sudan, where the issue of religion has come into play since the Muslim government worked to implement Islamic law in the predominantly Christian South. Their efforts eventually contributed to a national peace agreement in 2005 between the government and the major rebel army, as well as between some Muslim and Christian communities.

Another example of an outstanding initiative is Diyar's Consortium headquartered in Bethlehem under the leadership of Rev. Dr. Mitri Raheb. Diyar is an ecumenically oriented organization serving the whole Palestinian community, with emphasis on children, youth, women, and the elderly through unique programs that are contextual and holistic in nature. Founded in 1995, Diyar Consortium serves more than 60,000 persons annually. Since the Arab Spring, Diyar ministry has expanded to reach out to the neighboring countries of Jordan, Lebanon, Iraq, and Egypt, by inviting their youth to explore issues such as constitutions, the rule of law, the role of the state in securing religious liberties, and religious laws and practices against women. These efforts resulted in an outstanding statement on citizenship titled: "From the Nile to the Euphrates: The Call of Faith and Citizenship."[13]

A final example of effective political participation on the regional level is the role of Christian media. In this day and age, the public square is no longer a physical space, rather, it is an abstract common space in which different parties meet through a variety of media (print, electronic, TV, internet, etc.). And since more than 50 percent of the MENA region population

---

13. Diyar Consortium, "From the Nile to the Euphrates." A document by the Christian Academic Forum for Citizenship in the Arab World. Diyar Consortium, ed., *From the Nile to the Euphrates: The Call of Faith and Citizenship*, 2015. The document highlights the main challenges facing the Middle East in the post-"Arab Spring" era and a possible contribution of Christians towards the future of this region.

is urban, and the median age is twenty-five years, this is especially true among younger urban generations.

Media holds great power to both *express* and *form* public opinions. It does so by orienting the public towards acknowledging and accepting Christian values and beliefs, which can foster national unity and peace-building—values that help overcome distorted prejudices towards those who belong to a different community. Media can also enhance political participation by reporting on positive social action, ecumenical movements, and collaborative community projects, as well as reporting on injustices carried against minority groups, and motivating responses to battle such injustices. For instance, a major Arabic-speaking Christian satellite channel committed itself to developing educational programs based on the Syrian elementary school curriculum, and to airing them for several hours daily, so that Syrian children stuck in refugee camps do not miss out on their education.

As to public theology at home on the *national* level, the Egyptian Revolution of 2011 was a point of re-entry for Christians into political life, in a practical visible incarnational way. The sixty years prior to 2011 were marked by a palpable decline in the Christians' political participation—a decline that was sparked by Nasser's Revolution in 1952.[14] Before that, the Christians of Egypt were present and interwoven in the fabric of Egypt's society, contributing especially to the social, political, and economic making of the modern Egyptian state. But Nasser's Revolution, with its pan-Arabism rhetoric, posed a threat to the Egyptian Church, and Christians feared that it would eventually lead to a doctrine that could foster religious divides in Egyptian society, which would lead to sectarian tension and a removal of Copts from national life. Unfortunately, their fears were realized as Nasser focused on the unification of the Arab peoples under the United Arab Republic, "Copts had become foreigners in their own country at a time when every foreign Muslim was considered a citizen."[15] The Copts were effectively ousted from economic and political life at the national level in the Arab state that Nasser was building. Ever since then, the Christians of the region have had their suspicions of the military state, yet they were willing to tolerate it, because they knew that the alternative would be nothing less than a fundamentalist Islamic state.

But in January 2011, it was as if a scene from a pre-Nasser era was drawn out of our collective history and memory,[16] where Christians and Muslims were standing side by side demanding freedom, dignity, and social

---

14. Leveugle, *The Copts and the Egyptian State*, 13–24.
15. Leveugle, *The Copts and the Egyptian State*, 13–24.
16. Namely, the revolution of 1919 against British Occupation of Egypt and Sudan.

justice for all, and "priests and sheikhs visited one another and attended each other's religious services."[17] Then, although the Muslim Brotherhood tried to hijack the 2011 Revolution, and intentionally pushed Christians out of the scene, Egypt's military leaders stepped in during the second revolution of June 2013, and put the revolution back on track, going as far as including the Coptic Orthodox pope in the scene, as the figure representing all Christians in Egypt, including Protestants.

It is noteworthy that the pope's peaceful and wise response to the attacks on sixty churches, and on tens of Christian institutions only six weeks after the second revolution of 2013, single-handedly undid the Muslim Brotherhood's scheme for an Egyptian civil war. In response, President El-SiSi ordered the military to rebuild all the damaged churches at the government's expense. Since then, he has been careful to visit the Coptic Orthodox cathedral, the seat of the pope, for both Christmas and Easter Mass, to send a clear message to Muslim fundamentalists and the Muslim Brotherhood that he is the president for *all* Egyptians, and that Egypt is a home for Christians and Muslims.[18]

I will conclude with a brief mention of a few stellar examples of how the Egyptian Church shifted from survival to engagement mode in public life, by breaking down the barrier of fear, emerging from decades of hiding within her walls, and finally taking a central and visible role in weaving the fabric of the New Egypt. For instance, at crucial times of violent conflicts in the streets, churches transformed their buildings into makeshift clinics, inviting both Muslims and Christians to receive treatment. Others hosted blood drives to meet the shortages in the blood banks, due to ongoing acts of violence. Elsewhere, local churches offered public lectures and panels open to Muslims and Christians on political awareness and engagement, and some even formed "Citizenship Committees" to encourage their members with the right resources to participate in the political process. Finally, in the sphere of governance, Christians leaders sought to exercise more thoughtfulness in choosing who represents the Christian community in parliamentary elections and among the various political parties. Knowing that they would inevitably be under-represented meant that Christians had to be strategic peace-makers.

17. Carter, *The Copts in Egyptian Politics*, 62.

18. This message was further confirmed by the Saudi crown prince's visit to the Coptic Orthodox pope in 2018.

Interfaith engagement

Public theology always involves dialogue with and critique from both the Church itself and society as a whole. It must be open to being confronted with the question of congruence between what we believe and how we act. It asks: what are we saying about ourselves and about the gospel we proclaim when we act in the ways we do?

One example of this process done well comes from Muscat, Oman, where the Amana Center was given the responsibility by the government to represent Christians fairly, to develop programs to train visiting Church-leaders for interfaith dialogue, to help resolve interfaith disputes, and to strengthen national unity in diversity.

But, as we have already alluded to, interfaith engagement is much bigger than interfaith dialogue. Other examples of public Christian expressions of interfaith engagement that are visible in different parts of the MENA region include:

- Christian ministries hosting concerts of "religious chanting" featuring prominent Muslim and Christian singers together to promote national unity and peace-building, overcoming the barriers of traditional churches and mosques.

- The use of Middle Eastern instruments and melodies in Christian worship, in order to express and embrace our culture and be hospitable to others from other faith communities. Similarly, incorporating common Islamic floral patterns and varied calligraphies in Christian art and architecture, not just for evangelistic purposes, but also with the goals of contextualization and to affirm our citizenship. One Orthodox retreat center designed their chapel to look like a Muslim place of prayer, where people take their shoes off and sit on carpets on the ground as a way to reach our neighbors.

Social services through development and education

Finally, opportunities abound when it comes to social services through development and education. Public Theology is often practiced incarnationally on a humanitarian level in the MENA region. It is not confined to the church but is meant to be relevant to people outside of it as well. This has been the strength of the Christian faith in the MENA region, as it has succeeded in building trust and laying a foundation for social engagement. It takes seriously God's heart for the poor and the vulnerable, which was one of God's people's—and now the Church's—most distinctive priorities and commandments.

Social services are offered through several *development* initiatives. For instance, Christian hospitals, orphanages, child-care nurseries, and employment centers—all serve Muslims and Christians alike. The largest non-profit organization in the Middle East is a Christian NGO called The Coptic Evangelical Organization for Social Services (CEOSS) headquartered in Cairo, serving more than 2 million people in 150 communities each year through its comprehensive development programs in the areas of: agriculture, micro loans, Christian publishing, literacy, housing, people with disabilities, children at risk, health, and peace-building.

There are also social projects done in partnership between local churches and mosques in various communities to provide sports tournaments, cultural evenings, and the cleaning and greening of slum areas. An inspiring example of such a project is in the Garbage Villages, whose residents are 90 percent Christians. The work of the Christians among the garbage villages introduced Egypt to the concept of recycling, reflecting the Christian theology of creation care. In one of these garbage villages, in central Cairo, the garbage collectors sort and recycle a record 80 percent of Cairo's daily waste, yielding perhaps the highest rate of recycling efficiency and profitability in the world.[19]

Finally, social services are also offered through *Christian Education*. Some Protestant and Catholic schools have up to 70 percent Muslims in their student bodies, with the vision of raising reformed Muslims or whom some have referred to as "cultural Christians." Lengthy wait-lists are universal among these schools, because of their reputation for academic excellence and ethical distinction, as they teach ways of faithfully engaging culture through a Christian worldview.

Areas of Growth

As much as we have learned and been encouraged, the Church in the MENA region is far from perfect, and still has much growing to do. So, I will end by briefly identifying three areas for growth.

---

19. By comparison, most Western garbage companies only recycle 20–25 percent of the waste collected.

The need to overcome the minority-victim mentality

As a religious group that once dominated the land, and is now a shrinking minority, some segments of the Church have come to see themselves as marginalized, silenced, and even defeated. This manifests itself in a gripping fear that has led some Christians to justify their own self-interests, while ignoring the suffering and even dying of others. For example, in a terrorist attack we scan to see if there are Christian names among the deceased, before deciding whether to engage or not. This minority-victim mentality also makes us uninformed of and disengaged from the injustices perpetuated against other ethnic and religious minority groups, like the Nubians in North Sudan, or the Kurds in Syria, or the Amazighs in Algeria. We confess with our mouths the God of justice and compassion, yet our passive social and political responses to such incidents contribute to the suffering and oppression of others.

The need to engage the academy

David Tracy identifies three publics with whom one's public theology should try to engage in dialogue: the society, the academy, and the religious institution.[20] We have historically engaged society, have more recently engaged the religious institution, however, we have continued to fail to engage the academy. Through the academy, the Church will be able to engage other public spheres such as economics, law, the market, media, and other religious communities with effective interdisciplinary methodology. To do this effectively, we must carefully examine our form of speech and range of vocabulary. If we are going to succeed in addressing the public spheres in society, the language and rationale we use should be openly assessable by all, and not couched in theologically elitist terms. This is done by presenting the Christian position in a way that is publicly comprehensible, and thus, open to public debate and critical enquiry.

The need to develop constructive public theology

Public theology ought to be performed, not just printed in books or only done within our specialized circles. Law, physics, and medicine make contributions to the wider society. So should theology. This field of theology should not be theoretical first and then developed for application. Rather,

20. Tracey, *The Analogical Imagination*, 3–5.

it is a theology that develops and evolves while being expressed in society. The Church has a biblical, spiritual, pastoral, and prophetic role. Public theology helps the Church keep these four things in balance in her distinct Christian witness.

I believe this is a *kairos moment*, and the Church needs to rise to the occasion. With recent events in our region, the invisible hand of God is peeling the mask from extremist Islam and increasing numbers of Muslims are disillusioned with political Islam, having experienced first-hand its empty promises, incompetency, and irrelevance to the modern world. Intertwined with this disillusion is a search for truth, justice, and security, not only in this life, but in the life after. They are looking at us, their Christian neighbors more appreciatively, and are openly asking questions of faith and understanding.

Conclusion

I am convinced that public theology presents a cogent argument for the lordship of Christ over all of life, that challenges Christians to live out loud their ministry of reconciliation and peace-making with their Muslim neighbors. "As people seeking to live in the Kingdom of God, every time we confess 'Jesus is Lord,' we are in fact demanding that all other powers must be reframed in light of His Lordship."[21]

Perhaps a parable will make my point more lucid. While waiting to board my flight on a recent trip, I watched in amazement very small, low-profile vehicles towing and directing enormous aircrafts. They are called "Pushback tractors," and no major airport can function without them. They are used to push backwards large aircrafts away from airport gates, because although many aircrafts are capable of moving themselves backwards on the ground using reverse thrust, the resulting jet blast may cause damage to the terminal building or nearby equipment. Using a pushback tractor is therefore the preferred method to move the aircraft away from the gate.

While the church in the MENA region is small, we know from Ephesians 1:19 that we are empowered and filled with the same strength that raised Jesus from the dead. Therefore, we must remember that we are strong enough to push back the injustices of an entire socio-political structure, and powerful enough to tow this world in the right direction, ensuring the common good for all.

Even though the church in the MENA region has often been forced to be speechless, she has refused to be voiceless. May it be so for us all.

21. Labberton, "Political Dealing: The Crisis of Evangelicalism."

Bibliography

Anna. *The Church in the Square: Negotiations of Religion and Revolution at an Evangelical Church in Cairo, Egypt*. Cairo: American University in Cairo Press in Cairo, 2012.

Carter, B. L. *The Copts in Egyptian Politics*. Dover, NH: Croom Helm, 1986.

Day, Katie, and Sebastian Kim. "Introduction." In *A Companion to Public Theology*, 1–21. Brill's Companion to Modern Theology. Leiden: Brill, 2017.

The Epistle of Diognetus. Translated by Henry Meecham. Manchester, UK: Manchester University, 1949.

Epperly, Bruce. *Wisdom & Wonder: Common Grace in Science & Art, Abraham Kuyper*. Grand Rapids: Christian's Library, 2012.

Kairos Palestine. *A Moment of Truth: A Word of Faith, Hope and Love from the Heart of Palestinian Suffering*, 2009. https://www.kairospalestine.ps/index.php/about-kairos/kairos-palestine-document/.

Labberton, Mark. "Political Dealing: The Crisis of Evangelicalism." A speech addressed at a private meeting of Evangelical leaders held at Wheaton College in Chicago, on April 16, 2018.

Leveugle, Samantha. "The Copts and the Egyptian State: The Economic and Political Marginalization of the Coptic Christians of Egypt from Muhammad Ali to the Present." *The University of California Undergraduate Research Journal* XVI (2013) 1–12. https://archive.urop.uci.edu/journal/journal13/02_leveugle.pdf

Tracey, David. *The Analogical Imagination: Christian Theology and the Culture of Pluralism*. London: SCM, 1981.

Zaki, Andrea. *The Copts and The Revolution*. Cairo: Dar Al-Thaqafa, 2015.

Timeline

THIS TIMELINE IDENTIFIES SIGNIFICANT dates in the development of Christianity in the Middle East and the Persian Gulf. Some of these are part of the trajectory of the early Church in the Greco-Roman world, but in general, events located in Turkey are not included if they have a focus solely on the western Roman Empire.

The spelling, pointing, and accenting of Arabic and other names in the timeline are derived from Badr et al., *Christianity: A History in the Middle East* and Yarshater et al., *Encyclopaedia Iranica*.

Year	Event
*ca.*30	Forty days after the crucifixion and resurrection of Jesus Christ, the promised Holy Spirit fills the disciples on the Day of Pentecost and the witness of the Church begins. [**Palestine**]
49	The first Church council meets at Jerusalem and discusses whether the requirements of the Jewish law are binding on gentile converts to Christianity. [**Palestine**]
50–*ca.*95	The formation of the New Testament begins with Paul's letters to the churches in Asia Minor, Greece, and Rome (50–*ca.*65); the Gospels are written later, with Mark recording the first Gospel (possibly in Rome) *ca.*65 and John composing the last of the canonical Gospels in *ca.*95. [**Syria, Palestine, and Turkey**]
*ca.*80–100	An unknown writer compiles "The Lord's Instruction (i.e., the *Didachē*) to the Gentiles through the Twelve Apostles," a compendium of recommendations on morality, community organization, and liturgy; this is possibly the earliest extant Christian writing outside the New Testament. [**Syria**]

104	Addai ordains Pkidha as the first Christian bishop of Arbela in Adiabene. [Iraq]
ca.170	Tatian writes his *Diatessarōn* (lit. "through four"), the first harmony of the Gospels, in Arbela, Adiabene. [Iraq]
Before 195	Following the conversion of Abgar VIII, king of Osrhoene, Edessa becomes, in the Syrian tradition, the capital of the first Christian kingdom. [Turkey]
201	The records of Edessa (the *Chronicle of Edessa*) note the destruction of the first recorded church building ("the church of the Christians") by a major flood in the city. [Turkey]
225	The sixth-century Syriac *Chronicle of Arbela*, written by Měšīḥā-Zěḵā, records that there were more than twenty bishops in Mesopotamia by this date. [Turkey, Iraq, Iran (Persia), and Qaṭar]
ca.270	Antony of Egypt goes into the desert as an ascetic hermit, laying the foundations for the monastic movement; this solitary asceticism develops into an organized community by 305. [Egypt]
325	The Council of Nicaea condemns Arianism and issues the Nicene Creed as a statement of orthodox Christian belief. [Turkey]
336–45	The Syriac author Afrahāṭ writes his *Demonstrations*, a twenty-three-volume series of homilies on Christian doctrine. [Iraq and Iran (Persia)]
340–63	The Great Persecution of the Persian church begins under King Šāpur II, lasting until the accession of Julian "the Apostate" as emperor of the Roman Empire (when the Persian Christians could no longer be accused of being allies of a Christian Roman emperor); after some years of peace, the persecution is reignited sporadically from ca.379 until ca.401. [Iraq and Iran (Persia)]
356	A Roman mission to India under the Arian Theophilus the deacon (also known as "Theophilus the Indian," since he was a native of the Maldives Islands, southwest of Kerala) visits Southwest Arabia, converting its Ḥimyarite ruler, and building short-lived churches at Aden, Ẓafār, Sanʿāʾ, and Hormuz;

more enduring results follow from the activity of the Nestorian Arab convert Ḥayyān from 399 to 420. [**Yemen**]

373 Māwiyya, the first Christian Arab queen, becomes leader of the western Tanukh in the Syrian/Arabian desert on the death of her husband, the tribal sheik; the tribe had been converted through the influence of miracle-working priests and monks about ten years earlier. [**Syria, Jordan, and Saudi Arabia**]

390 The Persian Nestorian missionary ʿAbdisho establishes a monastery in Bahrain; delegates from Bahrain and Qatar would attend the Nestorian "Synod of Isaac" at Seleucia-Ctesiphon twenty years later. [**Bahrain, Qaṭar, Iraq, and Iran (Persia)**]

Fifth and sixth centuries Christianity becomes widespread on the pre-Islamic Arabian Peninsula; examples include the Christian kingdoms of the Lakhmids (Northern Arabia/Iraq) and of Kinda (central Arabia), the flourishing dioceses of Bahrain, Qaṭar, and ʿOman, and the martyr bishops of Yemen. [**Saudi Arabia, Iraq, Bahrain, Qaṭar, ʿOman, and Yemen**]

410 Following an Edict of Toleration issued the previous year by Shah Yazdegerd I, the Persian Church organizes itself as a separate, distinct, and autonomous Church at the "Synod of Isaac"; the synods of Dādīšoʿ (Dadyeshu) in 424, Mār ʿAqaq (Acacius) in 486, and Seleucia-Ctephison in 499 later extend this independence, leading to the adoption of a Nestorian definition of the Trinity, and the severance of all connections between the Persian Church and the West. [**Iraq and Iran (Persia)**]

410 The consecration of Hosea as bishop is the earliest attestation of role of the city of Ḥira as an episcopal see and as a center for Christian mission; its Christian population were known as al-ʿIbād, "the servants [i.e., of Christ]." [**Iraq**]

431 The Council of Ephesus excommunicates Nestorius because of his imputed teaching on the two *distinct* natures (divine and human) of Christ. [**Turkey**]

451 The Council of Chalcedon issues the classical orthodox definition of the divine and human natures of Christ *united* in the one person (sometimes referred to as "dyophysite," or "two natures" theology). [**Turkey**]

452–57	A theological revolt against Chalcedonian dyophysite orthodoxy breaks out in Egypt in 452, leading to the establishment of Coptic (i.e., Monophysite, "one nature") churches in Egypt and Ethiopia; five years later, the Chalcedonian patriarch of Alexandria is killed in a street riot. [**Egypt**]
489	The Metropolitan Archbishop Bar Ṣaumā founds a Nestorian school at Nisibis (then in Persian territory), which becomes the key institution in the revitalization and Nestorianizing of the Persian Church in the sixth century. [**Turkey, Iraq, and Iran (Persia)**]
520	Kaleb, the king of Aksum, invades Yemen (where the Ḥimyarite king Dhū Nuwās was persecuting Christians in Yemen and especially at Najrān, the key Christian center in Southern Arabia); Kaleb defeats Dhū Nuwās and appoints the native Christian Sumuafaʾ Ashawaʾ as viceroy, and as a result Southern Arabia becomes a Christian territory under Ethiopian hegemony for the next fifty years. [**Yemen and Saudi Arabia**]
540	Mār Aḇā becomes the patriarch of the East and introduces reforms in the Persian Church, reorganizing its discipline, reinvigorating its theological education, reviving its spiritual and moral tone, and attempting to bring unity. [**Iraq and Iran (Persia)**]
ca.542–78	A network of monophysite (i.e., Jacobite Syrian Orthodox) Churches expands from Syria to India, largely through the journeys of Jacob al-Barādʿi. [**Syria, Iraq, and Iran (Persia)**]
555	The Nestorian merchant and explorer Cosmas Indicopleustes encounters Christians in Socotra during his voyage to Taprobane (Sri Lanka) and Kerala (South India). [**Yemen**]
569–71	A Persian monastic revival begins under Abraham of Kashkar, the founder of the Mount Izla monastery, and its abbot, Mār Bābay, typified by education, mobility, and outreach (which extends as far as China by 635). [**Iraq and Iran (Persia)**]
610	The Prophet Muḥammad begins to receive revelations and is commanded to recite these (*Iqraʾ*, from which the word *Qurʾān*, i.e., "what is recited," is derived); twelve years later he flees from Mecca to Medina (the *Hijra* or *Hejira*: "emigration"

or "journey"), his flight marking the beginning of Islam and the starting point of the Islamic calendar. [**Saudi Arabia**]

631   Muḥammad signs an agreement with the Christians of Najrān, guaranteeing their personal safety and the right to their possessions and religion (subject to their submission to Muslim authorities, especially the payment of the *jizya* capitulation tax); this forms the basis of later agreements with Christians as *dhimmi* (subordinate communities). [**Saudi Arabia**]

638   The Arab Muslim armies under 'Umar I conquer Jerusalem, where 'Umar declines an invitation from the Christian bishop to pray in the Church of the Holy Sepulcher (since this would have furnished the precedent for a claim on the part of zealous Muslims to the church as a mosque), thus preserving it as a Christian house of worship. [**Palestine**]

661   The Umayyad Caliphate begins in Damascus; this acted like a civilized Byzantine successor state, employing Christian and Jewish civil servants to assist in its administration. [**Syria**]

741   Pope Gregory III, the fifth (and last) of an intermittent series of Syrian popes from 685 to 741, dies; he would be the last non-European pope until the election of the Argentinian Pope Francis I in 2013. [**Syria**]

750   The Umayyad dynasty falls and is replaced by the 'Abbasids at Baghdād; this more Asian and more strictly orthodox new Muslim dynasty placed greater importance on religious, rather than racial, identity and gradually introduced greater restrictions on Christians; nevertheless, it also began the translation of Greek texts into Syriac and thence into Arabic, leading to the development of Islamic philosophical, medical, and scientific learning. [**Iraq**]

779   The *Catholicos* Timotheos I, a native of Adiabene and the greatest of the Nestorian patriarchs, rules the Church of the East from 779 to 823, moving his seat from Seleucia-Ctesiphon to Baghdād, the new capital, where he was active in the 'Abbasid court. [**Iraq**]

781   The *Catholicos* Timotheos I engages in a public debate with the Caliph Mahdī on Islam and Christianity; the year was also a significant high point for Nestorian Christianity with the erection of a Christian monument (under imperial patronage)

	in the Chinese capital city Xi'an and Timotheos's appointment of a Nestorian bishop for Tibet. [**Iraq**]
1009–16	Abu 'Ali al-Ḥākim bi-'Amr-Allāh (the "mad Caliph") persecutes the Coptic Church in Egypt, executing Christian officials, and ordering the destruction of the Church of the Holy Sepulcher in Jerusalem. [**Egypt and Palestine**]
1026	A debate takes places at Nisibis between the Nestorian bishop Elijah and a Muslim vizier, during which the bishop argues for the superiority of Syriac learning, arguing that the Arabs had learned most of their science from these sources, rather than *vice versa*. [**Turkey**]
1071	The Byzantine Empire loses much of Asia Minor to the Saljuq (Seljuk) Turks at the Battle of Manzikert, with the result that Asia Minor becomes largely a Muslim territory and has remained so ever since. [**Turkey**]
1099	The crusaders capture Jerusalem after a prolonged siege and subject its Muslim and Jewish inhabitants to an appalling massacre in which more than 40,000 are believed to have perished. [**Palestine**]
1187	The Sunni Kurdish general Ṣalāḥ-al-dīn Yūsof ibn Ayyūb (Saladin) reconquers Jerusalem, allowing the defeated crusaders to leave the city in peace, and, in striking contrast to the crusaders eighty-eight years previously, treating Christian refugees with mercy and compassion. [**Palestine**]
1250	The Mamluks, a non-Arab knightly "slave soldier" caste, seize power in Egypt from the Ayubbid dynasty, adopting a hostile stance towards the Coptic Christians and decisively advancing the Islamization of Egypt; this repression intensifies after 1279, with churches being destroyed and refusals to recite the *Šahāda* (the Muslim confession of faith) leading to the threat of being burned alive. [**Egypt**]
1258	The Mongols under the Il-Khan Hülegü sack Baghdād and bring about the end of the 'Abbasid Caliphate. [**Iraq**]
1281	The Church of the East chooses the Mongol Nestorian monk Mark (despite his inability to speak Syriac, the language of the Church) as Patriarch Yaballaha III and enthrones him at Mār Koka near Baghdād. [**Iraq**]

1287	The Il-Khan Arġūn sends the Mongol monk Ṣaumā (by now a Nestorian bishop) from Iran on an ambassadorial mission to the pope and to the Christian courts of Europe, visiting Rome, Paris, and Gascony (where he celebrates Mass for the English King, Edward I). [**Iran (Persia)**]
1318	A Nestorian synod meets in Persia for the enthronement of a new patriarch (Timothy II) following the death of Yaballaha III; although there may have been subsequent patriarchs, this was the last recorded synod of the Nestorian Church of the East. [**Iran (Persia)**]
1453	Constantinople falls to the Ottoman Turks under Muḥammad II, who kill the Emperor Constantine XI and bring the Eastern Roman (Byzantine) Empire to an end after more than eleven hundred years. [**Turkey**]
1683	The defeat of the Ottoman armies at Vienna, the furthest western point of their advance into Europe, marks the beginnings of the Ottoman Empire's decline, leading to its eventual dissolution in the twentieth century. [**Turkey**]
1736	The Synod of Mount Lebanon, held in the monastery of Our Lady of Loueizeh, completes the Latinization of the Maronite Church and establishes the jurisdiction of the Roman Catholic Church over Maronite Christians. [**Lebanon**]
1834	Justin Perkins, an American missionary in Northwest Persia, discovers the surviving remnants of the Nestorian Church (who he calls "the Protestants of Asia") around Urmia in the mountainous areas of Kurdistan. [**Iran (Persia)**]
1860	Following the massacre of 11,000 Christians in Lebanon and Damascus, Syria and Lebanon become, through French intervention, an autonomous province with a Christian governor, while remaining part of the Ottoman Empire. [**Syria and Lebanon**]
1900	By the beginning of the twentieth century, Lebanon remains the only country in the Middle East that has Christians forming a religious majority in the population. [**Lebanon**]
1922	The dissolution of the Ottoman Empire leads to the emergence of a secular Turkish state the following year and the end of the Caliphate in 1924. [**Turkey**]

1923	The exchange of Muslim and Christian populations between Greece and Turkey results in the almost total elimination of Byzantine Orthodox Christians from modern-day Turkey. [**Turkey**]
1933	The Simele massacre of Assyrians and Christians in a systematic program of killing by the armed forces of the Kingdom of Iraq leads to the coining of the term "genocide" by Jewish Polish lawyer Raphael Lemkin. [**Iraq**]
1948	The British mandate over Palestine ends on May 14, 1948, in line with United Nations Resolution 181, and the establishment of the State of Israel is proclaimed the same day by David Ben-Gurion (its first prime minister). [**Israel**]
1968	Renewal takes place in the Coptic Church following several apparitions of the Virgin Mary over a period of nearly a year at a church in Zeitoun, Cairo, leading to reports of miracles and healings (including among Muslims). [**Egypt**]
1971	Influential Coptic leader Shenouda III becomes the pope of Alexandria and the patriarch of All Africa on the Holy Apostolic See of Saint Mark the Evangelist of the Coptic Orthodox Church of Alexandria; he would hold this office for forty-one years. [**Egypt**]
1981	President Anwār al-Sādāt effectively outlaws the Coptic Church, arresting Patriarch Shenouda III and other bishops and priests (who Sādāt had accused of having political ambitions and of fostering sectarianism); however, this persecution was short-lived, as Sādāt was assassinated a month later. [**Egypt**]

Bibliography

Badr, Ḥabīb, et al., eds. *Christianity: A History in the Middle East.* Beirut: Middle East Council of Churches, 2005.

Davidson, Ivor J. *The Birth of the Church: From Jesus to Constantine, AD 30–312.* Monarch History of the Church, vol. 1. Oxford: Monarch, 2005.

———. *A Public Faith: From Constantine to the Medieval World, AD 312–600.* Monarch History of the Church, vol. 2. Oxford: Monarch, 2005.

Hill, Jonathan, ed. *Zondervan Handbook to the History of Christianity.* Oxford: Lion, 2006.

Isichei, Elizabeth. *A History of Christianity in Africa: From Antiquity to the Present.* London: SPCK, 1995.

Jenkins, Philip. *The Lost History of Christianity: The Thousand-Year Golden Age of the Church in the Middle East, Africa, and Asia—and How It Died.* New York: HarperOne, 2008.

Knowles, Brett. *A Timeline of Global Christianity: One Thousand Significant Dates for Christianity across the Planet—and Beyond.* With a foreword by Tim Cooper. Eugene, OR: Resource, 2020.

Marty, Martin. *The Christian World: A Global History.* New York: Modern Library, 2009.

McManners, John, ed. *The Oxford Illustrated History of Christianity.* Oxford: Oxford University Press, 1995.

Moffett, Samuel Hugh. *A History of Christianity in Asia. Volume I: Beginnings to 1500.* San Francisco: Harper, 1992.

Neill, Stephen. *A History of Christian Missions.* Pelican History of the Church, vol. 6. 2nd ed. Harmondsworth, UK: Penguin, 1986.

Yarshater, Ehsan, et al., eds. *Encyclopaedia Iranica.* Online edition. New York: Columbia University, 2009–10. http://www.iranicaonline.org/.

Appendix

Christian Communities in the East

Church of the East (Syriac)—so-called "Nestorians"; instructed by the exegesis and doctrinal language of Theodore of Mopsuestia (c.350–428) as articulated in the synods of Seleucia-Ctesiphon (fifth to seventh centuries); major theologians: Narsai of Nisibis (d.c.503), Babai the Great (c.550–628), Patriarch Timothy I (728–823).
Today:

- The Assyrian Church of the East
- Chaldean Catholic Church
- The Syro-Malabar Catholic Church

The Oriental Orthodox Churches (Syriac, Armenian, Coptic)—so-called "Jacobites," after Jacob Baradaeus (c.500–578); instructed by the theology of St. Cyril of Alexandria (d.444) as presented in the cathedral homilies of Severus of Antioch (c.465–538, r.512–18); major theologians, Philoxenus of Mabbug (c.440–523), Jacob of Edessa (d.708), Bar Hebraeus (1226–86).
Today:

- The Syrian Orthodox Church
- The Coptic Orthodox Church
- The Armenian Apostolic Church
- The Armenian Catholic Church
- The Coptic Catholic Church and the Syrian Catholic Church
- The Malankara Orthodox Syrian Church and the Syro-Malankara Catholic Church

The Orthodox Churches (Greek, Syriac, Arabic, Old Church Slavonic)—until eighteenth century called "Melkites" in Arabic-speaking milieux; instructed by the decisions and definitions of the seven councils of Nicaea (325), Constantinople I (381), Ephesus (431), Chalcedon (451), Constantinople II (553), Constantinople III (681), and Nicaea II (787); major theological authorities, Maximus the Confessor (d. 662), John of Damascus (d. 749), *Synodicon of Orthodoxy* (after 843).
Today:

- Patriarchates of Constantinople, Alexandria, Antioch, Jerusalem, Moscow, and associated autocephalous churches (Greek, Bulgarian, Serbian, Rumanian, Ukrainian, etc.)
- The Orthodox Church in America (OCA)
- Churches in union with Rome (so-called Uniate Churches), e.g., Melkite Catholic Church, Ruthenians, Greeks, Ukrainians, Rumanians, etc.

The Maronites (Syriac, Arabic)—so-called because of their ancestral, charismatic leader St. Maron (d. before 423)—instructed by the seven councils of Orthodoxy; heirs of the ancient Syriac patristic and liturgical traditions of Antioch and Edessa; never formally broken communion with Rome, formalized since 1182.

The Middle Eastern Council of Churches—a modern ecumenical organization whose members include both Catholic and non-Catholic families of churches, and churches with parental relationships to Protestant churches in Europe and America. Special arrangement for the Assyrian Church of the East.

Mozarabs, a term used by modern historians to refer to the Arabic-speaking Christians of Muslim Spain. It is derived from the Arabic term *must'arib*, which has a range of meanings extending from "pretend Arab," "Arabizer," to "Arabist." It first appears in Christian texts from the eleventh century onwards, after the re-conquest of Toledo in 1085, "used as a pejorative term for Christians of Arabic origin living in the medieval Christian kingdoms [of Spain], particularly Toledo" (De Epalza, "Mozarabs," *Legacy of Muslim Spain I*, 149). The adjective "Mozarabic" is sometimes applied to the "Visigothic" or "Old Spanish" rite of the Iberian church up to the eleventh century.

Index

Abbasid Caliphate, 105, 140
Abboud, Hosn, 199
'Abd al-Masih ibn Buqaila, 96
Abdisho IV Maron, 156
Abdul-Hamid, 104
Abdullah, King, 58
Abgar of Edessa, 90–91
Abraham Ardzivian, 114, 154
Abraham of Kashkar, 138
Acacian schism, 149
Accad, Martin, 225ff.
Adalian, Rouben Paul, 104
Addai II, 144
Adyan Foundation, 205
Aflaq, Michel, 55
Ahiqar, the Aramean Sage, 91
Ahudemmeh, 96
Al-Akhtal, 95
Al-Baladhuri, 96
Alexander, Michael Solomon, 170
Alexandria, 71–73
    Greek Orthodox Church of, 120–21, 131
Al-Hakim bi-Amr Allah, 97
al-Hira, 95
al-Mahdi, 137
al-Mansur, 137
Al-Sayyīd, 220ff.
al-Tabari, 136
Aluoben, 140
American Board of Commissioners for Foreign Missions, 165, 166
American University of Cairo, 177
Ammar al-Basri, 89, 138

Andonian friars, 107
Andrew Akhijan, 158
Anglican presence in the Middle East, 170
    Anglicans in Palestine, Egypt, Sudan, and Iran, 165
Anglo-Egyptian rule, 172
Ankawa, 145
Antioch, Greek Orthodox Church of, 122–23, 131
    Rum (Roman) Orthodox Christians, 122
Antiochene, 9, 12
Antiochian Christology, 135, 136
Aphrahat, the Persian sage, 89, 90, 92
Apolliinaris of Laodicea, 8–9
Arab Evangelical Episcopal Church, 59, 171
Arab Orthodox Congresses, 53
Arab socialism, 58–59
Arab Spring, 167–8, 234
Arabic language, 38–39
Arab-Israeli War of 1948, 57–58, 106, 109
Arabization, 75–76
Aram I, 112, 113
Aramaic, 86, 96, 97
Arghun, 141
Armenian Church, 49–50
Armenian Cilicia Kingdom, 109
Armenian Evangelical Churches, 168
    union of, 168
Armenian genocide, 168

Armenian Missionary Association of
    America (AMAA), 177
Armenian Missionary Association of
    America, 108
Armenian Orthodox Church, 107, 108,
    112
Armenian Protestant community, 168
Armenian Relief Red Cross, 108
Armenian Revolutionary Federation
    (Tashnagtsoutyoun), 108
Armenian, 39, 98
    alphabet/language, 89, 110
    Apostolic Church, 113
    Catholic Church, 105, 107, 108, 109,
        114, 115, 154
    Church of Armenia, 112
    Eastern Orthodox Church, 112
    Evangelical Church, 105, 107, 108,
        109, 113, 114, 115
        Protestant millet, 113
        union of, 114
    genocide, 104–5-106, 109, 111, 113
    Jerusalem, 109, 110, 111
    newspapers, 108
    Oriental Orthodox Church, 112
    orphanages, 108
    Prelacy, 105, 110, 111
    Republic of, 105
    schools, 108, 109, 111
"ar-rum," 119
Arsacid Dynasty, 134
Ashot I, 154
Asia Minor, 4
Asori, 89
Assyrian Church
    Apostolic Church of the East, 133,
        139, 140, 142–43, 144, 156
    Chalcedonian Church, 136; East
        Syrian Church, 133, 135, 136,
        139, 145, 155
    "Syriac" dialect, 133, 155–56
Assyrians, 55
Athanasius of Alexandria, 73
Audo, Antoine, 148
Awad, Najib, 175
Awwad, Johnny, 199
Ayoub, Mahmoub, 222
Aziz El Towlen, 110

Babai the Great, 136
Babylon, 142
Baghdad, 28, 137, 140, 142, 143, 144
BaHira, 19–20
Baibars, 141
Balamand document, 131
Banna, Hassan al-, 57
Bāqillānī, Abū Bakr Muhammad al-, 32
Baqubah, 143
Bar 'Ebroyo (Ibn al-Ibri), 93
Bar Bahlul, 89
Bar Hebraeus, 141
Bardaisan, 6, 91, 92, 95
Barsauma, 135
Basha, Daoud, 107
Basil (the aritst), 87
Basra, 135
Battle of Ain Jalut, 141
Bet Abe, 139
Bet Hale (monastery), 137
Bet Lapat, 135
Beth Qatraye, 89
Bibliothecca Orientalis, 151
Biography of the Prophet, 28
Bir Zeit University, Palestine, 177
bishops, early, 5
Bkerke, 151
Black Death, 40
Bnay Ayama ("Children of the
    Covenant"), 91
Book of Laws and Lands, 133
Book of Questions and Answers, 138
Book of the Laws of the Countries, *See*
    Bardaisan
*Book of the Nature of the General and
    the Private*, 89
Botroseya Church bombing in
    December 2016, 192
Bourj Hamoud, 109
Bournoutian, George, 103
British Mandate government, 55
Brock, Sebatian, 94
Buddhism, 140
Bulayiq, 139
Byblos, 108
Byzantine rite, 87
Bzoumar, 107, 114–15

Cardinal Bechara Boutros Rai, 206

Catholic Church in Middle East
    Apostolic Letters
        Ecclesia in Medio Oriente, 149
        Orientale Lumen, 147
        Orientalium Dignitas, 148
        Orientalium Ecclesiarum, 148
        Rerum Orientalium, 148)
    Armenian Catholic Church, 154–55
        Armenian Catholic Sisters of Immaculate Conception, 155
        massacre, 155
        Patriarchal Institute and Seminary, 155
        Pontifical Armenian College, 155
    Chaldean Catholic Church, 155–57
        Church of the East, 155–56
        massacre, 157
        missionaries to, 156
        schools, 157
    Coptic Catholic Church, 159–60
        leadership, 159
        Miaphysite Oriental Orthodox Church, 159
        schools, 159–60
    Council of Catholic Patriarchs of the Orient, 151, 154
        Latin-Rite Roman Catholic Church in Middle East, 160–63
        Assembly of Organizations for Aid to the Oriental Churches, 162
        Congregation for the Propagation of the Faith, 160
        religious orders, 161
        schools, 161–62
    Maronite Church, 87, 92, 107, 149–52
        Jeremiah al-Amshiti, 151
        John al-Jaji, 150
        Lebanon, 151
        Maron (Saint and monastery), 149, 150
        religious orders, 151
        schools, 150, 151, 152
        Youssif al-Jurjissi, 150
    Melkite Greek Catholic Church, 152–54
        Chalcedonian, 152
        media, 153
        Patriarchs, 152–53
        religious orders, 154 161
        rites, 149
        Armenian, 149
        Byzantine, 149
        Coptic, 149
        Syriac, 149
    sui iuris (of their own laws), 147
    Syriac Catholic Church, 86, 99, 157–59
        Patriarchs, 158
        schools, 158
Catholic missionaries, 44, 46
Catholic, Melkite, 44–45
Catholicos, 135
Catholicosate of; Cilicia, 107, 108, 111, 113
    Etchmiadzin [in Armenia], 105, 111, 155
Catholics, Eastern-rite, 44
Center for the Armenian Handicapped (CAHL), 109
Chalcedonian, 36
    Chalcedonian Creed, *see* Council of Chalcedon
Chaldean Church, 142–43, 145, 152
Choosing Life: Christians in the Middle East: Towards Renewed Geo-Political and Theological Choices, 65.
Christian Arab/Arab Christian, 86
    Ghassanite, 89, 94
    Tanukhite, 89
Christian Missionary Alliance, 173
Christian Palestine Aramaic, 86
Christian-Jewish dialogue, 176
Christian-Muslim relations, 215ff., 224ff.
    interfaith relationships, 219ff.
    interrelational perception, 216-7
    SEKAP spectrum of Christian-Muslim interaction, 226
    Sunnite, Shi'ite, and Eastern Orthodox voices on interreligious dialogue, 227
    symbiotic interaction and, 216
Christology, 9–10

262 INDEX

Church Missionary Society, 171
Church of God, 173
Church of the East, 24–25, 28, 92, 93, 94, 95, 98, 155, 157
Church of the Holy Sepulcher, 77
Church of the Nativity, 43, 87
Church of the Nazarene, 173–74
Church of the Resurrection, 98
Cilicia
    Church of, 154
    Great House of, 113
    kingdom of, 110, 154
Citadel of Aleppo, 110
Commission for Inter-Ecclesial Relations, 145
Common Christological Declaration, 145
Community Reconciliation Sessions, Egypt, 238
Congregation for the Propagation of the Faith, 44
Congregationalists in Anatolia, Turkey, and Lebanon, 165
Constantine, 134
Constantinople, 41, 46
Coptic Catholic Church, 80
Coptic church, 39–41
Coptic culture and language, 76, 186
Coptic diaspora, 184ff.
    theology of, 184
Coptic Evangelical Church, 59, 170
Coptic Evangelical Organization for Social Services (CEOSS) in Cairo, 170, 244
Coptic Orthodox Church 55, 82–83, 183, 187
    liturgy and hymnology, 185
Coptic survival centers, 196
Coptic, 45–6, 120–21
Coptic-American community, 193
Copts, 71, 76, 78–84
Council of,
    Antiochian (Synod), 130
    Chalcedon, 10–16, 24, 26, 92–93, 94, 112, 119
    Chaldean (Synod), 142
    Constantinople, 8, 150
    Dvin (Second Council), 113
    East Syrian (Synod), 135
    Ephesus, 94, 119
    Florence, 147, 150, 152, 154, 157, 159
    Lateran, 150, 157
    Markabtha (Synod), 95
    Nicea, 8, 94, 118, 126
    Seleucia-Ctesiphon (Synod), 135
    Trent, 150
    Vatican II, 148, 151, 153, 155
Crusades, 33, 77, 97, 114, 154
Cyril of Alexandria, 9, 12–13

Damascus, 25
Dar al-Kalima University, 177
Dar-Al-Islam, 75
Darmo, Thomas, 144, 145
Deir al-Za'faran, 98
Democratic Front for the Liberation of Palestine, 61
devshirme system, 43
dhimmis, 42, 48–49, 76
    millet system, 42–43
Diaspora; Armenian, 104–5, 112, 155
    Melkite, 153
    Syriac, 100
Diocletian persecution, 75
Diodorus of Tarsus, 9, 136
Dioscurus of Alexandria, 10
Diyar's Consortium in Bethlehem, 240
Dominican, 38
Doquz Khatun, 141
Dunhuang, 139
Dutch Reformed Church in the Gulf, 165
Dyophysite, 24–25, 28

ecumenism, 60
Edessa, 6–7, 9, 11–12, 90, 92, 133
Edict of Gühane, 164
Edward I, 141
Egypt, 37, 45–46; churches, cooperation, 83; emigration, 84
    missionaries, 75
    persecution, 74–75, 82, 84
    Protestant presence, 80–81
    scripture translation, 73
    theological education, 75

INDEX 263

Egyptian Church, challenges of, 234
  internal theological challenges, 234
  regional and international
    challenges, 234
Egyptian Presbyterian Synod, 169
  Synod of the Nile, 169
ekklesia-congregation, 6
Elias of Nisibis, 138
Emmanuel II Thomas, 156
Empress Theodora, 94
Ephrem, 91, 92
Episcopal Evangelical Church
  (Anglican), 171
Era of the Martyrs, 75
Erbil, 135, 145
Eusebius of Caesarea, 91, 134
Eutyches, 10
Evagrius Ponticus, 138
Evangelical Episcopal Church, Synod of
  the, 54
Evangelical Lutheran Church in Jordan
  (ELCJ), 59, 169
Evangelical Presbyterian Church of
  Egypt (EPCE), 170, 206
Evangelical Theological Seminary in
  Cairo (ETSC), 170

Family Status Laws, 202
Farra, Therese, 199
Fellowship of the Middle East Churches
  (FMEEC), 60, 167
female education, 177ff.
feminist (and gender equality) views,
  201
feminist approaches within Christian
  communities, 205
  reformists/moderates, 205
  rejectionists, 205
  traditionalists, 205
Fisk, Pliny, 165–6
Formula of Union, 9
Fount of Knowledge, 27
Franciscan, 38
  Franciscans of the Holy Land, 160
Frederic Wilhelm IV, 168
*From the Nile to the Euphrates: The Call
  of Faith and Citizenship*, 65
future of Middle Eastern Church, xxvii

Galal, Lise, 199
Garbage Villages, 244
Genghis Khan, 140
geographical expansion and missionary
  strategies, xxii
George of Sadad, 98
Gewargis III, 145
Ghazan, 141
global Christianity, ix; entanglement
  in, xiv
global south versus global north, xxiiff
Gobat, Samuel, 171
Greek Orthodox, 53
  Basil the Great, 126, 129
  ecumenism, 131
  eucharist, 128–30
  interaction with Islam, 131–32
  John Chrysostom, 126
  liturgy, 123–30
  local church vs. universal church,
    124–25
Gregorius al-Kurji, 98
Gregory bar Hebraeus (Abu al-Far), 157
Gundishapur, 134, 135

Habash, George, 58, 61
Habib b. Khidma Abu Ra'ita, 89
Habib, Samuel, 59, 170
Hagopiantz, 110
Haigazian University, Beirut, 108, 111,
  177
Hakim, Al-, 77
Hakkari, 143, 144, 156
Harun al-Rashid, 137
Hatt-I Hümaysun, *See* Tanzimat
Hatti Humayun, 164
Hatt-I Serif of Gülhane, *See* Tanzimat
Hawatmch, Nayef, 61
Hebraeus, Bar, 41
Henotikon, 12
Herodotus, 105
hijra, first, 22–23
Hishām, Sira of Ibn, 22
Holy Land, 169
Holy Sepulcher, 43
Hotel Baron, 111
Hovannisian, Richard, 115
Hulagu Khan, 140
Hunain ibn Ishaq, 137

hypostases, 28, 93, 136
hypostasis, See Council of Chalcedon

Ibas, Bishop, 10
Ibn Abi Usaybi'a, 86
Ignatius Ephram II Rahman, 158
Ignatius Gabriel I Tappouni, 158
Ignatius III (Patriarch), 157
Ignatius IV (Patriarch), 131
Ignatius Ni'matallah, 98
Ignatius of Antioch, 124
Ilkan, 140
Independent Churches in the Middle East, xxv
Institute for Women's Studies in the Arab World, 201
Integrated and Isolated Ecclesiology, 234–5
interfaith engagement, 243
Intibah Association, 99
Intifada, 64–65
Iraq, 55, 64
Isaac of Nineveh, 89, 92, 138
Ishaq, Hunayn ibn, 29
Ishoyahb III, 136–37
Islamization, 63–64

Jabra, Nancy, 199
Jacob Burd'ono, 94
  Jacobites, 94
Jacob of Serug, 95
Jarjour, Riad, 240
Jarjour, Rose, 178
Jerusalem, 25, 36, 43–44
  Dome of the Rock, 26
  Church of the Resurrection, 33
  Greek Orthodox Church of, 121–22
Jinishian Center, 108
jizya (tax), 96
John of Apameia, 138
John of Dalyatha, 138
John of Damascus, 25, 27–28
John Paul II, Pope, 206
John Sulaqa, 142
Joseph Hazzaya, 138
Joseph of Amid, 156
Joseph Simon Assemani, 151
Joseph VI Audo, 156
Julius III, 142

Justin I, 12–14, 118
Justinian, 13

Kabara, Maria, 199, 203
Kalām, 29
Karaguezian Center, 108
Karekin II, 113
Karka de Bet Selok, 135
Kartir, 134
Kasr El Dobarah Evangelical Church, 236
Kerala, 139
Khabur River, 144
Khalid b. al-Walid, 96
Khanbaliq, 141
Kharput, 100
Khodr, Georges, 130, 223
Khoury, Archbishop Elia, 175
Khrish, Patriarch, 62
Khuzistan, 134
King's People, See Milkites
Kirkuk, 135
Kitbuqa, 141
Kokhe, 133
Kouyoumjian, Hovhannes Basha, 107
Krikor Bedros XV, 155
Kurdish, 143, 144
Kurdistan, 141
Kyrill, Pope, 62

Labberton, Mark, 237
Lakhmid, 95
Lebanese American University, 177
Lebanon, 54–55, 64, 150–51
linguistic traditions, 14–16
liturgy (Greek Orthodox), 123–12
  Basil the Great, 126, 129
  John Chrysostom, 126
Lutheran Church in the Holy Land, 169
  in southern Palestine, 165
  Lutheran World Federation (LWF) in Palestine, 169
Lutheran World Federation, 58

Maghribī, Abū al-Qāsim ibn al-, 32
Mahdī, Abbasid Caliph al-, 29–30
Mahdist movement, 172
Mamluk, 40, 42–43, 141
  Mamelukes, 77–80

Mandate years (1920–48), 171
Manichaeism, 140
Maphrian Basileios Shem'un II, 90
Maqrizi, Al-, 78
Mar Aprem, 145
Mar Awa Royel, 145
Mar Dinkha IV, 145
Mar Raphael I Bidawid, 145–46
Marcian, Emperor, 10
Markschies, Christoph, 17
Maronite Church, 54
Maronite, See Catholic Church in Middle East
martyrdom, 188ff.
Marutha of Maypherkat, 135
Marwan II, 150
Mary, 9
Mary's Path movement, Lebanon, 204
Masargawayh, Physician of Basra, 86
Mazloumian (brothers), 111
Mecca, 22
Medina, 22–23
Meletius Al-Doumani, 122
Melkite (Rum Orthodox), 24, 26, 28, 92
Mende, Claudia, 199, 206
Merv, 136, 139
Merw, 135
Meskeen, Matta al-, 62
Mesopotamia, 40–41
Mesrob Mashdotz, 110
Messianic Jews, 173
  Christian Zionist movement, 174–75
  movement, 174–5
  Ethiopian Jews, 174
  Russian Jews in the 1990s;
  of Russian Orthodox heritage, 174
Miaphysite, 136, 159
Michael I (Patriarch), 157
Michael Jarweh, 158
Michael the Syrian, 26
Middle East Council of Churches (MECC), 60, 131, 151, 154
Middle Eastern Christian communities, 183
  as struggle, sacrifice, and survival, xxiii
  in decline, xiv
  social hostilities and governmental restrictions of, xxvi
Mikhael, Mary, 178, 199, 202, 210
millet (nation), 79. 98, 99
millet system, See dhimmis
mission stations, establishment of, 165
missionaries; American Evangelical, 48–49; Egypt, 75; activity, 53
missions; Catholic, 80; German, 54
Mkhitar of Sebastia, 114, 155
  Mhkitarist, 114, 155
monasteries, 25, 43, 62
monasticism, 39
  Coptic, 193ff.
  monastic movement, 73–74
Mongols, 39–41, 140, 141
Monophysites, 24–25
Mor Gabriel Monastery, 92
Mount Izla, 138
mubāhala, 23
Mubarak, 82
MuHallami tribe, 98
MuHammad al-Bakhti, 90
Muhammad Ali Pasha, 164
Muhammad, 19–23, 25–26, 29, 33, 137
  Hadīth, 20
  Sīra al-Nabawiyya, 20
Muslim Brotherhood, 57
myrun, 46

Najla Kassab, 178
Narsai, 136
Nasser Revolution of 1952, 169, 241
Nasser, 58, 81
National Evangelical Church of Beirut, 166
National Evangelical Synod of Syria and Lebanon, 59, 166–67
National Evangelical Union of Lebanon, 59
national identity in mission, 174
  Catholic missions as French, Austrian, and Italian, 174
  Orthodox mission as Russian, 174
  Protestant missions as British, American, and German, 174
National Pact (al-Mithaq al-Watani), 54–55
National Tarkmanchatz, 112

Nazoreans, 134
Near East Council of Churches,
    See Middle East Council of
    Churches
Near East School of Theology (NEST),
    167
    Centre for Middle Eastern Christian
    Heritage, 167
Negus of Axum, 23
Nestorius/Nestorian, 9, 24, 36, 94, 133,
    135, 142
Nicene Creed, 10, 135
Nineveh Plain, 55, 97, 145
Nisibis, 92, 135
Nusaybin, 135

Obedience paradigm, Coptic, 193
October Revolution, 143
Orient, early believers, 6
Oriental Churches, the revival of, 166
Origen, 7
Orthodox Youth Movement (MJO),
    123, 130
Orthodox, 37
Our Lady of Qannubin, 150

Pact of 'Umar, 27
Pakradouniatz (kingdom of), 110
Palestine Kairos Document, 65
Palestine, 58–59, 61–62
Palestinian Liberation Organization
    (PLO), 61
Palm Sunday bombings in Tanta and
    Alexandria, 192
Palut, 7
Pan-Arabism, 60
Papa bar Aggai, 134
Parsons, Levi, 165–6
Parthians, 4
Paternal Instruction, 48
Paul of Samosata, 9
Paul, 4
Pentarchy, 118
Pentecostal Church of Sudan, 172
Persis, 135
Peter III (Patriarch), 98
Philip the Fair, 141

Philoxenos of Mabbug, 95
Pontifical Oriental Institute, 145, 148
Pope
    Agapetus I, 150
    Benedict XIV, 154
    Benedict XV, 148
    Clement VI, 160
    Gregory XV, 160
    Hormisdas, 149
    John Paul II, 145, 151
    Julius III, 156
    Leo XIII, 148, 159
    Nicholas I, 154
    Nicholas IV, 156
    Pius IV, 158
    Pius VIII, 156
    Pius IX, 148
    Pius XI, 148
Popular Front for the Liberation of
    Palestine (PFLP), 61
Prat de Maishan, 135
Presbyterians in Syria, Lebanon, and
    Egypt, 165
Protestant mission in the Middle East,
    164; four features of, 166ff.
Pseudo-Macarius, 138
public theology in Middle Eastern
    Christianity, 232

Qatarite, 89
Qudshanis, 142
Qur'an, 19, 26
Qurra, Theoldore Abū, 30–31

Rabban Hormizd, 142, 156
Rabban Sauma, 141
Raheb, Mitri, 175, 240
Raheb, Viola, 178, 199, 202
Ramgavar Liberal Party, 108
Red Lips High Heels movement, 200
Refutation of the Three Christian Sects,
    32
Republic of Armenia, 105
Rev Ardashir, 135, 139
Robber Council, *See* Dioscurus of
    Alexandria
Rome, 38

Roman Empire, 4, 7
Rum Orthodox, 86, 87, 89, 92, 96
Russia, 45
Russian Orthodox Church, 142

Saadeh, Anton, 56
Sadat, Anwar al-, 62, 81–82
Said, Edward, 176
Samarkand, 141
Sasanians, 4
Sasanid dynasty, 134
Sayfo genocide, 100
Schmidt-Leukel, Perry, 229
School of Alexandria, 119
School of Antioch, 119
School of Edessa/School of the Persians, 135, 136
Second World Mission Conference, 75
Seleucia-Ctesiphon, 133, 134, 135, 137
Semile massacre, 143
Sessons of Elias bar Shinaya of Nisibis, 32
Severus of Antioch, 94, 95,
Sfeir, Nasrallah, 62–63
Shapur I and II, 134
Shenouda III, Pope, 185, 191, 195–96
Shenouda III, Pope, 62
Shimun VII, 142
Shimun XIII, 156
Shimun XIX Benjamin, 143
Shimun XX Paulos, 143
Shimun XXI Eshai, 143, 144
Silk Road, 139
Simeon the Stylite, 95
Simon bar Sabbae, 134
Sleiman, Rola, 178
Social Democratic Henchag Party, 108
Soghdians, 139
Sourp Asdvadsazin (church), 110
Sourp Manoug (church), 111, 112
Sourp Nishan (church), 107
Sourp Tateos (St. Thaddeus Church), 106
Sourp Yedghia (church), 107
St. Anthony, 73
St. Athanasius, 195
St. Demiana, 192

St. George's College, Jerusalem, 171
St. Mark's Monastery, 98
St. Mina, doxology of, 190
St. Pachomius, 73
Stele for the Propagation of the Luminous Religion of Da Qin, 140
Stephen al-Duwayli, 151
storytelling components, ix, xiv
    history, contexts, and communities, x
    migration and global diaspora, xv
    movement, xv
    public theologies, xv
    translation, xv
Sudan Council of Churches, 172
Sudan Interior Church (Baptist), 172
Sudanese Church of Christ, 172
Sudanese Reformed Presbyterian Church, 172
Suez Crisis of 1956, 169
Sura Al-'Imran, 23
Surma, 143
Suryani, 87, 96
Swiss-Armenian Friendship Organization, 109
Sykes-Picot Agreement, 52–53, 161
Synaxarium, 189
Syria, 55
Syriac dialect/liturgical language, 133, 139, 155–56
Syriac Orthodox (West Syriac Church), 86, 89, 92, 93, 94, 95, 96, 97, 98 99, 100, 140
    diaspora, 100
Syrian Protestant College, Beirut in 1866; American University of Beirut, 177
Syrian Social Nationalist Party, 57
Syro-Palestian region, *See* Asia Minor

Tabet, Gihane, 199
Taif Accord, 63
Tālib, Jàfar ibn Abū, 22
Tamerlane, 156
Tang Dynasty, 140
Tanzimat, 48–49

INDEX

Tarim Basin, 139
tawhīd, 31–32
Tayyaye, 95
Tchillingirian, Hratch, 114
Teaching of Addai, 90
Thaddeus (Addai), 155
The Life of Anthony, 73
Theodore (an Arab), 94
Theodore of Mopsuestia, 9, 13–14, 94, 135–36
Theodoret of Cyrus, 10
Theodoros Abu Qurra, 89
Theodosius II, Emperor, 9
theological education, *see* Egypt
theologies for political power, especially in Africa and the Americas, xvi
    influence of evangelicalism, liberation theologies, and Pentecostal practices for, xvi
Third Ecumenical Council, 9
Thomas (apostle), 133, 139, 155
Thomas, David, 31
Thrissur, 139, 145
Tigran II (Tigranes), 105, 106, 109, 110
Timotheos I, 137, 138, 139
Timothy I, 30
Timur Lenk, 141
Transoxania, 139
Trichur, 144
Tur Abdin, 97, 99
Turayk, Patriarch Gabriel II ibn, 38
Turco-Tartar people, 140
Turfan, 139
Turkish Committee of Union and Progress (CUP), 99
Turkmenistan, 135

Uighur, 141
Umar ibn Khattab, 96
Uniat Schism, 122
uniatism, 147
Union of Lebanon and the National Evangelical Synod of Syria and Lebanon, 167
Union of the Armenian Evangelical Churches in the Near East (UAECNE), 108, 168, 177
United Evangelical Church of the Arab East, 59–60
Upper Dvin, Armenia, 87
Urma, 87
Urmia, 142, 143, 156

Vita Constantini IV, 134

Wahhabism, 63
Waraqa, 21
Warrāq, Abū Harūn ibn MuHammad al-, 32
West Syriac Church, (See Syriac Orthodox)
women in Middle Eastern Christianity, 199
    and religious authority, 206
world Christianity versus global Christianity, xi
Wuzong, 140

Xi'an (stele), 140

Yaballaha III, 156
Yassine-Hamdan, Nahla, 200
Yazdgird I and III, 135, 136
Yesu/Isaac the Armenian, 89
Yohannon Sulaqa, 156
Yohanon Hormizd, 156
Yuzbashian-Gulbenkian, 106

Zaki, Andrea, 175
Zaki, Anne, 199, 206
Zeno, 135